# Fodors 98

# Seattle & Vancouver

**The complete guide, thoroughly up-to-date**

Packed with details that will make your trip

**The must-see sights, off and on the beaten path**

What to see, what to skip

**Vacation itineraries, walking tours, day trips**

Smart lodging and dining options

**Essential local do's and taboos**

Transportation tips

**Key contacts, savvy travel advice**

When to go, what to pack

**Clear, accurate, easy-to-use maps**

Books to read, videos to watch, background essays

Portions of this book appear in *Fodor's Canada '98*

Fodor's Travel Publications, Inc.
New York • Toronto • London • Sydney • Auckland
www.fodors.com/

# Fodor's Seattle & Vancouver

**EDITOR:** Daniel Mangin

**Editorial Contributors:** Stephanie Adler, Alex Aron, Glen Berger, David Brown, Linda Cabasin, Julie Fay, Wier Harman, Christina Knight, Melissa Rivers, Heidi Sarna, M. T. Schwartzman (Gold Guide editor), Dinah A. Spritzer

**Editorial Production:** Laura M. Kidder

**Maps:** David Lindroth, *cartographer;* Steven K. Amsterdam, *map editor*

**Design:** Fabrizio La Rocca, *creative director;* Guido Caroti, *associate art director;* Jolie Novak, *photo editor*

**Production/Manufacturing:** Mike Costa

**Cover Photograph:** David Barnes/The Stock Market

## Copyright

## Special Sales

Fodor's Travel Publications are available at special discounts for bulk purchases for sales promotions or premiums. Special editions, including personalized covers, excerpts of existing guides, and corporate imprints, can be created in large quantities for special needs. For more information, contact your local bookseller or write to Special Markets, Fodor's Travel Publications, 201 East 50th Street, New York, NY 10022. Inquiries from Canada should be directed to your local Canadian bookseller or sent to Random House of Canada, Ltd., Marketing Department, 1265 Aerowood Drive, Mississauga, Ontario L4W 1B9. Inquiries from the United Kingdom should be sent to Fodor's Travel Publications, 20 Vauxhall Bridge Road, London SW1V 2SA, England.

PRINTED IN THE UNITED STATES OF AMERICA

10 9 8 7 6 5 4 3 2 1

# CONTENTS

## Maps

# ON THE ROAD WITH FODOR'S

**W**E'RE ALWAYS THRILLED to get letters from readers, especially one like this:

*It took us an hour to decide what book to buy and we now know we picked the best one. Your book was wonderful, easy to follow, very accurate, and good on pointing out eating places, informal as well as formal. When we saw other people using your book, we would look at each other and smile.*

Our editors and writers are deeply committed to making every Fodor's guide "the best one"—not only accurate but always charming, brimming with sound recommendations and solid ideas, right on the mark in describing restaurants and hotels, and full of fascinating facts that make you view your destination in a rich new light.

## About Our Writers

Freelance writer **Alex Aron,** who revised and updated the Side Trips from Seattle chapter, lived full-time in Washington State for eight years and continues to spend half the year working in and around the Seattle area. The rest of her year is spent in Brooklyn teaching in the New York City public schools.

After seven invigorating years in Seattle— exploring its restaurants and parks, frequenting its theaters and cinemas, and actually *enjoying* its climate (well, at least in summer)—**Wier Harman** now endures a self-imposed exile in New Haven, Connecticut, at the Yale School of Drama. He does, however, hold a return-trip ticket.

**Melissa Rivers,** who updated the Vancouver and Side Trips from Vancouver chapters, travels throughout the Pacific Northwest on assignments for Fodor's.

## New This Year

This year we've added terrific Great Itineraries that will lead you through the best of Seattle and Vancouver, plus new side trips, new neighborhood walking tours, and expanded dining, lodging, and nightlife coverage in both cities.

And this year, Fodor's joins Rand McNally, the world's largest commercial mapmaker, to bring you a detailed color map of Seattle and Vancouver. Just detach it along the perforation and carry it with you on your travels.

We're also proud to announce that the American Society of Travel Agents has endorsed Fodor's as its guidebook series of choice. ASTA is the world's largest and most influential travel trade association, operating in more than 170 countries, with 27,000 members pledged to adhere to a strict code of ethics reflecting the Society's motto, "Integrity in Travel." ASTA shares Fodor's devotion to providing smart, honest travel information and advice to travelers, and we've long recommended that our readers consult the experienced and professional ASTA member agents.

On the Web, check out Fodor's site (www.fodors.com/) for information on major destinations around the world and travel-savvy interactive features. The Web site also lists the 85-plus radio stations nationwide that carry the *Fodor's Travel Show,* a live call-in program that airs every weekend. Tune in to hear guests discuss their adventures—or call in for answers to your most pressing travel questions.

## How to Use This Book

### Organization

Up front is the **Gold Guide,** an easy-to-use section divided alphabetically by topic. Under each listing you'll find tips and information that will help you accomplish what you need to in Seattle and Vancouver. You'll also find addresses and telephone numbers of organizations and companies that offer destination-related services and detailed information and publications.

The first chapter in the guide, **Destination: Seattle & Vancouver,** helps get you in the mood for your trip. New and Noteworthy cues you in on trends and happenings, What's Where gets you oriented, Fodor's Choice showcases our top picks, and Books and Videos describes works in print and on tape in which Seattle, Vancouver, or their surrounding regions figure. Festivals and Seasonal Events alerts you to special events you'll want to seek out.

**Each city chapter** begins with an Exploring section subdivided by neighborhood; each subsection recommends a walking or driving tour and lists sights in alphabetical order. The remainder of the chapter is arranged in alphabetical order by subject—dining, lodging, nightlife and the arts, outdoor activities and sports, shopping. The **side trips chapters** cover day and overnight destinations near Seattle and Vancouver. Throughout, Off the Beaten Path sights appear after the places from which they are most easily accessible. And within town sections, all restaurants and lodgings are grouped together.

To help you decide what to visit in the time you have, all chapters begin with recommended itineraries; you can mix and match those from several chapters to create a complete vacation. The A-to-Z section that ends all chapters covers getting there and getting around. It also provides helpful contacts and resources.

## Icons and Symbols

★ Our special recommendation
✕ Restaurant
🏠 Lodging establishment
✕🏠 Lodging establishment whose restaurant warrants a special trip
☺ Good for kids (rubber duckie)
☞ Sends you to another section of the guide for more information
✉ Address
☎ Telephone number
FAX Fax number
☉ Opening and closing times
🎟 Admission prices (those we give apply to adults; substantially reduced fees are almost always available for children, students, and senior citizens)

Numbers in white and black circles (e.g., ② or ❷ ) that appear on the maps, in the margins, and within the tours correspond to one another.

## Dining and Lodging

The restaurants and lodgings we list are the cream of the crop in each price range. In the Seattle and Vancouver chapters, price charts appear before the first restaurant listing. In the side trips chapters, you'll find the charts in the Pleasures and Pastimes section that follows the chapter introduction. Prices are in U.S. dollars for Seattle and environs and in Canadian dollars for Vancouver and environs.

## Hotel Facilities

We always list the facilities that are available—but we don't specify whether they cost extra: When pricing accommodations, always ask what's included. Assume that all rooms have private baths unless otherwise noted.

## Restaurant Reservations and Dress Codes

Reservations are always a good idea; we note only when they're essential or when they are not accepted. Book as far ahead as you can, and reconfirm when you get to town. Unless otherwise noted, the restaurants listed are open daily for lunch and dinner. We mention dress only when men are required to wear a jacket or a jacket and tie.

## Credit Cards

The following abbreviations are used: **AE**, American Express; **D**, Discover; **DC**, Diners Club; **MC**, MasterCard; and **V**, Visa.

# Please Write to Us

You can use this book in the confidence that all prices and opening times are based on information supplied to us at press time; Fodor's cannot accept responsibility for any errors. Time inevitably brings changes, so always confirm information when it matters—especially if you're making a detour to visit a specific place. When making reservations, be sure to mention if you have a disability or are traveling with children, if you prefer a private bath or a certain type of bed, or if you have specific dietary needs or other concerns.

Were the restaurants we recommended as described? Did our hotel picks exceed your expectations? Did you find a museum we recommended a waste of time? If you have complaints, we'll look into them and revise our entries when the facts warrant it. If you've discovered a special place that we haven't included, we'll pass the information along to our correspondents and have them check it out. So send us your feedback, positive and negative: E-mail us at editors@fodors.com (specifying the name of the book on the subject line) or write the *Seattle & Vancouver '98* editor at Fodor's, 201 East 50th Street, New York, New York 10022. Have a wonderful trip!

*Karen Cure*

Karen Cure
*Editorial Director*

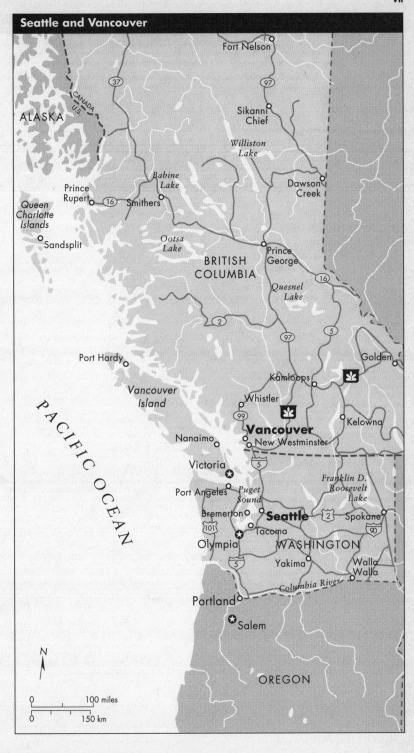

## Seattle and Vancouver

ALASKA

CANADA
U.S.

37

Fort Nelson

97

Sikanni
Chief

Williston
Lake

Babine
Lake

Prince
Rupert

16

Smithers

Queen
Charlotte
Islands

Sandsplit

Dawson
Creek

Ootsa
Lake

BRITISH
COLUMBIA

Prince
George

16

Quesnel
Lake

2

97

5

Golden

Port Hardy

Vancouver
Island

Kamloops

Whistler

99

Vancouver

New Westminster

Kelowna

PACIFIC OCEAN

Nanaimo

Victoria

Port Angeles

Puget
Sound

5

Franklin D.
Roosevelt
Lake

Bremerton

101

Seattle

2

Spokane

Olympia

Tacoma

WASHINGTON

90

5

Yakima

Walla
Walla

Columbia River

Portland

OREGON

Salem

N

0        100 miles

0        150 km

# The United States

# Canada

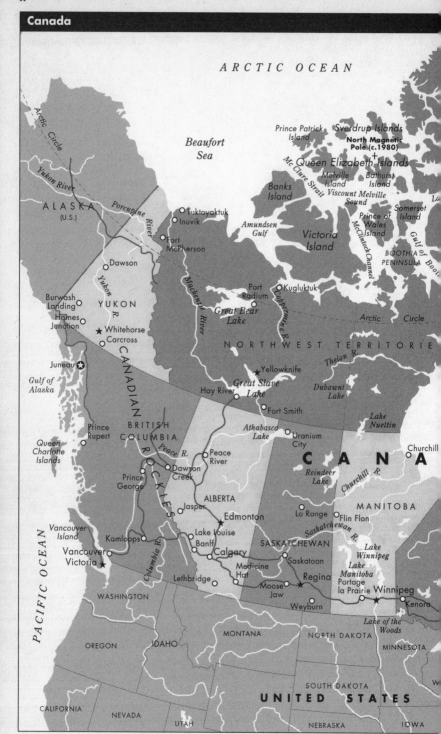

ARCTIC OCEAN

Beaufort Sea

Prince Patrick Island
Sverdrup Islands
**North Magnetic Pole (c.1980)**
+
Mc Clure Strait
Queen Elizabeth Islands
Melville Island
Bathurst Island
Viscount Melville Sound
Banks Island
Prince of Wales Island
Somerset Island
McClintock Channel
BOOTHIA PENINSULA
Gulf of Booth

ALASKA (U.S.)

Yukon River
Porcupine River
Arctic Circle

Amundsen Gulf
Victoria Island

Tuktoyaktuk
Inuvik
Fort McPherson
Dawson

Mackenzie River
Port Radium
Kugluktuk
Coppermine R.

Burwash Landing
Haines Junction
YUKON
Yukon R.
Whitehorse
Carcross

Great Bear Lake

Arctic Circle

Juneau

CANADIAN
NORTHWEST TERRITORIE

Gulf of Alaska

Yellowknife
Great Slave Lake
Hay River
Thelon R.
Dubawnt Lake
Lake Nueltin

Fort Smith

Prince Rupert

Queen Charlotte Islands

BRITISH COLUMBIA

Athabasca Lake
Uranium City
CANA
Churchill

Peace R.
Peace River
Dawson Creek

Reindeer Lake
Churchill R.

Prince George

ROCKIE

Jasper
ALBERTA
Edmonton
La Ronge
Flin Flon
MANITOBA

PACIFIC OCEAN

Vancouver Island

Kamloops

Columbia R.

Lake Louise
Banff
Calgary

Saskatchewan R.

SASKATCHEWAN

Saskatoon

Lake Winnipeg

Vancouver
Victoria

Medicine Hat

Lethbridge

Moose Jaw

Regina

Lake Manitoba
Portage la Prairie
Winnipeg

Weyburn

Kenora

WASHINGTON

Lake of the Woods

OREGON
IDAHO
MONTANA
NORTH DAKOTA
MINNESOTA

CALIFORNIA
NEVADA
UTAH

SOUTH DAKOTA

UNITED STATES

NEBRASKA
IOWA

# SMART TRAVEL TIPS A TO Z

*Basic Information on Traveling in Seattle and Vancouver, Savvy Tips to Make Your Trip a Breeze, and Companies and Organizations to Contact*

## A

### AIR TRAVEL

#### MAJOR AIRLINE OR LOW-COST CARRIER?

Most people choose a flight based on price. Yet there are other issues to consider. Major airlines offer the greatest number of departures; smaller airlines—including regional, low-cost, and no-frill airlines—usually have a more limited number of flights daily. Major airlines have frequent-flyer partners, which allow you to credit mileage earned on one airline to your account with another. Low-cost airlines offer a definite price advantage and fewer restrictions, such as advance-purchase requirements. Safety-wise, low-cost carriers as a group have a good history, but **check the safety record before booking** any low-cost carrier; call the Federal Aviation Administration's Consumer Hotline (☞ Airline Complaints, *below*). For information about airline service to particular areas covered in this book, *see* the A to Z section at the end of the city chapters or the Essentials section following the coverage of each region in the side trips chapters.

➤ MAJOR AIRLINES: **Air Canada** (☎ 800/776–3000). **Alaska** (☎ 800/426–0333). **American** (☎ 800/433–7300). **America West** (☎ 800/235–9292). **British Airways** (☎ 800/247–9297). **Continental** (☎ 800/525–0280). **Delta** (☎ 800/221–1212). **EVA Airways** (☎ 800/695–1188). **Hawaiian** (☎ 800/367–5320). **Japan** (☎ 800/525–3663). **Northwest** (☎ 800/225–2525). **Thai** (☎ 800/426–5204). **TWA** (☎ 800/221–2000). **United/United Express** (☎ 800/ 241–6522). **US Airways/US Airways Express** (☎ 800/428–4322). **Western Pacific** (☎ 800/930–3030).

➤ SMALLER AIRLINES: **Canadian** (☎ 800/426–7000). **Horizon Air** (☎ 800/547–9308). **Reno Air** (☎ 800/

736–6247). **Southwest** (☎ 800/435–9792).

➤ REGIONAL AIRLINES: **Air B.C.** (☎ 604/688–5515 or 250/360–9074; 800/776–3000 in the U.S.). **Harbor Air** (☎ 800/359–3220). **Helijet Airways** (☎ 604/682–1468). **Horizon Air** (☎ 800/547–9308). **Kenmore Air** (☎ 206/486–8400 or 800/543–9595). **West Isle Air** (☎ 800/874–4434). **Westjet** (☎ 800/538–5696).

➤ FROM THE U.K.: **American** (☎ 0345/789–789). **British Airways** (☎ 0345/222–111). **Delta** (☎ 0800/414–767). **United** (☎ 0800/888–555).

#### GET THE LOWEST FARE

The least-expensive airfares to Seattle and Vancouver are priced for round-trip travel. Major airlines usually require that you **book in advance and buy the ticket within 24 hours,** and you may have to **stay over a Saturday night.** It's smart to **call a number of airlines, and when you are quoted a good price, book it on the spot**—the same fare may not be available on the same flight the next day. Airlines generally allow you to change your return date for a fee of $25–$50. If you don't use your ticket you can apply the cost toward the purchase of a new ticket, again for a small charge. However, most low-fare tickets are nonrefundable. To get the lowest airfare, **check different routings.** If your destination or home city has more than one gateway, compare prices to and from different airports. Also price off-peak flights, which may be significantly less expensive. Remember that penalties for refunds or scheduling changes are stiffer for international tickets, usually about $150. International flights are also sensitive to the season: **plan to fly in the off season** for the cheapest fares.

To save money on flights from the United Kingdom and back, **look into an APEX or Super-PEX ticket.** APEX tickets must be booked in advance and have certain restrictions. Super-PEX tickets can be purchased at the airport on the day of departure—subject to availability.

## DON'T STOP UNLESS YOU MUST

When you book, **look for nonstop flights** and **remember that "direct" flights stop at least once.** International flights on a country's flag carrier are almost always nonstop; U.S. airlines often fly direct. Try to **avoid connecting flights,** which require a change of plane. Two airlines may jointly operate a connecting flight, so ask if your airline operates every segment—you may find that your preferred carrier flies you only part of the way.

## USE AN AGENT

Travel agents, especially those who specialize in finding the lowest fares (☞ Discounts & Deals, *below*), can be especially helpful when booking a plane ticket. When you're quoted a price, **ask your agent if the price is likely to get any lower.** Good agents know the seasonal fluctuations of airfares and can usually anticipate a sale or fare war. However, waiting can be risky: The fare could go *up* as seats become scarce, and you may wait so long that your preferred flight sells out. A wait-and-see strategy works best if your plans are flexible, but if you must arrive and depart on certain dates, don't delay.

## AVOID GETTING BUMPED

Airlines routinely overbook planes, knowing that not everyone with a ticket will show up, but sometimes everyone does. When that happens, airlines ask for volunteers to give up their seats. In return, these volunteers usually get a certificate for a free flight and are rebooked on the next flight out. If there are not enough volunteers, the airline must choose who will be denied boarding. The first to get bumped are passengers who checked in late and those flying on discounted tickets, **so get to the gate and check in as early as possible,** especially during peak periods.

## ENJOY THE FLIGHT

For better service, **fly smaller or regional carriers,** which often have higher passenger-satisfaction ratings.

Sometimes you'll find leather seats, more legroom, and better food.

For more legroom, **request an emergency-row seat;** don't, however, sit in the row in front of the emergency aisle or in front of a bulkhead, where seats may not recline.

If you don't like standard airline food, **ask for special meals when booking.** These can be vegetarian, low-cholesterol, or kosher, for example.

## COMPLAIN IF NECESSARY

If your baggage goes astray or your flight goes awry, complain right away. Most carriers require that you file a claim immediately.

➤ AIRLINE COMPLAINTS: U.S. Department of Transportation **Aviation Consumer Protection Division** (✉ C-75, Room 4107, Washington, DC 20590, ☎ 202/366–2220). **Federal Aviation Administration (FAA) Consumer Hotline** (☎ 800/322–7873).

### AIRPORTS

The major gateways are **Sea-Tac (Seattle-Tacoma) International Airport** and **Vancouver International Airport.** Nonstop flying time from New York to Seattle is approximately 5 hours; flights from Chicago are about 4–4½ hours; flights between Los Angeles and Seattle take 2½ hours. Flights from New York to Vancouver take about 8 hours with connections; from Chicago, about 4½ hours nonstop; and from Los Angeles, about 3 hours nonstop. For information about airport transfers to downtown, *see* the A to Z sections at the end of the Seattle and Vancouver chapters.

➤ AIRPORT INFORMATION: **Vancouver International Airport** (☎ 604/276–6101). **Sea-Tac International Airport** (☎ 206/431–4444).

### B

### BUS TRAVEL

**Greyhound Lines** operates regular intercity bus routes to points throughout the Pacific Northwest. **Gray Line of Seattle** has daily bus service between Seattle and Victoria via the Washington State ferry at Anacortes. Smaller bus companies provide service within local areas. One such

**THE GOLD GUIDE / SMART TRAVEL TIPS**

service, **Pacific Coach Lines,** runs from downtown Vancouver to Victoria (via the British Columbia ferry system). **Quick Shuttle** provides bus service between Seattle's Sea-Tac Airport and Vancouver's major hotels and cruise terminal.

Several companies operate charter bus service and scheduled sightseeing tours that last from a few hours to several days. Most tours can be booked locally and provide a good way for visitors to see the sights comfortably within a short period of time. **Gray Line** companies in Seattle and Vancouver run such sightseeing trips.

➤ BUS COMPANIES: **Greyhound Lines** (☎ 800/231–2222). **Gray Line** (☎ 206/624–5077 in Seattle; 604/681–8687 in Vancouver; 250/388–5248 in Victoria). **Pacific Coach Lines** (☎ 800/661–1725). **Quick Shuttle** (☎ 604/244–3744; 800/665–2122 in the U.S.).

## BUSINESS HOURS

Most retail stores in Washington are open from 9:30 to 6 seven days a week in downtown locations and later at suburban shopping malls. Downtown stores sometimes stay open late Thursday and Friday nights. Normal banking hours are weekdays from 9 to 6; some branches are also open Saturday morning.

In British Columbia, most stores are open Saturday to Tuesday from 9 to 6, and Wednesday to Friday from 9 AM to 9 PM. Normal banking hours in Canada are from 9 to 4 on weekdays and from 9 to 3 on Saturday. Some branches may be closed Monday.

## C

## CAMERAS, CAMCORDERS, & COMPUTERS

Always **keep your film, tape, or computer disks out of the sun.** Carry an extra supply of batteries, and **be prepared to turn on your camera, camcorder, or laptop** to prove to security personnel that the device is real. Always **ask for hand inspection of film,** which becomes clouded after successive exposure to airport x-ray machines, and **keep videotapes and computer disks away from metal detectors.**

➤ PHOTO HELP: **Kodak Information Center** (☎ 800/242–2424). *Kodak Guide to Shooting Great Travel Pictures,* available in bookstores or from Fodor's Travel Publications (☎ 800/533–6478), $16.50 plus $4 shipping.

## CAR RENTAL

➤ MAJOR AGENCIES: **Alamo** (☎ 800/327–9633; 0800/272–2000 in the U.K.). **Avis** (☎ 800/331–1212; 800/879–2847 in Canada). **Budget** (☎ 800/527–0700; 0800/181181 in the U.K.). **Dollar** (☎ 800/800–4000; 0990/565656 in the U.K., where it is known as Eurodollar). **Hertz** (☎ 800/654–3131; 800/263–0600 in Canada; 0345/555888 in the U.K.). **National InterRent** (☎ 800/227–7368; 01345/222525 in the U.K., where it is known as Europcar Inter-Rent).

## CUT COSTS

To get the best deal, **book through a travel agent who is willing to shop around.** When pricing cars, **ask about the location of the rental lot.** Some off-airport locations offer lower rates, and their lots are only minutes from the terminal via complimentary shuttle. You also may want to **price local car-rental companies,** whose rates may be lower still, although their service and maintenance may not be as good as those of a name-brand agency. Remember to ask about required deposits, cancellation penalties, and drop-off charges if you're planning to pick up the car in one city and leave it in another.

Also **ask your travel agent about a company's customer-service record.** How has it responded to late plane arrivals and vehicle mishaps? Are there often lines at the rental counter, and, if you're traveling during a holiday period, does a confirmed reservation guarantee you a car?

## NEED INSURANCE?

When driving a rented car you are generally responsible for any damage to or loss of the vehicle. You also are liable for any property damage or personal injury that you may cause while driving. Before you rent, **see** what coverage you already have under the terms of your personal auto-insurance policy and credit cards.

For about $14 a day, rental companies sell protection, known as a collision- or loss-damage waiver (CDW or LDW), that eliminates your liability for damage to the car; it's always optional and should never be automatically added to your bill.

In most states you don't need a CDW if you have personal auto insurance or other liability insurance. However, **make sure you have enough coverage to pay for the car.** If you do not have auto insurance or an umbrella policy that covers damage to third parties, purchasing a CDW or LDW is highly recommended.

## BEWARE SURCHARGES

Before you pick up a car in one city and leave it in another, **ask about drop-off charges or one-way service fees,** which can be substantial. Note, too, that some rental agencies charge extra if you return the car before the time specified on your contract. To avoid a hefty refueling fee, **fill the tank just before you turn in the car,** but be aware that gas stations near the rental outlet may overcharge.

## MEET THE REQUIREMENTS

In Canada your own driver's license is acceptable.

In the United States you must be 21 to rent a car, and rates may be higher if you're under 25. You'll pay extra for child seats (about $3 per day), which are compulsory for children under five, and for additional drivers (about $2 per day). Residents of the United Kingdom will need a reservation voucher, a passport, a U.K. driver's license, and a travel policy that covers each driver in order to pick up a car.

## CHILDREN & TRAVEL

Be sure to plan ahead and **involve your youngsters** as you outline your trip. When packing, include things to keep them busy en route. On sightseeing days try to schedule activities of special interest to your children. If you are renting a car, don't forget to **arrange for a car seat** when you reserve.

## HOTELS

Most hotels in Seattle and Vancouver allow children under a certain age to stay in their parents' room at no extra charge, but others charge them as extra adults; be sure to **ask about the cutoff age for children's discounts.**

## FLYING

As a general rule, infants under two not occupying a seat fly free in the United States and at greatly reduced fares or for free on international flights. If your children are two or older **ask about children's airfares.**

In general, the adult baggage allowance applies to children paying half or more of the adult fare. When booking international flights, **ask about carry-on allowances for those traveling with infants.** In general, for babies charged 10% of the adult fare, you are allowed one carry-on bag and a collapsible stroller, which may have to be checked; you may be limited to less if the flight is full.

According to the FAA, it's a good idea to use safety seats aloft for children weighing less than 40 pounds. Airlines, however, can set their own policies: U.S. carriers allow FAA-approved models but usually require that you buy a ticket, even if your child would otherwise ride free, because the seats must be strapped into regular seats. Airline rules vary regarding their use, so it's important to **check your airline's policy about using safety seats during takeoff and landing.** Safety seats cannot obstruct any of the other passengers in the row, so get an appropriate seat assignment as early as possible.

When making your reservation, **request children's meals or a free-standing bassinet** if you need them; the latter are available only to those seated at the bulkhead, where there's enough legroom. Remember, however, that bulkhead seats may not have their own overhead bins, and there's no storage space in front of you—a major inconvenience.

## GROUP TRAVEL

If you're planning to take your kids on a tour, look for companies that specialize in family travel.

➤ FAMILY-FRIENDLY TOUR OPERATORS: **Grandtravel** (✉ 6900 Wisconsin Ave.,

Suite 706, Chevy Chase, MD 20815, ☎ 301/986–0790 or 800/247–7651) for people traveling with grandchildren ages 7–17. **Families Welcome!** (⊠ 92 N. Main St., Ashland, OR 97520, ☎ 541/482–6121 or 800/326–0724, FAX 541/482–0660).

## CONSUMER PROTECTION

Whenever possible, **pay with a major credit card** so you can cancel payment if there's a problem, provided that you can provide documentation. This is a good practice whether you're buying travel arrangements before your trip or shopping at your destination.

If you're doing business with a particular company for the first time, **contact your local Better Business Bureau and the attorney general's offices** in your state and the company's home state, as well. Have any complaints been filed?

Finally, if you're buying a package or tour, always **consider travel insurance** that includes default coverage (☞ Insurance, *below*).

➤ LOCAL BBBs: **Council of Better Business Bureaus** (⊠ 4200 Wilson Blvd., Suite 800, Arlington, VA 22203, ☎ 703/276–0100, FAX 703/525–8277).

## CRUISES

Cruise ships travel the Inside Passage and Gulf of Alaska from mid-May through late September. The most popular ports of embarkation are Vancouver and Seward (port city for Anchorage), but cruises also leave from San Francisco and Seattle. One of the best ways to see the state is to **combine your cruise with a land tour.**

To get the best deal on a cruise, **consult a cruise-only travel agency.** For a low-priced cruise alternative, **consider traveling by ferry.**

## CUSTOMS & DUTIES

### ENTERING THE U.S.

Visitors age 21 and over may import the following into the United States: 200 cigarettes or 50 cigars or 2 kilograms of tobacco, 1 liter of alcohol, and gifts worth $100. Prohibited items include meat products, seeds, plants, and fruits.

### RETURNING TO THE U.S.

You may bring home $400 worth of foreign goods duty-free if you've been out of the country for at least 48 hours and haven't already used the $400 allowance or any part of it in the past 30 days.

Travelers 21 and older may bring back 1 liter of alcohol duty-free. In addition, regardless of your age, you are allowed 200 cigarettes and 100 non-Cuban cigars. (At press time, a federal rule restricting tobacco access to persons 18 years and older did not apply to importation.) Antiques, which the U.S. Customs Service defines as objects more than 100 years old, enter duty-free, as do original works of art done entirely by hand, including paintings, drawings, and sculptures.

You may also send packages home duty-free: up to $200 worth of goods for personal use, with a limit of one parcel per addressee per day (and no alcohol or tobacco products or perfume worth more than $5); label the package PERSONAL USE, and attach a list of its contents and their retail value. Do not label the package UNSOLICITED GIFT, or your duty-free exemption will drop to $100. Mailed items do not affect your duty-free allowance on your return.

➤ INFORMATION: **U.S. Customs Service** (Inquiries, ⊠ Box 7407, Washington, DC 20044, ☎ 202/927–6724; complaints, ⊠ Office of Regulations and Rulings, 1301 Constitution Ave. NW, Washington, DC 20229; registration of equipment, ⊠ Resource Management, 1301 Constitution Ave. NW, Washington, DC 20229, ☎ 202/927–0540).

### ENTERING CANADA

If you've been out of Canada for at least seven days, you may bring in C$500 worth of goods duty-free. If you've been away for fewer than seven days but more than 48 hours, the duty-free allowance drops to C$200; if your trip lasts 24–48 hours, the allowance is C$50. You may not pool allowances with family members. Goods claimed under the C$500 exemption may follow you by mail; those claimed under the lesser exemptions must accompany you.

Alcohol and tobacco products may be included in the seven-day and 48-hour exemptions but not in the 24-hour exemption. If you meet the age requirements of the province or territory through which you reenter Canada, you may bring in, duty-free, 1.14 liters (40 imperial ounces) of wine or liquor *or* 24 12-ounce cans or bottles of beer or ale. If you are 16 or older, you may bring in, duty-free, 200 cigarettes and 50 cigars; these items must accompany you.

You may send an unlimited number of gifts worth up to C$60 each duty-free to Canada. Label the package UNSOLICITED GIFT—VALUE UNDER $60. Alcohol and tobacco are excluded.

➤ INFORMATION: **Revenue Canada** (✉ 2265 St. Laurent Blvd. S, Ottawa, Ontario K1G 4K3, ☎ 613/993–0534; 800/461–9999 in Canada).

### ENTERING THE U.K.

From countries outside the European Union, including the United States and Canada, you may import, duty-free, 200 cigarettes or 50 cigars; 1 liter of spirits or 2 liters of fortified or sparkling wine or liqueurs; 2 liters of still table wine; 60 milliliters of perfume; 250 milliliters of toilet water; plus £136 worth of other goods, including gifts and souvenirs.

➤ INFORMATION: **HM Customs and Excise** (✉ Dorset House, Stamford St., London SE1 9NG, ☎ 0171/202–4227).

### D
#### DISABILITIES & ACCESSIBILITY

### TIPS & HINTS

The Seattle/King County Convention Visitor Information Bureau (✉ 520 Pike St., Suite 1300, 98101, ☎ 206/461–5800) notes the wheelchair-accessibility of attractions and lodgings in its Seattle Visitor and Lodging Guides. If you drop by the Vancouver Tourist Information Centre (✉ 200 Burrard St., ☎ 604/683–2000), you can look in the Centre's General Information binder for a list of area attractions that are wheelchair-accessible.

When discussing accessibility with an operator or reservationist, **ask hard questions.** Are there any stairs, inside *or* out? Are there grab bars next to the toilet *and* in the shower/tub? How wide is the doorway to the room? To the bathroom? For the most extensive facilities meeting the latest legal specifications, **opt for newer accommodations,** which are more likely to have been designed with access in mind. Older buildings or ships may offer more limited facilities. Be sure to **discuss your needs before booking.**

➤ COMPLAINTS: **Disability Rights Section** (✉ U.S. Dept. of Justice, Box 66738, Washington, DC 20035-6738, ☎ 202/514–0301 or 800/514–0301, FAX 202/307–1198, TTY 202/514–0383 or 800/514–0383) for general complaints. **Aviation Consumer Protection Division** (☞ Air Travel, *above*) for airline-related problems. **Civil Rights Office** (✉ U.S. Dept. of Transportation, Departmental Office of Civil Rights, S-30, 400 7th St. SW, Room 10215, Washington, DC 20590, ☎ 202/366–4648) for problems with surface transportation.

### TRAVEL AGENCIES & TOUR OPERATORS

The Americans with Disabilities Act requires that travel firms serve the needs of all travelers. That said, you should note that some agencies and operators specialize in making travel arrangements for individuals and groups with disabilities.

➤ TRAVELERS WITH MOBILITY PROBLEMS: **Access Adventures** (✉ 206 Chestnut Ridge Rd., Rochester, NY 14624, ☎ 716/889–9096), run by a former physical-rehabilitation counselor. **Hinsdale Travel Service** (✉ 201 E. Ogden Ave., Suite 100, Hinsdale, IL 60521, ☎ 630/325–1335), a travel agency that benefits from the advice of wheelchair traveler Janice Perkins. **Wheelchair Journeys** (✉ 16979 Redmond Way, Redmond, WA 98052, ☎ 425/885–2210 or 800/313–4751), for general travel arrangements.

➤ TRAVELERS WITH DEVELOPMENTAL DISABILITIES: **New Directions** (✉ 5276 Hollister Ave., Suite 207, Santa Barbara, CA 93111, ☎ 805/967–2841, FAX 805/964–7344). **Sprout** (✉ 893 Amsterdam Ave., New York, NY 10025, ☎ 212/222–9575 or 888/222–9575, FAX 212/222–9768).

## DISCOUNTS & DEALS

Be a smart shopper and **compare all your options before making a choice.** A plane ticket bought with a promotional coupon may not be cheaper than the least expensive fare from a discount ticket agency. For high-price travel purchases, such as packages or tours, keep in mind that what you get is just as important as what you save. Just because something is cheap doesn't mean it's a bargain.

### LOOK IN YOUR WALLET

When you use your credit card to make travel purchases, you may get free travel-accident insurance, collision-damage insurance, and medical or legal assistance, depending on the card and the bank that issued it. American Express, MasterCard, and Visa provide one or more of these services, so **get a copy of your credit card's travel-benefits policy.** If you are a member of the American Automobile Association (AAA) or an oil-company-sponsored road-assistance plan, always **ask hotel or car-rental reservationists about auto-club discounts.** Some clubs offer additional discounts on tours, cruises, or admission to attractions. And don't forget that auto-club membership entitles you to free maps and trip-planning services.

### DIAL FOR DOLLARS

To save money, **look into "1-800" discount reservations services,** which use their buying power to get a better price on hotels, airline tickets, and car rentals. When booking a room, always **call the hotel's local toll-free number** (if one is available) rather than the central reservations number—you'll often get a better price. Always ask about special packages or corporate rates.

➤ AIRLINE TICKETS: ☎ 800/FLY–4–LESS. ☎ 800/FLY–ASAP.

➤ HOTEL ROOMS: **Central Reservation Service (CRS)** (☎ 800/548–3311).

### SAVE ON COMBOS

Packages and guided tours can both save you money, but don't confuse the two. When you buy a package, your travel remains independent, just as though you had planned and booked the trip yourself. Fly-drive packages, which combine airfare and car rental, are often a good deal. In cities, ask the local visitors bureau about hotel packages. These often include tickets to major museum exhibits and other special events.

### JOIN A CLUB?

Many companies sell discounts in the form of travel clubs and coupon books, but these cost money. You must use participating advertisers to get a deal, and only after you recoup the initial membership cost or book price do you begin to save. If you plan to use the club or coupons frequently, you may save considerably. Before signing up, find out what discounts you get for free.

➤ DISCOUNT CLUBS: **Entertainment Travel Editions** (✉ 2125 Butterfield Rd., Troy, MI 48084, ☎ 800/445–4137), $23–$48, depending on destination. **Great American Traveler** (✉ Box 27965, Salt Lake City, UT 84127, ☎ 800/548–2812), $49.95 per year. **Moment's Notice Discount Travel Club** (✉ 7301 New Utrecht Ave., Brooklyn, NY 11204, ☎ 718/234–6295), $25 per year, single or family. **Privilege Card International** (✉ 237 E. Front St., Youngstown, OH 44503, ☎ 330/746–5211 or 800/236–9732), $74.95 per year. **Sears's Mature Outlook** (✉ Box 9390, Des Moines, IA 50306, ☎ 800/336–6330), $14.95 per year. **Travelers Advantage** (✉ CUC Travel Service, 3033 S. Parker Rd., Suite 1000, Aurora, CO 80014, ☎ 800/548–1116 or 800/648–4037), $49 per year, single or family. **Worldwide Discount Travel Club** (✉ 1674 Meridian Ave., Miami Beach, FL 33139, ☎ 305/534–2082), $50 per year family, $40 single.

## DRIVING

### FROM THE U.S.

The U.S. interstate highway network provides quick and easy access to the Pacific Northwest in spite of imposing mountain barriers. From the south, Interstate 5 (I–5) runs from the U.S.-Mexican border through California, into Oregon and Washington, and ends at the U.S.-Canadian border. Most of the population is clustered along this corridor. From the east, I–90 stretches from Boston to Seattle.

I–84 runs from the midwestern states to Portland.

The main entry point into Canada by car is on I–5 at Blaine, Washington, 30 mi south of Vancouver. Two major highways enter British Columbia from the east: the Trans-Canada Highway (the longest highway in the world, running more than 5,000 mi from St. John's, Newfoundland, to Victoria, British Columbia) and the Yellowhead Highway, which runs through northern British Columbia from the Rocky Mountains to Prince Rupert.

Border-crossing procedures are usually quick and simple (☞ Passports and Visas, *below*). The I–5 border crossing at Blaine, Washington, is open 24 hours a day and is one of the busiest border crossings anywhere between the United States and Canada. The peak traffic time at the border northbound into Canada is daily at 4 PM. Southbound, delays can be expected evenings and weekend mornings. Try to plan on reaching the border at off-peak times. There are smaller highway border stations at various other points between Washington and British Columbia, but they may be closed at night.

### INSURANCE

Vehicle insurance is compulsory in the United States and Canada. Motorists are required to produce evidence of insurance if they become involved in an accident. Upon arrival, visitors from foreign countries should contact an insurance agent or broker to obtain the necessary insurance for North America.

### SPEED LIMITS

The speed limit on U.S. interstate highways is 65 mi per hour in rural areas and 55 mi per hour in urban zones and on secondary highways. In Canada (where the metric system is used), the speed limit is usually 100 kph (62 mph) on expressways and 80 kph (50 mph) on secondary roads.

### WINTER DRIVING

In coastal areas, the mild, damp climate contributes to roadways that are frequently wet. Winter snowfalls are not common (generally only once or twice a year), but when snow does fall, traffic grinds to a halt and the roadways become treacherous and stay that way until the snow melts.

Tire chains, studs, or snow tires are essential equipment for winter travel in mountain areas such as Leavenworth, Washington, or Whistler, British Columbia. If you're planning to drive into high elevations, be sure to check the weather forecast beforehand. Even the main-highway mountain passes can be forced to close because of snow conditions. During the winter months, state and provincial highway departments operate snow advisory telephone lines that give pass conditions.

### F
### FERRY TRAVEL

Ferries play an important part in the transportation network of the Pacific Northwest. In some areas, ferries provide the only form of access into and out of communities. In other places, ferries transport thousands of commuters a day to and from work in the cities. For visitors, ferries are one of the best ways to get a feel for the region and its ties to the sea.

### BRITISH COLUMBIA

**B.C. Ferries** operates ferries between the mainland and Vancouver Island and elsewhere, carrying passengers, cars, campers, RVs, trucks, and buses. Peak traffic times are Friday afternoon, Saturday morning, and Sunday afternoon, especially during summer months and holiday weekends.

**Black Ball Transport**'s MV *Coho* makes daily crossings year-round, from Port Angeles to Victoria. The *Coho* can carry 800 passengers and 100 cars across the Strait of Juan de Fuca in 1½ hours. Advance reservations are not accepted.

**Clipper Navigation** operates three passenger-only jet catamarans between Seattle and Victoria. One makes the trip in two hours, another makes it in three hours, and the third, which takes the scenic route, makes it in five hours. The company also operates the *Princess Marguerite III* car and passenger ferry between Seattle and Victoria, with one round-trip daily from mid-May to mid-September. The sailing times is 4½ hours each way.

➤ FERRY COMPANIES: **B.C. Ferries** (✉ 1112 Fort St., Victoria, BC V8V 4V2, ☎ 250/386–3431 in Victoria; 604/277–0277 in Vancouver; 888/223–3779 in British Columbia only). **Black Ball Transport** (✉ 430 Belleville St., Victoria, BC V8V 1W9, ☎ 604/386–2202 in Victoria; 360/457–4491 in Port Angeles). **Clipper Navigation** (✉ 2701 Alaskan Way, Pier 69, Seattle, WA 98121, ☎ 250/480–5555 in Victoria; 206/448–5000 in Seattle; 800/888–2535 in the U.S. only).

➤ DISCOUNT PASSES: The **AlaskaPass Travelpass** (✉ Box 351, Vashon Island, WA 98070, ☎ 800/248–7598) provides transportation aboard any British Columbia ferry as well as many connecting bus and train services. Passes of varying lengths enable the independent traveler to exercise a high degree of flexibility in choosing an itinerary.

## WASHINGTON

If you are planning to use the Washington State Ferry System, try to **avoid peak commuter hours.** The heaviest traffic flows are eastbound in the mornings and on Sunday evening and westbound on Saturday morning and weekday afternoons. The best times for travel are 9–3 and after 7 PM on weekdays. In July and August, you may have to wait up to three hours to take a car aboard one of the popular San Juan Islands ferries. Walk-on space is always available; if possible, **leave your car behind.**

**Washington State Ferries** carries more than 23 million passengers a year between points on Puget Sound and the San Juan Islands. Reservations are not available on any domestic routes.

➤ FERRY COMPANY: **Washington State Ferries** (✉ Colman Dock, Pier 52, Seattle, WA 98104, ☎ 206/464–6400; 800/843–3779 in WA).

## G
### GAY & LESBIAN TRAVEL

➤ GAY- & LESBIAN-FRIENDLY TRAVEL AGENCIES: **Advance Damron** (✉ 1 Greenway Plaza, Suite 800, Houston, TX 77046, ☎ 713/850–1140 or 800/695–0880, FAX 713/888–1010). **Club Travel** (✉ 8739 Santa Monica Blvd., West Hollywood, CA 90069, ☎ 310/358–2200 or 800/429–8747, FAX 310/358–2222). **Islanders/Kennedy Travel** (✉ 183 W. 10th St., New York, NY 10014, ☎ 212/242–3222 or 800/988–1181, FAX 212/929–8530). **Now Voyager** (✉ 4406 18th St., San Francisco, CA 94114, ☎ 415/626–1169 or 800/255–6951, FAX 415/626–8626). **Yellowbrick Road** (✉ 1500 W. Balmoral Ave., Chicago, IL 60640, ☎ 773/561–1800 or 800/642–2488, FAX 773/561–4497). **Skylink Women's Travel** (✉ 3577 Moorland Ave., Santa Rosa, CA 95407, ☎ 707/585–8355 or 800/225–5759, FAX 707/584–5637), serving lesbian travelers.

➤ LOCAL PUBLICATIONS: **Seattle Gay News** (☎ 206/324–4297). **Angles** (☎ 604/688–0265); for Vancouver.

## I
### INSURANCE

Travel insurance is the best way to **protect yourself against financial loss.** The most useful policies are trip-cancellation-and-interruption, default, medical, and comprehensive insurance.

Without insurance you will lose all or most of your money if you cancel your trip, regardless of the reason. It's essential that you **buy trip-cancellation-and-interruption insurance,** particularly if your airline ticket, cruise, or package tour is nonrefundable and cannot be changed. When considering how much coverage you need, look for a policy that will cover the cost of your trip plus the nondiscounted price of a one-way airline ticket, should you need to return home early. Also **consider default or bankruptcy insurance,** which protects you against a supplier's failure to deliver.

Medicare generally does not cover health-care costs outside the United States, nor do many privately issued policies. If your own policy does not cover you outside the United States, **consider buying supplemental medical coverage.** Remember that travel health insurance is different from a medical-assistance plan.

Citizens of the United Kingdom can buy an annual travel-insurance policy valid for most vacations during the year in which it's purchased. If you are pregnant or have a preexisting medical condition, make sure you're covered. According to the Association of British Insurers, a trade association representing 450 insurance companies, it's wise to buy extra medical coverage when you visit the United States.

If you have purchased an expensive vacation, comprehensive insurance is a must. **Look for comprehensive policies that include trip-delay insurance,** which will protect you in the event that weather problems cause you to miss your flight, tour, or cruise. A few insurers sell waivers for preexisting medical conditions. Companies that offer both features include Access America, Carefree Travel, Travel Insured International, and Travel Guard (☞ *below*).

Always **buy travel insurance directly from the insurance company**; if you buy it from a travel agency or tour operator that goes out of business you probably will not be covered for the agency or operator's default—a major risk. Before you make any purchase, **review your existing health and home-owner's policies** to find out whether they cover expenses incurred while traveling.

➤ TRAVEL INSURERS: In the United States, **Access America** (☒ 6600 W. Broad St., Richmond, VA 23230, ☎ 804/285–3300 or 800/284–8300), **Carefree Travel Insurance** (☒ Box 9366, 100 Garden City Plaza, Garden City, NY 11530, ☎ 516/294–0220 or 800/323–3149), **Near Travel Services** (☒ Box 1339, Calumet City, IL 60409, ☎ 708/868–6700 or 800/654–6700), **Travel Guard International** (☒ 1145 Clark St., Stevens Point, WI 54481, ☎ 715/345–0505 or 800/826–1300), **Travel Insured International** (☒ Box 280568, East Hartford, CT 06128-0568, ☎ 860/528–7663 or 800/243–3174), **Travelex Insurance Services** (☒ 11717 Burt St., Suite 202, Omaha, NE 68154-1500, ☎ 402/445–8637 or 800/228–9792, ᶠᴬˣ 800/867–9531), **Wallach & Company** (☒ 107 W. Federal St., Box 480, Middleburg, VA 20118, ☎ 540/687–3166 or 800/237–6615). In Canada, **Mutual of Omaha** (☒ Travel Division, 500 University Ave., Toronto, Ontario M5G 1V8, ☎ 416/598–4083; 800/

268–8825 in Canada). In the United Kingdom, **Association of British Insurers** (☒ 51 Gresham St., London EC2V 7HQ, ☎ 0171/600–3333).

## L
### LODGING

## APARTMENT & VILLA RENTALS

If you want a home base that's roomy enough for a family and comes with cooking facilities, **consider a furnished rental.** These can save you money, however some rentals are luxury properties, economical only when your party is large. Home-exchange directories list rentals (often second homes owned by prospective house swappers), and some services search for a house or apartment for you (even a castle if that's your fancy) and handle the paperwork. Some send an illustrated catalog; others send photographs only of specific properties, sometimes at a charge. Up-front registration fees may apply.

➤ RENTAL AGENTS: **Europa-Let/Tropical Inn-Let** (☒ 92 N. Main St., Ashland, OR 97520, ☎ 541/482–5806 or 800/462–4486, ᶠᴬˣ 541/482–0660). **Rent-a-Home International** (☒ 7200 34th Ave. NW, Seattle, WA 98117, ☎ 206/789–9377 or 800/488–7368, ᶠᴬˣ 206/789–9379). **Hideaways International** (☒ 767 Islington St., Portsmouth, NH 03801, ☎ 603/430–4433 or 800/843–4433, ᶠᴬˣ 603/430–4444) is a travel club whose members arrange rentals among themselves; yearly membership is $99.

## BED-AND-BREAKFASTS

➤ RESERVATION SERVICES: **Best Canadian Bed & Breakfast Network** (☒ 1090 W. King Edward Ave., Vancouver, BC V6H 1Z4, ☎ 604/738–7207). **Hometours International, Inc.** (☒ 1170 Broadway, Suite 614, New York, NY 10001, ☎ 212/689–0851 or 800/367–4668). **Northwest Bed & Breakfast Reservation Service** (☒ 610 S.W. Broadway, Portland, OR 97205, ☎ 503/243–7616). **Traveller's Bed & Breakfast** (☒ Box 492, Mercer Island, WA 98040, ☎ 206/232–2345). In the United Kingdom: **American Bed & Breakfast, Inter-Bed Network** (☒ 31 Ernest Rd., Colchester, Essex CO7 9LQ, ☎ 0206/223162).

## HOME EXCHANGES

If you would like to exchange your home for someone else's, **join a home-exchange organization,** which will send you its updated listings of available exchanges for a year and will include your own listing in at least one of them. Making the arrangements is up to you.

➤ EXCHANGE CLUB: HomeLink International (✉ Box 650, Key West, FL 33041, ☎ 305/294–7766 or 800/638–3841, FAX 305/294–1148) charges $83 per year.

## HOTELS

Many big-city hotels offer special weekend rates, sometimes up to 50% off regular prices. However, these deals are usually not extended during peak summer months, when hotels are normally full.

➤ MAJOR CHAINS: **Canadian Pacific** (☎ 800/828–7447). **Delta** (☎ 800/877–1133). **Doubletree** (☎ 800/528–0444). **Embassy Suites Hotels** (☎ 800/362–2779). **Four Seasons** (☎ 800/332–3442). **Hilton** (☎ 800/445–8667). **Holiday Inn** (☎ 800/465–4329). **Hyatt** (☎ 800/233–1234). **Marriott** (☎ 800/228–9290). **Ramada** (☎ 800/228–2828). **Sheraton** (☎ 800/325–3535). **Renaissance** (☎ 800/468–3571). **West Coast Hotels/Coast Hotels** (☎ 800/426–0670). **Westin** (☎ 800/228–3000).

## MOTELS/MOTOR INNS

Chain-run motels and motor inns can be found throughout the Pacific Northwest. Some of these establishments offer basic facilities; others provide restaurants, swimming pools, and other amenities.

➤ MAJOR CHAINS: **Best Western** (☎ 800/528–1234). **Days Inn** (☎ 800/325–2525). **La Quinta Inns** (☎ 800/531–5900). **Motel 6** (☎ 800/440–6000). **Quality Inns** (☎ 800/228–5151). **Shilo Inns** (☎ 800/222–2244). **Super 8 Motels** (☎ 800/848–8888). **Travelodge** (☎ 800/255–3050).

➤ REGIONAL CHAINS: **Cavanaugh's** (☎ 800/843–4667). **Nendel's** (☎ 800/547–0106). **Sandman Inns** (☎ 800/726-3626).

## YMCAS/YWCAS

YMCAs or YWCAs are usually a good bet for clean, no-frills, reliable lodging in large towns and cities. These buildings are often centrally located, and their rates are significantly lower than those at city hotels. Nonmembers are welcome, but they may pay slightly more than members. A few very large Ys have accommodations for couples, but sleeping arrangements are usually segregated.

# M

## MAIL

### RATES

Postage rates vary for different classes of mail and destinations. Check with the local post office for rates before mailing a letter or parcel. At press time, it cost 32¢ to mail a standard letter anywhere within the United States. Mail to Canada costs 40¢ per first ounce and 23¢ for each additional ounce; mail to Great Britain and other foreign countries costs 50¢ per half ounce.

First-class rates in Canada are 45¢ for up to 30 grams of mail delivered within Canada, 52¢ for up to 30 grams delivered to the United States, 70¢ for 30 to 50 grams. International mail and postcards run 90¢ for up to 20 grams, $1.37 for 20–50 grams.

### RECEIVING MAIL

Visitors can have letters or parcels sent to them while they are traveling by using the following address: Name of addressee, c/o General Delivery, Main Post Office, City and State/Province, U.S./Canada, Zip Code (U.S.) or Postal Code (Canada). Contact the nearest post office for further details. Any item mailed to "General Delivery" must be picked up by the addressee in person within 15 days or it will be returned to the sender.

## MONEY

The United States and Canada both use the same currency denominations—dollars and cents—although each currency has a different value on the world market. At press time (fall 1997), one Canadian dollar was worth U.S. 72¢. One U.S. dollar was worth $1.38 Canadian. A good way to be sure you're getting the best exchange rate is by using your credit card. The issuing bank will convert your bill at the current rate. Prices in

Canada are always quoted in Canadian dollars.

### ATMS

Before leaving home, **make sure that your credit cards have been programmed for ATM use.**

➤ ATM LOCATIONS: **Cirrus** (☎ 800/424–7787). **Plus** (☎ 800/843–7587).

## N
### NATIONAL PARKS

You may be able to **save money on park entrance fees** by getting a discount pass. The Golden Eagle Pass ($25) gets you and your companions free admission to all parks for one year. (Camping and parking are extra.) Both the Golden Age Passport, for U.S. citizens or permanent residents age 62 and older, and the Golden Access Passport, for travelers with disabilities, entitle holders to free entry to all national parks plus 50% off fees for the use of many park facilities and services. Both passports are free; you must show proof of age and U.S. citizenship or permanent residency (such as a U.S. passport, driver's license, or birth certificate) or proof of disability. All three passes are available at all national park entrances. Golden Eagle and Golden Access passes are also available by mail.

If you're traveling in Canada, you may want to invest in Parks Canada's pass to the nation's parks. This pass covers the cost of admission and parking for one year, and is available to Canadian and non-Canadian citizens. One pass ($70; $53 for visitors age 65 and older) pays for a carload of up to 10 people. Information is available by phone or mail.

➤ PASSES: **National Park Service** (✉ Dept. of the Interior, Washington, DC 20240). **Parks Canada** (✉ 220 4th Ave. SE, Room 552, Calgary T2G 4X3, ☎ 403/292–4401).

## P
### PACKING FOR SEATTLE & VANCOUVER

Residents of the Pacific Northwest are generally informal by nature and wear clothing that reflects their disposition. Summer days are warm but evenings can cool off substantially. Your best bet is to **dress in layers**— sweatshirts, sweaters, and jackets are removed or put on as the day progresses. If you plan to explore the region's cities on foot, or if you choose to hike along mountain trails or beaches, bring comfortable walking shoes.

Dining out is usually an informal affair, although some restaurants require a jacket and tie for men and dresses for women. Residents tend to dress conservatively when going to the theater or symphony, but it's not uncommon to see some patrons wearing jeans. In other words, almost anything is acceptable for most occasions.

If you plan on hiking or camping during the summer, insect repellent is a must. Bring an extra pair of eyeglasses or contact lenses in your carry-on luggage, and if you have a health problem, **pack enough medication** to last the entire trip. It's important that you **don't put prescription drugs or valuables in luggage to be checked**: It might go astray.

### LUGGAGE

In general, you are entitled to check two bags on flights within the United States and Canada and on international flights leaving the United States and Canada. A third piece may be brought on board, but it must fit easily under the seat in front of you or in the overhead compartment. Air Canada and some other Canadian airlines allow a fourth carry-on bag.

Airline liability for baggage is limited to $1,250 per person on flights within the United States and $750 on most Canadian airlines for flights within Canada. On international flights, Canadian and U.S. airline liability amounts to $9.07 per pound or $20 per kilogram for checked baggage (roughly $640 per 70-pound bag) and $400 per passenger for unchecked baggage. Insurance for losses exceeding these amounts can be bought from the airline at check-in for $5–$10 per $1,000 of coverage; note that this coverage excludes a rather extensive list of items, which is shown on your airline ticket.

Before departure, **itemize your bags' contents** and their worth, and label the bags with your name, address, and phone number. (If you use your home address, cover it so that potential thieves can't see it readily.) Inside each bag, **pack a copy of your itinerary.** At check-in, **make sure that each bag is correctly tagged** with the destination airport's three-letter code. If your bags arrive damaged or fail to arrive at all, file a written report with the airline before leaving the airport.

### PASSPORTS & VISAS

Once your travel plans are confirmed, **get a passport even though you don't need one to enter Canada**—it's always the best form of ID.

### U.S. CITIZENS

Citizens and legal residents of the United States do not need a passport or a visa to enter Canada, but proof of citizenship (a birth certificate or valid passport) and photo identification may be requested. Naturalized U.S. residents should carry their naturalization certificate or "green card." U.S. residents entering Canada from a third country must have a valid passport, naturalization certificate, or "green card."

### CANADIAN CITIZENS

A passport is not required for entry into the United States.

### U.K. CITIZENS

Citizens of the United Kingdom need only a valid passport to enter Canada for stays of up to 90 days.

British citizens need a valid passport to enter the United States. If you are staying for fewer than 90 days on vacation, with a return or onward ticket, you probably will not need a visa. However, you will need to fill out the Visa Waiver Form, 1-94W, supplied by the airline.

➤ INFORMATION: **London Passport Office** (☎ 0990/21010) for fees and documentation requirements and to request an emergency passport. **U.S. Embassy Visa Information Line** (☎ 01891/200–290) for U.S. visa information; calls cost 49p per minute or 39p per minute cheap rate. **U.S. Embassy Visa Branch** (✉ 5 Upper Grosvenor St., London W1A 2JB) for U.S. visa information; send a self-addressed, stamped envelope. Write

the **U.S. Consulate General** (✉ Queen's House, Queen St., Belfast BT1 6EO) if you live in Northern Ireland.

## S

### SENIOR-CITIZEN TRAVEL

To qualify for age-related discounts, **mention your senior-citizen status up front** when booking hotel reservations (not when checking out) and before you're seated in restaurants (not when paying the bill). Discounts may be limited to certain menus, days, or hours. When renting a car, **ask about promotional car-rental discounts,** which can be cheaper than senior-citizen rates.

➤ EDUCATIONAL TRAVEL PROGRAMS: **Elderhostel** (✉ 75 Federal St., 3rd floor, Boston, MA 02110, ☎ 617/426–8056).

### SPORTS

### BICYCLING

Bicycling is a popular sport in Seattle and Vancouver, appealing to both families out for a leisurely ride and avid cyclists seeking a challenge on rugged mountain trails. Several cycling organizations sponsor trips of various lengths and degrees of difficulty, both on- and off-road.

➤ BICYCLE CLUBS: **Cascade Bicycle Club** (☎ 206/522–2453). **Bicycling Association of British Columbia** (✉ 332–1367 W. Broadway, Vancouver, BC V6H 4A9, ☎ 604/737–3034).

### CLIMBING/MOUNTAINEERING

➤ CLIMBING CLUB: **The Mountaineers** (✉ 300 3rd Ave. W, Seattle, WA 98119, ☎ 206/284–6310).

### FISHING

➤ INFORMATION/LICENSES: **Department of Fisheries and Oceans** (✉ 555 W. Hastings St., Suite 400, Vancouver, BC V6B 5G3, ☎ 604/666–0384) for saltwater fishing. **Ministry of Environment, Fish and Wildlife Information** (✉ Parliament Bldgs., Victoria, BC V8V 1X5, ☎ 604/387–9740) for freshwater fishing. **Washington Department of Fish and Wildlife** (✉ 600 Capitol Way N, Olympia, WA 98501, ☎ 360/902–2200) for all types of fishing.

## HIKING

**National Parks and Forests Outdoor Recreation Information Center** (✉ 222 Yale Ave. N, Seattle, WA 98109, ☎ 206/470–4060) has maps of regional trails.

## HUNTING

➤ FACILITIES/LICENSES: **Washington Department of Fish and Wildlife** (✉ 600 Capitol Way N, Olympia, WA 98501, ☎ 360/902–2200). **British Columbia Ministry of Environment, Wildlife Branch** (✉ 810 Blanshard St., Victoria, BC V8W 2H1, ☎ 604/ 387–9740).

## SCUBA DIVING

The crystal-clear waters of Puget Sound present excellent opportunities for scuba diving and underwater photography.

➤ RENTALS & INFORMATION: **Underwater Sports** (✉ 10545 Aurora St., Seattle, WA 98133, ☎ 206/362–3310). **Dive B.C.** (✉ 707 Westminster Ave., Powell River, BC V8A 1C5, ☎ 604/485–6267).

## SKIING

Washington operates a system of more than 40 **SnoParks.** The cost to ski these groomed cross-country trails within state parks is $7 per day, $10 for three days, and $20 for a seasonal pass.

➤ PASSES & INFORMATION: **Office of Winter Recreation, Parks and Recreation Commission** (✉ 7150 Cleanwater La., Box 42650, Olympia, WA 98504, ☎ 360/902–8500).

## STUDENTS

➤ STUDENT IDs & SERVICES: **Council on International Educational Exchange** (✉ CIEE, 205 E. 42nd St., 14th floor, New York, NY 10017, ☎ 212/822–2600 or 888/268–6245, FAX 212/822–2699), for mail orders only, in the United States. **Travel Cuts** (✉ 187 College St., Toronto, Ontario M5T 1P7, ☎ 416/979–2406 or 800/ 667–2887) in Canada.

➤ HOSTELING: **Hostelling International—American Youth Hostels** (✉ 733 15th St. NW, Suite 840, Washington, DC 20005, ☎ 202/783–6161, FAX 202/783–6171). **Hostelling International—Canada** (✉ 400-205 Catherine St., Ottawa, Ontario K2P 1C3, ☎ 613/237–7884, FAX 613/

237–7868). **Youth Hostel Association of England and Wales** (✉ Trevelyan House, 8 St. Stephen's Hill, St. Albans, Hertfordshire AL1 2DY, ☎ 01727/855215 or 01727/845047, FAX 01727/844126). Membership in the United States, $25; in Canada, C$26.75; in the United Kingdom, £9.30.

➤ STUDENT TOURS: **Contiki Holidays** (✉ 300 Plaza Alicante, Suite 900, Garden Grove, CA 92840, ☎ 714/ 740–0808 or 800/266–8454, FAX 714/740–2034).

## T

### TAXES

The sales tax in Washington varies from 7% to 8.6%. Seattle adds 5% to the rate for hotel rooms. In British Columbia, consumers pay an 8% to 10% provincial and municipal tax. The percentage varies from one municipality to another.

### GST

Canada's Goods and Services Tax (GST) is 7%, applicable on virtually every purchase except basic groceries and a small number of other items. Visitors to Canada may claim a full rebate of the GST on any goods taken out of the country as well as on short-term accommodations. Rebates can be claimed either immediately on departure from Canada at participating duty-free shops or by mail. Instant cash rebates up to a maximum of $500 are provided by some duty-free shops when leaving Canada, and most provinces do not tax goods that are shipped directly by the vendor to the purchaser's home. Always **save your original receipts** from stores and hotels, and **be sure the name and address of the establishment is shown on the receipt.** Original receipts are not returned. The total amount of GST on each receipt must be at least $3.50, and visitors have to claim at least $14 in tax per rebate application form. Rebate forms can be obtained at most stores and hotels in Canada or by writing to Revenue Canada.

➤ INFORMATION: **Revenue Canada** (✉ Visitor Rebate Program, Summerside Tax Centre, Summerside, Prince Edward Island C1N 6C6, ☎ 800/ 668-4748 in Canada; 902/432–5608 from outside of Canada).

## TELEPHONES

The telephone area codes are 206 for Seattle and 253, 425, or 360 for other western Washington locales. Vancouver's area code is 604; the code in Victoria and the Gulf Islands is 250.

Pay telephones cost 25¢ for local calls. Charge phones are also found in many locations. These phones can be used to charge a call to a telephone-company credit card, your home phone, or the party you are calling: You do not need to deposit 25¢. For directory assistance, dial 1, the area code, and 555–1212. For local directory assistance, dial 1 followed by 555–1212. You can dial most international calls direct. Dial 0 to reach an operator.

## CALLING HOME

AT&T, MCI, and Sprint long-distance services make calling home relatively convenient and let you avoid hotel surcharges. Typically you dial an 800 number in the United States.

➤ To Obtain Access Codes: AT&T USADirect (☎ 800/874–4000). MCI Call USA (☎ 800/444–4444). Sprint Express (☎ 800/793–1153).

## TIPPING

Tips and service charges are usually not automatically added to a bill in the United States or Canada. If service is satisfactory, customers generally give waiters, waitresses, taxi drivers, barbers, hairdressers, and so forth, a tip of from 15% to 20% of the total bill. Bellhops, doormen, and porters at airports and railway stations are generally tipped $1 for each item of luggage.

## TOUR OPERATORS

Buying a prepackaged tour or independent vacation can make your trip to Seattle and Vancouver less expensive and more hassle-free. Because everything is prearranged you'll spend less time planning.

Operators that handle several hundred thousand travelers per year can use their purchasing power to give you a good price. Their high volume may also indicate financial stability. But some small companies provide more personalized service; because they tend to specialize, they may also be more knowledgeable about a given area.

### A GOOD DEAL?

The more your package or tour includes, the better you can predict the ultimate cost of your vacation. Make sure you know exactly what is covered, and **beware of hidden costs.** Are taxes, tips, and service charges included? Transfers and baggage handling? Entertainment and excursions? These can add up.

If the package or tour you are considering is priced lower than in your wildest dreams, **be skeptical.** Also, **make sure your travel agent knows the accommodations** and other services. Ask about the hotel's location, room size, beds, and whether it has a pool, room service, or programs for children, if you care about these. Has your agent been there in person or sent others you can contact?

### BUYER BEWARE

Each year consumers are stranded or lose their money when tour operators—even very large ones with excellent reputations—go out of business. So **check out the operator.** Find out how long the company has been in business, and ask several agents about its reputation. **Don't book unless the firm has a consumer-protection program.**

Members of the National Tour Association and United States Tour Operators Association are required to set aside funds to cover your payments and travel arrangements in case the company defaults. Nonmembers may carry insurance instead. Look for the details, and for the name of an underwriter with a solid reputation, in the operator's brochure. Note: When it comes to tour operators, **don't trust escrow accounts.** Although the Department of Transportation watches over charter-flight operators, no regulatory body prevents tour operators from raiding the till. You may want to protect yourself by buying travel insurance that includes a tour-operator default provision. For more information, *see* Consumer Protection, *above.*

It's also a good idea to choose a company that participates in the Tour Operator Program (TOP) of the American Society of Travel Agents. This gives you a forum if there are any disputes between you and your tour operator; ASTA will act as mediator.

➤ TOUR-OPERATOR RECOMMENDATIONS: **American Society of Travel Agents** (☞ *below*). **National Tour Association** (⊠ NTA, 546 E. Main St., Lexington, KY 40508, ☎ 606/226–4444 or 800/755–8687). **United States Tour Operators Association** (⊠ USTOA, 342 Madison Ave., Suite 1522, New York, NY 10173, ☎ 212/599–6599, FAX 212/599–6744).

## USING AN AGENT

In fact, large operators accept bookings made only through travel agents. But it's a good idea to **collect brochures from several agencies,** because some agents' suggestions may be influenced by relationships with tour and package firms that reward them for volume sales. If you have a special interest, **find an agent with expertise in that area**; ASTA (☞ Travel Agencies, *below*) has a database of specialists worldwide. Do some homework on your own, too: Local tourism boards can provide information about lesser-known and small-niche operators, some of which may sell only direct.

## SINGLE TRAVELERS

Prices for packages and tours are usually quoted per person, based on two sharing a room. If traveling solo, you may be required to pay the full double-occupancy rate. Some operators eliminate this surcharge if you agree to be matched with a roommate of the same sex, even if one is not found by departure time.

## GROUP TOURS

Among companies that sell tours to Seattle and Vancouver, the following are nationally known, have a proven reputation, and offer plenty of options. The classifications used below represent different price categories, and you'll probably encounter these terms when talking to a travel agent or tour operator. The key difference is usually in accommodations, which run from budget to better, and better-yet to best.

➤ DELUXE: **Globus** (⊠ 5301 S. Federal Circle, Littleton, CO 80123-2980, ☎ 303/797–2800 or 800/221–0090, FAX 303/347–2080).

**Maupintour** (⊠ 1515 St. Andrews Dr., Lawrence, KS 66047, ☎ 913/843–1211 or 800/255–4266, FAX 913/843–8351). **Tauck Tours** (⊠ Box 5027, 276 Post Rd. W, Westport, CT 06881-5027, ☎ 203/226–6911 or 800/468–2825, FAX 203/221–6828).

➤ FIRST CLASS: **Brendan Tours** (⊠ 15137 Califa St., Van Nuys, CA 91411, ☎ 818/785–9696 or 800/421–8446, FAX 818/902–9876). **Collette Tours** (⊠ 162 Middle St., Pawtucket, RI 02860, ☎ 401/728–3805 or 800/832–4656, FAX 401/728–1380). **Mayflower Tours** (⊠ Box 490, 1225 Warren Ave., Downers Grove, IL 60515, ☎ 708/960–3430 or 800/323–7064).

➤ BUDGET: **Cosmos** (☞ Globus, *above*).

## PACKAGES

Like group tours, independent vacation packages are available from major tour operators and airlines. The companies listed below offer vacation packages in a broad price range.

➤ AIR-HOTEL: **Air Canada Vacations** (☎ 514/876–4141). **American Airlines Fly AAway Vacations** (☎ 800/321–2121). **Delta Dream Vacations** (☎ 800/872–7786, FAX 954/357–4687).

➤ AIR-HOTEL-CAR: **Air Canada Vacations** (☎ 514/876–4141). **United Vacations** (☎ 800/328–6877).

## TRAIN TRAVEL

**Amtrak,** the U.S. passenger rail system, has daily service to Seattle from the Midwest and California. The *Empire Builder* takes a northern route from Chicago to Seattle. The *Coast Starlight* begins in Los Angeles, makes stops throughout western Oregon and Washington, and terminates its route in Seattle. The once-daily *Mt. Baker International* takes a highly scenic coastal route from Seattle to Vancouver.

Canada's passenger service, **VIA Rail Canada,** operates transcontinental routes on the *Canadian* three times weekly between eastern Canada and Vancouver.

➤ RAIL COMPANIES: **Amtrak** (☎ 800/872–7245). **VIA Rail Canada** (☎ 800/665–0200).

## WITHIN THE PACIFIC NORTHWEST

The Pacific Northwest has a number of scenic train routes in addition to those operated by Amtrak and VIA Rail Canada. The **Rocky Mountaineer** is a two-day rail cruise between Vancouver and the Canadian Rockies, May–October. There are two routes—one to Banff/Calgary and the other to Jasper—through landscapes considered to be the most spectacular in the world. An overnight hotel stop is made in Kamloops.

On Vancouver Island, **VIA Rail** runs the *E&N Railway* daily from Victoria north to Nanaimo. **BC Rail** operates daily service from its North Vancouver terminal to the town of Prince George. At Prince George it is possible to connect with VIA Rail's *Skeena* service east to Jasper and Alberta or west to Prince Rupert. BC Rail also operates a summertime excursion steam train, the *Royal Hudson*, between North Vancouver and Squamish, at the head of Howe Sound.

➤ RAIL COMPANIES: **Rocky Mountaineer** (✉ Great Canadian Railtour Co., Ltd., 340 Brooksbank Ave., Suite 104, North Vancouver, BC V7J 2C1, ☎ 800/665–7245). **BC Rail** (✉ Box 8770, Vancouver, BC V6B 4X6, ☎ 604/631–3500). **VIA Rail** (☎ 888/842–7245).

## DISCOUNT PASSES

**VIA Rail Canada** offers a **Canrailpass** that is good for 30 days. System-wide passes cost $282 (January 6–June 6 and October–December 14) and $420 (June 7–September). Youth passes (age 24 and under) are $377 in peak season and $257 during the off-season. Prices are quoted in U.S. dollars. Tickets can be purchased in the United States or the United Kingdom from a travel agent, from **Long Haul Leisurail,** or upon arrival in Canada. This offer does not apply to Canadian citizens.

The **AlaskaPass Travelpass** provides transportation aboard any British Columbia ferry as well as many connecting bus and train services. Passes of varying lengths enable the independent traveler to exercise a high degree of flexibility in choosing an itinerary.

➤ INFORMATION: **VIA Rail Canada** (☎ 800/665–0200). **Long Haul Leisurail** (✉ Box 113, Peterborough PE1 1LE, ☎ 0733/51780). **Alaska-Pass Travelpass** (✉ Box 351, Vashon Island, WA 98070, ☎ 800/248–7598).

## TRAVEL AGENCIES

A good travel agent puts your needs first. Look for an agency that has been in business at least five years, emphasizes customer service, and has someone on staff who specializes in your destination. In addition, **make sure the agency belongs to the American Society of Travel Agents** (ASTA). If your travel agency is also acting as your tour operator, *see* Tour Operators, *above*).

➤ LOCAL AGENT REFERRALS: **American Society of Travel Agents** (ASTA, ☎ 800/965–2782 24-hr hot line, FAX 703/684–8319). **Alliance of Canadian Travel Associations** (✉ 1729 Bank St., Suite 201, Ottawa, Ontario K1V 7Z5, ☎ 613/521–0474, FAX 613/521–0805). **Association of British Travel Agents** (✉ 55–57 Newman St., London W1P 4AH, ☎ 0171/637–2444, FAX 0171/637–0713).

## TRAVEL GEAR

Travel catalogs specialize in useful items, such as compact alarm clocks and travel irons, that can **save space when packing.**

➤ MAIL-ORDER CATALOGS: **Magellan's** (☎ 800/962–4943, FAX 805/568–5406). **Orvis Travel** (☎ 800/541–3541, FAX 540/343–7053). **TravelSmith** (☎ 800/950–1600, FAX 800/950–1656).

# U

## U.S. GOVERNMENT

The U.S. government can be an excellent source of inexpensive travel information. When planning your trip, **find out what government materials are available.**

➤ PAMPHLETS: **Consumer Information Center** (✉ Consumer Information Catalogue, Pueblo, CO 81009, ☎ 719/948–3334) for a free catalog that includes travel titles.

# V

## VISITOR INFORMATION

*See also* Visitor Information *in* the A to Z sections at the end of the Seattle and Vancouver chapters, and the Essentials sections throughout the Side Trips from Seattle and Side Trips from Vancouver chapters.

➤ SEATTLE: **Visitors Information Centre** (✉ Washington State Convention Center, 8th Ave. and Pike St., Seattle, WA 98104, ☎ 206/461–5840).

➤ VANCOUVER: **Vancouver Tourist Info Center** (✉ 200 Broward St., Vancouver, BC Z6C 3L6, ☎ 604/683–2000, FAX 604/682–6839).

# W

## WHEN TO GO

The Pacific Northwest's climate is the most enjoyable from June through September. Hotels in the major tourist destinations are often filled in July and August, so it's important to book reservations in advance. Summer temperatures generally range in the 70s, and rainfall is usually minimal. Nights, however, can be cool, so if you're going to enjoy the nightlife, take along a sweater or jacket.

Spring and fall are also excellent times to visit. The weather usually remains quite good, and the prices for accommodations, transportation, and tours can be lower (and the crowds much smaller) in the most popular destinations.

In winter, the coastal rain turns to snow in the nearby mountains, making the region a skier's dream.

## CLIMATE

Tempered by a warm Japan current and protected by the mountains from the extreme weather conditions found inland, the coastal regions of Washington and British Columbia experience a uniformly mild climate.

Average daytime summer highs are in the 70s; winter temperatures are generally in the 40s. Snow is uncommon in the lowland areas. If it does snow (usually in December or January), everything grinds to a halt—but children love it!

The area's reputation for rain is somewhat misleading, as the amount of rainfall in the Pacific Northwest varies greatly from one locale to another. In the coastal mountains, for example, 160 inches of rain fall annually, creating temperate rain forests. In Washington and British Columbia, near-desert conditions prevail, with rainfall as low as 6 inches per year.

Seattle has an average of only 36 inches of rainfall a year—less than New York, Chicago, or Miami. The wetness, however, is concentrated during the winter months, when cloudy skies and drizzly weather persist. More than 75% of Seattle's annual precipitation occurs from October through March.

➤ FORECASTS: **Weather Channel Connection** (☎ 900/932–8437), 95¢ per minute from a Touch-Tone phone.

The following are average daily maximum and minimum temperatures for Seattle and Vancouver.

THE GOLD GUIDE / SMART TRAVEL TIPS

## Climate in Seattle and Vancouver

**SEATTLE**

| | | | | | | | | |
|------|------|-----|------|------|-----|-------|------|-----|
| Jan. | 45F | 7C | May | 66F | 19C | Sept. | 69F | 20C |
| | 35 | 2 | | 47 | 8 | | 52 | 11 |
| Feb. | 50F | 10C | June | 70F | 21C | Oct. | 62F | 16C |
| | 37 | 3 | | 52 | 11 | | 47 | 8 |
| Mar. | 53F | 12C | July | 76F | 24C | Nov. | 51F | 10C |
| | 38 | 3 | | 56 | 13 | | 40 | 4 |
| Apr. | 59F | 13C | Aug. | 75F | 24C | Dec. | 47F | 8C |
| | 42 | 5 | | 55 | 13 | | 37 | 3 |

**VANCOUVER**

| | | | | | | | | |
|------|------|-----|------|------|-----|-------|------|-----|
| Jan. | 41F | 5C | May | 63F | 17C | Sept. | 64F | 18C |
| | 32 | 0 | | 46 | 8 | | 50 | 10 |
| Feb. | 46F | 8C | June | 66F | 19C | Oct. | 57F | 14C |
| | 34 | 1 | | 52 | 11 | | 43 | 6 |
| Mar. | 48F | 9C | July | 72F | 22C | Nov. | 48F | 9C |
| | 36 | 2 | | 55 | 13 | | 37 | 3 |
| Apr. | 55F | 13C | Aug. | 72F | 22C | Dec. | 45F | 7C |
| | 41 | 5 | | 55 | 13 | | 34 | 1 |

# 1 Destination: Seattle & Vancouver

# TWO CHAIRS ARE BETTER THAN THREE

**T**HE FIRST TIME I visited Seattle, I took with me preconceived ideas about the Pacific Northwest. A friend who had moved here was full of stories about camping on the weekends, biking after work, and theater tickets that cost the same as movie tickets in New York. Articles in the national press raved about the region's natural beauty, cultural vibrancy, and healthy economy. "America's Most Livable City," they touted, referring to Seattle. So I arrived with high expectations.

The weather was ideal. We went to Orcas Island—a short drive and ferry ride from Seattle—and camped on a bluff overlooking Puget Sound. My friend fell asleep, and I lay on my back in front of a dying fire, beneath stellar patterns I had rarely noticed before, and considered how inadequate my life in New York was, how suited I was to the natural, more wholesome lives people led in the Great Northwest. All of what I had heard seemed true: I felt I had found the ideal blend of natural splendor and urban sophistication, where a rain forest could mingle in perfect harmony with a modern metropolis. The next day we drove to the top of Mount Constitution, the highest peak on the island. From this privileged perspective, I surveyed virtually the whole pristine region, including Puget Sound, Vancouver Island, and the Olympic Mountains. I decided to move west.

Needless to say, I suffered some disillusionment. I can remember waiting for a taxi at Sea-Tac Airport on my first day in Seattle, trying to decide if the mist demanded an umbrella and wondering why everything suddenly looked so dreary. Two days later I made my first major purchase in Seattle—a mountain bike. Eager to prove myself an outdoorsman, that evening I pedaled to a party on Queen Anne Hill; the terrain—typical for Seattle—was a little steeper than I had expected. Cursing every step, I ended up climbing the arduous hill, with bike alongside me. I was beginning to learn that, while the image of the great outdoors meeting the great metropolis evokes drama, if not romance, the two forces don't always create the most comfortable situations.

One December not too long ago, for instance, a snowstorm hit Seattle, leaving the steep hills sheathed in ice. As a New York native, I expected salt on the sidewalks, sand on the streets, and a fairly active city the next day. Not a chance. Many of the busiest streets hadn't been plowed, cars were abandoned by the side of the road, and businesses and schools were shut down. The message was clear: If you live in the Pacific Northwest, you must accept nature's tendency to disrupt and inconvenience you. Houses slide down eroded slopes into Puget Sound, volcanoes erupt, and it rains and rains and rains. Rigidity, outrage, obstinate determination, or any other form of hubris can get you into trouble. I was the only passenger on a bus one night, and the bus driver drove three blocks off his route to drop me at the door of my destination. Sure, he was being kind, but it's more than that. Native northwesterners are used to adjustments, and they make them without thinking twice.

My enchanted experience on Orcas Island was no fluke. If nature disrupts, its grace and power also inspires. On a clear day in Seattle, Mount Rainier floats, dreamlike, over the industrial southern end of the city; the peaks of the Cascade Range reign in the east, looming over Lake Washington; in the west, the Olympics rise over Bainbridge Island and Elliott Bay, and ragged clouds turn an evening sky into an explosion of color. Standing at the seawall in Vancouver's Stanley Park, the mountains rest at what seems like just an arm's reach across Burrard Inlet. Take just a few steps onto one of the park trails and you feel as though you're lost in a virgin forest, with no sign of city life.

If the weather has been especially depressing, I seize the first clear day and rent a canoe at the University of Washington waterfront in Seattle. The channels at the Arboretum give way to Lake Washington, fringed by the Cascade Range. Inevitably, I feel serene, as I did on Orcas Island, and the Northwest once again becomes the ideal place to live.

But residents of Seattle and Vancouver don't just paddle away their days. Politics run hot here, and local leaders work hard to maintain legislation that has helped to protect the environment of the cities and their surroundings. Likewise, advocates deserve credit for their efforts to restore some of the history that went into the makings of Seattle and Vancouver. In 1971, the Canadian Government bought Granville Island, which was originally used to store logging supplies. Today, only businesses that deal with maritime activities, the arts, and a public market are permitted to set up shop on the island. A walk around the island will lead you past produce stalls, crafts merchants, food vendors, and artists' studios. Around the same time as the Granville Island purchase, Vancouver embarked on the restoration of Gastown, a historic area by the waterfront and named for "Gassy" Jack Deighton, who opened the settlement's first saloon. By the time Deighton died in 1875, a bawdy and sometimes lawless town had sprouted in the vicinity of his saloon. In one way, the area remained faithful to his vision, as it proceeded for the next 100 years to attract an abundance of drunks. In 1960, more than two-thirds of all arrests in Vancouver were made in the vicinity of the old Deighton House. Some of the old buildings remain, but until the rehabilitation the squalor of the neighborhood was more prominent than its history. Today boutiques, galleries, restaurants, and a steam-powered clock line the cobblestone streets of this touted tourist spot—a worthy tribute to the old codger.

Vancouver's history predates Gassy Jack Deighton and the first white entourage. When the settlers arrived in Vancouver, there were, according to one witness, 10 Suquamish villages in the area. A few years later, most of the land had been claimed by the newcomers, and the villages had vanished. Fortunately, the native culture survived, and today Vancouver is the center for producing and selling native Pacific coast crafts. Local Haida carver Bill Reid has his studio on Granville Island; galleries display the works of Inuit, Tlingit, Tsimshian, Kwakiutl, Haida, and Salish artisans; students can study the craft at the University of British Columbia; and the university's Museum of Anthropology houses one of the finest collections of native art in the world. Western techniques have been studied and incorporated into the works, but the dominant styles and the mythological references—usually related to the animal wildlife of the region—are firmly rooted in Pacific coast cultures.

SEATTLE'S EARLY history began with the native Suquamish people, and the city has devoted much energy to preserving its historic neighborhoods. In the late 1800s, Seattle began to expand around a steam-powered lumber mill at the foot of a hill, in the area of what is now called Pioneer Square. Loggers cut the trees near the hilltop and skidded them down to the mill along a road that came to be known as "skid road." "Road" soon became "row," and the term lost its original significance.

By the early 1960s, Pioneer Square had lost its historic character, going the same sordid route as Gastown had in Vancouver. So Seattle undertook a massive rehabilitation of its own. Historic buildings were restored, shops and galleries moved in, and, in keeping with the theme, the city put 1890s-style uniforms on the police officers who walked the local beat.

Fortunately, Pioneer Square hasn't become overly sanitized. On my first visit to Seattle, a friend took me to a small bar on the block between the square and the waterfront. A quiet place to have a beer, she said. Soon after we sat down, a man with a gruff voice broke into a chorus of "Barnacle Bill the Sailor." When a younger man dressed in black told him to be quiet, a fight broke out. So much for the quiet beer. Most urban rehabilitations leave only the pure and clean, but Pioneer Square retains its old rowdiness, lending authenticity to the restoration. A church that feeds the homeless is right across the street from the Elliott Bay Bookstore, where well-known writers read from their latest works. On weekend nights, the OK Hotel (not really a hotel) may host bands that appeal to young leather-adorned rock fans, while just a block away Il Terrazzo Carmine serves gourmet Italian fare to a decidedly upscale clientele. Seattle's unrefined elements nicely balance all the historical charm, making this part of town feel lived-in and real.

The city's other major restoration project was the Pike Place Market, which was originally built in 1907. The complex of lofts and stalls overlooking Elliott Bay nearly faced the demolition ball in the 1960s, but it was saved by a voter referendum. Amid a maze of ramps and hallways, today's visitors shop for gourmet foods, spices, posters, jewelry, crafts, clothes, fish, and produce.

I go down to the market to get my hair cut. On my way, I pass a fish stall that's on the first level. A seller—I call him the fish-thrower—stands before an array of sea creatures displayed on beds of ice. Hoarsely, the man calls out the specials and jokes with a few potential customers. No takers, yet. Now the man is discussing a particular salmon with an older woman. He holds up the fish and lets it fly, over the heads of potential customers and into a piece of wax paper held by one of the counter merchants. Successful completion, as usual.

Now I walk down to the barbershop. Kim, my barber of choice, raises the radio volume, prattles for a while about her love life, and needles the owner, who is tending to the customer in the only other chair. He takes her ribbing in stride. The cut costs $8, and without fail there's a line out the door. My impulse is to ask the owner why he doesn't expand—get a bigger shop, with room for a new chair and another assistant. Clearly, there's a demand for it. But I can imagine his response: "You transplants are all the same, all bent on expansion." In this city, I remind myself, two chairs can be better than three. It's the same message that the Pike Place merchants are now sending to the Preservation and Development Authority, which manages the complex.

Of course, no one can deny that both cities have reaped at least some economic and cultural benefits from all the growth and renewal of the past few decades. Vancouver is among the busiest ports in North America, and Seattle—recognized in the past as the home of airline manufacturer Boeing—is now a center for computer technology as well, thanks to Bill Gates and Microsoft. You can go to the theater for less than $10 in Seattle and, although a chandelier may not fall from the ceiling à la *Phantom of the Opera*, the performance is generally first-rate. Vancouver's Jazz Festival ranks among the best in the world.

All the success is also making people think. Highways are more crowded; sprawling suburbs encroach on the forests; and homelessness, drugs, and street gangs are on the rise. In Seattle, some locals have responded by forming a group called Lesser Seattle, devoted to discouraging people from moving here. "Keep the Bastards Out," they say, only half-jokingly. But beneath the tough talk lies a simple wish they share with Vancouverites: to maintain at least some control over the recent changes in their cities. If you plan to spend some time in either Seattle or Vancouver, don't be too concerned with this talk. No one will blame you outright for all the congestion and untrammeled growth; folks out here are too polite for that. They may instead hint at it, or bait you into a statement that you'll later regret. "This rain can be depressing, huh?" A resident might feel you out with this kind of question, to see what kind of appreciation you really have. Keep your answers short, and remember that out here, two chairs are often better than three.

— By Philip Joseph

A native New Yorker, Phil has found his way to Seattle, where he is a freelance writer and editor.

# NEW AND NOTEWORTHY

## Seattle

Nearly every top-of-the-line arts organization and sports franchise in Seattle has undergone or is planning a major remodeling or venue change. The **Paramount Theatre** recently completed a stunning renovation, the Seattle Repertory Theatre and **A Contemporary Theatre** just celebrated the opening of new spaces, and the **Seattle Symphony** is due for a 1998 move into a new $99 million downtown facility. The recently rebuilt **Key Arena** (formerly the Coliseum) at last provides a worthy home for perennial National Basketball Association contenders the Seattle Supersonics, and the Seattle Mariners baseball team and the Seattle Seahawks football team will both have new facilities within the next few years.

Vancouver

An increase in direct flights—a result of the **Open Skies agreement** signed by the United States and Canada—has further enhanced Vancouver's status as a Pacific Rim player, as did Amtrak's restoration of daily train service between the city and Seattle. A ride on the *Mt. Baker International* train, which follows the coast most of the way, is a truly glorious way to take in the region's scenery.

# WHAT'S WHERE

Seattle Area

Seattle, justly celebrated for its laid-back lifestyle, is the metropolitan hub of **Puget Sound,** a fast-growing region of more than 2.5 million residents. The city's natural splendors at times make one forget its standing as a center of industry and an economic and cultural portal to the Pacific Rim. But most visitors can't help noticing that for all its dynamism, the city still seems to have one speed: slow. Seattleites live on and among lakes and hills. Getting from place to place sometimes takes a while because, frankly, the geography demands it. Few cities are as defined by and identified with their environment as Seattle. This harmony, which has an incalculable effect on the city's quality of life, is also the key to its appeal.

One of the great attractions of Seattle is how quickly you can leave it all behind. In a minute, the gray mist that commonly enshrouds the city can evaporate, revealing "The Mountain," as locals call **Mount Rainier,** or a ferry gliding gently across **Elliott Bay.** To truly escape the (relative) hustle of city life, take the 35-minute drive east to the town of **Snoqualmie,** gateway to the Cascades. Merely stepping on a ferry at Coleman Dock seems to take you light years away from the city, but within 30 minutes you're standing on **Bainbridge Island,** a perfect launching pad to **Port Townsend** and the **Olympic Peninsula.** In the summer months, you'll find a wait of three or more hours for boats to the **San Juan Islands.** In a very real sense, you haven't seen Seattle until you leave Seattle, so be sure to plan enough time for at least one excursion to the other side of the mist.

Vancouver Area

The spectacular setting of cosmopolitan Vancouver has inspired people from around the world to settle here. The Pacific Ocean and the mountains of the **North Shore** form a dramatic backdrop to gleaming towers of commerce downtown and make it easy to pursue no end of outdoor pleasures. You can trace the city's history in **Gastown** and **Chinatown,** savor the wilderness only blocks from the city center in **Stanley Park,** or dine on superb ethnic or Pacific Northwest cuisine before you sample the city's nightlife. People from every corner of the earth create a young and vibrant atmosphere.

Museums and buildings of architectural and historical significance are the primary draw in **downtown Vancouver.** There's also plenty of fine shopping to provide breaks (or to distract, depending on your perspective) along the way. Vancouver is a new city, when compared to others, but one that's rich in culture and diversity.

As with Seattle, you can steal away from the hubbub of the city in just minutes to the lush inland valleys, Pacific beaches, rugged mountains, and forested islands of **British Columbia.** There are plenty of opportunities for whale- and nature-watching, as well as year-round skiing and superb fishing and kayaking. And whether your visit takes you to the Anglophile city of **Victoria** or nearby coastal and island towns, you'll encounter the diversity of the area's residents.

# FODOR'S CHOICE

## Seattle

Magic Seattle Moments

★ **Coffee from a drive-through.** You'll certainly never forget your first double-tall nonfat latte, especially if it's from a drive-through espresso bar. If you're trying to lay off the caffeine, substitute a double shot of wheat grass from a juice bar.

★ **Floatplane flight from Lake Union to Friday Harbor.** Hop on the plane that lands on the sea for unforgettable views of Puget Sound and the San Juan Islands.

★ **Pike Place Market on a Saturday afternoon.** It's fun here anytime, but there's no place in the world quite like Pike Place Market in full swing on a Saturday afternoon. "If we get separated, I'll meet you by the pig in an hour." But watch for low-flying fish!

★ **Sunset over Elliott Bay from a westbound ferry.** Catch a late-afternoon ferry heading toward the ocean. You'll get an unobstructed view of the snowcapped Olympics silhouetted against the setting sun, with a return trip toward a gradually dimming Seattle skyline.

## Parks

★ **Washington Park Arboretum.** The Arboretum is a true Seattle gem, a 200-acre mixed-use park that's perfect for a picnic, a stroll through the greenhouse, or a quiet afternoon in the immaculate Japanese garden.

★ **Woodland Park Zoo.** Many of the animals in this award-winning botanical garden roam free in climate-specific habitats. The African savanna, the elephant forest, and the recently added Northern Trail (housing brown bears, wolves, mountain goats, and otters) are of particular interest.

## Sights and Attractions

★ **Ballard Locks.** Follow the fascinating progress of fishing boats and pleasure craft through the locks, part of the Lake Washington Ship Canal, then watch as salmon and trout make the same journey via a "fish ladder" from saltwater to freshwater.

★ **Museum of Flight.** Exhibits on the history of human flight fill the Red Barn, Boeing's original airplane factory, and the Great Gallery contains more than 20 classic airplanes, dating from the Wright brothers to the jet era.

★ **Pike Place Market.** Read the hundreds of names etched into the floor tiles as you wander among stalls selling fresh seafood, produce, cheese, Northwest wines, bulk spices, tea, coffee, and arts and crafts.

★ **Space Needle.** There's nothing like the view of the city at night from the observation deck of this Seattle landmark.

## Restaurants

★ **Fullers.** Locals' restaurant of choice for special occasions hangs the works of Pacific Northwest artists over the booths in its dining room. Chef Monique Andrée Barbeau is a James Beard Award winner. $$$$

★ **Lampreia.** The subtle beige-and-gold interior of this Belltown restaurant is the perfect backdrop for owner and chef Scott Carsberg's clean, sophisticated cuisine. $$$$

★ **Rover's.** An intimate escape from the energy of downtown, Rover's offers exceptional French cooking with a menu (changing daily) founded on fresh, locally available ingredients, selected and prepared by chef-owner Thierry Rautureau. $$$$

★ **Dahlia Lounge.** The easygoing ambience of the Dahlia Lounge suits chef Tom Douglas's penchant for simple, if uncommon, preparations. His signature Dungeness crab cakes lead an ever-evolving menu focused on regional ingredients. $$$

★ **Metropolitan Grill.** This clubby downtown spot serves custom-aged mesquite-broiled steaks—the best in Seattle—in a classic steak-house atmosphere. $$$

★ **Palace Kitchen.** Northwest ingredients are again the centerpiece of Tom Douglas's latest venture, which has a gorgeous curved bar and an open kitchen. $$$

★ **Ray's Boathouse.** The view of Puget Sound may be the drawing card, but the seafood is impeccably fresh, well prepared, and complemented by one of the area's finest wine lists. $$$

★ **Saigon Gourmet.** This small café in the International District is about as plain as they get, but the Vietnamese food is superb and the prices are incredibly low. $

## Hotels and Inns

★ **Four Seasons Olympic Hotel.** Seattle's most elegant hotel has a 1920s Renaissance Revival–style grandeur. Public rooms are appointed with marble, wood paneling, potted plants, and thick rugs, and furnished with plush armchairs. $$$$

★ **Sorrento.** Sitting high on First Hill, this deluxe European-style hotel, designed to look like an Italian villa, has wonderful views overlooking downtown and the waterfront. $$$$

★ **Inn at the Market.** This sophisticated but unpretentious hotel, right up the street from the Pike Place Market, combines the best aspects of a small French country inn with the informality of the Pacific Northwest. $$$–$$$$

★ **Gaslight Inn.** Rooms at this Capitol Hill–area B&B range from a cozy crow's nest to suites with antique carved beds and gas fireplaces. $$–$$$

# Vancouver

## Sights and Attractions

★ **Dr. Sun Yat-Sen Gardens.** Fifty-two artisans from Suzhou, China, built these gardens in the 1980s using no power tools, screws, or nails.

★ **Granville Island.** This small sandbar, once a derelict factory district, was redeveloped. Former industrial buildings and tin sheds, painted in upbeat primary colors, house restaurants, a public market, marine activities, and artisans' studios.

★ **Museum of Anthropology.** Vancouver's most spectacular museum displays aboriginal art from the Pacific Northwest and around the world. See dramatic totem poles, ceremonial archways, and dugout canoes; exquisite carvings of gold, silver, and argillite; and masks, tools, and costumes from many cultures.

★ **Stanley Park.** An afternoon in this 1,000-acre wilderness park, just blocks from downtown, can include beaches, the ocean, the harbor, Douglas fir and cedar forests, and a good look at the North Shore mountains.

## Restaurants

★ **Chartwell.** Named after Sir Winston Churchill's country home, the flagship dining room at the Four Seasons Hotel offers robust, inventive Continental food in a British-club atmosphere. $$$–$$$$

★ **Star Anise.** Pacific Rim cuisine with a French flair shines in this intimate restaurant on the west side of town. $$$

★ **Tojo's.** Hidekazu Tojo is a sushi-making legend here, with more than 2,000 preparations tucked away in his creative mind. $$$

★ **Villa del Lupo.** Vancouver's top chefs head to this elegant restaurant for Italian food. The country-house decor sets a romantic tone, but come prepared to roll up your sleeves and mop up the sauce with a chunk of crusty bread. $$$

★ **Imperial Chinese Seafood.** This Cantonese restaurant in the art deco Marine Building has two-story floor-to-ceiling windows with stupendous views of Stanley Park and the North Shore mountains across Coal Harbour. $$–$$$

★ **Rubina Tandoori.** For the best East Indian food in the city, try Rubina Tandoori, 20 minutes from downtown. The large menu spans most of the subcontinent's cuisines. $$

★ **Phnom Penh Restaurant.** Part of a small cluster of Southeast Asian shops on the fringes of Chinatown, Phnom Penh serves unusually robust Vietnamese and Cambodian fare. $

## Hotels and Inns

★ **Sutton Place.** This property feels more like an exclusive guest house than a large hotel: Its lobby has sumptuously thick carpets, enormous displays of flowers, and European furniture; the rooms are even better. $$$$

★ **Waterfront Centre Hotel.** Dramatically elegant, the 23-story glass hotel is across from Canada Place, which can be reached from the hotel by an underground walkway. $$$$

★ **Hotel Vancouver.** The copper roof of this grand château-style hotel dominates Vancouver's skyline. The hotel itself, opened in 1939 by the Canadian National Railway, commands a regal position in the center of town across from the art gallery and Cathedral Place. $$$

★ **Rosedale on Robson.** If you plan to be in town a while and want to keep expenses down by doing some of your own cooking, consider this all-suites property downtown. $$–$$$

★ **English Bay Inn.** In this renovated 1930s Tudor house a block from the ocean, the guest rooms have wonderful sleigh beds with matching armoires. A small, sunny English country garden brightens the back of the inn. $$

★ **West End Guest House.** This lovely Victorian house, built in 1906, is a true "painted lady," from its gracious front parlor, cozy fireplace, and early 1900s fur-

niture to its green-trimmed pink exterior.
$$

★ **Hostelling International Vancouver Downtown.** Vancouver's newest hostel, conveniently located in the West End downtown, is tidy and secure. $

# BOOKS AND VIDEOS

## Seattle

*Above Seattle,* with photos by Robert Cameron and text by Emmett Watson, provides, literally, an overview of the city, via historical and contemporary aerial photographs.

The late Bill Spiedel, one of Seattle's most colorful characters, wrote about the early history of the city in books replete with lively anecdotes and legends; *Sons of the Profits* and *Doc Maynard* are two of his best. David Buerge's *Seattle in the Eighteen Eighties* is difficult to find but worth the effort; it documents a period of great growth and turmoil. Buerge also compiled the history and photographs in *Chief Seattle,* part of a series about the Northwest. Quintard Taylor's scholarly *The Forging of a Black Community: Seattle's Central District, From 1870 Through the Civil Rights Era* studies race relations in the city through anecdotal and other research.

John T. Gaertner's *North Bank Road: The Spokane, Portland and Seattle Railway* outlines the impact that railroads had on the Northwest. The book is one of several titles on the subject published by Washington State University Press, whose other titles include *The Way We Ate: Pacific Northwest Cooking 1843–1900* and *Raise Hell and Sell Newspapers: Alden J. Blethen and The Seattle Times.*

In her memoir *Nisei Daughter,* Monica Itoi Sone recalls her time in Seattle before World War II, the social and other struggles of her family and other Japanese-Americans during the war, and life in the postwar era. The treatment of Japanese-Americans during World War II is one of the subjects of David Guterson's *Snow Falling on Cedars.* The novel, which takes place in the 1950s on an island north of Puget Sound, won the PEN/Faulkner award for fiction.

*Screaming Music: A Chronicle of the Seattle Music Scene,* by Charles Peterson and Michael Azerrad, delivers the dish on the grunge and other musical eras. Rock music reporter Clark Humphrey covers the city's music scene from the 1960s into the 1990s in *Loser: The Real Seattle Music.*

Seattle has the largest municipal gardening program in the United States. You'll get a minitour of the city and some great recipe ideas from *The City Gardener's Cookbook: Totally Fresh, Mostly Vegetarian, Decidedly Delicious Recipes from Seattle's P-Patches.*

For a pulpy good time, read John Saul's best-selling *Black Lightning,* in which a Seattle journalist who has spent years tracking a serial killer finds herself facing new horrors when similar murders begin occurring after his execution.

One of the first talking pictures with scenes shot in Seattle was the 1930s comedy *Tugboat Annie,* starring Marie Dressler (as the title character) and Wallace Beery. (Dressler's famous line: "And I didn't get the name pushin' toy boats around the bathtub either.") Lizabeth Scott, a star of the late 1940s and early 1950s, debuted in the sentimental *You Came Along* (gal on warbond tour falls in love with a GI), parts of which were filmed in Seattle. Elvis Presley flew into town—literally; he played a crop-dusting pilot—for *It Happened at the World's Fair,* shot in 1962. The film is no great shakes, but has some fine views of the fair and the city.

Stars continued to pass through Seattle in the 1970s as film production in and around the city increased. All or part of the James Caan sailor-on-leave vehicle *Cinderella Liberty,* John Wayne's *McQ* (he plays a Seattle police detective), and Warren Beatty's paranoid political thriller *The Parallax View,* take place in the city.

Car thief Stockard Channing drove through Seattle in *Dandy the All-American Girl* (a.k.a. *Sweet Revenge*). Michael Sarrazin, James Coburn, and Walter Pidgeon picked pockets in Seattle and Salt Lake City in the peculiar *Harry in Your Pocket,* now more memorable for Pidgeon's performance and the location shots in the two cities (and also Vancouver) than the plot. The San Juan Islands were among the places through which Jack Nicholson drifted in director Bob Rafelson's *Five Easy Pieces,* which also includes scenes in British Columbia. The town of Redmond, south of Seattle, appeared in Peter Fonda's futuristic *Idaho Transfer,* which was shot and released to little fanfare in the 1970s but revived in the 1990s as a "lost American independent classic."

Scenes from *Eleanor and Franklin* and other made-for-TV movies were shot in Seattle in the 1970s, but the pace of television production picked up in the 1980s with the feature-length *The Divorce Wars* (in which Tom Selleck and Jane Curtin spar) and *Jacqueline Bouvier Kennedy.* Parts of the pilot for David Lynch's idiosyncratic *Twin Peaks* series were shot in North Bend, Snoqualmie, and Everett. Major theatrical films shot during the 1980s in the area included *An Officer and a Gentleman, War Games, Trouble in Mind, Starman,* and *The Fabulous Baker Boys.*

The hits continued in the 1990s with *Singles* director Cameron Crowe's tale of Seattle twentysomethings; *The Hand That Rocks the Cradle,* in which nanny from hell Rebecca de Mornay terrorizes a yuppie couple; *Disclosure,* in which corporate boss Demi Moore terrorizes employee Michael Douglas; and *Sleepless in Seattle,* in which the town provides a backdrop for love to conquer all for Tom Hanks and Meg Ryan. Most of the American footage in *Little Buddha,* Bernardo Bertolucci's tale of an American lama, was shot in the Seattle area. Scenes from *Free Willy* and *Free Willy II* were shot in the San Juan Islands. The contemporary Seattle skyline is seen to great effect in the television show *Frasier,* whose title character has a radio talk show on a top-rated city station.

Seattle became a haven for independent producers in the 1990s. Jeff Bridges starred in the major studio release *The Vanishing,* parts of which were shot here, but received better notices for his performance in the independently financed *American Heart,* also shot in the area, in which he plays a convict whose 12-year-old son rejoins him upon his release from prison. A grim view of the city can be seen in *Black Circle Boys,* in which a southern California swimmer moves to Seattle and gets caught up in Satanic rituals, drugs, and the underground music scene. For a cheerier

portrait, see *Steaming Milk,* a hit at the 1997 Seattle International Film Festival. Its lead character, a struggling screenwriter, encounters a cross-section of Seatleites at his day job at a Queen Anne espresso café. The 1997 documentary *Hype* is an alternately enlightening and creepy glimpse at the rise and fall of the grunge music scene.

## Vancouver

Photographer Morton Beebe's beautiful *Cascadia: A Tale of Two Cities, Seattle and Vancouver, B.C.* explores the cultural and natural wonders of Seattle, Vancouver, and the regions surrounding each city.

Pauline Johnson's *Legends of Vancouver* is a colorful compilation of regional native myths. Longtime Vancouver resident George Bowering wrote the lively *British Columbia: A Swashbuckling History of the Province.* Lois Simmie's children's book *Mister Got-to-Go* takes place in the Sylvia Hotel. Annette, the protagonist of Margaret A. Robinson's *A Woman of Her Tribe,* leaves her village to study in Victoria but feels alienated upon her return.

Wayson Joy's 1997 novel *The Jade Peony,* which takes place in 1940, tells the tale of three children of a Chinese immigrant family in Vancouver's Chinatown.

Rhodri Windsor Liscombe explores the city's architecture in *The New Spirit: Modern Architecture in Vancouver 1938–1963.* Gerald B. Straley's *Trees of Vancouver* is a good survey of the major and less-common varieties. Straley's book is one of many titles published by the press of University of British Columbia about the Canadian Northwest.

Film and television production is a big business in British Columbia—in 1996, $537 million was spent making 34 feature films, 52 made-for-TV movies or feature-length pilots, and 16 series. Vancouver is the scene of much of this action, including animation produced at a recently opened Disney facility.

Vancouver often stands in for other urban areas—including New York City in *Rumble in the Bronx* (1994) and *Friday the 13th: Jason Takes Manhattan* (1989)—but occasionally plays itself. The 1995 Canadian feature *The War Between Us* recreates 1940s Vancouver as it explores the fate of a well-to-do family of Japanese descent whose members are interned in a camp in interior British Columbia following the outbreak of World War II. *Once in a Blue Moon* (1995), another period piece shot in British Columbia, concerns a 10-year-old boy who comes of age in the suburbs of Vancouver in the late 1960s. For a peek at Vancouver's 1990s slacker culture, check out *Live Bait,* a 1995 homage to Woody Allen. The sometimes goofy sci-fi flick *Cyberjack* (1995) conjures up the Vancouver of the 21st century, complete with flying SeaBuses.

The 1990s are the heyday of British Columbia film production, but the area's cinematic roots go back several decades. Estelle Taylor, Thomas Meighan, and Anna May Wong starred in *The Alaskan,* a 1924 Paramount drama about a man who rescues Alaska from the clutches of corrupt robber barons. The 1945 *Son of Lassie* is not one of the lovable collie's best pictures, but does contain scenes shot in British Columbia. Rugged Sterling Hayden starred in *Timberjack,* a 1954 offering from Republic Pictures. Oliver Reed starred in the 1966 film *The Trap,* about a 19th-century trapper and his wife in British Columbia.

Robert Altman shot scenes for two of his early films in British Columbia, *That Cold Day in the Park* and *McCabe and Mrs. Miller.* The well-crafted 1976 remake of the Orson Welles thriller *Journey Into Fear,* starring Vincent Price, Shelley Winters, and Sam Waterston, was shot in and around Vancouver, as was the 1980 *The Grey Fox,* based on the life of an early-1900s stagecoach bandit. *Klondike Fever,* a 1979 picture starring Rod Steiger, concerns the 1897–98 gold rush.

Among the productions filmed in whole or in part in British Columbia in the past decade or so are *Roxanne, Stakeout, The Accused,* the *Look Who's Talking* movies, the Jean Claude Van Damme action picture *Time Cop, The Crush, Cousins, This Boy's Life, Stay Tuned, Jennifer Eight,* the Robin Williams fantasy *Jumanji,* the Adam Sandler comedy *Happy Gilmore,* the remake of *Little Women, Cyberteens in Love* (check your local video store for this curious Canadian production), *Bounty Hunters II, Mr. Magoo,* and *Deep Rising.*

The TV series *21 Jump Street,* which made Johnny Depp a star, was one of several 1980s television series filmed in Vancouver. Since then, production has increased greatly. Other small-screen shows shot here include *Poltergeist, Highlanders, Millennium,* and *The X-Files. Neon Rider, Northwood, The Odyssey,* and *Mom P.I.* are among the Canadian series produced in Vancouver or elsewhere in British Columbia in the 1990s.

# FESTIVALS AND SEASONAL EVENTS

## WINTER

➤ JAN.: The **Polar Bear Swim** on New Year's Day in Vancouver is said to bring good luck all year. **Skiing competitions** take place at most alpine ski resorts throughout the province (through Feb.).

➤ MAR.: The **Pacific Rim Whale Festival** on Vancouver Island's west coast celebrates the spring migration of gray whales with guided tours by whale experts and accompanying music and dancing. Sip the world's best at the **Vancouver International Wine Festival.**

## SPRING

➤ LATE MAR.–MID-APR.: The **Skagit Valley Tulip Festival** enchants visitors with more than 1,000 acres of tulips in full bloom, as well as with music, crafts, and parades in nearby Mount Vernon, Washington, midway between Seattle and Vancouver.

➤ MAY: The **Seattle International Children's Festival** brings international music, dance, and theatre to young audiences. The **Seattle International Film Festival** presents more than 200 features in three weeks at various locations around Seattle. Highlights include the New Directors Showcase, the Children's Film

Fest, and the Secret Festival. The **Vancouver Children's Festival,** said to be the largest event of its kind in the world, presents dozens of performances in mime, puppetry, music, and theater.

➤ LATE MAY: **Northwest Folklife Festival** lures musicians and artists to Seattle for one of the largest folk fests in the United States. The **Pike Place Market Festival** celebrates the enduring contribution of the market to the life and character of Seattle, with entertainment, food booths, and an even higher than usual concentration of crafts artisans and vendors. **Swiftsure Race Weekend** draws more than 300 competitors to Victoria's harbor for an international yachting event. **Victoria Day,** a national holiday, is usually celebrated throughout Canada on the penultimate weekend in May.

## SUMMER

➤ JUNE: The **Fremont Street Fair** is the best of Seattle's summer neighborhood street fairs (others are held in Capitol Hill and the University District). Vancouver's **Canadian International Dragon Boat Festival** in late June features races between long, slender boats decorated with huge dragon heads, an event based on a Chinese "awakening the dragons"

ritual; the festival also includes community and children's activities, dance performances, and arts exhibits. The **Du Maurier International Jazz Festival,** also in late June, celebrates a broad spectrum of jazz, blues, and related improvised music, with more than 200 performances in 20 locations in Vancouver.

➤ JUNE–SEPT.: **Bard on the Beach** is a series of Shakespearean plays performed under a huge seaside tent at Vanier Park in Vancouver.

➤ JULY 1: **Canada Day** inspires celebrations around the country in honor of Canada's birthday. In Vancouver, **Canada Place** hosts an entire day of free outdoor concerts followed by a fireworks display in the inner harbor. Victoria hosts the daylong **Great Canadian Family Picnic** in Beacon Hill Park. The event usually includes children's games, bands, food booths, and fireworks.

➤ JULY 4: **Independence Day** in Seattle means two spectacular celebrations. Gasworks Park is the site of a day of entertainment, culminating in orchestral music (usually provided by the Seattle Symphony) and a fireworks display over Lake Union. A full slate of cultural and other activities unwinds on the other side of Queen Anne Hill at the Fourth of Jul-Ivar Celebration before the skies light up over Elliott Bay.

➤ JULY: **Bite of Seattle** serves up sumptuous specialties from the city's finest restaurants. People travel from all over Canada to attend Vancouver's **Folk Music Festival.** The **Vancouver Sea Festival** celebrates the city's nautical heritage with the World Championship Bathtub Race, sailing regattas, and windsurfing races, plus a parade, fireworks, entertainment, and a carnival.

➤ MID-JULY–EARLY AUG.: **Seafair,** Seattle's biggest festival of the year (really a collection of smaller regional events), kicks off with a torchlight parade through downtown and culminates in hydroplane races on Lake Washington.

➤ MID-AUG.–EARLY SEPT.: The **Pacific National Exhibition,** western Canada's biggest annual fair, brings top-name entertainment and a variety of displays to Vancouver.

➤ LATE AUG.–EARLY SEPT.: **Bumbershoot,** a Seattle festival of the arts, presents more than 400 performers in music, dance, theater, comedy, and the visual and literary arts.

**AUTUMN**

➤ SEPT.: Cars speed through downtown Vancouver in the **Molson Indy**

**Formula 1 race.** The **Fringe Theater Festival** attracts cutting-edge artists to Vancouver's smaller stages.

➤ OCT.: The **Vancouver International Film Festival** brings top Canadian and international films and film directors to the city. Bookish types opt for the **International Writers & Readers Festival,** also in Vancouver.

# 2 Seattle

*Coffeehouses, brew pubs, grunge music, and lots of rain—these are what many people associate with the hippest city in the U.S. Northwest. But Seattle has more to offer than steaming lattes and garage bands. You can wander historic neighborhoods, browse amid the sights and smells of the Pike Place Market, explore lakes and islands, or just eat, eat, eat—Seattle restaurants are among the nation's most innovative and diverse.*

**S**EATTLE IS DEFINED BY WATER. There's no use deny-
ing the city's damp weather, or the fact that its skies
are cloudy for much of the year. Residents of Seat-
tle don't tan, goes the joke, they rust. But Seattle is also defined by the
rivers, lakes, and canals that bisect its steep green hills, creating a series of distinctive areas along the water's edge. Funky fishing boats,
floating homes, swank yacht clubs, and waterfront restaurants exist
side by side.

By Wier
Harman

But a city is defined by its people as well as by its geography, and the
people of Seattle—a half million within the city proper, another 2 million in the surrounding Puget Sound region—are a diversified bunch.
Seattle has long had a vibrant Asian and Asian-American population,
as well as well-established communities of Scandinavians, African-
Americans, Jews, Native Americans, and Latinos. It's impossible to gen-
eralize about such a varied group, but the prototypical Seattleite was
once pithily summed up by a *New Yorker* cartoon in which one arch-
eyebrowed East Coast matron says to another, "They're backpacky,
but nice."

Seattle's climate fosters an easygoing indoor lifestyle. Overcast days
and long winter nights have made it a haven for moviegoers and book
readers. Hollywood often tests new films here, and residents' per-
capita book purchases are among the country's highest. The town
that Sir Thomas Beacham once described as a "cultural wasteland" now
has all the trappings of a metropolitan hub—two daily newspapers, a
state-of-the-art convention center, professional sports teams, a diverse
music-club scene, and top-notch ballet, opera, symphony, and theater
companies. A major seaport, Seattle is a vital link in Pacific Rim trade.
Evidence of this internationalism is everywhere, from the discreet Japanese script identifying downtown department stores—for example,
"Nordstrom" written as "Katakana"—to the multilingual recorded messages at Seattle-Tacoma International Airport.

Seattle's expansion has led to the usual big-city problems: increases in
crime, drug abuse, homelessness, poverty, and traffic congestion, along
with a decline in the quality of the public schools. Many residents have
fled to the nearby suburb of Bellevue, which has swollen from a quiet
farming community to become Washington's fifth-largest city. But despite the growing pains they've endured, Seattleites as a whole mani-
fest a great love for their city and a firm commitment to maintaining
its reputation as one of the most livable areas in the country.

## Pleasures and Pastimes

### Dining

The best Seattle restaurants build their menus around local ingredients.
The city has an invaluable resource in the Pike Place Market, which
warehouses bountiful supplies of seafood and produce. A quick scan
of the stalls will tell you what to expect on restaurant plates in any
given season: strawberries in June; Walla Walla Sweets—a mild soft-
ball-size onion—in July; wild blackberries in August; and Washington's
renowned apples during autumn. All year long, you'll find Washington wines and beer at Seattle eateries. This reliance on locally produced
ingredients, along with the synthesis of European and Asian cooking
techniques and a touch of irreverence, makes for what has come to be
known as Pacific Northwest cuisine.

## Nightlife and the Arts

Seattle achieved fleeting notoriety as the birthplace of grunge rock. Some of the better-known bands to emerge from the local scene include Nirvana, Pearl Jam, and Soundgarden. But jazz, blues, and R&B have been perennial favorites, and you'll find clubs that showcase everything from tinny garage bands to subtle stylists. Beyond music, you can catch a comedian or a movie—or just have a drink while watching the lights flicker on the water. On any given night there are usually several worthwhile dance or theater offerings. Seattle's galleries support an active community of painters, sculptors, woodworkers, and glass artists. The annual Northwest Folklife Festival on Memorial Day weekend celebrates their creativity.

## Parks and Gardens

"Seattle possesses extraordinary landscape advantages. . . . In designing a system of parks and parkways the primary aim should be to secure and preserve for the use of the people as much as possible of these advantages of water and mountain views and of woodlands . . . as well as some fairly level land for field sports and the enjoyment of scenery." These words appeared in a surveyors report prepared in 1903 for Seattle's fledgling parks commission and established the foundation for an ambitious master plan, the spirit of which has been maintained to this day. Seattle's extensive parks system retains that delicate (and often elusive) balance between the fanciful and functional—from the primeval growth of West Seattle's Schmitz Park to the manicured ball fields around Green Lake, from the epic sprawl of the Washington Park Arboretum to Parson's Garden, a prim urban oasis.

# EXPLORING SEATTLE

Seattle, like Rome, is built on seven hills. As a visitor, you're likely to spend much of your time on just two of them (Capitol Hill and Queen Anne Hill), but the seven knobs are indeed the most definitive element of the city's natural and spiritual landscape. Years of largely thoughtful zoning practices have kept tall buildings from obscuring the lines of sight, maintaining vistas in most directions and around most every turn. The hills are lofty, privileged perches from which Seattleites are constantly reminded of the beauty of the forests, mountains, and water lying just beyond the city. That is, when it stops misting long enough to see your hand in front of your face.

To know Seattle is to know its distinctive neighborhoods. Below is a thumbnail sketch of the major ones. Because of the hills, comfortable walking shoes are a must.

**Ballard,** home to Seattle's fishing industry and fun-to-tour locks, is at the mouth of Salmon Bay, northwest of downtown.

**Capitol Hill,** northeast of downtown on Pine Street, east of Interstate 5 (I–5), is the center of youth culture in this very young city.

**Downtown** is bounded on the west by **Elliott Bay,** on the south by **Pioneer Square** (the city's oldest neighborhood) and the **International District,** on the north by the attractive residences lining the slopes of **Queen Anne Hill,** and by I–5 to the east. You can reach most points of interest by foot, bus, trolley, or the monorail that runs between the Seattle and Westlake centers.

**Fremont,** Seattle's eccentric and artsy hamlet, is just north of **Lake Union** and the **Lake Washington Ship Canal,** east of Ballard, west of **Wallingford,** and south of **Woodland Park.**

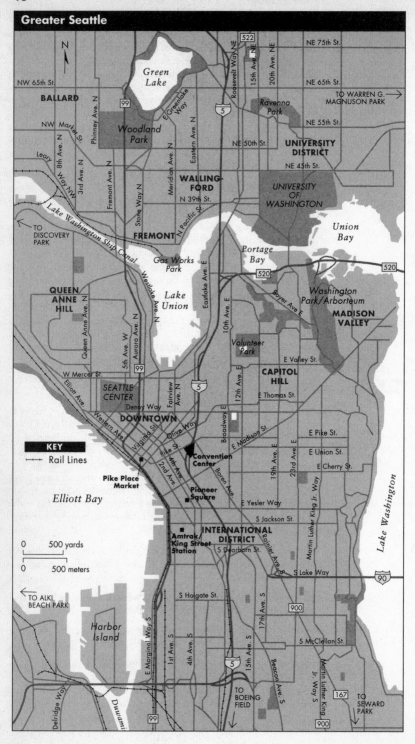

N

NE 75th St.

NW 65th St.

Green
Lake

NE 65th St.

**BALLARD**

TO WARREN G.
MAGNUSON PARK

Ravenna
Park

NE 55th St.

Woodland
Park

NE 50th St.

**UNIVERSITY
DISTRICT**

NW Market St.

NE 45th St.

**WALLING-
FORD**

**UNIVERSITY
OF
WASHINGTON**

N 39th St.

Leary

Lake Washington Ship Canal

**FREMONT**

Union
Bay

TO
DISCOVERY
PARK

Gas Works
Park

Portage
Bay

520

520

**QUEEN
ANNE
HILL**

Lake
Union

Washington
Park/Arboretum

**MADISON
VALLEY**

Volunteer
Park

W Mercer St.

99

E Valley St.

**CAPITOL
HILL**

**SEATTLE
CENTER**

Denny Way

**DOWNTOWN**

E Thomas St.

5

Olive Way

E Pike St.

**KEY**

Pike St.

Convention
Center

E Union St.

— Rail Lines

E Cherry St.

**Pike Place
Market**

**Pioneer
Square**

E Yesler Way

Lake Washington

*Elliott Bay*

S Jackson St.

**INTERNATIONAL
DISTRICT**

0        500 yards

**Amtrak/
King Street
Station**

S Dearborn St.

0        500 meters

S Lake Way

90

TO ALKI
BEACH PARK

S Holgate St.

900

*Harbor
Island*

S McClellan St.

5

Duwamish

TO
BOEING
FIELD

167

TO
SEWARD
PARK

99

900

**Magnolia,** dotted with expensive (and precariously perched) homes, is at the northwestern edge of Elliott Bay, west of Queen Anne Hill.

**University District,** the area around the University of Washington, is north of Capitol Hill and Union Bay.

## Great Itineraries

IF YOU HAVE 1 DAY

If you've come to Seattle on business or for another reason only have a day for sightseeing, focus your energy on downtown. Weather permitting, an after-dinner ferry ride to Bainbridge Island (☞ Chapter 3) and back is a perfect way to conclude your day.

IF YOU HAVE 3 DAYS

Get a feel for what makes Seattle special at Pike Place Market and then explore more of downtown and the waterfront. Start your second day at the Ballard Locks, reaching Fremont in time for lunch. After a stroll through the neighborhood's galleries and shops, grab a beer at the Redhook Brewery before heading to the Space Needle, where the views are the most spectacular as sunset approaches. Venture outside the city on I–90 to Snoqualmie Falls (☞ Chapter 3) on day three. Hike to the falls and lunch at Salish Lodge. To get a true sense of the pace of life in the Northwest, on your return to Seattle, detour north from I–90 on Highway 203 and stop in tiny Duvall, home to antiques shops, boutiques, and cafés. You can easily make it back to Seattle in time for dinner or a night on the town.

IF YOU HAVE 5 TO 7 DAYS

Follow the three-day itinerary above. Take a morning bay cruise on day four and spend the afternoon at the Washington Park Arboretum before heading to Capitol Hill for dinner and some nightclubbing. If you can only stay in the Seattle area one more day, take the ferry to Port Townsend on day five. If you have a few days, take the ferry to one or more of the San Juan Islands.

# Pike Place Market, the Waterfront, and Seattle Center

*Numbers in the text correspond to numbers in the margin and on the Downtown Seattle map.*

## A Good Tour

Spend some time at **Pike Place Market** ① before walking south a block on 1st Avenue to the **Seattle Art Museum** ②, whose postmodern exterior is worth a look even if you're not going inside. From the museum, walk west across 1st Avenue and descend the **Harbor Steps.** At the bottom of the steps is the waterfront. Head north (to the right). At Pier 59, you'll find the **Seattle Aquarium** ③ and the **Omnidome Film Experience** ④. You can walk out on Piers 62 and 63 for a good view of Elliott Bay. The newly refurbished **Bell Street Pier** (Pier 66) contains a marina, several restaurants, and the **Odyssey: The Maritime Discovery Center** ⑤, which is scheduled to open in July 1998.

Continue up the waterfront to **Myrtle Edwards Park,** just past Pier 70. It's a good place to rest a moment before making the several-block walk up **Broad Street** through the northern part of the Belltown neighborhood (be forewarned: the first three blocks are a tad steep) to the **Seattle Center** and the **Space Needle** ⑥. Especially if you've got kids in tow, you'll want to arrive here before the **Pacific Science Center** ⑦ and **Seattle Children's Museum** ⑧ close. Take the **Seattle Center Monorail** to return to downtown. The monorail stops at **Westlake Center** ⑨, at the corner of 5th Avenue and Pine Street. To get to the **Washington State Convention and Trade Center** ⑩, walk one block southeast to Pike

Street and east to 8th Avenue. Seattle's main **Visitor Information Center** is inside the street-level mall at Convention Place.

TIMING

It would take about half the day to complete the above route stopping only a little, but you'll need to devote the whole day or more to fully appreciate the various sights. A visit to Pike Place Market can easily fill two hours. Plan on an hour for the art museum. The aquarium is a two-hour stop at most. You could spend half a day or more in Seattle Center. The Space Needle is especially fun at sunset. Most of the sights listed below are open daily; the Frye Art Museum and the Seattle Art Museum are closed Monday and open until 9 PM on Thursday.

## Sights to See

**Frye Art Museum.** Among the pivotal late-19th- and early-20th-century American and European realist works at this gallery east of downtown are German artist Franz von Stuck's *Sin,* a painting with Impressionist leanings that predates the movement, and Alexander Koester's *Ducks,* an example of the Academy school of German painting. The Frye, which opened in 1952, underwent a mid-1990s redesign that has added more exhibition space, an outdoor garden courtyard, and a reflecting pool. ⊠ *704 Terry Ave.,* ☎ *206/622–9250.* ⌨ *Free.* ☉ *Tues.–Sat. 10–5 (Thurs. until 9), Sun. noon–5.*

**Myrtle Edwards Park.** Sandwiched between the Burlington Northern Railroad to the east and the gently lapping waters of Elliott Bay to the west, this sliver of a park just north of Pier 70 is popular with Seattleites for jogging, walking, and picnicking. As a place to catch the sunset in the city, it's rivaled only by the deck of a westbound Bainbridge Island ferry. ⊠ *Alaskan Way between W. Bay and W. Thomas Sts.*

**❺ Odyssey: The Maritime Discovery Center.** Cultural and educational maritime exhibits on Puget Sound and ocean trade will be the focus of this facility that is scheduled to open in July 1998 (though its debut has already been delayed a couple of times). Already open at the center are a conference center, a short-stay boat basin, fish-processing terminals, a gourmet fish market, and a restaurant. ⊠ *Pier 66 off Alaskan Way,* ☎ *206/623–2120.* ⌨ *$6.50.* ☉ *Daily 10–6.*

**❹ Omnidome Film Experience.** The theater next to the aquarium shows short films on a large, curved screen about the eruption of Mount St. Helens, mountain gorillas, real-life storm chasers, and the Great Barrier Reef. ⊠ *Pier 59 off Alaskan Way,* ☎ *206/622–1868.* ⌨ *$6.95; combination tickets including aquarium admission, $12.75.* ☉ *Daily 10–5.*

**✆ ❼ Pacific Science Center.** An excellent stop for children and adults, the Pacific Science Center has 200 hands-on exhibits. The large, brightly colored machines of Body Works amusingly analyze cardiovascular activity, the motion of limbs, and other aspects of physiology. Text Zones contains robots and virtual-reality diversions that participants can control. The dinosaurs exhibit is wildly popular. Imax screenings and laser light shows take place daily. A *Jetsons*-style outdoor plaza, with fountains and concrete towers, dates from the 1962 World's Fair. ⊠ *200 2nd Ave. N,* ☎ *206/443–2001.* ⌨ *$7.50.* ☉ *Weekdays 10–5, weekends 10–6.*

**★ ❶ Pike Place Market.** The heart of the Pike Place Historical District, this Seattle institution began in 1907 when the city issued permits to farmers allowing them to sell produce from their wagons parked at Pike Place. Later the city built stalls for the farmers. At one time the market was a madhouse of vendors hawking their produce and haggling over prices; some of the fishmongers still carry on this kind of frenzied banter, but chances are you won't get them to waver on their prices.

Urban renewal almost killed the market, but city voters, led by the late architect Victor Steinbreuck, rallied and voted it a historical asset. Many buildings have been restored, and the project is now connected to the waterfront by stairs and elevators. Besides a number of restaurants, you'll find booths selling fresh seafood—which can be packed in dry ice for your flight home—produce, cheese, Northwest wines, bulk spices, tea, coffee, and arts and crafts.

If the weather is nice, gather a picnic of market foods—fresh fruit and smoked salmon, of course, but soups, sandwiches, pastries, and various ethnic snacks are also available in the market or from the small shops facing it along Pike Place. Carry your bounty north, past the market buildings, to **Victor Steinbreuck Park,** a small green gem named for Pike Place's savior. ⊠ *Pike Pl. at Pike St., west of 1st Ave.,* ☎ *206/682–7453.* ☉ *Mon.–Sat. 9–6, Sun. 11–5.*

NEED A
BREAK?
**Three Girls Bakery** (⊠ Pike Pl. Market, 1514 Pike Pl., ☎ 206/622–1045), a 13-seat glassed-in lunch counter that's tucked behind a bakery outlet, serves sandwiches, soups, and pastries to hungry folks in a hurry. Go for the chili and a hunk of Sicilian sourdough, or buy a loaf at the take-out counter, pick up some smoked salmon at the fish place next door, and head for a picnic table in Waterfront Park.

③ **Seattle Aquarium.** Pacific Northwest marine life is the emphasis at this waterfront facility. At the Discovery Lab you'll see baby barnacles, minute jellyfish, and other "invisible" creatures through high-resolution video microscopes. The Tide Pool exhibit re-creates Washington's rocky coast and sandy beaches at low tide; there's even a 6,000-gallon wave that sweeps in over the underwater life—spectators standing close by may get damp from the simulated sea spray. Sea otters and seals swim and dive in their pools, and the "State of the Sound" exhibit shows the aquatic life and ecology of Puget Sound. ⊠ *Pier 59 off Alaskan Way,* ☎ *206/386–4320.* ☜ *$7.50.* ☉ *Memorial Day–Labor Day, daily 10–8, Labor Day–Memorial Day, daily 10–6.*

② **Seattle Art Museum.** Postmodern architect Robert Venturi designed this five-story museum, which is a work of art in itself. The 1991 building has a limestone exterior with large-scale vertical fluting accented by terra-cotta, cut granite, and marble. Sculptor Joseph Borofsky's several-stories-high *Hammering Man* pounds away outside the front door. The museum displays an extensive collection of Asian, Native American, African, Oceanic, and pre-Columbian art and has a café and gift shop. A ticket to the Seattle Art Museum is valid for admission to the Seattle Asian Art Museum (☞ *below*) in Volunteer Park if used within one week. ⊠ *100 University St.,* ☎ *206/654–3100.* ☜ *$6; free 1st Thurs. of month.* ☉ *Tues.–Sun. 10–5 (Thurs. until 9).*

**Seattle Center.** The 74-acre Seattle Center complex was built for the 1962 World's Fair. A rolling green campus organized around the massive International Fountain, the center includes an amusement park, theaters, exhibition halls, museums, shops, a skateboard park, Key Arena, the Pacific Science Center (☞ *above*), and the Space Needle (☞ *below*). Among the arts groups headquartered here are Seattle Repertory Theatre, Intiman Theatre, the Seattle Opera, and the Pacific Northwest Ballet. (The Seattle Symphony will perform here until the opening of Benaroya Hall downtown in 1998.) The center hosts several professional sports teams: the Seattle Supersonics (NBA basketball), Reign

**20**

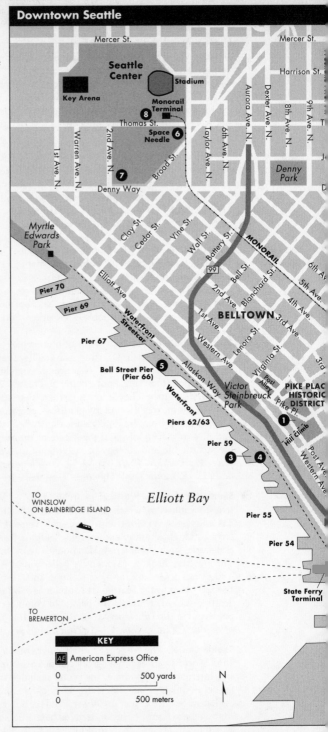

**Downtown Seattle**

Mercer St.    Mercer St.

Seattle Center    Stadium    Harrison St.

Key Arena

Monorail Terminal

Thomas St.    Space Needle **6**

**8**

**7**    Denny Park

Denny Way

Aurora Ave. N.    Dexter Ave. N.    8th Ave. N.    9th Ave. N.

Warren Ave. N.    2nd Ave. N.    Broad St.    6th Ave. N.    Taylor Ave. N.

1st Ave. N.

Myrtle Edwards Park

Clay St.    Cedar St.    Vine St.    Wall St.    Battery St.    MONORAIL

Elliott Ave.    99    Bell St.    6th Av

Pier 70    2nd Ave.    Blanchard    5th Ave.    St.

Pier 69    Waterfront Streetcar    1st Ave.    BELLTOWN    3rd Ave.    4th Ave.

Pier 67    Western Ave.    Lenora St.    3rd

Bell Street Pier (Pier 66)    **5**    Alaskan Way    Virginia St.

Waterfront    Victor Steinbreuck Park    Post Alley    PIKE PLAC HISTORIC DISTRICT

Piers 62/63    Pike Pl.    **1**

Pier 59    Hill Climb

**3**    **4**    Post Ave.    Western Ave.

*Elliott Bay*

TO WINSLOW ON BAINBRIDGE ISLAND    Pier 55

Pier 54

State Ferry Terminal

TO BREMERTON

**KEY**

AE  American Express Office

0                    500 yards

0                    500 meters

N

(women's basketball), Sounders (soccer), Seadogs (indoor soccer), and Thunderbirds (hockey). It's a bit cramped, and parking can be a nightmare, but Seattle Center is the undisputed hub of the city's leisure life. It's also the site of three of the area's largest summer festivals: the Northwest Folklife Festival, Bite of Seattle, and Bumbershoot. *See* Festivals and Seasonal Events *in* Chapter 1 for details about these. The Experience Music Project, a music museum financed by a nonprofit started by Microsoft cofounder Paul Allen and designed by architect Frank Gehry, will open near the Space Needle in 1999. The **Seattle Center Monorail** (☞ Getting Around *in* Seattle A to Z, *below*) travels between the center and Westlake Center. ⊠ *Between 1st and 5th Aves. N and Denny Way and Mercer St.,* ☎ *206/684–8582.*

👆 ❽ **Seattle Children's Museum.** The global village at this colorful and spacious facility introduces children to everyday life in Ghana, the Philippines, and other lands. A mountain wilderness area (including a slide and waterfall) educates kids about climbing, camping, and the Northwest environment. Cog City is a giant maze of pipes and pulleys. A pretend neighborhood contains a post office, café, fire station, and grocery store. An infant/toddler area is well padded for climbing and sliding. Arts-and-crafts activities, special exhibits, and workshops are also offered. ⊠ *Seattle Center House, fountain level, 305 Harrison St.,* ☎ *206/441–1768.* ☞ *$5.50 children, $4 adults.* ☉ *Weekdays 10–5, weekends 10–6.*

★ ❻ **Space Needle.** The distinctive exterior of the 520-ft-high Space Needle can be seen from almost any spot in the downtown area. The view from the inside out is even better—the observation deck, a 42-second elevator ride from street level—yields vistas of the entire region. Have a drink at the Space Needle Lounge or a latte at the adjacent coffee bar and take in Elliott Bay, Queen Anne Hill, and on a clear day the peaks of the Cascade Range. (If it's stormy, have no fear: 25 lightning rods protect the tower.) The needle's rotating restaurants, one family style and the other more formal, are not known for their innovative cuisine. ⊠ *5th Ave. and Broad St.,* ☎ *206/443–2111.* ☞ *Observation deck $8.50.* ☉ *Daily 8 AM–midnight.*

❿ **Washington State Convention and Trade Center.** Seattle's vine-covered exhibition hall straddles I–5. The design of verdant **Freeway Park** south of here is intended to convey the spirit and flavor of the Pacific Northwest, which it does fairly well, considering the urban location. The street-level **Visitor Information Center** has maps, brochures, and events listings. ⊠ *Visitor center: 800 Convention Pl., at 8th Ave. and Pike St.,* ☎ *206/461–5840.* ☉ *Memorial Day–Labor Day, daily 10–4; Labor Day–Memorial Day, weekdays 8:30–5, Sat. 10–4.*

❾ **Westlake Center.** This three-story mall (☞ Shopping, *below*) is also a major terminus for buses and the Seattle Center Monorail, which was built for the 1962 World's Fair and connects downtown to Seattle Center. The ground-level Made in Washington store showcases the state's products. ⊠ *1601 5th Ave.,* ☎ *206/467–1600.* ☉ *Mon.–Sat. 9:30–8, Sun. 11–6.*

## Pioneer Square and the International District

A walk through Seattle's Pioneer Square and International districts provides a glimpse into the city's days as a logging and shipping center and a haven for immigrants from Asia and the Pacific Islands.

*Numbers in the text correspond to numbers in the margin and on the Downtown Seattle map.*

## A Good Walk

Begin at **Pioneer Place,** at 1st Avenue and Yesler Way in the **Pioneer Square District.** Explore the shops and historic buildings along 1st Avenue before heading to the **Klondike Gold Rush National Historical Park** ⑪, on Main Street two blocks south and one block east of Pioneer Place. A restful stop along Main Street heading east to the **International District** is **Waterfall Garden** park, designed by Masao Kinoshita on the site where the messenger service that became United Parcel Service began operations.

Head south (right) on 2nd Avenue South and east (left) at South Jackson Street. You'll see the **Kingdome** sports stadium and Amtrak's **King Street Station** on your right as you head up South Jackson to 7th Avenue, where the **Wing Luke Museum** ⑫ surveys the past and present of immigrants from Asia and the Pacific Islands and their descendants. The museum has walking-tour maps of historic buildings and businesses; one intriguing stop is the **Uwajimaya** store at 6th Avenue South and South King Street (head south one block on 7th Avenue South and turn right on South King Street). You can return to the harbor in one of the vintage **Waterfront Streetcar** trolleys—the southern terminus is at 5th Avenue South and Jackson Street. You can also catch a bus to downtown at the same corner.

TIMING

You can explore Pioneer Square and the International District in one to two hours unless you stop for lunch or like to shop. The Wing Luke Museum is closed Monday.

## Sights to See

**International District.** The 40-block "I.D.," as it's locally known, began as a haven for Chinese workers who came to the United States to work on the transcontinental railroad. The community has remained largely intact despite anti-Chinese riots and the forcible eviction of Chinese residents during the 1880s and the internment of Japanese-Americans during World War II. About one third of the I.D.'s residents are Chinese, one third are Filipino, and another third come from elsewhere in Asia or the Pacific Islands. The district, which includes many Chinese, Japanese, and Korean restaurants, also contains herbalists, massage parlors, acupuncturists, antiques shops, and private clubs for gambling and socializing. Among the I.D.'s many great markets is the huge **Uwajimaya** Japanese supermarket and department store (☞ Shopping, *below*). ⊠ *Between Main and S. Lane Sts. and 4th and 8th Aves.*

⑪ **Klondike Gold Rush National Historical Park.** This indoor center provides insight into Seattle's role in the 1897–98 gold rush in northwestern Canada's Klondike Region through film presentations, permanent exhibits, and gold-panning demonstrations. ⊠ *117 S. Main St.,* ☎ *206/553-7220.* ▣ *Free.* ☉ *Daily 9–5; closed major holidays.*

**Pioneer Square District.** The ornate iron-and-glass pergola at **Pioneer Place,** at 1st Avenue and Yesler Way, marks the site of the pier and sawmill owned by Henry Yesler, one of Seattle's first businessmen. Timber logged off the hills was sent to the sawmill on a "skid road"—now Yesler Way—made of small logs laid crossways and greased so that the freshly cut trees would slide down to the mill. The area grew into Seattle's first business center; in 1889, a fire destroyed many of the district's wood-frame buildings, but the industrious residents and businesspeople rebuilt them with brick and mortar.

With the 1897 Klondike gold rush, however, this area became populated with saloons and brothels; businesses gradually moved north, and the old pioneering area deteriorated. Eventually, only drunks and bums hung out in the neighborhood that had become known as Skid Row, and the name became synonymous with "down and out." The Pioneer Square District encompasses about 18 blocks and includes restaurants, bars, shops, and the city's largest concentration of art galleries, but it is once again known as a hangout for those down on their luck. Incidents of crime in the neighborhood have increased lately, especially after dark, but few find it intimidating during the day.

⓬ **Wing Luke Museum.** The small but well-organized museum named for the first Asian-American elected official in the Northwest surveys the history and cultures of people from Asia and the Pacific Islands who have settled in the Pacific Northwest. The emphasis here is on how immigrants and their descendants have transformed and been transformed by American culture. The permanent collection includes costumes, fabrics, crafts, basketry, photographs, and Chinese traditional medicines. ✉ *407 7th Ave. S,* ☎ *206/623–5124.* ✆ *$2.50.* ☉ *Tues.– Fri. 11–4:30, weekends noon–4.*

## Capitol Hill Area

With its mix of theaters and churches, coffeehouses and nightclubs, stately homes and student apartments, Capitol Hill demonstrates Seattle's diversity better than any other neighborhood. There aren't many sights in the traditional sense, but you can while away an enjoyable day here and perhaps an even more pleasurable evening.

*Numbers in the text correspond to numbers in the margin and on the Downtown Seattle and North Seattle maps.*

### A Good Walk

If you're prepared for some hills, this walk will give you a great overview of the area. From downtown, walk up Pine Street to the corner of Melrose Avenue, where you can fortify yourself with a jolt of java at the **Bauhaus** coffeehouse. This hip area of the hill is known as the **Pike–Pine corridor** ⑬. Continue east on Pine Street to Broadway and turn left (but don't miss the art deco Egyptian Theater to the right). Passing Seattle Central Community College you'll cross Denny Way, the unofficial threshold of the **Broadway shopping district** ⑭. After six energetic blocks, the road bears to the right, becoming 10th Avenue East.

You'll notice many beautiful homes on the side streets off 10th Avenue East in either direction as you continue north to Prospect Street. Turn right at Prospect and gird yourself for another hill. Continue on to 14th Avenue East and turn left (north) to enter **Volunteer Park** ⑮. After walking around a picturesque water tower (with a good view from the top), you'll see the **Volunteer Park Conservatory** straight ahead, the **reservoir** to your left, and the **Seattle Asian Art Museum** to your right. Leave the park to the east via Galer Street. At 15th Avenue East, you can turn left (north) to visit **Lakeview Cemetery** (where Bruce Lee lies in repose), or turn right (south) and walk four blocks to shops and cafés. To return to downtown, continue walking south on 15th Avenue East and west on Pine Street (if you've had enough walking, catch Metro Bus 10 at this intersection; it heads toward Pike Place Market). At Broadway, cut one block south to Pike Street for the rest of the walk.

The above tour is a good survey of Capitol Hill, but it's by no means complete. The area's best attraction, the **Washington Park Arboretum** ⑯, is too far to walk; you'll need to take the bus (catch Metro Bus 11 heading northeast along East Madison Street) or drive.

TIMING

Simply walking this tour, which is a bit strenuous, requires about four hours—two if you start and end in the Broadway shopping district. You'll want to allow at least one to two hours for shopping the Pike–Pine corridor and Broadway, one to two hours for the Asian Art Museum, and a half hour for the conservatory. Any time you spend at Bruce Lee's grave site is between you and Mr. Lee. Plan on at least a few hours for a visit to the arboretum, where losing track of time, and yourself, is pretty much the point.

## Sights to See

⑭ **Broadway shopping district.** Seattle's youth-culture, old-money, and gay scenes all converge on the lively stretch of Broadway East between East Denny Way and East Roy Street. A great place to stroll and sip coffee or have a brew, the strip contains the obligatory art-house movie theater (☞ Harvard Exit *in* Nightlife and the Arts, *below*), record shops and new and vintage clothing stores, and plenty of cafés. The three-story Broadway Market (⊠ 401 Broadway E) has the Gap, Urban Outfitters, and other slick merchandisers, along with some smaller boutiques. You won't be able to miss the glaring sign for the open-air **Dick's Drive-In** (⊠ 115 Broadway E). Dropping in for a Dick's Deluxe Burger and a shake at 1 AM is a quintessential Seattle experience.

**Lakeview Cemetery.** Kung-fu star **Bruce Lee's grave** is the most-visited site at this cemetery directly north of Volunteer Park. Inquire at the office for a map. ⊠ *1554 15th Ave. E,* ☎ *206/322–1582.* ☜ *Free.* ☉ *Weekdays 9–4:30.*

⑬ **Pike–Pine corridor.** A hip new center of activity, this strip that runs toward downtown from the south end of the Broadway shopping district holds galleries, thrift shops, music stores, restaurants, and rock clubs.

**Seattle Asian Art Museum.** This facility in the former Seattle Art Museum holds thousands of paintings, sculptures, pottery, and textiles from China, Japan, India, Korea, and several southeast Asian countries. You can sip any of nearly three dozen distinctive teas at the tranquil **Kado Tea Garden.** A ticket to the Asian Art Museum is valid for admission to the Seattle Art Museum (☞ Pike Place Market, the Waterfront, and Seattle Center, *above*) if used within one week. ⊠ *Volunteer Park, 1400 E. Prospect St.,* ☎ *206/654–3100.* ☜ *$6; free 1st Thurs. of month.* ☉ *Tues.–Sun. 10–5 (Thurs. until 9) and some Mon. holidays; call for tour schedule.*

⑮ **Volunteer Park.** High above the mansions of North Capitol Hill sits 45-acre Volunteer Park, a grassy affair perfect for picnicking, sunbathing, reading, and strolling. It's a mere 108 steps to some great views at the top of the water tower near the main entrance. Beside the lake in the center of the park is the **Seattle Asian Art Museum** (☞ *above*), and across from the museum is the romantic **Volunteer Park Conservatory** (☎ 206/684–4743). The greenhouse, which was completed in 1912, has accumulated its inhabitants largely by donation, including an extensive collection of orchids begun in 1919. Rooms here are dedicated to ferns, palms, cacti, and exotic flowers. Admission is free; hours are seasonal, so call ahead. ⊠ *Park entrance: 14th Ave. E, at Prospect St.*

⑯ **Washington Park Arboretum.** The 200-acre arboretum's Rhododendron Glen and Azalea Way are in full bloom from March through June. During the rest of the year, other plants and wildlife flourish. From March through October, visit the peaceful **Japanese Garden,** a compressed world of mountains, forests, rivers, lakes, and tablelands. The **Graham Visitors Center** at the north end provides explanations of the

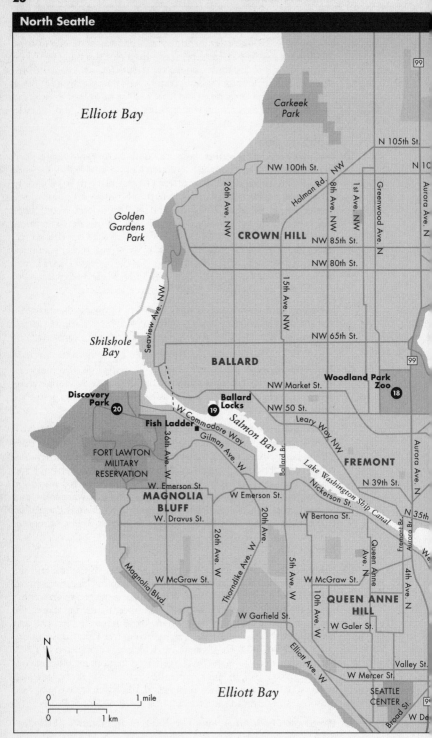

*Elliott Bay*

Carkeek
Park

N 105th St.

NW 100th St.

99

N 10

Holman Rd. NW

8th Ave. NW

1st Ave. NW

Greenwood Ave. N

Aurora Ave. N

*Golden
Gardens
Park*

26th Ave. NW

**CROWN HILL**

NW 85th St.

NW 80th St.

15th Ave. NW

Seaview Ave. NW

*Shilshole
Bay*

NW 65th St.

**BALLARD**

99

NW Market St.

**Woodland Park
Zoo**

18

**Discovery
Park**

20

**Ballard
Locks**

19

NW 50 St.

Leary Way NW

W Commodore Way

**Fish Ladder**

*Salmon Bay*

Ballard Br.

Lake Washington Ship Canal

**FREMONT**

Aurora Ave. N

36th Ave. W

Gilman Ave. W

N 39th St.

N 35th

**FORT LAWTON
MILITARY
RESERVATION**

W. Emerson St.

Nickerson St.

Fremont Br.

Aurora Br.

**MAGNOLIA
BLUFF**

W. Dravus St.

W. Emerson St.

20th Ave.

W Bertona St.

Magnolia Blvd

26th Ave. W

Thorndike Ave. W

5th Ave. W

Queen Anne Ave. N

N 35th

4th Ave. N

W McGraw St.

W McGraw St.

10th Ave. W

**QUEEN ANNE
HILL**

W Garfield St.

W Galer St.

N

*Elliott Ave. W*

Valley St.

W Mercer St.

**SEATTLE
CENTER**

9

N

0 ——— 1 mile

0 ——— 1 km

Broad St.

W De

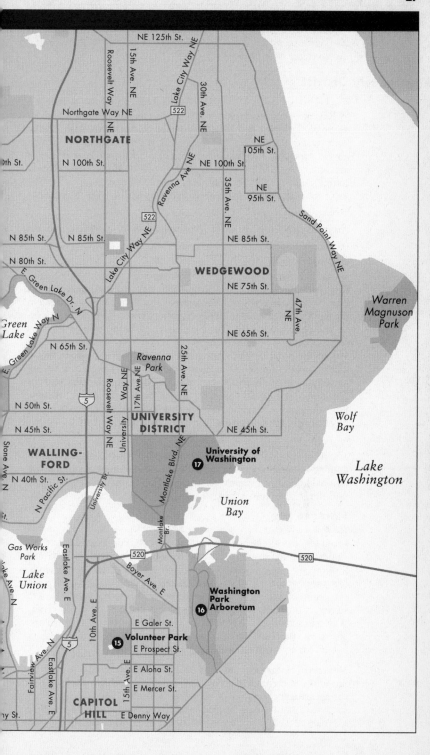

arboretum's flora and fauna and has brochures with self-guided walking tours. Or you can dispense with maps and follow your bliss. ⊠ *2300 Arboretum Dr. E,* ☎ *206/325–4510.* ▭ *Free.* ☉ *Park daily 7 AM–sunset, visitor center daily 10–4.*

---

## University District

The U District, as the University District is known locally, is bounded by Ravenna Boulevard to the north, the Montlake Cut waterway (connecting Lake Union and Lake Washington) to the south, 25th Avenue Northeast to the east, and I–5 to the west. A stroll through the sprawling University of Washington campus can include stops at its museums and other cultural attractions. To get a whiff of the slightly anarchic energy that fuels this part of town, head off campus to "The Ave," the student-oriented shopping area along University Way Northeast.

*Numbers in the text correspond to numbers in the margin and on the North Seattle map.*

### A Good Walk

Start at the corner of Northeast 45th Street and University Way Northeast. Turn left at Northeast Campus Parkway, stopping by the visitor center at the **University of Washington** ⑰. Straight ahead at the end of the block is the **Henry Art Gallery.** Continue east to Central Plaza, better known as **Red Square.** On clear days, you'll be rewarded with views of Mount Rainier to the southeast. Walk down Rainier Vista (past the Frosh Pond and fountain) to Stevens Way, turning left into **Sylvan Grove,** a gorgeous outdoor theater. Return via Rainier Vista to Red Square and strike out due north. A walk along shady Memorial Way past the commuter lot deposits you at the **Burke Museum of Natural History.** From the Burke step out onto Northeast 45th Street, walking two longish blocks to the left to return to University Way Northeast.

#### TIMING

The route above should only take about two hours, but factor in an hour or so each for the Henry gallery and Burke museum and an additional hour if you want to shop along The Ave. It's quite possible to tour the U District in a long morning or a short afternoon.

### Sights to See

**The Ave.** University Way Northeast, the hub of University of Washington social life, has all the activities (and the grungy edge) one expects in a student-oriented district—great coffeehouses, cinemas (☞ the Grand Illusion *and* Varsity theaters *in* Nightlife and the Arts, *below*), clothing stores, and cheap restaurants, along with panhandlers and pockets of grime. The major action along The Ave is between 42nd and 50th streets, though there are more shops and restaurants as University Way continues north to 58th Street and the entrance to Ravenna Park. Stop in the **Big Time Brewery** (☞ Brew Pubs *in* Nightlife and the Arts, *below*) for a pint of ale and a gallon of local color.

☾ **Museum of History and Industry.** An 1880s-era room and a Seattle time line at this museum depict the city's earlier days. Other displays from the permanent collection are shown on a rotating basis—a recent one surveyed Pacific Coast League baseball teams—along with traveling exhibits. ⊠ *2700 24th Ave. E,* ☎ *206/324–1125.* ▭ *$5.50.* ☉ *Daily 10–5.*

⑰ **University of Washington.** Locals know this university with 35,000 students as "U-Dub." Founded in 1861 downtown, the university moved in 1895 to Denny Hall, the first building on the present campus. The

Alaska-Yukon-Pacific Exposition, which the school hosted in 1909, brought the Northwest national attention. The University of Washington is respected for its research and graduate programs in medicine, nursing, oceanography, drama, physiology, and social work, among many others. Its athletic teams—particularly football and women's basketball—have strong regional followings. A **Visitor Information Center** (⊠ 4014 University Way NE, ☎ 206/543–9198) is open daily from 8 to 5.

**Red Square** is the nerve center for student activity and politics. The "red" refers to its brick paving, not students' political inclinations—this is a decidedly nonactivist campus, though it's in the square that you'll see animal-rights, environmental, and other advocates attempting to rouse the masses. On sunny days the steps are filled with students sunbathing, studying, or hanging out.

The extensive collection of works by Northwest artists in the **Henry Art Gallery** (⊠ 15th Ave. NE and N.E. 41st St., ☎ 206/543–2280) on the west side of campus includes photography, 19th- and 20th-century paintings, and textiles; the facility often presents important touring exhibitions. Among the improvements that were part of a redesign completed in 1997 were added gallery space and a light-filled central atrium. The Henry is open Tuesday through Sunday from 11 to 5 (Thursday until 8). Admission is $5.

Exhibits at the **Burke Museum of Natural History** (⊠ 17th Ave. NE and N.E. 45th St., ☎ 206/543–5590), on the northwest edge of campus, survey the cultures of the Pacific Northwest and Washington State's 35 Native American tribes. The museum is open daily from 10 until 5 (Thursday until 8). Admission is $3.

OFF THE
BEATEN PATH

**WARREN MAGNUSON PARK –** Jutting into Lake Washington northeast of the University District, "Sand Point" (as it's called by locals) is one of the best beaches in the city for quiet sunbathing. The sound garden, a grassy area filled with metal sculptures that emit tones when the wind blows, is in the northern part of the park, through the turnstile and across *Moby Dick* Bridge (embedded with quotes from Melville's novel). ⊠ *Park entrance: Sand Point Way NE at 70th St.*

## Fremont and Environs

Around Seattle, the word "Fremont" is invariably preceded by the words "funky," "artsy," or "eclectic." And why not? The neighborhood's residents—largely artists—do little to challenge the image. "The Artists Republic of Fremont," as many prefer to call it, brims with sass and self-confidence. Signs on the outskirts proclaim it THE CENTER OF THE UNIVERSE and instruct visitors to set their watches back five minutes, or to throw them away entirely. Given the area's many assets—galleries, restaurants, coffeehouses, brew pubs, antiques shops, and the like—dispensing with time can be a very good idea. To the east of Fremont is Wallingford, an inviting neighborhood of bungalow homes and boutique shopping. You'll find Phinney Ridge and the Woodland Park Zoo to the north of Fremont. Ballard, a neighborhood with a strong Scandinavian flavor, and the center of Seattle's fishing industry, lies to the west.

*Numbers in the text correspond to numbers in the margin and on the North Seattle map.*

### A Good Tour

Coming from downtown, you'll probably enter Fremont via the **Fremont Bridge,** one of the busiest drawbridges in the world. Central Fremont is tiny and can easily be explored by intuition. Here's one strategy: Proceed north on Fremont Avenue North, turning right at North 35th Street. Walk two blocks to the **Aurora Bridge** (you'll be standing underneath it). Turn left and walk one block, but approach with care; the "Fremont troll"—a whimsical concrete monster that lurks beneath the bridge—jealously guards his Volkswagen Beetle. Head back along North 36th Street, making a hard left at the **statue of Lenin** (seriously) at Fremont Place, the first street after you cross Fremont Avenue North. Walk a half block southeast, go right at the crosswalk, and then make a right onto to North 35th Street. At the end of the block is the 53-ft **Fremont Rocket,** officially designating the center of the universe. Walk straight ahead one long block to Phinney Avenue to **Redhook Brewery** (tours are conducted daily) and the **Trolleyman** (☞ Brew Pubs *in* Nightlife and the Arts, *below*). Turn left and continue one block to the **Ship Canal.** On the right is **Canal Park.** Linger there, or turn left onto North 34th Street and return to the Fremont Bridge. On the way you'll pass a parking lot that hosts two important Fremont traditions: the Sunday Flea and Crafts Market (spring to fall, weather permitting) and the Outdoor Cinema (bring a chair on Saturdays after dusk in the summer).

The major Fremont-area attractions are best reached by car, bus, or bike. The **Woodland Park Zoo** ⑱ is due north of Fremont via Fremont Avenue North (catch Bus 5 heading north from the northeast corner of Fremont Avenue North and North 39th Street). The **Ballard Locks** ⑲ are west of Fremont (take Bus 28 from Fremont Avenue North and North 35th Street to Northwest Market Street and 8th Avenue North and transfer to Bus 44 or, on weekdays only, Bus 46, heading west). **Discovery Park** ⑳ is a walk of less than a mile from the south entrance to the Ballard Locks. Head west (right) on Commodore Way and south (left) on 40th Street.

TIMING

The walk above takes an hour at most, but Fremont is meant for strolling, browsing, sipping, and shopping. Plan to spend a full morning or a good part of an afternoon. You could easily spend two hours at the Ballard Locks and several hours at Discovery Park or the zoo.

## Sights to See

★ ✋ ⑲ **Ballard Locks.** Officially the Hiram M. Chittenden Locks, this part of the 8-mi Lake Washington Ship Canal connects Lake Washington and Lake Union with the salt water of Shilshole Bay and Puget Sound. The locks, which were completed in 1917, service 100,000 boats yearly by raising and lowering water levels anywhere from 6 to 26 ft. On the north side of the locks is a 7-acre **ornamental garden** of native and exotic plants, shrubs, and trees. Also on the north side are a staffed visitor center with displays on the history and operation of the locks as well as several fanciful sculptures by local artists. Along the south side is a 1,200-ft promenade with a footbridge, a fishing pier, and an observation deck.

Take some time to watch the progress of fishing boats and pleasure craft through the locks, then observe how the marine population makes the same journey from saltwater to fresh: On the **fish ladder,** whose 21 levels form a gradual incline that allows an estimated half-million salmon and trout each year to swim upstream. Several windows at the waterline afford views of the fish struggling against the current as they migrate to their spawning grounds. Most of the migration takes place from late June through October. (The fish ladder, by the way, is where various attempts are being carried out to prevent sea lions, including the locally notorious Herschel, from depleting the salmon population.) If you're coming via bus from downtown, take Bus 15 or 18 to the stop at Northwest Market Street and 15th Avenue Northwest and transfer to Bus 44 or (weekdays only) 46 heading west on Market. ⊠ *3015 N.W. 54th St.; from Fremont, head north on Leary Way NW, west on N.W. Market St., and south on 54th St.,* ☎ *206/783–7059.* ⊡ *Free.* ☉ *Locks daily 7* AM*–9* PM*, visitor center June–Sept., daily 10–7; Oct.–May, Thurs.–Mon. 11–5; call for tour information.*

**Center for Wooden Boats.** Though slightly off the main drag at the south end of Lake Union, the center is a great place to launch your expedition if you're interested in exploring the water (or just the waterfront). You can check out the 1897 schooner *Wawona* and the other historic vessels on display, watch the staff at work on a restoration, or rent a boat at the Oarhouse for a sail around the lake. Picnic facilities are also available. ⊠ *1010 Valley St.,* ☎ *206/382–2628.* ⊡ *Free.* ☉ *Memorial Day–Labor Day, daily 11–6 (boat rentals until 7); Labor Day–Memorial Day, daily 11–5 (museum and rentals).*

**❷⓪ Discovery Park.** Formerly a military base, Seattle's largest park (520 acres) now serves as a sprawling wildlife sanctuary. Visitors can hike through cool forests, explore saltwater beaches, or take in views of Puget Sound and Mount Rainier. A 2.8-mi trail traverses this urban wilderness. From Fremont, take Leary Way Northwest to 15th Avenue Northwest, turn left, and head south on 15th Avenue over the Ballard Bridge. Turn right onto West Emerson Street, right onto Gilman Avenue West, left onto West Fort Street, and right onto East Government Way. From downtown, take Elliott Avenue north until it becomes 15th Avenue Northwest, turn left onto West Emerson, and follow the previous directions the rest of the way. ⊠ *3801 E. Government Way,* ☎ *206/386–4236.* ⊡ *Free.* ☉ *Park daily 6* AM*–11* PM*, visitor center daily 8:30–5.*

**Fremont Center.** The self-styled Republic of Fremont is one of Seattle's most distinctive neighborhoods. The center is an eclectic strip of Fremont Avenue stretching from the Ship Canal at the south end to North 36th Street, with shops and cafés two blocks to either side. The area also contains many lighthearted "attractions," including a statue of Lenin, a 53-ft rocket, and the Fremont troll.

**Gasworks Park.** Summer afternoons at Gasworks Park, on the north end of Lake Union, bring colorful displays of kites in the air and spinnakers on the water. Get a glimpse of your future (and downtown Seattle) from the locally famous zodiac sculpture at the top of the hill, or feed the ducks at sea (make that *lake*) level. In the summer, Gasworks is the site of outdoor concerts, including an annual Independence Day fireworks display and a performance by the Seattle Symphony with fireworks. ⊠ *N. Northlake Way and Meridian Ave. N.*

**Green Lake.** Just across Highway 99 (Aurora Avenue North) from the Woodland Park Zoo (☞ *below*), Green Lake is the recreational hub of the city's park system. A 3-mi jogging and bicycling trail rings the lake, and there are facilities for basketball, tennis, baseball, and soccer. The park is generally packed (and the facilities overbooked) on weekday evenings, which has made this the best time for active Seattleites to see and be seen (truth be told, it's something of a young-singles' scene). ⊠ *E. Green Lake Dr. N and W. Green Lake Dr. N.*

**☙ ⓲ Woodland Park Zoo.** Many of the 300 species of animals in this 92-acre botanical garden roam freely in habitat areas that have won several design awards. The African Savanna, the elephant forest, and the Northern Trail, which shelters brown bears, wolves, mountain goats, and otters, are of particular interest. Wheelchairs and strollers can be rented. A memorial to musician Jimi Hendrix, a Seattle native, overlooks the African Savanna exhibit; appropriately enough, it's a big rock. ⊠ *5500 Phinney Ave. N,* ☎ *206/684–4800.* 🖭 *$8.* ☉ *Mid-Mar.–mid-Oct., daily 9:30–6; mid-Oct.–mid-Mar., daily 9:30–4.*

## On Seattle's Outskirts and Beyond

**Chateau Ste. Michelle Winery.** One of the oldest wineries in the state is 15 mi northeast of Seattle on 87 wooded acres that were once part of the estate of lumber baron Fred Stimson. Trout ponds, a carriage house, a caretaker's cottage, formal gardens, and the 1912 family manor house—which is on the National Register of Historic Places—are part of the original estate. Visitors are invited to picnic and explore the grounds; the wine shop sells delicatessen items. During the summer, Chateau Ste. Michelle hosts nationally known performers and arts events in its amphitheater. ⊠ *14111 N.E. 145th St., Woodinville,* ☎ *206/488–1133. From downtown Seattle take I–90 east to north I–405. Take Exit 23 east (S.R. 522) to the Woodinville exit. Complimentary wine tastings and cellar tours daily 10–4:30, except holidays.*

**Jimi Hendrix Grave Site.** The famed guitarist's grave is in Greenwood Cemetery in Renton. From Seattle, take I–5 south to the Renton exit, then I–405 past Southcenter to Exit 4B. Bear right under the freeway. Take a right onto Sunset Boulevard and another right one block later at 3rd Street. Continue 1 mi, turning right at the third light. ⊠ *Corner of 3rd and Monroe Sts.,* ☎ *206/255–1511.* ☉ *Daily until dusk. Inquire at the office; a counselor will direct you to the site.*

★ ☻ **Museum of Flight.** Boeing, the world's largest builder of aircraft, is based in Seattle, so it's not surprising that this facility at Boeing Field is one of the city's best museums, and one that kids particularly enjoy. The Red Barn, Boeing's original airplane factory, houses an exhibit on the history of human flight. The Great Gallery, a dramatic structure designed by Seattle architect Ibsen Nelson, contains more than 20 vintage airplanes. ⊠ *9404 E. Marginal Way S (take I–5 south to exit 158; turn right on Marginal),* ☎ *206/764–5720.* 🖭 *$8.* ☉ *Daily 10–5 (Thurs. until 9).*

# DINING

*See* the Downtown Seattle and Capitol Hill Dining map to locate restaurants in those areas and the North Seattle Dining map for establishments north of the Lake Washington Ship Canal and Union Bay.

| CATEGORY | COST* |
|----------|-------|
| $$$$ | over $35 |
| $$$ | $25–$35 |
| $$ | $15–$25 |
| $ | under $15 |

*per person for a three-course meal, excluding drinks, service, and sales tax (about 9.1%, varies slightly by community)*

## Downtown Seattle and Capitol Hill

### American

$$$ ✕ **Metropolitan Grill.** Meals at this favorite lunching spot of the white-
★ collar crowd are not for timid eaters: Custom-aged mesquite-broiled steaks—the best in Seattle—are huge and come with baked potatoes or pasta. Even the veal chop is extra thick. Lamb, chicken, and seafood entrées are also on the menu. Among the accompaniments, the onion rings and the sautéed mushrooms are tops. ⊠ *818 2nd Ave.,* ☎ *206/624–3287. AE, D, DC, MC, V. No lunch weekends.*

$$–$$$$  ✕ **Wolfgang Puck Cafe.** A laid-back, amiable staff serves postmodern
★ comfort food—barbecued-duck quesadillas, jerk-chicken Caesar sal-
ads, linguine with seared jumbo sea scallops—at this vivacious Puck
enterprise across 1st Avenue from the Seattle Art Museum. You can
slurp down some oyster shooters or "sip" a jumbo gulf-shrimp "mar-
tini" at the seafood bar. ✉ *1225 1st Ave.,* ☎ *206/621–9653. AE, D,
DC, MC, V.*

## Asian

$$$  ✕ **Wild Ginger.** The seafood and Southeast Asian fare at this restau-
rant near Pike Place Market ranges from mild Cantonese to spicier Viet-
namese, Thai, and Korean dishes. House specialties include *satay*
(chunks of beef, chicken, or vegetables skewered and grilled, and usually served with a spicy peanut sauce), live crab, sweetly flavored duck,
wonderful soups, and some fine vegetarian options. The satay bar, where
you can sip local brews and eat skewered tidbits until 2 AM, is a local
hangout. The clubby, old-fashioned dining room has high ceilings and
lots of mahogany and Asian art. ✉ *1400 Western Ave.,* ☎ *206/623–
4450. AE, D, DC, MC, V. No lunch Sun.*

$  ✕ **Noodle Ranch.** Tongue planted firmly in cheek, Noodle Ranch bills
itself as Belltown's purveyor of "Pan-Asian vittles." Standouts on the
inexpensive menu include sugar-cane shrimp, Japanese eggplant in
ginger, and a spicy basil stir-fry. The sense of humor evident in the name
is borne out in the freewheeling decor. ✉ *2228 2nd Ave.,* ☎ *206/728–
0463. AE, MC, V. Closed Sun.*

## Chinese

$  ✕ **Chau's Chinese Restaurant.** This small, very plain place on the
northwest edge of Seattle's International District near Pioneer Square
serves great seafood—steamed oysters in garlic sauce, Dungeness crab
with ginger and onion, and geoduck. Avoid the standard Cantonese
dishes and stick to the seafood and specials. ✉ *310 4th Ave. S,* ☎ *206/
621–0006. MC, V. No lunch weekends.*

## Deli

$  ✕ **Bakeman's Restaurant.** Low on frills but high on atmosphere, this
well-lighted lunchery attracts a steady stream of business suits with its
signature turkey and meat-loaf sandwiches, served on fluffy white
bread. Bakeman's, open weekdays from 10 to 3, is within easy striking distance of Pioneer Square, but the feel here is far from touristy.
✉ *122 Cherry St.,* ☎ *206/622–3375. Reservations not accepted. No
credit cards. Closed weekends. No dinner.*

## Eclectic

$$$$  ✕ **Fullers.** Consistently ranked at or near the top of Seattle's restau-
★ rants in local and national publications, Fullers delivers a rare commodity:
a dining experience of exceptional poise and restraint born of uncon-
ventional, even visionary, risk-taking. The menu, a playground for acclaimed chef Monique Andrée Barbeau, is a perpetual work-in-progress
that always seems exquisitely finished; with evident humor, Barbeau
calls her cuisine "Americanized Northwest gourmet with French techniques, Pacific Rim influences, and some rustic touches." Among the
signature dishes are Moroccan-spiced quail with preserved lemons and
oregano, house-marinated kasu salmon with gingered Asian slaw, and
herb-encrusted sea scallops with curried pesto broth. Works by Northwest artists adorn an otherwise austere dining room. ✉ *Seattle Sheraton Hotel and Towers, 1400 6th Ave.,* ☎ *206/447–5544. Reservations
essential. AE, D, DC, MC, V. Closed Sun. No lunch Sat.*

$$$–$$$$  ✕ **Axis.** Restaurant as theater is the angle at this Belltown restaurant
with a wood-fire grill—diners can view the kitchen from just about every

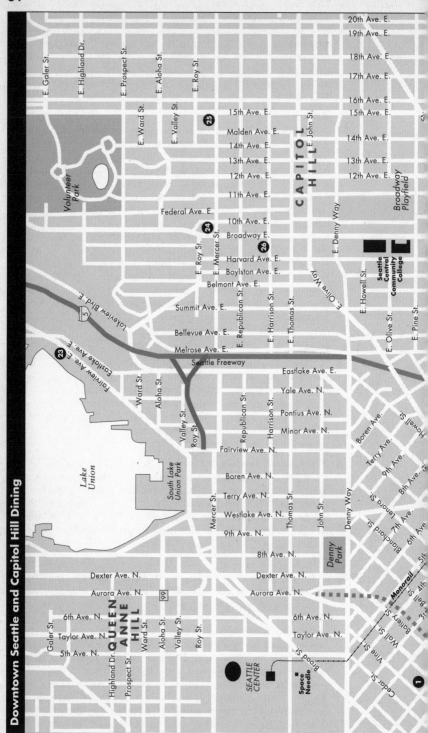

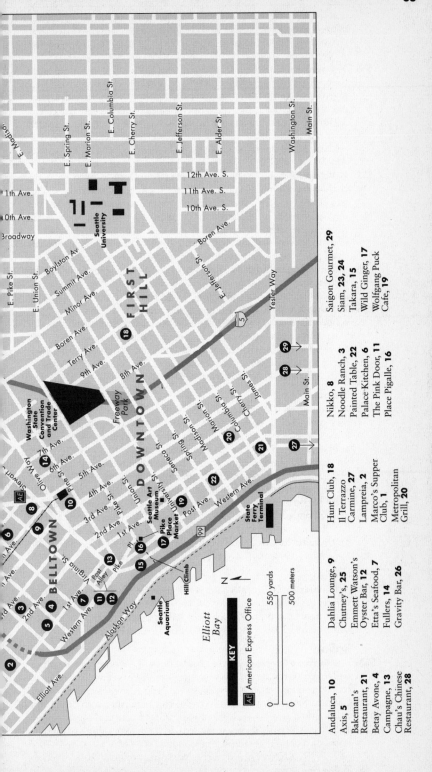

Andaluca, **10**
Axis, **5**
Bakeman's
Restaurant, **21**
Betay Avone, **4**
Campagne, **13**
Chau's Chinese
Restaurant, **28**

Dahlia Lounge, **9**
Chutney's, **25**
Emmett Watson's
Oyster Bar, **12**
Etta's Seafood, **7**
Fullers, **14**
Gravity Bar, **26**

Hunt Club, **18**
Il Terrazzo
Carmine, **27**
Lampreia, **2**
Marco's Supper
Club, **1**
Metropolitan
Grill, **20**

Nikko, **8**
Noodle Ranch, **3**
Painted Table, **22**
Palace Kitchen, **6**
The Pink Door, **11**
Place Pigalle, **16**

Saigon Gourmet, **29**
Siam, **23, 24**
Takara, **15**
Wild Ginger, **17**
Wolfgang Puck
Cafe, **19**

**KEY**

[AE] American Express Office

**Seattle University**

**FIRST HILL**

**DOWNTOWN**

**BELLTOWN**

Washington
State
Convention
and Trade
Center

Freeway
Park

Seattle Art
Museum

Pike
Place
Market

State
Ferry
Terminal

Seattle
Aquarium

Hill Climb

Elliott
Bay

Elliott Ave.

seat in the house. But the cuisine proves worthy of the show, with appetizers like crispy eggplant wonton and an entrée of oven-roasted Dungeness crab with Cajun seasonings. ⊠ *2214 1st Ave.,* ☎ *206/441–9600. Reservations essential. AE, DC, MC, V. No lunch.*

**$$$  ✕ Andaluca.** Chef Don Curtiss oversees the kitchen at this secluded spot downstairs at the Mayflower Park Hotel. A synthesis of fresh local ingredients and Mediterranean techniques, the fare includes small plates that can act as starters or be combined to make a satisfying meal. A Dungeness crab tower with avocado, hearts of palm, and gazpacho salsa is cool and light, while the Cabrales crusted beef tenderloin with pears and blue cheese is neither. ⊠ *407 Olive Way,* ☎ *206/382–6999. AE, D, DC, MC, V.*

**$$$  ✕ Palace Kitchen.** The latest venture of Tom Douglas, who's also the
**★** chef-owner of Dahlia Lounge and Etta's Seafood, is simultaneously chic and convivial. The star of the stylish room may be the 45-ft bar, but the real show takes place within the giant open kitchen at the back. Sausages, sweet-pea ravioli, salmon carpaccio, and a nightly selection of exotic cheeses vie for your attention on an ever-changing menu of small plates, a few entrées, and 10 fantastic desserts. There's always a rotisserie special from the apple-wood grill as well. Especially rare for early-to-bed Seattle, dinner is served until 1 AM. ⊠ *2030 5th Ave.,* ☎ *206/448–2001. AE, D, DC, MC, V. No lunch.*

**$$  ✕ Marco's Supper Club.** Multiregional cuisine is the specialty of this casual former tavern with shrimp-color walls and mismatched flatware. Start with the fried sage-leaf appetizer with garlic aioli and salsa, then move on to sesame-crusted ahi tuna, Jamaican jerk chicken, or a pork porterhouse in an almond mole sauce. ⊠ *2510 1st Ave.,* ☎ *206/441– 7801. AE, MC, V. No lunch weekends.*

## French

**$$$$  ✕ Campagne.** The white walls, picture windows, snowy linens, candles, and fresh flowers at this intimate and urbane restaurant evoke Provence, as does the menu—French cuisine here means the robust flavors of the Midi, not the more polished tastes of Paris. To start, try the seafood sausage or the calamari fillets with ground almonds. Main plates include panfried scallops with a green-peppercorn and tarragon sauce, cinnamon-roasted quail served with carrot and orange essence, and Oregon rabbit accompanied by an apricot-cider and green-peppercorn sauce. Campagne, which overlooks Pike Place Market and Elliott Bay, is open only for dinner, but its sister café serves breakfast and lunch daily. ⊠ *Inn at the Market, 86 Pine St.,* ☎ *206/728–2800. Reservations essential. AE, DC, MC, V. No lunch.*

## Indian

**$  ✕ Chutney's.** The local chain (☞ Indian *in* North Seattle Dining, *below*) has a Capitol Hill branch. The outstanding dishes include tandoori halibut and prawns, chicken kabobs, five curries, and rack of lamb. ⊠ *605 15th Ave. E,* ☎ *206/726–1000. AE, D, DC, MC, V.*

## Italian

**$$$  ✕ Il Terrazzo Carmine.** On the ground floor of a Pioneer Square office building, this restaurant owes its comfortable but refined ambience to ceiling-to-floor draperies, genteel service, and quiet music. Chef-owner Carmine Smeraldo prepares flavorful chicken dishes with prosciutto and fontina, and his veal baked with spinach and scallops is simply excellent. The pasta dishes are superb. In the summer, you can eat outdoors on a patio that faces a large fountain. ⊠ *411 1st Ave. S,* ☎ *206/ 467–7797. AE, D, DC, MC, V. Closed Sun. No lunch Sat.*

**$$  ✕ The Pink Door.** This restaurant with a "secret" entrance off Post Alley dishes up a generous portion of atmosphere along with solid Italian fare. The roasted garlic and *tapenada* (a caper, anchovy, and black-olive spread) are eminently sharable appetizers; spaghetti *alla puttanesca* (with anchovies, capers, and tomatoes) and cioppino are the standout entrées. The quirky bar is often crowded with young people, and cabaret acts regularly perform on a small stage in the corner. But the real draw here is the outdoor deck, rimmed in flowers, topped with a canopy of colored lights, and perched perfectly over Pike Place Market, with a terrific view of the water beyond. ⊠ *1919 Post Alley,* ☎ *206/443–3241. AE, MC, V. Closed Sun.–Mon.*

## Japanese

$$$ ✕ **Nikko.** Given that the sushi bar is the architectural centerpiece of this restaurant's low-light and black-lacquer decor, it's not surprising that Nikko serves some of the best sushi and sashimi in Seattle. The Kasuzuke cod and teriyaki salmon are also both highly recommended. ⊠ *Westin Hotel, 1900 5th Ave.,* ☎ *206/322–4641. AE, D, DC, MC, V. Closed Sun. No lunch Sat.*

$$ ✕ **Takara.** In full action, the sushi chef here can look like a character from a Japanese wood-block print, perhaps a master swordsman preparing to fight heaven and earth. His real calling, however, is carving up the freshest of seafood for sushi and sashimi. No wonder Japanese businessmen flock here for lunch. The dining room serves classic Japanese dishes using Northwest ingredients. The salmon teriyaki is top-notch, as is the steamed black cod. ⊠ *Pike Pl. Market Hillclimb, 1501 Western Ave.,* ☎ *206/682–8609. AE, MC, V. Closed Sun. in winter.*

## Kosher

$$$ ✕ **Betay Avone.** The Mediterranean-inspired dishes at this restaurant inside an unassuming Belltown storefront are administered under rabbinical supervision. Moroccan *bysteeyas* (braised chicken with scallions, cinnamon, cayenne, and cumin wrapped in phyllo) are a fantastic starter, and the salmon fillet with caramelized onions and tahini over couscous is an imaginative spin on a Northwest staple. ⊠ *113 Blanchard St.,* ☎ *206/448–5597. AE, MC, V. No dinner Fri.–Sat., no lunch Fri.–Mon.*

## Pacific Northwest

$$$ ✕ **Dahlia Lounge.** Romantic Dahlia worked its magic on Tom Hanks
★ and Meg Ryan in *Sleepless in Seattle*—with valentine-red walls lighted so dimly that you can't see much farther than your dinner companion's eyes, this place is cozy and then some. But the food plays its part, too. Locally legendary crab cakes, served as an entrée or an appetizer, lead an ever-changing regionally oriented menu. Other standouts are seared ahi tuna and near-perfect gnocchi. Desserts that include coconut cream pie and fresh cobblers are among the best in town. Chef-owner Tom Douglas is Seattle's most energetic restaurateur. He also owns Etta's Seafood in Pike Place Market, and the excellent Palace Kitchen on 5th Avenue, but Dahlia is the one to make your heart go pitter-pat. ⊠ *1904 4th Ave.,* ☎ *206/682–4142. Reservations essential. AE, D, DC, MC, V. No lunch weekends.*

$$$ ✕ **Hunt Club.** Dark wood and plush seating provide a comfortable if surprisingly traditional setting for chef Eric Leonard's interpretations of Pacific Northwest meat and seafood. The potato pancakes with caviar or the squash ravioli are excellent starters. Entrées on the seasonal menu include swordfish with an almond-herb crust, pork chops stuffed with artichokes and sun-dried tomatoes, and roast venison with a peppercorn-and-cranberry game-based demi-glace, served with candied yams. ⊠ *Sorrento, 900 E. Madison St.,* ☎ *206/622–6400. AE, DC, MC, V.*

$$$   ✕ **Lampreia.** The beige-and-gold interior of this Belltown restaurant
★    is the perfect backdrop for chef-owner Scott Carsberg's sophisticated
cuisine. After an appetizer of cream of polenta with shiitake mushrooms,
try one of the seasonal menu's intermezzo or light main courses—per-
haps squid and cannelloni filled with salmon—or a full entrée such as
pheasant with apple-champagne sauerkraut or lamb with pesto and
whipped potatoes. The clear flavors of desserts like lemon mousse with
strawberry sauce bring a soothing conclusion to an exciting experience.
✉ *2400 1st Ave.,* ☎ *206/443–3301. Reservations essential. AE, MC,
V. Closed Sun.–Mon. No lunch.*

$$$   ✕ **Painted Table.** Chef Tim Kelly selects the freshest regional ingredi-
ents for dishes that are served on hand-painted plates. His seasonal menu
might include spicy rock-shrimp linguine, wild-mushroom risotto, or
herb-crusted lamb with grilled Japanese eggplant, fennel, and polenta.
Desserts include a frozen banana soufflé and a jasmine-rice custard made
with coconut milk. The restaurant's sand-color hues and local artwork
make for an all-around stylish experience. ✉ *Alexis Hotel, 1007 1st
Ave.,* ☎ *206/624–3646. Reservations essential. AE, D, DC, MC, V.
No lunch weekends.*

$$$   ✕ **Place Pigalle.** Large windows look out onto Elliott Bay from this
intimate restaurant tucked behind a meat vendor in Pike Place Mar-
ket's main arcade; in nice weather, they're left ajar to admit the fresh
salt breeze. Bright flower bouquets lighten up the café tables, and the
friendly staff makes you feel right at home. Despite its French name,
this is a very American restaurant. Seasonal meals showcase seafood
and regional ingredients. Go for the rich oyster stew, the Dungeness
crab (available only when it is truly fresh), or the fish of the day baked
in hazelnuts. ✉ *81 Pike Pl. Market,* ☎ *206/624–1756. AE, MC, V.
Closed Sun.*

## Seafood

$$$   ✕ **Etta's Seafood.** Tom Douglas's restaurant near Pike Place Market
has a sleek and slightly whimsical design and views of Victor Stein-
breuck Park. In season try the Dungeness crab cakes, roasted king salmon
with cornbread pudding, or the various Washington oysters on the half
shell. Brunch, served on weekends, always includes zesty seafood
omelets, but the chef also does justice to French toast, eggs and bacon,
and Mexican-influenced breakfast fare. ✉ *202 Western Ave.,* ☎ *206/
443–6000. AE, D, DC, MC, V.*

$   ✕ **Emmett Watson's Oyster Bar.** This unpretentious spot can be hard
to find—it's in the back of the Pike Place Market's Soames-Dunn
Building, facing a small flower-bedecked courtyard—but for Seattleites
and visitors who know their oysters, it's worth the special effort. Not
only are the oysters very fresh and the beer icy cold, but both are inexpensive and available in any number of varieties. If you don't like
oysters, try the salmon soup or the fish-and-chips—flaky pieces of fish
with very little grease. ✉ *1916 Pike Pl.,* ☎ *206/448–7721. Reservations not accepted. No credit cards.*

## Thai

$   ✕ **Siam.** Thai cooking is ubiquitous in Seattle—it can almost be con-
sidered a mainstream cuisine. Start your meal at popular Siam with a
satay skewer or the city's best *tom kah gai,* a soup of coconut, lemon-
grass, chicken, and mushrooms. Entrées include curries, noodle dishes,
and many prawn, chicken, and fish preparations. You can specify one
to five stars according to your tolerance for heat. The location on Fairview
Avenue near Lake Union has a more relaxed atmosphere than the energetic Capitol Hill original on Broadway. ✉ *616 Broadway,* ☎ *206/*

*324–0892; 1880 Fairview Ave. E,* ☎ *206/323–8101. AE, MC, V. No lunch weekends.*

### Vegetarian

$ ✕ **Gravity Bar.** Sprouty sandwiches and other "modern food," all healthful and then some, are dished up at this congenial juice bar with a sci-fi–industrial ambience at its Capitol Hill location. The juices—from all number of fruits and vegetables, solo or in combo form—are often zippier than the solid food, which in the old days would have been called "bland but grand." ✉ *415 Broadway E,* ☎ *206/325–7186. No credit cards.*

### Vietnamese

$ ✕ **Saigon Gourmet.** This small café in the International District is
★ about as plain as they get, but the food is superb and incredibly inexpensive. Aficionados make special trips for the Cambodian soup and the shrimp rolls, but also consider the unusual papaya with beef jerky. Parking can be a problem, but the food rewards your patience. ✉ *502 S. King St.,* ☎ *206/624–2611. Reservations not accepted. MC, V. Closed Mon.*

## North Seattle

### American

$$$$ ✕ **Canlis.** Little has changed at this Seattle institution since the '50s, when steak served by kimono-clad waitresses represented the pinnacle of high living. Recent renovations have made for a less old-boy clubby feel than before, but the restaurant is still very expensive, very good at what it does, and very popular. The view across Lake Union is almost as good as ever, though it now includes a forest of high-rises. Besides the famous steaks, there are equally famous oysters from Quilcene Bay and fresh fish in season. In 1997 the restaurant was one of only five restaurants in the United States to earn a Grand Award from *Wine Spectator* magazine for its wine list and service. ✉ *2576 Aurora Ave. N,* ☎ *206/283–3313. Reservations essential. AE, DC, MC, V. Closed Sun. No lunch.*

$$$ ✕ **Kaspar's.** A decidedly unglamorous atmosphere and its location amid lower Queen Anne Hill's low-rise office buildings and light industry shifts the attention at this restaurant where it belongs—on chef-owner Kaspar Donier's finely wrought contemporary cuisine. Seafood, steak, and poultry options abound—the five-course Northwest seafood dinner will prove a lifeline to the indecisive. Its proximity to Seattle Center makes Kaspar's a natural destination before or after your evening's entertainment, but the food insists that you take your time. ✉ *19 W. Harrison St., west of Queen Anne Ave. N,* ☎ *206/298–0123. AE, MC, V. Closed Sun.–Mon. No lunch.*

$$ ✕ **Five Spot.** Just up the hill from Seattle Center, the Five Spot is comfortable and unpretentious. Its regional American menu makes a new stop every four months or so—Little Italy, New Orleans, and Florida are previous ones. The Five Spot is also popular for Sunday brunch. At the restaurant's kitchen cousins, Jitterbug in Wallingford and the Coastal Kitchen in Capitol Hill, the same rotating menu strategy, with more international flavor but equally satisfying results, applies. ✉ *1502 Queen Anne Ave. N,* ☎ *203/285–7768. MC, V. Jitterbug:* ✉ *2114 N. 45th St.,* ☎ *206/547–6313. MC, V. Coastal Kitchen:* ✉ *429 15th Ave. E,* ☎ *206/322–1145. MC, V.*

# North Seattle Dining

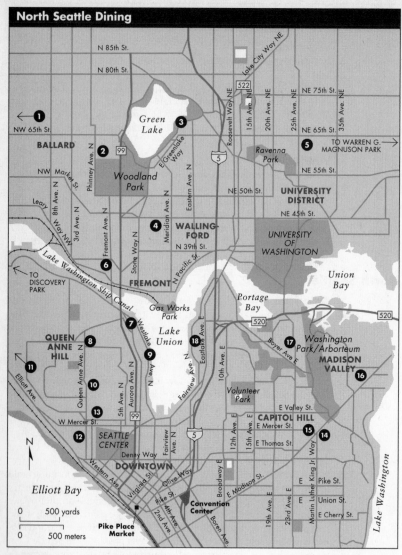

Adriatica, **9**

Bandoleone, **18**

Cactus, **16**

Cafe Flora, **14**

Cafe Lago, **17**

Canlis, **7**

Chutney's, **4, 13**

El Camino, **6**

Five Spot, **10**

Kaspar's, **12**

Palisade, **11**

Pirosmani, **8**

Ray's Boathouse, **1**

Rover's, **15**

Saleh Al Lago, **3**

Santa Fe Cafe, **2, 5**

## Eclectic

**$$–$$$** ✕ **Bandoleone.** Here's a place that leads a double life. The dining room is simple and austere, even rustic, but the deck out back is festive and fun, decorated with colorful Mexican paper cutouts. Both spaces are perfect for a romantic dinner. Though the prevailing atmosphere at Bandoleone is decidedly unpretentious, the sophisticated menu of large and small plates roams Spain, the Caribbean, and Central and South America. A sweet and clean grilled ahi tuna entrée comes with papaya black-bean salsa; the eggplant relleno is a swampy blend of squash, summer corn, sweet onions, and goat cheese. Tequila-cured salmon gravlax and a banana-macadamia empanada with a tamarind dipping sauce are two of several outstanding tapas. The gravlax also appears on the imaginative and inexpensive menu for Saturday and Sunday brunch (served between 9 AM and 2 PM). ✉ *2241 Eastlake Ave. E,* ☎ *206/329–7559. MC, V. No lunch.*

## French

**$$$$** ✕ **Rover's.** The restaurant of Thierry Rautereau, one of the Northwest's
★ most imaginative chefs, is an essential destination on any culinary tour of Seattle. Most patrons order off a multicourse tasting menu (vegetarian selections available) of Rautereau's latest creations; sea scallops, venison, squab, lobster, and rabbit are frequent offerings. The incomparable sauce work and reliance on delicacies such as foie gras and truffles pay homage to Rautereau's French roots, but bold combinations of ingredients are evidence of his wanderlust. The service at Rover's is excellent—friendly but unobtrusive—the setting romantic, and the presentation stunning. ✉ *2808 E. Madison St.,* ☎ *206/325–7442. Reservations essential. AE, MC, V. Closed Sun.–Mon. No lunch.*

## Georgian

**$$$$** ✕ **Pirosmani.** This restaurant in a 1906 house on Queen Anne Hill is named for folk painter Niko Pirosmani. The Georgian dishes are notable for their clever use of herbs and lack of heavy sauces: Duck is seared, then braised with coriander and savory. Skewered lamb is grilled with basil, garlic, and cilantro and served with a plum sauce. Other entrées have their origins in North Africa or the south of France. The signature dessert is a walnut-date rosewater tart, but you wouldn't go wrong with the baklava-ricotta cheesecake either. ✉ *2220 Queen Anne Ave. N,* ☎ *206/285–3360. AE, MC, V. Closed Sun.–Mon. No lunch.*

## Indian

**$** ✕ **Chutney's.** The aromas of cardamom, cumin, and jasmine wafting through the air may make you feel like you've been transported to another continent. The outstanding dishes include tandoori halibut and prawns, chicken kabobs, five different curries, and rack of lamb. Consistently rated as one of Seattle's top restaurants, Chutney's has a flagship location in Queen Anne, a branch in Wallingford, and another in Capitol Hill (☞ Downtown Seattle and Capitol Hill Dining, *above*). ✉ *Queen Anne: 519 1st Ave. N,* ☎ *206/284–6799.* ✉ *Wallingford: 1815 N. 45th St.,* ☎ *206/634–1000. AE, D, DC, MC, V.*

## Italian

**$$$** ✕ **Saleh Al Lago.** Some of the best Italian fare in the city can be found north of downtown. The well-lighted dining room here is done in soft colors and, with its view of Green Lake and Woodland Park, invites slow-paced dining. The antipasti, fresh pasta, and veal dishes are always excellent, as is the chef's special ravioli. Even deceptively plain fare like grilled breast of chicken with olive oil and fresh herbs is superb. ⊠ *6804 E. Greenlake Way N,* ☎ *206/522–7943. AE, DC, MC, V. Closed Sun.–Mon. No lunch Sat.*

**$$**    ✕ **Cafe Lago.** Hugely popular with locals, Cafe Lago specializes in wood-fired pizzas and light handmade pastas. The lasagna—ricotta, béchamel and cherry-tomato sauce amid paper-thin pasta sheets—perfectly represents the menu's inclination toward the simply satisfying. Spare table settings, high ceilings, and a friendly atmosphere make the restaurant suitable for a night out with friends or a romantic getaway. ⊠ *2305 24th Ave. E,* ☎ *206/329–8005. D, MC, V. Closed Mon. No lunch.*

## Mediterranean

**$$$**    ✕ **Adriatica.** This place gathered a loyal local following, became a virtual Seattle institution, and then was discovered by visitors who spread the word. The dining room and upstairs bar in this hillside Craftsman-style house have terrific views of Lake Union. The fare here could best be described as Pacific Northwest–influenced Greek and Italian cuisine. Regular offerings include fresh fish, pasta, risotto, and seafood souvlaki. Phyllo pastries with honey and nuts are among the tasty dessert choices. ⊠ *1107 Dexter Ave. N,* ☎ *206/285–5000. Reservations essential. AE, DC, MC, V. No lunch.*

## Mexican

**$$**    ✕ **El Camino.** The atmosphere at this loose, loud, and funky Fremont storefront perfectly mirrors El Camino's irreverent Northwest interpretation of Mexican cuisine. Rock-shrimp quesadillas, chipotle-pepper and garlic sea bass, and duck with a spicy green sauce are typical of the gentle spin applied by chef Joe Curry. Even a green salad becomes transformed with toasted pumpkin seeds on crispy romaine with a cool dressing of garlic, lime juice, and cilantro. As for cool, there's no better place to chill on a summer afternoon than El Camino's deck. A tart scratch margarita, served in a pint glass with plenty of ice, makes the perfect accessory. ⊠ *607 N. 35th St.,* ☎ *206/632–7303. AE, DC, MC, V. No lunch weekdays.*

## Seafood

**$$$**    ✕ **Ray's Boathouse.** The view of Puget Sound may be the big draw here,
★     but the seafood is impeccably fresh and well prepared. Perennial favorites include broiled salmon, kasu sake cod, Dungeness crab, and regional oysters on the half shell. Ray's has a split personality: There's a fancy dining room downstairs and a casual café and bar upstairs. In warm weather, you can sit on the deck outside the café and watch the parade of fishing boats, tugs, and pleasure craft floating past, almost right below your table. ⊠ *6049 Seaview Ave. NW,* ☎ *206/789–3770. Reservations essential for dining room; reservations not accepted for café. AE, DC, MC, V.*

**$$**    ✕ **Palisade.** The short ride to the Magnolia neighborhood yields a stunning view back across Elliott Bay to the lights of downtown. And there's no better place to take in the vista than this restaurant at the Elliott Bay Marina. Palisade scores points for its playfully exotic ambience—complete with a burbling indoor stream. As for the food, the simpler preparations, especially a signature plank-broiled salmon, will prove most satisfying. Maggie Bluffs, an informal café downstairs, is a great spot for lunch on a breezy summer afternoon. ⊠ *2601 W. Marina Pl.; from downtown, take Elliott Ave. northwest across Magnolia Bridge to Elliott Bay Marina exit,* ☎ *206/285–1000. AE, D, DC, MC, V.*

## Southwestern

**$$**    ✕ **Cactus.** It's worth the drive to Madison Park to experience the rich flavors and colorful atmosphere of Cactus. The food, which displays Native American, Spanish, and Mexican influences, will satisfy wide-ranging palates, from the sensibly vegetarian to the utterly carnivorous. From the tapas bar, sample the marinated eggplant, garlic shrimp, or the tuna *escabeche* (spicy cold marinade). Larger plates include the vegetarian chili relleno, the grilled pork with orange and chipotle peppers, and a flavorful ancho-chili and cinnamon roasted chicken. ⊠ *4220 E. Madison St.,* ☎ *206/324–4140. D, DC, MC, V.*

$$ ✕ **Santa Fe Cafe.** Visitors from New Mexico say that this is about as authentic as southwestern fare gets in these parts—maybe because that's where the restaurant buys the red and green chilies for its sauces. Interesting brews on tap help mitigate the heat of such delicious dishes as green-chili burritos made with blue-corn tortillas. Try the red or green enchiladas or house specialties like the artichoke ramekin, the chili-relleno torte, and a roast-garlic appetizer. Of Santa Fe's locations, the 65th Street one, with its woven rugs and dried flowers, is cozier. The Phinney Avenue restaurant is slicker and more chic; skylights bring in rays that further brighten a pink-and-mauve color scheme. ⊠ *2255 N.E. 65th St.,* ☎ *206/524–7736. MC, V. No lunch Sat.–Mon.* ⊠ *5910 Phinney Ave. N,* ☎ *206/783–9755. MC, V. No lunch Sun.–Fri.*

### Vegetarian

$$ ✕ **Cafe Flora.** This sophisticated Madison Valley café attracts vegetarians and meat eaters for artistically presented, full-flavored meals. An adventurous menu includes Portobello mushroom Wellington, fajitas, and polenta topped with onion, rosemary, and mushrooms. Sunday brunch draws a crowd. ⊠ *2901 E. Madison St.,* ☎ *206/325–9100. MC, V. Closed Mon. No dinner Sun.*

# LODGING

By Julie Fay

Seattle has lodgings to suit most budgets, but though the city has many rooms, you need to book as far in advance as possible if you're coming between May and September. The most elegant properties are downtown; less expensive but still tasteful options, usually smaller in size (and with more of a Seattle feel), can be found in the University District. Many of the lower-price motels along Aurora Avenue North (Highway 99) were built for the 1962 World's Fair. Air travelers often stay along Pacific Highway South (also Highway 99), near Seattle-Tacoma International Airport. Always inquire about special rates based on occupancy or weekend stays; many hotels below give discounts to AARP or AAA members.

| CATEGORY | COST* |
|----------|-------|
| $$$$ | over $170 |
| $$$ | $110–$170 |
| $$ | $60–$110 |
| $ | under $60 |

*All prices are for a standard double room, excluding 15.2% combined hotel and state sales tax.*

## Downtown

$$$$ 🏨 **Alexis Hotel.** The intimate, European-style Alexis occupies two re-
★ stored buildings near the waterfront. Complimentary sherry awaits you in the lobby bar upon your arrival, a prelude to the attentive service you'll receive throughout your stay at this property managed by the Kimpton Group. Rooms are decorated in subdued colors and imported Italian and French fabrics, with at least one piece of antique furniture. Some suites have whirlpool tubs or wood-burning fireplaces and some have marble fixtures. Unfortunately, views are limited and rooms facing 1st Avenue can be noisy. Amenities include complimen-

**44**

**Seattle Lodging**

Mercer St.

Mercer St.

Seattle Center

Stadium

Key Arena

Harrison St.

Monorail Terminal

Thomas St.

Space Needle

Denny Park

Denny Way

Myrtle Edwards Park

Clay St.

Cedar St.

Vine St.

Wall St.

Battery St.

MONORAIL

Elliott Ave.

99

Bell St.

Blanchard St.

Pier 70

2nd Ave.

BELLTOWN

Pier 69

Waterfront Streetcar

1st Ave.

Lenora St.

Western Ave.

Pier 67

Bell Street Pier (Pier 66)

Virginia St.

Post Alley

PIKE PLAC
HISTORIC
DISTRICT

Waterfront

Alaskan Way

Pike Pl.

Piers 62/63

Hill Climb

Pier 59

Western Ave.

Elliott Bay

TO WINSLOW ON BAINBRIDGE ISLAND

Pier 55

Pier 54

TO BREMERTON

State Ferry Terminal

**KEY**

AE  American Express Office

0 _____ 500 yards

0 _____ 500 meters

N

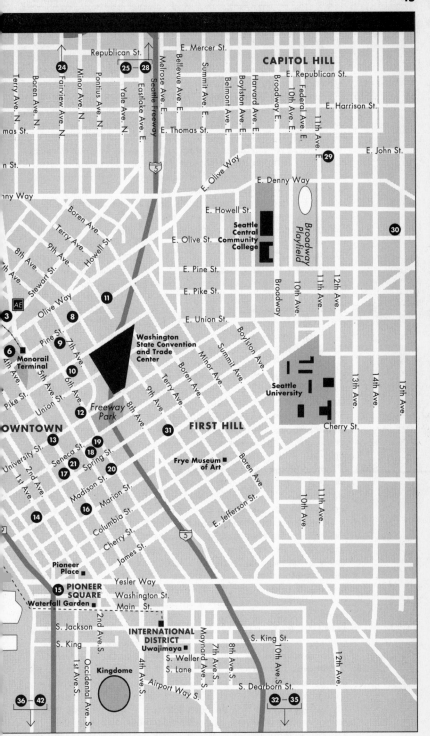

tary Continental breakfast, shoe shines, the morning newspaper, and access to workout facilities. Pets are welcome. ⊠ *1007 1st Ave., 98104,* ☎ *206/624–4844 or 800/426–7033,* ℻ *206/621–9009. 65 rooms, 44 suites. Restaurant, bar, in-room modem lines, minibars, room service, spa, steam room, exercise room, laundry service, meeting rooms, parking (fee). AE, DC, MC, V.*

**\$\$\$\$**   🖀 **Four Seasons Olympic Hotel.** The 1920s Renaissance Revival–style
★ Olympic is the grande dame of Seattle hotels. Marble, wood paneling, potted plants, thick rugs, and plush armchairs adorn the public spaces. Palms and skylights in the Garden Court provide a relaxing background for lunch, afternoon tea, or dancing to a live swing band on the weekends. The Georgian Room, the hotel's premier dining room, exudes Italian Renaissance elegance. The Shuckers oyster bar is more casual. Guest rooms, decorated with period reproductions and floral print fabrics, are less luxurious than the public areas but have a homey feel. All have sofas, comfortable reading chairs, and desks. Amenities include valet parking, chocolates on your pillow, complimentary shoe shines, the morning newspaper, and a bathrobe. ⊠ *411 University St., 98101,* ☎ *206/621–1700 or 800/223–8772,* ℻ *206/682–9633. 450 rooms. 3 restaurants, lounge, room service, indoor pool, health club, children's programs, laundry service, concierge, meeting rooms, parking (fee). AE, DC, MC, V.*

**\$\$\$\$**   🖀 **Hotel Monaco.** Seattle's newest luxury hotel, a Kimpton Group
★ property, opened inside a former office building in 1997. The redesign by Cheryl Rowley, who was also responsible for the equally playful Monaco in San Francisco, has a nautical theme. Rooms are plush but have amenities such as voice mail and fax machines that business travelers will appreciate. All rooms have stereos with compact disc players, irons, hair dryers, coffeemakers. The hotel welcomes pets. ⊠ *1101 4th Ave., 98101,* ☎ *206/621–1770 or 800/845–2240,* ℻ *206/621–7779. 144 rooms, 45 suites. Restaurant, bar, in-room modem lines, no-smoking rooms, room service, exercise room, dry cleaning, laundry service, concierge, business services, meeting rooms, airport shuttle, parking (fee).*

**\$\$\$\$**   🖀 **Hotel Vintage Park.** As a tribute to the state's growing wine industry, each accommodation in this small hotel is named for a Washington winery or vineyard. The theme is extended to complimentary servings of local wines each evening in the lobby, where patrons can relax on richly upholstered sofas and chairs arranged around a marble fireplace. The rooms, which are decorated in color schemes of dark green, plum, deep red, taupe, and gold, are furnished with custom-made cherry-wood pieces and original works by San Francisco artist Chris Kidd. For literary-minded guests, hotel staff will check out and deliver your choice of titles from the nearby Seattle Public Library. The more athletically inclined can have exercise equipment brought to their rooms. ⊠ *1100 5th Ave., 98101,* ☎ *206/624–8000 or 800/624–4433,* ℻ *206/623–0568. 126 rooms. Restaurant, in-room modem lines, minibars, no-smoking floors, refrigerators, room service, spa, laundry service, concierge, meeting rooms, parking (fee). AE, D, DC, MC, V.*

**\$\$\$\$**   🖀 **Sorrento.** The Sorrento, built in 1909 for the Alaska-Yukon Exposition, was designed to look like an Italian villa. The dramatic entrance is along a circular driveway around a fountain ringed by palm trees. Sitting high on First Hill, the hotel has views overlooking downtown and Elliott Bay. The rooms, smaller than those in more modern hotels, are nevertheless quiet and comfortable. The largest are the corner suites, which have some antiques and spacious baths. The Hunt Club (☞ Dining, *above*) serves Pacific Northwest dishes. The dark-paneled Fireside Lounge in the lobby is an inviting spot for coffee, tea, or cocktails. Other amenities include complimentary limousine service within the downtown area and privileges at a nearby athletic club. ⊠ *900 Madison St., 98104,* ☎ *206/622–6400 or 800/426–1265,* 𝔽𝔸𝕏 *206/ 343–6155. 76 rooms, 42 suites. Restaurant, bar, in-room modem lines, minibars, room service, laundry service, concierge, meeting rooms, parking (fee). AE, DC, MC.*

**$$$$** 🖫 **Warwick Hotel.** Despite its size, the Warwick has an intimate feel. Service is friendly and leisurely (but not slow), and the rooms are understated without being bland. Most have small balconies with views of downtown. There is live entertainment in the Liaison restaurant and lounge, and 24-hour courtesy transportation within downtown. ⊠ *401 Lenora St., 98121,* ☎ *206/443–4300 or 800/426–9280,* 𝔽𝔸𝕏 *206/448– 1662. 225 rooms, 4 suites. Restaurant, bar, in-room modem lines, no-smoking rooms, room service, indoor pool, hot tub, sauna, exercise room, concierge, parking (fee). AE, D, DC, MC, V.*

**$$$$** 🖫 **Westin Hotel.** The flagship of the Westin chain often hosts visiting dignitaries, including U.S. presidents. Just north and east of Pike Place Market, the hotel is easily recognizable by its twin cylindrical towers. With this design, all rooms have terrific views of Puget Sound, Lake Union, the Space Needle, or the city. Airy rooms are furnished in a plain but high-quality style. A number have been turned into guest office rooms equipped with fax machines, speakerphones, and modem hookups. ⊠ *1900 5th Ave., 98101,* ☎ *206/728–1000 or 800/228–3000,* 𝔽𝔸𝕏 *206/ 728–2259. 822 rooms, 43 suites. 3 restaurants, 2 bars, in-room safes, minibars, no-smoking floors, room service, indoor pool, beauty salon, massage, exercise room, children's programs, laundry service, concierge, business services, convention center, car rental, parking (fee). AE, D, DC, MC, V.*

**$$$–$$$$** 🖫 **Edgewater.** The spacious accommodations on the waterfront side of the only hotel on Elliott Bay have views of ferries, barges, and the Olympic Mountains. Rooms are decorated in rustic Northwest plaids and light-color unfinished wood furniture. From the lobby's comfortable sofas and chairs, you can sometimes see sea lions frolicking in the bay. A courtesy van shuttles patrons to the downtown area on a first-come, first-served basis. ⊠ Pier 67, 2411 Alaskan Way, 98121, ☎ 206/ 728–7000 or 800/624–0670, 𝔽𝔸𝕏 206/441–4119. 237 rooms. Restaurant, bar, in-room modem lines, minibars, no-smoking rooms, room service, exercise room, bicycles, laundry service, concierge, meeting rooms, parking (fee). AE, DC, MC, V.

**$$$–$$$$** 🖫 **Inn at the Market.** This sophisticated yet unpretentious property just ★ up the street from Pike Place Market is perfect for travelers who prefer originality, personality, and coziness. The good-size rooms are decorated with comfortable modern furniture and small touches such as fresh flowers and ceramic sculptures. Ask for a room with views of the market and Elliott Bay. Coffee and the morning newspaper are complimentary each morning. An added plus is the fifth-floor 2,000-square-ft deck, furnished with Adirondack chairs and overlooking the water and market. Guests have access to a health club and spa. The restaurants here include Campagne (☞ Dining, *above*), its less formal yet equally romantic café spin-off, and Bacco, which serves tasty variations on breakfast classics. ⊠ *86 Pine St., 98109,* ☎ *206/443–3600 or 800/446–4484,* 𝔽𝔸𝕏 *206/448–0631. 55 rooms, 10 suites. 3 restaurants, in-room modem lines, no-smoking rooms, refrigerators, room service, laundry service, concierge, meeting room, parking (fee). AE, D, DC, MC, V.*

**$$$–$$$$** 🖫 **Paramount Hotel.** The château-style Paramount opened in 1996 as a companion to the high-tech entertainment sites one block away, including Planet Hollywood, Gameworks, NikeTown, and a 16-screen Cineplex Odeon multiplex. Neither the Paramount nor these facilities has a particularly Seattle feel, but the hotel's lobby is cozy, with a fireplace, bookshelves, and period reproductions lending it the feel of a country gentleman's smoking parlor. Guest rooms, quiet but small, are decorated in hunter green and beige with gray accents. All have work areas, lounge chairs, large bathrooms, and state-of-the-art movie and game systems. ⊠ *724 Pine St., 98101,* ☎ *206/292–9500 or 800/426–0670,* ℻ *206/292–8610. 146 rooms, 2 suites. Restaurant, in-room modem lines, no-smoking rooms, room service, exercise room, laundry service, concierge, meeting rooms, parking (fee). AE, D, DC, MC, V.*

**$$$–$$$$** 🏨 **Seattle Sheraton Hotel and Towers.** Business travelers are the primary patrons of this large hotel near the Washington State Convention & Trade Center. Rooms on the top five floors, larger and more elegant than those on lower floors, include concierge service and complimentary Continental breakfast. Dining options within the complex include Fullers (☞ Dining, *above*), one of Seattle's best restaurants. The Pike Street Cafe serves all-American cuisine in a casual atmosphere. The lobby features an art-glass collection by well-known Northwest artist Dale Chihuly. ⊠ *1400 6th Ave., 98101,* ☎ *206/621–9000 or 800/325–3535,* ℻ *206/621–8441. 800 rooms, 40 suites. 4 restaurants, 2 bars, in-room modems, minibars, room service, indoor pool, health club, laundry service, concierge, meeting rooms, parking (fee). AE, D, DC, MC, V.*

**$$$** 🏨 **Crowne Plaza.** This favorite of business travelers is directly off I–5, midway between First Hill and the Financial District. The lobby is small and plainly appointed in teal and cream with brass accents and houseplants. Rooms are quiet and spacious, with views of the Kingdome and Harbor Island to the south and Elliott Bay and the Space Needle to the north; all have lounge chairs and work areas. The relaxed and friendly staff is very attentive. ⊠ *1113 6th Ave., 98101,* ☎ *206/464–1980 or 800/521–2762,* ℻ *206/340–1617. 415 rooms, 28 suites. Restaurant, bar, in-room modem lines, no-smoking rooms, room service, sauna, health club, laundry service, concierge, business services, meeting rooms, parking (fee). AE, D, DC, MC, V.*

**$$$** 🏨 **Madison.** Rooms at this high-rise between downtown and I–5 are decorated in deep green, burgundy, and brown, with metal accents and dark wood furniture. Good views of downtown, Elliott Bay, and the Cascade Range can be had from above the 10th floor—above the 20th they're excellent. Guests on club-level floors (25, 26, and 27) receive complimentary Continental breakfast and have their own concierge. Amenities on other floors include complimentary coffee, the morning newspaper, and shoe shines. The health club has a 40-ft rooftop pool and a hot tub. ⊠ *515 Madison St., 98104,* ☎ *206/583–0300 or 800/278–4159,* ℻ *206/622–8635. 466 rooms, 88 suites. 2 restaurants, bar, in-room modem lines, minibars, room service, laundry service, concierge, meeting rooms, parking (fee). AE, D, DC, MC, V.*

**$$$** 🏨 **Seattle Hilton.** This hotel west of I–5 hosts many conventions and meetings. Tastefully nondescript rooms have soothing color schemes. The Top of the Hilton serves well-prepared salmon dishes and other local specialties and has excellent views of the city. An underground passage connects the Hilton with the Rainier Square shopping concourse, the 5th Avenue Theater, and the Washington State Convention Center. ⊠ *1301 6th Ave., 98101,* ☎ *206/624–0500, 800/542–7700, or 800/426–0535,* ℻ *206/682–9029. 237 rooms, 3 suites. 2 restaurants, piano bar, in-room modem lines, no-smoking floors, room service, exercise room, laundry service, concierge, meeting rooms, parking (fee). AE, D, DC, MC, V.*

**$$$**    ⊞ **WestCoast Roosevelt Hotel.** An older hotel near the convention center and the shopping district, the Roosevelt has an elegant lobby with a grand piano, a fireplace, a Chinese lacquered screen, and walls of windows—a great place to relax and watch the foot traffic outside. Smallish rooms are furnished with period reproduction furniture upholstered in mellow pinks and greens. Thanks to the insulated windows you can enjoy city views without hearing street noise. Some bathrooms have their original tile work, though there isn't much counter space. ⊠ *1531 7th Ave.,* ☎ *206/621–1200 or 800/426–0670,* FAX *206/233–0335. 138 rooms, 13 suites. Restaurant, bar, in-room modem lines, no-smoking rooms, room service, exercise room, laundry service, meeting rooms, parking (fee). AE, D, DC, MC, V.*

**$$–$$$**    ⊞ **Mayflower Park Hotel.** The brass fixtures and antiques at this older property near the Westlake Center lend its public and private spaces a muted Asian feel. The service here is unobtrusive and smooth. Rooms are on the small side, but the Mayflower Park is so sturdily constructed that it is much quieter than many modern downtown hotels. Guests have privileges at a nearby health club. ⊠ *405 Olive Way, 98101,* ☎ *206/623–8700 or 800/426–5100,* FAX *206/382–6997. 159 rooms, 13 suites. Restaurant, bar, no-smoking rooms, room service, exercise room, laundry service, business services, meeting rooms, parking (fee). AE, D, DC, MC, V.*

**$$–$$$**    ⊞ **Pioneer Square Hotel.** This landmark building was built in 1914 as a workmen's hotel. A mid-1990s renovation trimmed the property down to 75 generously sized rooms, all with private bathrooms. Furnishings are standard issue; the color scheme is predominantly pink. The rooms on the back of the hotel face an air shaft, creating a dark but peaceful refuge. Guests have access to a nearby health club. Room rates include a Continental breakfast. ⊠ *77 Yesler Way, 98104,* ☎ *206/340–1234,* FAX *206/467–0707. 75 rooms, 3 suites. Coffee shop, pub, in-room modem lines, no-smoking rooms, room service, laundry service, concierge, business services, meeting rooms, parking (fee). AE, D, DC, MC, V.*

**$$**    ⊞ **Pacific Plaza.** This 1929 property that retains a '20s–'30s feel is a good bargain for singles or couples; families may find the nondescript rooms too small to accommodate them. A renovation of the hotel is scheduled for 1998. Room rates include a Continental breakfast. ⊠ *400 Spring St., 98104,* ☎ *206/623–3900 or 800/426–1165,* FAX *206/ 623–2059. 159 rooms. Restaurant, coffee shop, pizzeria, no-smoking rooms, concierge, parking (fee). AE, D, DC, MC, V.*

**$$**    ⊞ **Pensione Nichols.** The bad news first: This eclectic B&B occupies the top two floors above an adult movie theater. But the location one block from Pike Place Market can't be beat, and this stretch of 1st Avenue is hardly run-down; the unobtrusive theater is almost out of place. Suites on the second floor have enclosed balconies, full-size kitchens, private baths, separate bedrooms, and large open living rooms. Most rooms on the third floor have skylights rather than windows and are decorated in light colors with antique and contemporary furnishings. ⊠ *1923 1st Ave., 98101,* ☎ *206/441–7125 or 800/ 440–7125. 10 rooms share 4 baths, 2 suites. AE, D, DC, MC, V.*

**$$**    ⊞ **WestCoast Camlin Hotel.** The lobby of this 1926 apartment-hotel on the edge of downtown but near the convention center has Oriental carpets, large mirrors, and lots of marble. Rooms ending with the number 10 are the best—they have windows on three sides. All rooms have work spaces with a chair and a table, and a cushioned chair to relax in. One drawback here is the noisy heating, air-conditioning, and ventilation system, but these along with the rest of the hotel are slated for upgrading in 1998. ⊠ *1619 9th Ave., 98101,* ☎ *206/682–0100* or 800/426–0670, FAX 206/682–7415. *132 rooms, 4 suites. Restaurant, bar, in-room modem lines, room service, outdoor pool, dry cleaning, concierge, meeting rooms. AE, D, DC, MC, V.*

$    🏨 **Seattle YMCA.** Rooms at this member of the American Youth Hostels Association are clean and plainly furnished with a bed, a phone, a desk, and a lamp—all for about $40. Three bunk units, designed to accommodate four people each, cost about $20. ⊠ *909 4th Ave., 98104,* ☎ *206/382–5000. 3 rooms with private bath, 186 rooms with shared baths. Pool, health club, coin laundry. D, MC, V.*

$    🏨 **Youth Hostel: Seattle International.** You can bed down in dormitory style for about $20 a night at this hostel near Pike Place Market. Guests have kitchen and dining-room access. ⊠ *84 Union St., 98101,* ☎ *206/622–5443. 3 rooms, 191 dormitory beds share baths. Library, coin laundry. AE, MC, V.*

## Capitol Hill

$$–$$$    🏨 **Gaslight Inn.** The Capitol Hill district contains many trendy shopping, restaurant, and night-life establishments, all of which are within
★    walking distance of this B&B. Rooms range from a cozy crow's nest with peeled-log furniture and Navajo-print fabrics to suites with gas fireplaces and antique carved beds. There's also an apartment with a blown-glass chandelier and an expansive view of downtown and Elliott Bay. The large common areas have a masculine feel, with oak wainscoting, animal statuary, high ceilings, and hunter-green carpeting. One owner's past career as a professional painter is evident in the impeccable custom-mixed finishes throughout the inn. Room rates include a Continental breakfast and use of a laundry room; suite rates include the same amenities and off-street parking. ⊠ *1527 15th Ave., 98122,* ☎ *206/325–3654,* FAX *206/328–4803. 9 rooms, 7 suites. No-smoking rooms, pool. AE, MC, V.*

$–$$    🏨 **Hill House.** This Capitol Hill B&B is in an impeccably restored 1903 Victorian. Rooms, painted in rich colors, contain a mix of antique and contemporary furnishings. Two suites have phones and televisions. That the rates here include a filling breakfast and free off-street parking makes this one of the city's best bargains. Book well in advance for summer weekends. ⊠ *1113 E. John St.,* ☎ *206/720–7161 or 800/720–7161,* FAX *206/323–0772. 5 rooms, 3 with private bath. Free parking. AE, D, MC, V.*

## Queen Anne Hill and Fremont

$$$    🏨 **Williams House.** Something is usually in bloom year-round in the beautiful garden that surrounds this Queen Anne Hill mansion. Carved lions with fangs said to bring good luck to those who rub them flank the entryway fireplace. The living and dining rooms have high ceilings, antique furnishings, hardwood floors, and plush carpeting. Guest rooms are small but have good views. The Brass and Satin Room overlooking the rose arbor has a romantic view of the city beyond. The Skyline Room has an unusually good angle on the Space Needle. Room rates include a Continental breakfast. Children are welcome with prior notice. ⊠ *1505 4th Ave. N, 98109,* ☎ *206/285–0810 or 800/880–0810,* FAX *206/285–8526. 5 rooms. Free parking. AE, D, MC, V.*

$$    🏨 **Chelsea Station.** The feel is very Seattle at this B&B across the street from the Woodland Park Zoo. The parlor and breakfast rooms are decorated in sage green with mission-oak furniture, brocade upholstery, lace curtains, and works by local artists. Spacious guest rooms, each with a phone and a writing desk, have antique and contemporary furnishings. The accommodations in front have views of the

# In case you want to see the world.

**At American Express, we're here to make your journey a smooth one. So we have over 1,700 travel service locations in over 120 countries ready to help. What else would you expect from the world's largest travel agency?**

do more

http://www.americanexpress.com/travel

Travel

# In case you want to be welcomed there.

We're here to see that you're always welcomed at establishments everywhere. That's why millions of people carry the American Express® Card – for peace of mind, confidence, and security, around the world or just around the corner.

## do more

**Cards**

# In case you're running low.

We're here to help with more than 118,000 Express Cash locations around the world. In order to enroll, just call American Express before you start your vacation.

do more

**Express Cash**

# And just in case.

We're here with American Express® Travelers Cheques and Cheques *for Two*.® They're the safest way to carry money on your vacation and the surest way to get a refund, practically anywhere, anytime.

Another way we help you...

*do more* ®

**Travelers Cheques**

Cascade Range. One suite has an 1800s pump organ, another a kitchen. Several rooms have adjoining doors, useful for families or larger groups. Room rates include a full breakfast, tailored to your special dietary needs upon request. ⊠ *4915 Linden Ave. N, 98103,* ☎ *206/547–6077 or 800/400–6077,* FAX *206/632–5107. 2 rooms, 6 suites. In-room modem lines. AE, D, DC, MC, V.*

## University District and Lake Union

**$$$** 🏨 **Marriott Residence Inn.** An extended-stay hotel on scenic Lake Union, the Marriott is a perfect choice for families. All rooms are either one- or two-bedroom suites, each with a living room, a fully equipped kitchen, and a breakfast bar. Decorated in greens and blues, the comfortable suites get plenty of natural light. The lobby is within a seven-story atrium with a waterfall and many areas to relax, watch TV, play games, or look up recipes in cookbooks displayed on bookshelves. Room rates include Continental breakfast and complimentary shuttle service within a 2½-mi radius of the hotel. ⊠ *800 Fairview Ave. N, 98109,* ☎ *206/624–6000 or 800/331–3131 (central reservations),* FAX *206/223–8160. 234 suites. Room service, no-smoking rooms, indoor pool, sauna, spa, exercise room, children's programs, parking (fee). AE, D, DC, MC, V.*

**$$** 🏨 **Chambered Nautilus.** A resident teddy bear will keep you company at this Georgian Colonial B&B that was built in 1915 by a professor of Oriental studies at the University of Washington. Rooms all have private baths, some with antique dressers converted to serve as sinks and counters. Most rooms have private porches, and all come with robes and a well-stocked bookshelf. Breakfast might include stuffed French toast with orange syrup, rosemary buttermilk biscuits, or a breakfast pie made with salmon, dill, and Swiss cheese. ⊠ *5005 22nd Ave. NE, 98105,* ☎ *206/522–2536,* FAX *206/528–0898. 6 rooms. AE, MC, V.*

**$$** 🏨 **Edmond Meany Tower Hotel.** This 1931 property within blocks of the University of Washington underwent a $5.5 million restoration in 1997. Though the results were mixed, the hotel remains an important neighborhood landmark. Large-size rooms have fine views of the university campus, Mount Rainier, Green Lake, or Lake Union. Soothing shades of white bathe the rooms—green upholstered headboards and bright-red lounge chairs provide a striking contrast. The hallways are painted a none-too-subtle traffic-sign yellow. Our visit came while construction was still underway—the staff appeared stressed and the service was uneven. ⊠ *4507 Brooklyn Ave. NE, 98105,* ☎ *206/634–2000 or 800/899–0251,* FAX *206/547–6029. 155 rooms. Restaurant, bar, in-room modem lines, no-smoking rooms, room service, exercise room, laundry service, concierge, meeting rooms, free parking. AE, DC, MC, V.*

**$$** 🏨 **University Inn.** The no-nonsense accommodations at this modern hotel have writing desks and are decorated in light wood and floral patterns. Some rooms have decks. Units in back are quieter. The rates include a Continental breakfast. Enjoy the hot tub year-round and the outdoor pool in season. ⊠ *4140 Roosevelt Way NE, 98105,* ☎ *206/632–5055 or 800/733–3855,* FAX *206/547–4937. 102 rooms. Restaurant, in-room modem lines, in-room safes, no-smoking floors, outdoor pool, hot tub, exercise room, coin laundry, dry cleaning, meeting rooms, free parking. AE, D, DC, MC, V.*

**$$** 🏨 **University Plaza Hotel.** Families and business travelers like this full-service motor hotel just across I–5 from the University of Washington campus. The mock-Tudor decor gives the place a dated feel, but the service is cheerful and the rooms are spacious and pleasantly decorated in teak furniture. Ask for a room away from the freeway. ⊠ *400 N.E.*

*45th St., 98105,* ☎ *206/634–0100 or 800/343–7040,* ℻ *206/633–2743. 135 rooms. Restaurant, bar, no-smoking rooms, room service, pool, beauty salon, exercise room, meeting rooms, free parking. AE, D, DC, MC, V.*

## Seattle-Tacoma International Airport

**\$\$\$** ▥ **Doubletree Hotel Seattle Airport.** The Doubletree is a full-service convention hotel. Rooms, large and bright, all have balconies—corner "King Rooms" have wraparound ones with great views. Furnishings include chests of drawers, comfortable chairs, a dining table, and a desk. ⊠ *18740 Pacific Hwy. S, 98188,* ☎ *206/246–8600,* ℻ *206/431–8687. 837 rooms, 13 suites. 3 restaurants, 2 bars, in-room modem lines, room service, outdoor pool, beauty salon, exercise room, laundry service, meeting rooms, airport shuttle, parking (fee). AE, D, DC, MC, V.*

**\$\$\$** ▥ **Marriott Sea-Tac.** The luxurious Marriott has a five-story, 21,000-
★ square-ft tropical atrium that's complete with a waterfall, a dining area, an indoor pool, and a lounge. Rooms are decorated in greens and mauve with dark wood and brass furnishings. ⊠ *3201 S. 176th St., 98188,* ☎ *206/241–2000 or 800/643–5479,* ℻ *206/248–0789. 459 rooms. Restaurant, lobby lounge, in-room modem lines, no-smoking rooms, room service, indoor pool, hot tubs, sauna, health club, video games, laundry service, concierge, meeting rooms, airport shuttle, free parking. AE, D, DC, MC, V.*

**\$\$\$** ▥ **Seattle Airport Hilton.** With its cozy lobby fireplace and paintings of Northwest scenery, this hotel, only a half-hour drive from downtown, has a surprisingly intimate feel. Large rooms are bright and decorated in pastel colors. ⊠ *17620 Pacific Hwy. S, 98188,* ☎ *206/244–4800,* ℻ *206/248–4499. 175 rooms, 3 suites. Restaurant, bar, in-room modem lines, pool, exercise room, coin laundry, laundry service, concierge, business services, meeting rooms, airport shuttle, free parking. AE, D, DC, MC, V.*

**\$\$\$** ▥ **Wyndham Garden Hotel.** This hotel has the most convenient airport access. The elegant lobby has a fireplace, a marble floor, and comfortable furniture. Rooms have large desks, overstuffed chairs, irons and boards, coffeemakers, and hair dryers. ⊠ *18118 Pacific Hwy. S, 98188,* ☎ *206/244–6666,* ℻ *206/244–6679. 180 rooms, 24 suites. Restaurant, lobby lounge, in-room modem lines, no-smoking floors, room service, indoor pool, exercise room, coin laundry, laundry service, meeting rooms, airport shuttle, free parking. AE, D, DC, MC, V.*

**\$\$–\$\$\$** ▥ **Doubletree Inn, Doubletree Suites.** These two hotels across the street from each other are adjacent to the Southcenter shopping mall and convenient to business-park offices. The Inn is a classic Pacific Northwest–style lodge—its rooms are smaller and less lavish than those at the Suites, but they're perfectly fine and cost at least \$25 less. Accommodations at the Suites all have a sofa, a table and chairs, and a wet bar. The vanity area includes a full-size closet with mirrored doors. ⊠ *Doubletree Inn, 205 Strander Blvd., 98188,* ☎ *206/575–8220 or 800/325–8733,* ℻ *206/575–4743. 193 rooms, 5 suites. Bar, coffee shop, dining room, indoor pool, outdoor pool, meeting rooms, airport shuttle, free parking. Doubletree Suites, 16500 Southcenter Pkwy., 98188,* ☎ *206/575–8220 or 800/325–8733,* ℻ *206/575–4743. 221 suites. Restaurant, bar, refrigerators, indoor pool, hot tub, sauna, health club, racquetball, meeting rooms, airport shuttle, free parking. AE, D, DC, MC, V.*

**\$\$** ▥ **WestCoast Gateway Hotel.** Perfect for the traveler catching an early flight, this hotel contains quiet rooms in shades of burgundy and gray. All have coffeemakers; rates include a Continental breakfast. ⊠ *18415*

*Pacific Hwy. S, 98188,* ☎ *206/248–8200 or 800/426–0670,* ꜰᴀx *206/ 244–1198. 145 rooms. Breakfast room, in-room modem lines, no-smoking floors, room service, exercise room, dry cleaning, meeting room, airport shuttle, free parking. AE, D, DC, MC, V.*

**$$** 🏨 **WestCoast Sea-Tac Hotel.** The enthusiastic and helpful staff at this conveniently located property make it attractive to the business or leisure traveler. Guests are welcome to play the baby grand piano in the small but comfortable lobby. All rooms come equipped with Nintendo systems. Rooms in the rear have views of Bow Lake. ⊠ *18220 International Blvd., 98188,* ☎ *206/246–5535 or 800/426–0670,* ꜰᴀx *206/ 246–9733. 146 rooms. Restaurant, bar, room service, outdoor pool, hot tub, sauna, exercise room, business services, meeting rooms, airport shuttle, free parking. AE, D, DC, MC, V.*

## Bellevue/Kirkland

**$$$–$$$$** 🏨 **Doubletree Hotel Bellevue.** The 10-story Doubletree has an airy atrium filled with trees, shrubs, and flowering plants. The property also has a formal dining room, a lounge with two dance floors, and oversize guest rooms decorated in hunter green, burgundy, and beige. Rooms have either king- or queen-size beds. Two-room suites contain wet bars and whirlpool tubs. ⊠ *300 112th Ave. SE, Bellevue 98004,* ☎ *425/ 455–1300 or 800/733–5466,* ꜰᴀx *425/455–0466. 348 rooms, 5 suites. 2 restaurants, bar, in-room modem lines, room service, outdoor pool, exercise room, laundry service, concierge, business services, meeting rooms, free parking. AE, D, DC, MC, V.*

**$$$–$$$$** 🏨 **Hyatt Regency Bellevue.** This deluxe high-rise complex is in the heart of downtown Bellevue, within a few blocks of Bellevue Square and other shopping centers. The exterior looks pretty much like any other sleek high-rise, but the interior has Asian touches such as antique Japanese chests and huge displays of fresh flowers. The rooms are decorated in similarly understated ways, with floor-to-ceiling windows and dark wood and earth tones predominating. The service is impeccable. Deluxe suites include two bedrooms, bar facilities, and meeting rooms with desks and full-length tables; business-plan rooms have modem lines. Guests have access to a health club and pool. The restaurant serves excellent and reasonably priced breakfast, lunch, and dinner; an English-style pub and sports bar serves lunch and dinner. ⊠ *900 Bellevue Way NE, 98004,* ☎ *425/462–2626,* ꜰᴀx *425/646–7567. 353 rooms, 29 suites. Restaurant, sports bar, no-smoking rooms, room service, concierge, meeting rooms, parking (fee). AE, D, DC, MC, V.*

**$$$–$$$$** 🏨 **Woodmark Hotel.** Only steps away from downtown Kirkland, 7 mi
★ east of Seattle, this hotel is the only one on the shores of Lake Washington. Its contemporary-style rooms, which face the water, a courtyard, or the street, are done in exquisite shades of café au lait, taupe, and ecru. The numerous amenities include terry-cloth bathrobes, coffeemakers, irons, hair dryers, complimentary shoe shines, and the morning paper. Guests have privileges at the health club in the hotel complex. A circular staircase descends from the lobby to the Library Lounge, passing a huge bay window with a vast view of Lake Washington. Waters bistro serves Pacific Rim cuisine, dishes such as lemongrass steamed clams or grilled halibut with roasted onion-ginger relish. ⊠ *1200 Carillon Pt., Kirkland 98033,* ☎ *425/822–3700 or 800/822– 3700,* ꜰᴀx *425/822–3699. 79 rooms, 21 suites. Restaurant, bar, in-room modem lines, in-room safes, minibars, refrigerators, room service, exercise room, laundry service, concierge, business services, meeting rooms, parking (fee). AE, DC, MC, V.*

**$$**   🖬 **WestCoast Bellevue Hotel.** This hotel–motor inn has a number of town house suites, suitable for two to four people, with sleeping lofts and wood-burning fireplaces. Rooms are clean; those facing the court-yard are larger and quieter than the others. The hotel is a 20-minute walk from Bellevue Square. A substantial, complimentary appetizer buf-fet, served in the lounge weekdays between 5 and 7 PM, includes seafood and roast beef. ⊠ *625 116th Ave. NE, Bellevue 98004,* ☎ *425/455–9444,* 𝔽𝔸𝕏 *425/455–2154. 160 rooms, 16 suites. Restaurant, bar, room service, outdoor pool, exercise room, laundry service, business services, meeting rooms, free parking. AE, D, DC, MC, V.*

# NIGHTLIFE AND THE ARTS

The Thursday edition of the *Seattle Times* and the Friday *Seattle Post-Intelligencer* include pullout weekend sections that detail upcoming arts and entertainment events. *Seattle Weekly,* which hits most newsstands on Wednesday, has even more detailed coverage and reviews. *The Stranger,* a provocative free weekly, provides broad, though not nec-essarily deep, coverage of the city's cultural activities and is the unof-ficial bible of the music and club scenes.

**Ticketmaster** (☎ 206/628–0888) provides tickets to most arts, enter-tainment, and sports events in the Seattle area; for a rather steep fee, you can charge by phone. The two locations of **Ticket/Ticket** (⊠ Broad-way Market, 401 Broadway E, 2nd floor, ☎ 206/324–2744; ⊠ Pike Pl. Market Information Booth, 1st Ave. and Pike St., ☎ 206/682–7453, ext. 26) sell half-price tickets to many events on the day of the per-formance (or previous day for matinees). Sales are cash and in-person only.

## Nightlife

Neighborhoods with high concentrations of clubs and bars include **Bal-lard, Pioneer Square, Capitol Hill, and Belltown** (also known as the Denny Regrade, just north of Pike Place Market). The opening of **Planet Hol-lywood** (⊠ 6th Ave. and Pike St., ☎ 206/287–0001) and the Steven Spielberg–Sega collaboration **GameWorks** (⊠ 7th Ave. and Pike St., ☎ 206/521–0952) amusement center on the same block with Nike-Town (⊠ 6th Ave. and Pike St., ☎ 206/447–6453) instantly livened things up in the area around the convention center.

### Bars and Lounges

Bars with waterfront views are plentiful—you just have to pick your body of water. **Anthony's Home Port** (⊠ 6135 Seaview Ave. NW, ☎ 206/783–0780) overlooks Shilshole Bay. **Arnie's Northshore** (⊠ 1900 N. Northlake Way, ☎ 206/547–3242) has a great view of downtown from north Lake Union. **Duke's at Chandler's Cove** (⊠ 901 Fairview Ave. N, 206/382–9963) surveys south Lake Union. **Ernie's Bar & Grill** (⊠ Edgewater, 2411 Alaskan Way, Pier 67, ☎ 206/728–7000) has great views of Elliott Bay and the Olympic Mountains. The intimate deck at **Ponti** (⊠ 3014 3rd Ave. N, ☎ 206/284–3000) overlooks the Ship Canal.

If the view's not important, check out three of Seattle's hipper venues, all near Pike Place Market. The **Alibi Room** (⊠ 85 Post Alley, ☎ 206/623–3180) is the unofficial watering hole of the city's film commu-nity. The romantic **Il Bistro** (⊠ 93A Pike St., ☎ 206/682–3049) has low lights, low ceilings, and stiff drinks. Installations by local artists adorn the **Virginia Inn** (⊠ 1937 1st Ave., ☎ 206/728–1937).

In Pioneer Square check out **F. X. McRory's** (✉ 419 Occidental Ave. S, ☎ 206/623–4800), near the Kingdome, which is famous for its huge selection of single-malt whiskeys and fresh oysters. The **Garden Court** (✉ 411 University St., ☎ 206/621–1700) is without a doubt downtown's most elegant lounge. **Pioneer Square Saloon** (✉ 77 Yesler Way, ☎ 206/340–1234) is a great, easygoing, no-frills tavern.

## Brew Pubs

Seattle brew pubs—as drinking establishments attached to actual breweries are called—churn out many high-quality beers made for local distribution. All the pubs listed below serve food and nonalcoholic beverages. If live music is performed, a cover charge may be required; otherwise admission is free. Unless noted, the establishments listed below are open daily from at least noon to 11 PM; call ahead if you're planning a visit at other hours.

**Big Time Brewery** (✉ 4133 University Way NE, ☎ 206/545–4509) caters to the U District crowd and resembles an archetypal college-town pub, with the obligatory moose head on the wall and vintage memorabilia scattered about. Pale ale, amber, and porter are always on tap; the imaginative specialty brews change monthly.

**Hales Ales Brewery and Pub** (✉ 4301 Leary Way NW, ☎ 206/782–0737) serves up nine regular and seasonal taps in a cheerful Fremont setting. The pub's signature brews are its Honey Wheat and Moss Bay Amber ales; order a taster's "flight" to test the rest as well.

**Pike Pub and Brewery** (✉ 1415 1st Ave., ☎ 206/622–6044), a dandy downtown establishment, is operated by the brewers of the award-winning Pike Place Pale Ale. Proudly proclaiming itself Beer Central, the Pike also houses the Seattle Microbrewery Museum and an excellent shop with supplies for home brewing.

**Pyramid Alehouse** (✉ 91 S. Royal Brougham Way, at 1st Ave. S, ☎ 206/682–3377), just south of the Kingdome, brews the varied Pyramid Line—including a top-notch Hefeweizen and an Apricot Ale that tastes much better than it sounds—and Thomas Kemper Lagers. A loud, festive atmosphere makes Pyramid the perfect place to gather after a Mariners baseball game.

**Redhook Brewery** has an in-town location (☞ Trolleyman, *below*) and a larger complex—with a pub, a beer garden, and a gift shop in addition to brewing facilities ($1 tours available daily; call for hours and directions)—in Woodinville (✉ 14300 N.E. 145th St., ☎ 206/483–3232).

**Six Arms** (300 E. Pike St., ☎ 206/223–1698) features the same comfortably eccentric decor that has become the trademark of the chain of pubs operated by the McMenamin family of Portland, Oregon. The beer is equally memorable, especially the challenging Terminator Stout. The Six Arms displays considerably more charm than her Seattle cousins, McMenamin's (✉ 200 Roy St., ☎ 206/285–4722) and Dad Watson's (✉ 3601 Fremont Ave., ☎ 206/632–6505), though the beer at all three tastes the same.

**The Trolleyman** (✉ 3400 Phinney Ave. N, ☎ 206/548–8000), found near the north end of the Fremont Bridge, is the birthplace of local favorites Ballard Bitter and Redhook Ale. The pub mixes Northwest style (whitewashed walls and a no-smoking policy) with a relaxed atmosphere that includes a fireplace and ample armchairs. The original Redhook Brewery is right next door—take a 45-minute tour before you pop in for a pint. The pub opens at 8:30 AM except Sunday, when it opens at noon (and closes at 7). Call for tour times.

## Coffeehouses

Unlike the city's brew pubs, Seattle's coffeehouses are defined as much by the people they serve as the beverages they pour. Most cafés serve the same drinks, but some Seattleites will linger for hours over their latte, while others prefer a cup to go from a drive-through espresso stand. Every neighborhood has its own distinctive coffee culture—usually three or four, actually. Below are a few of the options on Capitol Hill and downtown.

### CAPITOL HILL

Local favorite **B&O Espresso** (⊠ 204 Belmont Ave. E, ☎ 206/322–5028) lures Capitol Hill hipsters and solitary types. The on-site bakery turns out gorgeous wedding cakes. A youngish crowd browses through the art and architecture books on the shelves of **Bauhaus** (⊠ 301 E. Pine St., ☎ 206/625-1600). Scribble and brood with the poetry set at **Cafe Paradiso** (⊠ 1005 E. Pike St., ☎ 206/322–6960). Take a trip to Paris when you enter **Septième** (⊠ 214 Broadway E, ☎ 206/860–8858), which, despite its white-linen tablecloths, has a calculatedly seedy feel. In back is an open patio, where during the summer you can listen to rhumba and salsa music and sip by the light of tiki torches. Exceptional, no-nonsense **Vivace Roasteria** (⊠ 901 E. Denny Way, ☎ 206/860–5869) roasts its own coffee and sells to other coffeehouses.

### DOWNTOWN

The rich smell of the roaster as you step through the door of tiny **Caffé Vitta** (⊠ 2621 5th Ave., ☎ 206/441–4351) is intoxicating; the café also supplies the bean to a number of Seattle restaurants. **Lux** (⊠ 2226 1st Ave., ☎ 206/443–0962) has a thrift-store opulence that's right at home among the fashionable boutiques of 1st Avenue and the Belltown arts scene. The **Sit & Spin** (⊠ 2219 4th Ave., ☎ 206/441–9484) café has a full-service laundromat on one side. Sit & Spin's rival for the award for the coffeehouse most likely to improve your time management is **Speakeasy** (⊠ 2304 2nd Ave., ☎ 206/728–9770) where you can download your e-mail along with your caffeine. Both cafés also double—or is it triple?—as performance spaces in the evening. **Zio Ricco** (⊠ 1415 4th Ave., ☎ 206/467–8616) is downtown's most elegant coffee bar, with a well-stocked newsstand and inviting leather couches.

## Comedy Clubs

**Comedy Underground** (⊠ 222 S. Main St., ☎ 206/628–0303), a Pioneer Square club that's literally underground, beneath Swannie's sports bar and restaurant, presents stand-up comedy nightly. Monday and Tuesday are open-mike nights.

**Giggles** (⊠ 5220 Roosevelt Way NE, ☎ 206/526–5653) in the University District books local and nationally known comedians from Thursday to Sunday, with late shows on Friday and Saturday.

## Music

For $8 you can purchase the Pioneer Square joint cover charge, which will admit you to up to 10 area clubs; contact the New Orleans Restaurant (☞ Jazz, *below*) for details.

### BLUES AND R&B

**Ballard Firehouse** (⊠ 5429 Russell St. NW, ☎ 206/784–3516), Ballard's music mecca, books local and national blues acts.

**Larry's** (⊠ 209 1st Ave. S, ☎ 206/624–7665) presents live blues and rhythm and blues nightly in an unpretentious, friendly, and usually jampacked tavern-restaurant in Pioneer Square.

**Old Timer's Cafe** (✉ 620 1st Ave., ☎ 206/623–9800), a popular Pioneer Square restaurant and bar, has live music—mostly rhythm and blues—nightly.

**Scarlet Tree** (✉ 6521 Roosevelt Way NE, ☎ 206/523–7153), a neighborhood institution just north of the University District, serves up great burgers and live rhythm and blues most nights.

DANCE CLUBS

The local chapter of the **U.S. Amateur Ballroom Dancing Association** (☎ 206/822–6686) holds regular classes and dances throughout the year at the Avalon Ballroom (✉ 1017 Stewart St.). The **Washington Dance Club** (✉ 1017 Stewart St., ☎ 206/628–8939) sponsors nightly workshops and dances in various styles.

**Downunder** (✉ 2407 1st Ave., ☎ 206/728–4053) is an old-school disco with a packed floor. Top-40 music is the lure at **Iguana Cantina** (✉ 2815 Alaskan Way, at Broad St., ☎ 206/728–7071). The moody **Romper Room** (✉ 106 1st Ave. N, ☎ 206/284–5003) specializes in '70s soul. **Re-Bar** (✉ 1114 Howell St., ☎ 206/233–9873) presents an eclectic mix of music nightly, including acid jazz, rock, and soul. The **Vogue** (✉ 2018 1st Ave., ☎ 206/443–0673) hosts reggae, industrial, and gothic dance nights. Several rock clubs (☞ *below*) have dance floors.

FOLK

**Backstage** (✉ 2208 N.W. Market St., ☎ 206/781–2805) is a basement venue in Ballard that hosts national and local acts, with the emphasis on world music, offbeat rock, and new folk.

**Kells** (✉ 1916 Post Alley, ☎ 206/728–1916), a snug Irish-style pub near Pike Place Market, books Celtic-music artists from Wednesday to Saturday.

**Murphy's Pub** (✉ 2110 45th St. NE, ☎ 206/634–2110), a cozy neighborhood bar, has Irish and other folk music on Friday and Saturday.

JAZZ

**Dimitriou's Jazz Alley** (✉ 2037 6th Ave., ☎ 206/441–9729), a downtown club, books nationally known, consistently high-quality performers every night but Sunday. Excellent dinners are served before the first show.

**Latona Pub** (✉ 6423 Latona Ave. NE, ☎ 206/525–2238) is a funky, friendly neighborhood bar at the south end of Green Lake that presents local folk, blues, or jazz musicians nightly.

**New Orleans Restaurant** (✉ 114 1st Ave. S, ☎ 206/622–2563), a popular Pioneer Square restaurant, has good food and live jazz nightly—mostly top local performers but occasionally national acts as well.

ROCK

The **Moore Theater** (✉ 1932 2nd Ave., ☎ 206/443–1744) and the **Paramount** (✉ 907 Pine St., ☎ 206/682–1414, or Ticketmaster, ☎ 206/628–0888) are elegant structures from the early 20th century that now host visiting big-name acts.

**Crocodile Café** (✉ 2200 2nd Ave., ☎ 206/448–2114), one of Seattle's most successful rock clubs, books alternative music acts nightly except Monday.

**The Fenix** (✉ 315 2nd Ave. S, ☎ 206/467–1111) is a crowded Pioneer Square venue with an ever-changing roster of local and national acts.

**Off-Ramp** (✉ 109 Eastlake Ave. E, ☎ 206/628–0232) presents a rock band nightly, often the loud and alternative kind.

**O.K. Hotel** (✉ 212 Alaskan Way S, ☎ 206/621–7903) hosts rock, folk, and jazz nightly in a small venue near Pioneer Square.

**Showbox** (✉ 1426 1st Ave., ☎ 206/628–3151) presents locally and nationally acclaimed artists near Pike Place Market.

## The Arts

On any given night in Seattle, you can attend first-rate symphony or ballet performances, or catch the world premiere of a play or a Hollywood blockbuster. Galleries and museums of every mission and description flourish here; scan the arts listings and see what catches your eye. With Seattle's often misty skies, it stands to reason that a city that spends this much time indoors has figured out how to make the best of it.

### THE ARTS FOR FREE

Seattle's summer concerts, the **Out to Lunch Series** (☎ 206/623–0340), happen every weekday at noon from mid-June to early September in various parks, plazas, and atriums downtown. Concerts showcase local and national musicians and dancers. Call ahead for schedules and locations.

**First Thursday Gallery Walk** (☎ 206/587–0260), an open house hosted by Seattle's art galleries, visits new local exhibits the first Thursday of every month, starting at 5.

### Dance

**Meany Hall for the Performing Arts** (✉ University of Washington campus, ☎ 206/543–4880) hosts important national and international companies, from September to May, with an emphasis on modern and jazz dance.

**On the Boards** (✉ Washington Performance Hall, 153 14th Ave., ☎ 206/325–7901) presents and produces contemporary performances including not only dance but theater, music, and multimedia events by local, national, and international artists. Although the main subscription series runs from October to May, events are scheduled nearly every weekend year-round. In fall 1998, OTB will take up residence in a larger space on lower Queen Anne Hill (✉ 100 W. Roy St.) near the Seattle Center.

**Pacific Northwest Ballet** (✉ Opera House at Seattle Center, Mercer St. at 3rd Ave., ☎ 206/441–2424) is a resident company and school that presents 60 to 70 performances annually. Attending its Christmastime production of *The Nutcracker,* with choreography by Kent Stowell and sets by Maurice Sendak, is a Seattle tradition.

### Film

The strongest evidence of Seattle's passion for the flickers is the wildly popular **Seattle International Film Festival** (☎ 206/324–9996), held each May. For show times and theater locations of current releases, call the **Seattle Times InfoLine** (☎ 206/464–2000, ext. 3456).

**Egyptian Theater** (✉ 801 E. Pine St., at Broadway, ☎ 206/323–4978), an art deco movie palace that was formerly a Masonic temple, screens first-run films and is the prime venue of Seattle's film festival.

**Grand Illusion Cinema** (✉ 1403 N.E. 50th St., at University Way, ☎ 206/523–3935) in the U District was a tiny screening room for exhibitors in the '30s. A venue for independent and art films, it has a terrific espresso bar.

**Harvard Exit** (✉ 807 E. Roy St., ☎ 206/323–8986), a first-run and art-film house, has Seattle's most inviting theater lobby—complete with couches and a piano.

**U.A. 150 Cinemas** (✉ 2131 6th Ave., ☎ 206/443–9591) screens second-run and classic films for the bargain price of $2.

**Varsity Theater** (✉ 4329 University Way NE, ☎ 206/632–3131), in the U District, usually dedicates two of its three screens to classic films.

## Music

ORCHESTRAS

**Northwest Chamber Orchestra** (✉ 1305 4th Ave., ☎ 206/343–0445) presents a full spectrum of music, from baroque to modern, at the University of Washington's Kane Hall. The subscription series, generally from September to May, includes a baroque-music festival every fall.

**Seattle Symphony** (✉ Opera House at Seattle Center and other locations, ☎ 206/215–4747) performs under the direction of Gerard Schwartz from September to June. The symphony is scheduled to move into its new home, Benaroya Hall (✉ 2nd Ave. and University St.) in September 1998.

## Opera

**Seattle Opera** (✉ Opera House at Seattle Center, Mercer St. at 3rd Ave., ☎ 206/389–7676), considered among the top operas in the United States, presents five productions during its season, which runs from August to May.

## Performance Venues

**Broadway Performance Hall** (✉ Seattle Central Community College, 1625 Broadway, ☎ 206/323–2623), small but acoustically outstanding, often hosts dance and music concerts.

**Cornish College of the Arts** (✉ 710 E. Roy St., ☎ 206/323–1400) serves as headquarters for distinguished jazz, dance, and other groups.

**Fifth Avenue Theater** (✉ 1308 5th Ave., ☎ 206/625–1900) is the home of the Fifth Avenue Musical Theater Company (☞ Theater Companies, *below*). When the company is on hiatus, this chinoiserie-style historic landmark, carefully restored to its original 1926 condition, hosts traveling musical and theatrical performances.

**Moore Theater** (✉ 1932 2nd Ave., ☎ 206/443–1744), a 1908 music hall, now presents dance concerts and rock shows.

**Paramount Theatre** (✉ 907 Pine St., ☎ 206/682–1414), a 3,000-seat building from 1929 that has seen duty as a music hall and a movie palace, hosts Best of Broadway touring shows and national pop-music acts.

**Seattle Center** (✉ 305 Harrison St., ☎ 206/684–8582) contains several halls that present theater, opera, dance, music, and performance art.

## Theater Companies

**Annex Theatre** (✉ 1916 4th Ave., ☎ 206/728–0933), run by a collective of artists, presents avant-garde works year-round.

**Bathhouse Theater** (✉ 7312 W. Greenlake Dr. N, ☎ 206/524–9108) produces six productions per year, often innovative updates of classics.

**A Contemporary Theater** (⊠ Eagle Auditorium, 700 Union St., ☎ 206/292–7676) specializes in regional premieres of new works by established playwrights. Every December the theater revives its popular production of *A Christmas Carol.*

**Crêpe de Paris** (⊠ 1333 5th Ave., ☎ 206/623–4111), a restaurant in the Rainier Tower building downtown, books sidesplitting cabaret theater and musical revues.

**Empty Space Theater** (⊠ 3509 Fremont Ave., ☎ 206/547–7500) has a reputation for introducing Seattle to new playwrights. Its season generally runs from November to June, with five or six main-stage productions and several smaller shows.

**Fifth Avenue Musical Theater Company** (⊠ Fifth Avenue Theater, 1308 5th Ave., ☎ 206/625–1900) is a resident professional troupe that mounts four lavish musicals between October and May.

**Group Theater** (⊠ Seattle Center, fountain level of Center House, 305 Harrison St., ☎ 206/441–1299) is a multicultural troupe that prides itself on presenting socially provocative works—old and new—from September to June. A constant is the annual Voices of Christmas, a look at the holidays from various ethnic and cultural perspectives.

**Intiman Theater** (⊠ Playhouse at Seattle Center, 2nd Ave. N and Mercer St., ☎ 206/626–0782) presents classics of the world stage in an intimate setting. The season generally runs from May to November.

**New City Theater and Arts Center** (⊠ 1634 11th Ave., ☎ 206/323–6800) hosts experimental performances by local, national, and international artists.

**Seattle Children's Theatre** (⊠ Charlotte Martin Theatre at Seattle Center, 2nd Ave. N and Thomas St., ☎ 206/441–3322), the second-largest resident professional children's theater company in the United States, has commissioned several dozen new plays, adaptations, and musicals. The theater's six-play season runs from September to June.

**Seattle Repertory Theater** (⊠ Bagley Wright Theater at Seattle Center, 155 Mercer St., ☎ 206/443–2222) performs six new or classic plays on its main stage from October to May, along with three smaller shows at an adjoining smaller venue.

**Village Theater** (⊠ 303 Front St. N, Issaquah, ☎ 206/392–2202) produces high-quality family musicals, comedies, and dramas from September to May in Issaquah, a town east of Seattle. The main stage is at 303 Front Street; the theater's original venue, at 120 Front Street, is now known as First Stage.

# OUTDOOR ACTIVITIES AND SPORTS

## Beaches

If you happen to be in town on a sunny day, catch those precious rays at Golden Gardens (⊠ Seaview Ave. NW, ☎ 206/684–4075), a bit north of the Ballard Locks, or at Alki Beach (⊠ Alki Ave. SW; from downtown, take Hwy. 99 west, then head north on Harbor Ave. SW, ☎ 206/684–4075) in West Seattle. Another option is Warren Magnuson Park (☞ University District *in* Exploring Seattle, *above*). Be forewarned that the water stays pretty cold in Seattle year-round.

# Participant Sports

**Seattle Parks and Recreation** (☎ 206/684–4075) has information about participant sports and facilities.

## Bicycling

The Burke-Gilman Trail and the trail that circles Green Lake are popular among recreational bicyclists and children, but at Green Lake joggers and walkers tend to impede fast travel. The city-maintained Burke-Gilman Trail extends 12.1 mi along Seattle's waterfront from Lake Washington nearly to Salmon Bay along an abandoned railroad line; it is a much less congested path. Myrtle Edwards Park, north of Pier 70, has a two-lane path for jogging and bicycling.

Many shops rent mountain bikes and standard touring or racing bikes and equipment. Call **Gregg's Greenlake Cycle** (✉ 7007 Woodlawn Ave. NE, ☎ 206/523–1822) in North Seattle. **Mountain Bike Specialists** (✉ 5625 University Way NE, ☎ 206/527–4310) serves the U District.

## Boating and Sailboarding

On sunny days, a virtual fleet of boats dots the Puget Sound waterways. Because of the region's mild climate, boating is a year-round endeavor. Charters, which are available with or without a skipper and crew, can be rented for a few hours or several days. Sea kayaking is another appealing way to explore the intertidal regions.

**Sailboat Rentals & Yachts** (✉ 301 N. Northlake Way, ☎ 206/632–3302), on the north side of Lake Union near the Fremont area, rents sailboats with or without skippers by the hour or day. **Seacrest Boat House** (✉ 1660 Harbor Ave. SW, ☎ 206/932–1050), in West Seattle, rents aluminum fishing boats by the hour or day. **Wind Works Rentals** (✉ 7001 Seaview Ave. NW, ☎ 206/784–9386), on Shilshole Bay, rents sailboats with or without skippers by the half day, day, or week.

Lake Union and Green Lake are Seattle's prime sailboarding spots. Sailboards can be rented year-round at **Urban Surf** (✉ 2100 N. Northlake Way, ☎ 206/545–9463) on Lake Union.

## Fishing

There are plenty of good spots for fishing on Lake Washington, Green Lake, and Lake Union, and there are several fishing piers along the Elliott Bay waterfront. Companies operating from Shilshole Bay operate charter trips for catching salmon, rock cod, flounder, and sea bass. **Ballard Salmon Charter** (☎ 206/789–6202) is a recommended local firm. Like most companies, **Pier 54 Adventures** (☎ 206/623–6364) includes the cost of a two-day fishing license ($3.50) in its fee.

## Golf

The city-run **Jackson Park** (✉ 1000 N.E. 135th St., 206/301–0472 or 206/363–4747) and **Jefferson Park** (✉ 4101 Beacon Ave. S, ☎ 206/762–4513 or 206/301–0472) golf facilities each have an 18-hole course (greens fee: $18.50, plus $20 for optional cart) and a nine-hole executive course ($8, plus $13 for optional cart).

## Jogging, Skating, and Walking

Green Lake is far and away Seattle's most popular spot for jogging, and the 3-mi circumference of this picturesque lake is custom-made for it. Walking, bicycling, roller-skating, fishing, lounging on the grass, and feeding the plentiful waterfowl are other possibilities. Several outlets clustered along the east side of the lake have skate and cycle rentals.

Other good jogging locales are along the Burke-Gilman Trail (☞ Bicycling, *above*), around the reservoir at Volunteer Park (☞ Capitol Hill Area *in* Exploring Seattle, *above*), and at Myrtle Edwards Park, north of Pier 70 downtown.

### Kayaking

Kayaking—around the inner waterways (Lake Union, Lake Washington, the Ship Canal) and open water (Elliott Bay)—affords some singular views of Seattle. The **Northwest Outdoor Center** (✉ 2100 Westlake Ave. N, ☎ 206/281–9694), on the west side of Lake Union, rents one- or two-person kayaks and equipment by the hour or week and provides both basic and advanced instruction.

### Skiing

There's fine downhill skiing in and around Snoqualmie (☞ Chapter 3). For Snoqualmie ski reports and news about conditions in the more distant White Pass, Crystal Mountain, and Stevens Pass, call 206/634–0200 or 206/634–2754. For recorded messages about road conditions in the passes, call 888/766–4636.

### Tennis

There are public tennis courts in many parks around the Seattle area. Many are located in the U District, and several are near Capitol Hill. For information, contact the athletics office of the **King County Parks and Recreation Department** (☎ 206/684–7093).

## Spectator Sports

**Ticketmaster** (☎ 206/628–8888) sells tickets to many local sporting events.

### Baseball

The **Seattle Mariners** (☎ 206/622–4487) of the American League play at the Kingdome (✉ 201 S. King St.).

### Basketball

The **Seattle SuperSonics** (☎ 206/283–3865) of the National Basketball Association play at Key Arena (✉ 1st Ave. N and Mercer St.) in the Seattle Center.

The women of the American Basketball League's **Seattle Reign** (☎ 206/285–5225) play their games at Seattle Center's Mercer Arena (4th Ave. N. and Mercer St.).

### Boat Racing

The **unlimited hydroplane races** (☎ 206/628–0888) are a highlight of Seattle's Seafair festivities from mid-July to the first Sunday in August. The races are held on Lake Washington near Seward Park. Tickets cost from $10 to $20. Weekly sailing regattas are held in the summer on Lakes Union and Washington. Call the Seattle Yacht Club (☎ 206/325–1000) for schedules.

### Football

**Seattle Seahawks** (☎ 206/827–9777) National Football League games take place in the Kingdome (✉ 201 S. King St.). The **University of Washington Huskies** (☎ 206/543–2200), every bit as popular as the Seahawks, play out their fall slate at Husky Stadium, off Montlake Boulevard Northeast on the UW campus.

### Horse Racing

Take in Thoroughbred racing from April to September at **Emerald Downs** (✉ 2300 Emerald Downs Dr., Auburn, ☎ 206/288–7000), a 166-acre track about 15 mi south of downtown, east of I–5.

**Soccer**

For outdoor soccer, catch the A-League **Seattle Sounders** at Memorial Stadium (✉ Seattle Center, 5th Ave. N and Harrison St., ☎ 800/796–54250).

# SHOPPING

Most Seattle stores are open daily. Mall hours are generally from 9:30 to 9 Monday through Saturday and from 11 to 6 on Sunday. Some specialty shops keep shorter evening and Sunday hours.

## Shopping Districts

**Broadway** in the Capitol Hill neighborhood is lined with clothing stores selling new and vintage threads and high-design housewares shops.

**Fremont Avenue** contains a funky mix of galleries, thrift stores, and boutiques around its intersection with North 35th Street, just above the Fremont Bridge. At **Armadillo & Co.** (✉ 3510 Fremont Pl. N, ☎ 206/633–4241), you'll find jewelry, T-shirts, and other armadillo-theme accessories and gifts. The eclectic **Bitters Co.** (✉ 513 N. 36th St., ☎ 206/632–0886), a general store, has a wine bar. **Dusty Strings** (✉ 3406 Fremont Ave. N, ☎ 206/634–1656) is the place to pick up hammered dulcimers. **Frank & Dunya** (✉ 3418 Fremont Ave. N, ☎ 206/547–6760) carries unique art pieces, from furniture to jewelry. **Guess Where** (✉ 615 N. 35th St., ☎ 206/547–3793) stocks vintage men's and women's clothing and antiques.

The **International District,** bordered roughly by South Main and South Lane streets and 4th and 8th avenues, contains many Asian herb shops and groceries. **Uwajimaya** (✉ 519 6th Ave. S, ☎ 206/624–6248), one of the largest Japanese stores on the West Coast, sells Asian foods and affordable china, gifts, fabrics, and housewares. Okazuya, the snack bar in Uwajimaya, prepares noodle dishes, sushi, tempura, and other Asian dishes to take out or to eat in.

**University Way Northeast,** in the University District between Northeast 41st and Northeast 50th streets, has a few upscale shops, many bookstores, and businesses that carry such student-oriented imports as ethnic jewelry and South American sweaters.

## Shopping Centers and Malls

**Bellevue Square** (✉ N.E. 8th St. and Bellevue Way, ☎ 425/454–8096), an upscale shopping center about 8 mi east of Seattle, holds more than 200 shops and includes a children's play area, the Bellevue Art Museum, and covered parking.

**Northgate Mall** (✉ I–5 and Northgate Way, ☎ 206/362–4777), 10 mi north of downtown, houses 118 stores, including Nordstrom, The Bon Marché, Lamonts, and JCPenney.

**Southcenter Mall** (✉ I–5 and I–405 in Tukwila, ☎ 206/246–7400) contains 140 shops and department stores.

**Westlake Center** (✉ 1601 5th Ave., ☎ 206/467–1600), in downtown Seattle, has 80 upscale shops and covered walkways to Seattle's two major department stores, Nordstrom and The Bon Marché.

# Specialty Shops

## Antiques
**Antique Importers** (⊠ 640 Alaskan Way, ☎ 206/628–8905), a large warehouselike structure, carries mostly English oak and Victorian pine antiques.

## Art Dealers
**Foster/White Gallery** (⊠ 311 Occidental Ave. S, ☎ 206/622–2833) represents many Northwest painters and sculptors, as well as glass artists of the Pilchuck School outside Seattle.

**Stonington Gallery** (⊠ 2030 1st Ave., ☎ 206/443–1108) specializes in contemporary Native American and other Northwest works.

## Art Glass
**The Glass House** (⊠ 311 Occidental Ave. S, ☎ 206/682–9939) has one of the largest displays of glass artwork in the city.

## Books and Maps
**Bailey/Coy Books** (⊠ 414 Broadway, ☎ 206/323–8842), on Capitol Hill, stocks contemporary and classic fiction and nonfiction, and has a magazine section.

**Elliott Bay Book Company** (⊠ 101 S. Main St., ☎ 206/624–6600), a mammoth general independent bookstore in Pioneer Square, hosts lectures and readings by local and international authors, and hosts a children's story hour at 11 AM on the first Saturday of the month.

**M. Coy Books** (⊠ 117 Pine St., ☎ 206/623–5354), in the heart of downtown, carries a large selection of contemporary literature and has a small espresso bar.

**Metsker Maps** (⊠ 702 1st Ave., ☎ 206/623–8747), on the edge of Pioneer Square, stocks many regional maps.

**University of Washington Bookstore** (⊠ 4326 University Way NE, ☎ 206/634–3403), which carries textbooks and general-interest titles, is one of Seattle's best bookshops.

**Wide World Books and Maps** (⊠ 1911 N. 45th St., ☎ 206/634–3453), north of downtown in the Wallingford neighborhood, carries travel books and maps.

## Chocolates
**Cafe Dilettante** (⊠ 416 Broadway E, ☎ 206/329–6463) is well known for its mouthwatering dark chocolates, whose recipe comes from the imperial court of Russia.

## Clothing
**Alhambra** (⊠ 101 Pine St., ☎ 206/621–9571) specializes in imported women's apparel, jewelry, and accessories.

**Baby and Co.** (⊠ 1936 1st Ave., ☎ 206/448–4077) sells stylish, contemporary fashions and accessories for women.

**Butch Blum** (⊠ 1408 5th Ave., ☎ 206/622–5760) carries contemporary menswear.

**C. C. Filson** (⊠ 1246 1st Ave. S, ☎ 206/622–3147) is a nationally renowned outdoor outfitter.

**Ebbets Field Flannels** (⊠ 406 Occidental Ave. S, ☎ 206/623–0724) specializes in replicas of vintage athletic apparel.

**Littler** (⊠ Rainier Sq., ☎ 206/223–1331) stocks classic fashions for women.

**Local Brilliance** (⊠ 1535 1st Ave., ☎ 206/343–5864) is a showcase for fashions from local designers.

## Crafts
**Hands of the World** (⊠ 1501 Pike Pl., ☎ 206/622–1696) carries textiles, jewelry, and art from around the world.

**Ragazzi's Flying Shuttle** (⊠ 607 1st Ave., ☎ 206/343–9762) displays handcrafted jewelry, whimsical folk art, hand-knit items, and handwoven garments.

## Gifts
**Ruby Montana's Pinto Pony** (⊠ 603 2nd Ave., ☎ 206/721–7669) is kitsch heaven. You'll find furniture, housewares, T-shirts, books, and other postmodern accessories here.

## Jewelry
**Fireworks Gallery** (⊠ 210 1st Ave. S, ☎ 206/682–8707; ⊠ 400 Pine St., ☎ 206/682–6462) sells handmade gifts, along with whimsical earrings and pins.

## Newspapers and Magazines
**Read All About It** (⊠ 93 Pike Pl., ☎ 206/624–1040) serves downtown.

**Steve's Broadway News** (⊠ 204 Broadway E, ☎ 206/324–7323) covers Capitol Hill.

**Steve's Fremont News** (⊠ 3416 Fremont Ave. N, ☎ 206/633–0731) is just north of the bridge in Fremont Center.

## Outdoor Wear and Equipment
**Recreational Equipment, Inc.** (⊠ 222 Yale Ave. N, ☎ 206/223–1944)—which everybody calls REI—has Seattle's most comprehensive selection of gear for the great outdoors at its state-of-the-art downtown facility. The nearly 80,000-square-ft store contains a mountain-bike test trail, a simulated rain booth for testing outerwear, and the REI Pinnacle, an enormous freestanding indoor climbing structure. It's unbelievable, but there's room left over for a wildlife art gallery, a café, and a 250-seat meeting room for how-to clinics.

## Toys
**Archie McPhee** (⊠ 3510 Stone Way N, ☎ 206/545–8344), Seattle's self-proclaimed "outfitters of popular culture," specializes in bizarre toys and novelties.

**Magic Mouse Toys** (⊠ 603 1st Ave., ☎ 206/682–8097) has two floors of toys, from small windups to giant stuffed animals.

## Wine
**Delaurenti Wine Shop** (⊠ 1435 1st Ave., ☎ 206/340–1498) has a knowledgeable staff and a large selection of Northwest Italian–style wines.

**Pike & Western Wine Merchants** (⊠ Pike Pl. and Virginia St., ☎ 206/441–1307 or 206/441–1308) carries Northwest wines from small wineries.

# SEATTLE A TO Z

## Arriving and Departing

### By Bus
**Greyhound Lines** (☎ 800/231–2222) serves Seattle at 8th Avenue and Stewart Street. (☎ 206/628–5508).

## By Car

Seattle is accessible by I–5 and Highway 99 from Vancouver (three hours north) and Portland (three hours south), and by I–90 from Spokane (six hours east).

## By Plane

Among the carriers serving **Seattle–Tacoma International Airport** (☎ 206/431–4444), also known as Sea-Tac, are Air Canada, Alaska, American, America West, British Airways, Continental, Delta, EVA Airways, Hawaiian, Horizon, Japan, Northwest, Southwest, Thai, TWA, United, United Express, and US Airways. *See* Air Travel *in* the Gold Guide for airline phone numbers.

**Between the Airport and the City:** Sea-Tac is about 15 mi south of downtown on I–5; a taxi costs about $30. **Gray Line Airport Express** (☎ 206/626–6088) service to downtown hotels costs $7.50. **Super Shuttle** (☎ 206/622–1424; 800/487–7433 in WA only) has 24-hour door-to-door service from $16 to $30, depending on the location of your pickup. **Metro Transit** (☎ 206/553–3000 or 800/542–7876) city buses (Express Tunnel Bus 194 and regular Buses 174 and 184) pick up passengers outside the baggage claim areas.

## By Train

**Amtrak** (800/872–7245) trains service downtown's King Street Station (⌧ 303 S. Jackson St., ☎ 206/382–4125). The *Mt. Baker International* runs once daily to Vancouver, British Columbia, in about four hours. Three trains make the four-hour trip each day from Seattle to Portland, Oregon. Seattle is also the terminus for Amtrak's daily *Empire Builder* from Chicago and *Coast Starlight* from Los Angeles.

# Getting Around

## By Bus and Streetcar

**Metropolitan Transit** (⌧ 821 2nd Ave., ☎ 206/553–3000) is convenient, inexpensive, and fairly comprehensive. For questions about specific destinations, call the Automated Schedule Line (☎ 206/287–8463). Most buses run until around midnight to 1 AM; some run all night. All buses are wheelchair accessible. The visitor center at the Washington State Convention and Trade Center has maps and schedules.

Between 6 AM and 7 PM, all public transportation is free within the **Metro Bus Ride Free Area,** bounded by Battery Street to the north, 6th Avenue to the east (and over to 9th Avenue near the convention center), South Jackson Street to the south, and the waterfront to the west; you'll pay as you disembark if you ride out of this area. At other times (or in other places), fares range from 85¢ to $1.60, depending on how far you travel and at what time of day. Onboard fare collection boxes have prices posted on them. On weekends and holidays you can purchase a **Day Pass** from bus drivers for $1.70, a bargain if you're doing a lot of touring.

The **Waterfront Streetcar** line of vintage 1920s-era Australian trolleys runs south along Alaska Way from Pier 70, past the Washington State Ferries terminal at Piers 50 and 52, turning inland on Main Street, and passing through Pioneer Square before ending in the International District. It runs at about 20-minute intervals daily from 7 AM to 9 or 10 PM (less often and for fewer hours in the winter). The fare is 85¢. The stations and streetcars are wheelchair accessible.

## By Car

Parking downtown is scarce and expensive. Metered parking is free after 6 PM and on Sunday. Be vigilant during the day—the parking enforcement officers here are notoriously efficient.

If you plan to be downtown longer than two hours (the maximum time allowed on the street), you may find parking in a garage easier. The Bon Marché garage (entrance on 3rd Avenue between Stewart and Pine streets) is centrally located. Many downtown retailers participate in the Easy Streets discount parking program. Tokens are good for $1 off parking in selected locations, and you receive more substantial reductions at the Shopper's Quick Park garages at 2nd Avenue and Union Street and at Rainier Square on Union Street between 4th and 5th avenues.

Right turns are allowed on most red lights after you've come to a full stop.

### By Ferry
**Washington State Ferries** (☎ 206/464–6400; 800/843–3779 in WA only) serves the Puget Sound and San Juan Islands area. For more information about the ferry system, *see* Ferry Travel *in* the Gold Guide.

### By Monorail
The **Seattle Center Monorail** (☎ 206/441–6038 or 206/684–7200), built for the 1962 World's Fair, shuttles between its terminals in Westlake Center and the Seattle Center daily from 9 AM to 11 PM every 15 minutes; the trip takes less than three minutes. The adult fare is $1.

### By Taxi
It's difficult but not impossible to flag a taxi on the street, though it's usually easier to call for a ride. **Orange Cab** (☎ 206/522–8800) is Seattle's friendliest company. **Graytop Cab** (☎ 206/622–4800) is the oldest. Taxis are readily available at most downtown hotels, and the stand at the **Westin Hotel** (✉ 1900 5th Ave.,☎ 206/728–1000) is generally attended all night.

## Contacts and Resources

### B&B Reservation Agencies
For information about bed-and-breakfast arrangements in western Washington, contact the **Bed & Breakfast Association of Seattle** (☎ 206/547–1020).

### Car Rental
Most major rental agencies have offices downtown as well as at Sea-Tac Airport, including **Avis** (✉ 1919 5th Ave., ☎ 800/331–1212), **Dollar** (✉ 7th Ave. and Stewart St., ☎ 800/800–4000), **Hertz** (✉ 722 Pike St., ☎ 800/654–3131) and **National** (✉ 1942 Westlake Ave. N, ☎ 206/448–7368).

### Consulates
**Canada** (✉ Plaza 600 Bldg., 6th Ave. and Stewart St., 4th Floor, ☎ 206/443–1777). **United Kingdom** (✉ First Interstate Center, 999 3rd Ave., Suite 820, ☎ 206/622–9255).

### Emergencies
**Ambulance** (☎ 911). **Fire** (☎ 911). **Police** (☎ 911).

**Doctors, Inc.** (✉ 1215 4th Ave., ☎ 206/622–9933) gives referrals of physicians and dentists in the Seattle area.

### Guided Tours
Three companies offer orientation tours of Seattle. The price of most tours is between $18 and $29, depending on the tour's length and mode of transportation. Custom packages cost more.

**Gray Line of Seattle** (☎ 206/626–5208 or 800/426–7532) operates bus and boat tours, including a six-hour Grand City Tour ($33) that includes many sights, lunch in Pike Place Market, and admission to the Space Needle observation deck.

**Show Me Seattle** (☎ 206/633–2489) surveys the major Seattle sights and also operates a tour that takes in the *Sleepless in Seattle* floating home, "the world's loveliest outdoor Jell-O mold collection," and other offbeat stops.

**Seattle Tours** (☎ 206/860–8687) conducts three-hour tours in customized vans. The tours cover about 50 mi, with plenty of stops for picture-taking.

### BALLOON
**Over the Rainbow** (☎ 206/364–0995) operates balloon tours in the spring and summer only, weather permitting. The cost ranges from $120 to $160.

### BICYCLING
**Terrene Tours** (☎ 206/325–5569) operates day and overnight bicycling and other tours of Seattle, the wine country surrounding the city, and points farther afield. The prices vary, depending on the destination and length of the tour.

### BOAT
**Argosy Cruises** (☎ 206/623–4252) sail around Elliott Bay (one hour, from Pier 55 several times daily, $14.50), the Ballard Locks (2½ hours, from Pier 57, twice daily, $23.75), and other area waterways.

**Pier 54 Adventures** (☎ 206/623–6364) arranges speedboat rides, and sailboat excursions around Elliott Bay, along with guided kayak and bicycle tours. Salmon-fishing and seaplane charters are also available, as well as custom packages. The rates vary.

### CARRIAGE
**Sealth Horse Carriages** (☎ 206/277–8282) narrated tours ($60 per hour) trot away from the waterfront and Westlake Center.

### PLANE
**Galvin Flying Service** (☎ 206/763–9706) departs from Boeing Field in southern Seattle on excursions as near as downtown or as far away as the San Juan Islands and Snoqualmie Falls. Prices begin at $89 ($10 for a second person).

**Seattle Seaplanes** (☎ 800/637–5553) operates a 20-minute scenic flight that takes in views of the Woodland Park Zoo, downtown Seattle, and the Microsoft "campus." Custom tours are also available. Prices begin at $42.50.

**Sound Flight** (☎ 206/255–6500) offers a 30-minute scenic flight for $59, custom sightseeing packages, and flights to secluded fishing spots.

### SAILING
**Let's Go Sailing** (☎ 206/624–3931) permits passengers to take the helm, trim the sails, or simply enjoy the ride aboard the *Obsession*, a 70-ft ocean racer. Three 1½-hour excursions ($20) depart daily from Pier 56. A 2½-hour sunset cruise ($35) is also available. Passengers can bring their own food on board. Private charters can also be arranged.

### WALKING
**Chinatown Discovery Tours** (☎ 206/236–0657) include two culinary excursions—one a light sampler, the other an eight-course banquet. The rates range from $9.95 to $34.95, based on a minimum of four participants.

**Seattle Walking Tours** (☎ 206/885–3173) through the city's historic areas, including the International District and Pioneer Square, cost $10.

**Underground Seattle** (☎ 206/682–4646) tours ($6.50) of the now-buried original storefronts and sidewalks of Pioneer Square are extremely popular, though many locals can't fathom why—it's somewhat like spending an hour and a half exploring your grandmother's extremely large basement. Then again, it does offer an effective primer on early Seattle history, and it may be a good place to take cover if your above-ground tour starts to get soggy.

## Late-Night Pharmacies
**Bartell Drugs** (✉ 600 1st Ave. N, at Mercer St., ☎ 206/284–1353) is a 24-hour pharmacy.

## Travel Agencies
**AAA Travel** (✉ 330 6th Ave. N, ☎ 206/455–9905). **American Express Travel Office** (✉ 600 Stewart St., ☎ 206/441–8622). **Doug Fox Travel** (✉ 1321 4th Ave., ☎ 206/628–6171).

## Visitor Information
**Seattle/King County Convention and Visitors Bureau** (✉ 520 Pike St., Suite 1300, 98101, ☎ 206/461–5800). **Seattle Visitor Center** (✉ 800 Convention Pl., ☎ 206/461–5840). **Washington State Convention & Trade Center** (✉ 800 Convention Pl., ☎ 206/447–5000). **Washington Tourism Development Division** (✉ Box 45213, Olympia, WA 98504, ☎ 360/753–5600).

# 3 Side Trips from Seattle

*Excursions from Seattle are usually into the mountains or out on the water. A trip of less than an hour by car or ferry will take you places that seem worlds away from the hubbub of the city.*

**T**HE WATERS OF PUGET SOUND SURROUND PEACEFUL, rural Whidbey Island, a one-hour ferry ride from Seattle. Port Townsend, across from Whidbey on the Olympic Peninsula, holds cultural and historical attractions in addition to its beautiful setting. Plan on more than a day trip to fully appreciate the remote San Juan Islands. If you head east to Snoqualmie, nestled in the Cascade Range and home to a towering waterfall, you can hike, bike, or take an historic train through forests and meadows. Farther east is alpine Leavenworth, a favorite Seattle getaway.

By Alex Aron

## Pleasures and Pastimes

### Dining

Spicy yet subtle flavorings testify to the strong Asian influence on the cuisine in the region surrounding Seattle. On the Olympic Peninsula, sweet, meaty Dungeness crab is the local specialty. Oysters, mussels, and clams are plentiful as well. Many of the finer coastal restaurants serve flavorful Ellensburg (in eastern Washington) beef and lamb.

| CATEGORY | COST* |
| --- | --- |
| $$$$ | over $35 |
| $$$ | $25–$35 |
| $$ | $15–$25 |
| $ | under $15 |

*per person for a three-course meal, excluding drinks, service, and sales tax (about 7.9%, varies slightly by community)*

### Ferries

The vessels of the Washington State Ferries system range from the Hiyu, which holds 40 cars, to jumbo craft capable of carrying more than 200 cars and 2,000 passengers each. A diversion in and of themselves, the boats, which connect points all around Puget Sound, the San Juan Islands, and beyond, are the *only* way to reach some areas of western Washington. For information about ferry runs to the regions covered in this chapter, *see* Getting Around *in* Essentials, at the end of the Bainbridge Island section; the Whidbey Island, Fidalgo Island, and Port Townsend section; and the San Juan Islands section. For general information about the Washington State Ferries, *see* Ferry Travel *in* the Gold Guide.

### Lodging

Spend the night in one of Puget Sound's waterfront or bed-and-breakfast inns, and you'll quickly understand the attraction the water holds for local residents. Most of the Northwest's smaller accommodations may lack the old-fashioned charm and historical ties of their counterparts in New England or the South, but they're often equipped with hot tubs and in-room fireplaces that take the edge off crisp coastal air. Prices generally run lower than those in Seattle, so you needn't break the bank to overnight here, in the Snoqualmie Valley, or even in popular Leavenworth.

| CATEGORY | COST* |
| --- | --- |
| $$$$ | over $170 |
| $$$ | $110–$170 |
| $$ | $60–$110 |
| $ | under $60 |

*All prices are for a standard double room, excluding taxes (generally 7.9%; slightly higher in some areas).*

### Outdoor Activities and Sports

The combination of flat and hilly terrain surrounding Seattle satisfies hikers and bikers of varying skills. Kayaking is a popular way to get close to otters, seals, whales, and other sea creatures; ample rental facilities are available at each of the destinations covered. Whale-watching tours are among the region's many more passive outdoor options.

# BAINBRIDGE ISLAND

Take the half-hour ride on the **Bainbridge Island ferry** (☞ *below*) for great views of the city skyline and the surrounding hills. The ferry trip itself lures most of the island's visitors—this is the least expensive way to cruise Puget Sound—along with Bainbridge's small-town atmosphere and scenic countryside. From the Bainbridge Island terminal, continue north up a short hill on Olympic Drive to Winslow Way. If you turn west (left), you'll find yourself in **Winslow,** where there are several blocks of antiques shops, clothing boutiques, galleries, bookstores, and restaurants.

Pass the Winslow Way turnoff and head about ¼ mi farther north on Olympic to the **Bainbridge Island Vineyard and Winery** (✉ 682 Hwy. 305, ☎ 206/842–9463), which is open for tastings and tours Wednesday–Sunday noon–5.

You'll need a car to get to the **Bloedel Reserve,** whose grounds, the 150-acre estate of Vancouver, B.C., lumber baron Prentice Bloedel, were designed to recapture the natural, untamed look of the island. Within the park are ponds with ducks and trumpeter swans, Bloedel's grand mansion, and 2 mi of trails. Dazzling displays of rhododendrons and azaleas bloom in spring, and the leaves of Japanese maples and other trees colorfully signal the arrival of autumn. There is no food service and picnicking is not permitted. ✉ *7571 N.E. Dolphin Dr. (from ferry follow signs on Hwy. 305),* ☎ *206/842–7631.* ⌑ *$6.* ☉ *Wed.–Sun. 10–4 (reservations essential).*

## Bainbridge Island Essentials

### Getting Around

The **Bainbridge Island ferry** (☎ 206/464–6400), which takes cars and walk-on passengers, leaves Seattle once an hour during the day from Pier 52 (Coleman dock), south of Pike Place Market, and stops at Winslow. Highway 305 is the main road through the island.

### Visitor Information

The **Bainbridge Island Chamber of Commerce** (✉ 590 Winslow Way, ☎ 206/842–3700), two blocks from the ferry dock, has maps and tourist information.

# WHIDBEY ISLAND, FIDALGO ISLAND, AND PORT TOWNSEND

*Numbers in the margin correspond to points of interest on the Puget Sound map.*

On a nice day there's no better short excursion from Seattle than a ferry trip across Puget Sound to **Whidbey Island.** It's a great way to watch the seagulls, sailboats, and massive container vessels in the sound—not to mention the surrounding scenery, which takes in the Kitsap Peninsula and Olympic Mountains, Mount Rainier, the Cascade Range, and the Seattle skyline. Even when the weather isn't all that terrific,

**Puget Sound** *(Box Refers to Detail Map)*

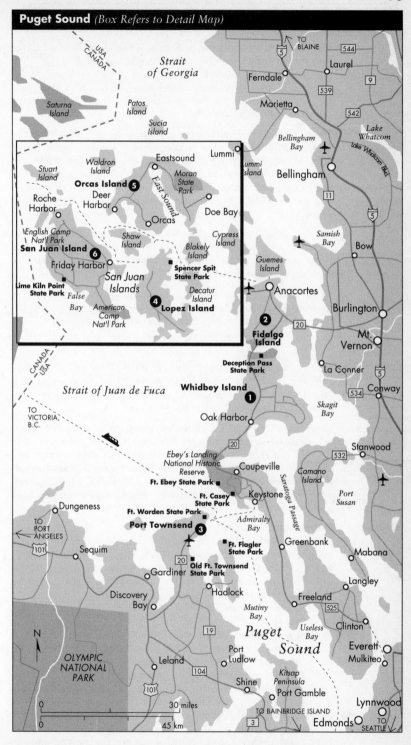

travelers can stay snug inside the ferry, have a snack, and listen to folk musicians.

The island, 30 mi northwest of Seattle, is one of the nearest escapes from the city. In fact, some folks escape to it nightly—they live on Whidbey and commute to work. The island is a blend of bucolic hills, forests, meadows, sandy beaches, and dramatic cliffs. It's a great place for country drives, bicycle touring, viewing sunsets, and exploring the shoreline by boat or kayak.

The best beaches are on the west side, where the sand stretches out to the sea and you have a view of the shipping lanes and the Olympic Mountains. Maxwelton Beach (⊠ Maxwelton Beach Rd.) is popular with the locals. Possession Point (⊠ off Coltas Bay Rd.) includes a park, a beach, and a boat launch. Fort Ebey in Coupeville has a sandy spread, and West Beach is a stormy patch north of the fort with mounds of driftwood.

Whidbey is easily accessible via a Washington State Ferries vessel from Mukilteo (pronounced muck-ill-*tee*-oh) to Clinton on the southern part of the island. Or you can drive across from the mainland on Highway 20 at the northern end of the island.

At 60 mi long and 8 mi wide, Whidbey is the second-longest island in the contiguous United States; only Long Island in New York stretches farther. The tour below begins at the island's southern tip.

## Langley

*From Seattle, take I–5 north 21 mi to Exit 189 (Whidbey Island–Mukilteo Ferry) and follow signs 7 mi to ferry landing. From Clinton (Whidbey Island ferry terminal), take Hwy. 525 north 2 mi to Langley Rd., turn right, and follow road 5 mi.*

Langley sits atop a 50-ft-high bluff overlooking Saratoga Passage on the southeastern shore. It's a great vantage point for viewing wildlife on land and sea. Upscale boutiques selling art, glass, jewelry, and clothing line 1st and 2nd streets in the heart of town. The **South Whidbey Historical Museum** (⊠ 312 2nd St., ☎ 360/579–4696), open weekends from 1 to 4 in a former one-room schoolhouse, displays old Victrolas, farm tools, kitchen utensils, and antique toys.

### Dining and Lodging

$$$ ✕ **Country Kitchen.** Tables for two unobtrusively line the walls of this intimate restaurant. On the other side of the fireplace is the "great table," which seats 10. The prix-fixe, five-course seasonal menu highlights local produce. Dinners may include locally gathered mussels in a black-bean sauce, breast of duck in a loganberry sauce, or rich Columbia River salmon. ⊠ *Inn at Langley, 400 1st St., ☎ 360/221–3033. Reservations essential. MC, V.*

$$ ✕ **Garibyan Brothers Café Langley.** Terra-cotta tile floors, antique oak tables, and the aroma of garlic, basil, and oregano set the mood at this Greek restaurant. The menu includes eggplant moussaka, Dungeness crab cakes, Mediterranean seafood stew, and lamb kabobs. All entrées are served with Greek salads. ⊠ *113 1st St., ☎ 360/221–3090. MC, V. Closed Tues. in winter. No lunch Tues.*

$$ ✕ **Star Bistro.** This slick 1980s-vintage bistro atop the Star Store serves up Caesar salads, shrimp-and-scallop linguine, and gourmet burgers. Popular for lunch, it remains crowded well into the late afternoon. ⊠ *201½ 1st St., ☎ 360/221–2627. Reservations not accepted. AE, MC, V. No dinner Mon.*

$   ✕ **Dog House Backdoor Restaurant.** Friendly and relaxed, this waterfront tavern and family restaurant, a recent addition to the National Register of Historic Places, is filled with collectibles that include a 1923 nickelodeon. Juicy burgers, homemade chili, and vegetarian entrées are made from low-salt recipes. The restaurant has a fine view of the Saratoga Passage. ⊠ 230 1st St., ☎ 360/221–9996. Reservations not accepted. No credit cards.

$$$$   ☷ **Inn at Langley.** Langley's classiest inn, a concrete-and-wood, Frank
★   Lloyd Wright–inspired structure, perches on the side of a bluff that descends to the beach. The Asian-style guest rooms have dramatic views of the Saratoga Passage and the Cascade Range. All have whirlpool tubs, fireplaces, outdoor terraces, and TVs. Meals are served in the inn's acclaimed restaurant, the Country Kitchen (☞ Dining, above). Dinner starts promptly at 7 with a glass of sherry and a tour of the wine cellar. ⊠ 400 1st St., 98260, ☎ 360/221–3033. 24 rooms. Restaurant. MC, V.

$–$$   ☷ **Drake's Landing.** Langley's most affordable lodging has fine views. At the edge of town and across the street from the harbor off 1st Street, the humble but clean rooms here are decorated with quilts. ⊠ 203 Wharf St., 98260, ☎ 360/221–3999. 3 rooms. MC, V.

## Outdoor Activities and Sports

### BICYCLING

In the Bayview area of Whidbey Island, just off Highway 525 near Langley, **The Pedaler** (⊠ 5603½ S. Bayview Rd., ☎ 360/321–5040), a bicycle sales and service shop, rents mountain bikes and hybrids year-round.

### BOATING AND FISHING

Langley's small **boat harbor** (☎ 360/221–6765) provides moorage for 35 boats, plus utilities and a 160-ft fishing pier, all protected by a timber-pile breakwater. You can catch salmon, perch, and cod, from the Langley pier. Supplies are available from the **Langley Marina** (⊠ 202 Wharf St., ☎ 360/221–1771).

## Shopping

**Childers/Proctor Gallery** (⊠ 302 1st St., ☎ 360/221–2978) exhibits and sells paintings, jewelry, pottery, and sculpture. The **Cottage** stocks vintage and imported women's clothing (⊠ 210 1st St., ☎ 360/221–4747). You can meet glass and jewelry artist Gwenn Knight at her shop, the **Glass Knight** (⊠ 214 1st St., ☎ 360/221–6283). The **Museo Piccolo** (⊠ 215 1st St., ☎ 360/221–7737), a gallery and gift shop, carries contemporary art by recognized and emerging artists.

At the **Blackfish Studio** (⊠ 5075 S. Langley Rd., ☎ 360/221–1274), outside Langley, you can see works-in-progress and finished pieces by Kathleen Miller, who produces enamel jewelry and hand-painted clothing and accessories, and Donald Miller, whose photographs depict the land and people of the Northwest.

# Freeland

*7 mi north of Langley on Hwy. 525.*

Unincorporated Freeland is home to two parks. You'll find picnic spots and a sandy beach at **Freeland Park** on Holmes Harbor. Bush Point Lighthouse is the main attraction at **South Whidbey State Park,** which has hiking trails, camping, and swimming.

## Lodging

$$$ – $$$$     ⊡ **Cliff House.** A winding drive through the woods leads to this secluded three-story house overlooking Admiralty inlet. The award-winning architectural design is uncompromisingly modern; one side is nearly all glass and provides sweeping views. Rain and occasionally snow whisk through the open-air atrium in the middle of the house. An adjacent cottage also has sea views. Guests in both accommodations are pampered with fresh flowers, every modern amenity, and miles of driftwood beach. ⊠ *5440 Windmill Rd., 98249,* ☎ *360/221–1566. 2 rooms. No credit cards.*

# Greenbank

*11 mi north of Freeland on Hwy. 525.*

About halfway up Whidbey is the town of Greenbank, home to the 125-acre **Greenbank Farm Winery,** which Island County purchased in late 1997. The vineyard here produces a small portion of the loganberries used for production of the island's unique spirit, Whidbey's Liqueur (available at the gift shop). Picnic tables are scattered throughout the farm. ⊠ *657 Wonn Rd.,* ☎ *360/678–7700.* ▧ *Free.* ☉ *Gift shop 10–5.*

The 53-acre **Meerkerk Rhododendron Gardens** contains 1,500 native and hybrid species of rhododendrons, numerous walking trails, and ponds. The flowers are in full bloom in April and May. ⊠ *Resort Rd.,* ☎ *360/678–1912.* ▧ *$2.* ☉ *Daily 9–4.*

## Lodging

$$$     ⊡ **Guest House Cottages.** The very private log cabins here, surrounded
★     by 25 forested acres, have feather beds, VCRs, whirlpool tubs, country antiques, and fireplaces. Fresh flowers, robes, and a fine Continental breakfast are among the other draws, along with an enormous two-story lodge filled with collectibles that include a working pump organ. ⊠ *835 E. Christianson Rd., 98253,* ☎ *360/678–3115. 6 units. Pool, exercise room. No credit cards.*

# Coupeville

*17 mi north of Greenbank, Hwy. 525 to 20.*

Restored Victorian houses grace many of the streets in quiet Coupeville, which has one of the largest national historic districts in Washington. Stores along the waterfront have maintained their second-story false fronts and old-fashioned character. Captain Thomas Coupe founded the town in 1852; his house, built in 1853, is one of the state's oldest.

The **Island County Historical Museum** has exhibits on the history of the island's fishing, timber, and agricultural industries, and conducts historical tours and walks. ⊠ *908 N.W. Alexander St.,* ☎ *360/678–3310.* ▧ *$2.* ☉ *May–Oct., daily 10–5; Nov.–Apr., Fri.–Mon. 11–4.*

**Ebey's Landing National Historic Reserve** encompasses two state parks and some privately held farmland. The reserve, the first and largest of its kind, holds nearly 100 nationally registered historical structures, most from the 19th century. A 22-acre beach area is the highlight of **Fort Ebey State Park**—the best view over Ebey's prairie can be had from the park's Sunnyside Cemetery. **Fort Casey State Park,** set on a bluff overlooking the Strait of Juan de Fuca, was one of three forts built in 1890 to protect Puget Sound. The park contains a small interpretive center, picnic sites, fishing spots, and a boat launch. ⊠ *Fort Ebey State Park: 2 mi west of Hwy. 20,* ☎ *360/678–4636; Fort Casey State Park: 3 mi west of Hwy. 20,* ☎ *360/678–4519. Follow signs from Hwy. 20 to each park.* ⊞ *Free (day use), $11–$16 for campsites.* ☉ *Daily 8 AM–sunset.*

### Dining and Lodging

**$$–$$$** ✕ **Rosi's.** Deceptively simple-looking Rosi's, set inside the Victorian
★ home of its chef-owners, serves outstanding Italian and Northwest cuisine. Chicken mascarpone, osso buco, scallops pesto, prime rib, and Penn Cove mussels are among the entrées. ⊠ *606 N. Main St.,* ☎ *360/ 678–3989. No lunch weekends.*

**$$** ✕ **Christopher's.** The ambience is warm and casual at this eclectically furnished restaurant whose tables are set with linens, fresh flowers, and candles. Penn Cove oysters broiled on the half shell with garlic, capers, and lemon butter are a few of the appealing appetizers; for the main course, try the pork medallions with blackberry-almond sauce or a daily vegetarian entrée such as curried lentils tossed with roasted vegetables and served on a bed of couscous. The wine list here is extensive. ⊠ *23 Front St.,* ☎ *360/678–5480. AE, D, MC, V. Closed Mon., Tues.*

**$$** 🏨 **Fort Casey Inn.** The inn's two-story Georgian Revival structures, which once served as officers' quarters, rest on a hillside overlooking Ebey's prairie. Each accommodation has a fireplace, two bedrooms, a living room, and a full country kitchen (with breakfast fixings on hand). Owners Gordon and Victoria Hoenig restored the house's tin ceilings and decorated the units with rag rugs, old quilts, hand-painted furniture, and sundry Colonial touches. Children are welcome here. ⊠ *1124 S. Engle Rd., 98239,* ☎ *360/678–8792. 9 units. Bicycles. AE, MC, V.*

## Oak Harbor

*10 mi north of Coupeville on Hwy. 20.*

Oak Harbor gets its name from the Garry oaks that grow in the area. Dutch and Irish immigrants settled the town in the mid-1800s; several windmills are still in existence. Unfortunately, suburban sprawl has overtaken Whidbey Island's largest city in the form of multiple strips of fast-food restaurants and service stations.

★ **Deception Pass State Park** hosts more than 4 million visitors each year. With 19 mi of saltwater shoreline, three freshwater lakes, and more than 38 mi of madrona-forest trails, it's easy to see why. Summertime picnickers blanket the secluded inlet and long but crowded sandy beach. The park is at the northernmost point of Whidbey Island, just over Deception Pass Bridge. If you walk across the bridge, you won't be able to miss the dramatic gorge below, well known for its swift tidal currents. ⊠ *Hwy. 20, 7 mi north of Oak Harbor,* ☎ *360/675–2417.* ⊞ *Park free; campsite fees vary.* ☉ *Apr.–Sept., daily 6:30 AM–sunset; Oct.–Mar., daily 8 AM–sunset.*

## Anacortes

*15 mi north of Oak Harbor on Hwy. 20; 76 mi from Seattle, north on I–5 (to Exit 230) and west on Hwy. 20.*

❷ Deception Pass Bridge links Whidbey to **Fidalgo Island.** From the bridge it's just a short distance to Anacortes, Fidalgo's main town and the terminus for ferries going to the San Juan Islands. Anacortes consists mostly of strip malls and chain stores, but a small historical waterfront section contains some well-preserved redbrick buildings. The frequently changing exhibits at the **Anacortes Museum** (⊠ 1305 8th

St., ☎ 360/293–1915) focus on the cultural heritage of Fidalgo and nearby Guemes Island.

### Lodging

$$$–$$$$   ⊞ **Majestic Hotel.** One of the finest small hotels in the Northwest
★         began life in 1889 as a mercantile building. From the Victorian-style lobby, you can enter the Rose & Crown pub and the banquet rooms or ascend a sweeping staircase to your room or an English-style library. The top-floor gazebo has views of the marina, Mount Baker, and the Cascades. The rooms are decorated with European antiques and down comforters; several contain whirlpool tubs. A complimentary Continental breakfast is served in the dining room. ⊠ *419 Commercial Ave., 98221,* ☎ *360/293–3355,* FAX *360/293–5214. 23 rooms. Restaurant, pub, library. MC, V.*

## Port Townsend

★ ❸   *45 mi from Seattle; I–5 north to Edmonds Ferry to Kingston; from landing drive northwest on Hwy. 307 to Rte. 3N, to Rte. 19. Port Townsend can be accessed from Whidbey Island by ferry at Keystone.*

Many writers, musicians, painters, and other artists live in Port Townsend, the largest city on the northern tip of the Olympic Peninsula. Handsome restored 1870s brick buildings that hold shops and restaurants line its waterfront; the many impressive yachts docked here attest to the area's status as one of greater Seattle's premier sailing spots.

The "Genuine Bull Durham Smoking Tobacco" ad on the **Lewis Building** (⊠ Madison and Water Sts.) is one of many charming relics of Port Townsend's glory days as a maritime center. The **bell tower** on Jefferson Street, at the top of the Tyler Street stairs, is the last of its kind in the country. Built in 1890, it was used to call volunteer firemen to duty; now it houses artifacts from the city museum, including a 19th-century horse-drawn hearse that you can peek at through the windows.

The 1892 City Hall building—Jack London languished briefly in the jail here on his way to the Klondike—contains the **Jefferson County Historical Museum,** four floors of Native American artifacts, historic photos of the Olympic Peninsula, and exhibits on Port Townsend's past. ⊠ *210 Madison St.,* ☎ *360/385–1003.* ⊠ *$2 suggested donation.* ☉ *Mon.–Sat. 11–4, Sun. 1–4.*

The neatly manicured grounds of 443-acre **Fort Worden State Park** include a row of restored Victorian officers' houses, a World War II balloon hangar, and a sandy beach that leads to the **Point Wilson Lighthouse,** built in 1879. The fort, which was built on Point Wilson in 1896 to defend Puget Sound, now hosts art events sponsored by Centrum (☞ Nightlife and the Arts, *below*). The **Marine Science Center** has aquariums and touch tanks where you can reach in and feel slimy sea creatures like crabs and anemones. ⊠ *200 Battery Way,* ☎ *360/385–4730.* ⊠ *Free (park day use); $2 (science center).* ☉ *Park daily dawn–dusk, Marine Science Center Tues.–Sun. noon–6.*

A 15- to 20-minute drive south of town takes you to the tip of Marrowstone Island and **Fort Flagler State Park.** The turn-of-the-century gun placements and bunkers are interesting, but the main attractions are the beaches, campgrounds, and 7 mi of wooded and oceanside hiking trails—the nameless remnants of old army roads that radiated from the perimeter road. The inlets of the island are great for paddling around, and you can rent canoes, kayaks, and pedalboats from the **Nordland General Store** (☎ 360/385–0777), near the park entrance. ⊠ *10341*

*Flagler Rd. (from Port Townsend take Hwy. 20 and Hwy. 19 south to Hwy. 116 east), Nordland,* ☎ *360/385–1259.* ⌲ *Free (day use), $10– $16 (campground).* ⊙ *Daily dawn–dusk.*

**Guided Historical Tours** (✉ 820 Tyler St., ☎ 360/385–1967) conducts several tours of Port Townsend, the most popular of which is a one-hour walking tour of the waterfront and downtown, focusing on the town's architecture, history, and humor.

## Dining and Lodging

**$$$** ✕ **Lonny's.** Chef-owner Lonny Ritter aims to provide a sensual dining experience. The handsome wooden furnishings and the texture of the ocher-color walls at his restaurant are as carefully selected as the professional staff and the extensive wine collection. Entrées on the seasonally changing menu might include a char-grilled Peking duck breast with Italian sausage stuffing or Lonny's signature Dungeness crab dish, prepared with basil butter, heavy cream, and sweet Gorgonzola cheese. The vegetarian entrées here are thoughtfully conceived. ✉ *2330 Washington St.,* ☎ *360/385–0700. MC, V. Closed Tues. No lunch.*

**$$** ✕ **Fountain Café.** The new owners of this funky, art- and knickknack-filled café retained favorite dishes such as Oysters Dorado but added creative grilled sandwiches for lunch and new entrées for dinner. Count on seafood and pasta specialties with imaginative twists—smoked salmon in a light cream sauce with a hint of Scotch, for example. Expect the occasional wait (call ahead to get your name on the list for tables) at this local hot spot. ✉ *920 Washington St.,* ☎ *360/385–1364. Reservations not accepted. MC, V. Closed Tues. in winter.*

**$–$$** ✕ **Salal Café.** Informal and bright, this restaurant prepares healthful cuisine and is especially beloved for its ample, all-day Sunday breakfasts (you can also get breakfast the rest of the week). The lunch menu mixes standard American fare with vegetarian options. Dinners are more exotic, with entrées such as tofu Stroganoff, mushroom risotto with oysters, and curried sea scallops pan-seared on a bed of spinach. Try to get a table in the glassed-in back room, which faces a plant-filled courtyard. ✉ *634 Water St.,* ☎ *360/385–6532. Reservations not accepted. No credit cards. No dinner Tues., Wed.*

**$$–$$$** 🏠 **James House.** This meticulously restored, antiques-filled Victorian-era inn rests proudly on the bluff overlooking downtown Port Townsend and the waterfront. Some guest rooms are spacious and have waterfront views, others are small and share baths. The hardwood floors, though exquisite, are creaky and the sounds of footsteps and conversations drift into the rooms. Gourmet breakfasts are served in the formal dining room, as is complimentary sherry in the evening. The gardener's cottage next door has a wood-burning fireplace, a whirlpool tub, and other modern amenities. ✉ *1238 Washington St., 98368,* ☎ *360/385–1238 or 800/385–1238,* 🅵🅰🆇 *360/379–5551. 12 rooms, 10 with bath. Dining room. MC, V.*

**$$** 🏠 **Palace Hotel.** The decor of this spacious hotel reflects the building's history as a bordello: One can easily imagine the exposed brick lobby filled with music and men waiting for the ladies whose names now grace hallway plaques. The large rooms have 14-ft ceilings and worn antiques. The outstanding corner suite—Miss Marie's—has full views of the Bay and the original working fireplace from Marie's days as a madam. ✉ *1004 Water St., 98368,* ☎ *360/385–0773 or 800/962–0741,* 🅵🅰🆇 *360/ 946–5287. 15 rooms, 12 with bath. AE, D, MC, V.*

**$$** 🏠 **Tides Inn.** You might recognize this place from the movie *An Officer and a Gentleman,* which was filmed around Port Townsend and Fort Worden: The waterfront inn was the setting for those steamy love scenes between Richard Gere and Debra Winger. Comfortable and unfancy, the Tides has a briny smell and a seaside-motel atmosphere. Some rooms have small private decks that extend over the water's edge. All the rooms have TVs and phones; some have kitchens, decks, hot tubs, or all three. A Continental breakfast (muffins and juice) is served each morning. ✉ *1807 Water St., 98368,* ☎ *360/385–0595 or 800/822–8696,* 𝖥𝖠𝖷 *360/385–7370. 21 rooms. AE, D, DC, MC, V.*

## Nightlife and the Arts

### NIGHTLIFE

**Back Alley** (✉ 923 Washington St., ☎ 360/385–2914), a favorite with locals, hosts live rock and roll on weekends. Secluded **Sirens** (✉ 832 Water St., 3rd floor, ☎ 360/379–0776) overlooks the water and books a variety of musical acts on the weekends. The old **Town Tavern** (✉ 639 Water St., ☎ 360/385–4706) has live music—from jazz to blues to rock—on weekends.

### THE ARTS

**Centrum** (✉ Box 1158, 98368, ☎ 800/733–3608), Port Townsend's well-respected performing-arts organization, presents performances, workshops, and conferences throughout the year at Fort Worden State Park. The **Centrum Summer Arts Festival** runs from June to September.

## Outdoor Activities and Sports

### BICYCLING

**P. T. Cyclery** (✉ 100 Taylor St., south of Water St., ☎ 360/385–6470) rents mountain bikes in July and August. The nearest place to go riding is Fort Worden, but you can range as far afield as Fort Flagler, the lower Dungeness trails (no bikes are allowed on the spit itself), or across the water to Whidbey Island.

### BOAT CRUISE

**P. S. Express** (✉ 431 Water St., ☎ 360/385–5288) operates narrated passenger tours to San Juan Island from April to October for $45 round-trip.

### KAYAK TOURS

**Kayak Port Townsend** (✉ 435 Water St., ☎ 360/385–6240) conducts guided kayak tours from April to October ($40 for about three hours or $70 for a full day with lunch).

## Shopping

The best shopping in Port Townsend can be found along the waterfront; many of the boutiques and stores here carry Northwest arts and crafts. **North by Northwest Gallery** (✉ 18 Water St., ☎ 360/385–0955) specializes in Eskimo and Native American art, artifacts, jewelry, and clothing. **Russell Jaqua Gallery** (✉ 21 Taylor St., ☎ 360/385–5262) exhibits blacksmith and other iron-work creations. **William James Bookseller** (✉ 829 Water St., ☎ 360/385–7313) stocks used and out-of-print books in all fields, with an emphasis on nautical, regional-history, and theology titles.

Three dozen dealers at the two-story **Port Townsend Antique Mall** (✉ 802 Washington St., ☎ 360/385–2590) flea market sell merchandise ranging from pricey Victorian collectors' items to cheap funky junk.

More shops are uptown on **Lawrence Street** near an enclave of Victorian houses.

# Whidbey Island, Fidalgo Island, and Port Townsend Essentials

## Arriving and Departing

### BY CAR

Whidbey Island can be reached by heading north from Seattle on I–5, west on Highway 20 onto Fidalgo Island, and south across Deception Pass Bridge. The all-land route from Seattle to Port Townsend is a long one, south on I–5 to Olympia and north on U.S. 101 and Highway 20.

### BY FERRY

**Washington State Ferries** (☎ 206/464–6400; 800/843–3779 in WA only) operates a ferry to Whidbey Island that leaves from Mukilteo, off I–5's Exit 189, 20 mi north of Seattle. Port Townsend can be reached by ferry from Whidbey Island at Keystone (in the middle of the island, where Highways 525 and 20 intersect). To get to Port Townsend from Seattle on the Edmonds Ferry, drive north on I–5 14 mi to Exit 177 and board the ferry. From the Kingston landing, take Highway 104 to Route 19 and follow the signs. An alternative route is to take the Bainbridge Ferry from downtown Seattle to Bainbridge Island and then drive northwest on Highway 305 to Route 3 North to Highway 104 to Route 19 and follow the signs.

### BY PLANE

**Harbor Airlines** (☎ 800/359–3220) flies to Whidbey Island from Friday Harbor and Sea-Tac Airport. **Kenmore Air** (☎ 206/486–1257 or 800/543–9595) can arrange charter floatplane flights to Whidbey Island. **Port Townsend Airways** (☎ 800/385-6554) flies charter planes between Sea-Tac airport and Port Townsend.

## Visitor Information

**Anacortes Chamber of Commerce** (✉ 819 Commercial Ave., Suite G, 98221, ☎ 360/293–7911). **Central Whidbey Chamber of Commerce** (✉ 5 S. Main St., Coupeville 98239, ☎ 360/678–5434). **Langley Chamber of Commerce** (✉ 124½ 2nd St., 98260, ☎ 360/221–6765). **Port Townsend Chamber of Commerce** (✉ 2437 E. Sims Way, 98368, ☎ 360/385–2722).

# THE SAN JUAN ISLANDS

*Numbers in the margin correspond to points of interest on the Puget Sound map.*

The San Juan Islands beckon to souls longing for quiet, whether it be kayaking in a cove, walking a deserted beach, or nestling by the fire in an old farmhouse. Unfortunately, solitude becomes a precious commodity in the summer, when tourists descend on the San Juans. Not surprisingly, tourism and development are hotly contested issues among locals.

You can reach the island only by ferry or plane. On weekends and even on some weekdays, expect to wait at least three hours in line once you arrive at the ferry terminal. You will face the same challenge or worse if you return on Sunday afternoon or evening. One way to avoid the crowds is to plan a trip in the spring, fall, or winter. Reservations are a must anytime in the summer and are advised for weekends in the off-season, too.

There are 176 named islands in the San Juan archipelago, although the islands total 743 at low tide and 428 at high tide. Sixty are populated and 10 are state marine parks. Ferries stop at the four largest islands:

Lopez, Shaw, Orcas, and San Juan; other islands, many privately owned, must be reached by private plane or boat. Naturalists love the San Juans because they are home to three pods of orca and a few minke whales, plus seals, dolphins, otters, and more than 80 active pairs of breeding bald eagles. Because of their location in the rain shadow of the Olympics, the San Juans average more than 250 days of sunshine a year. Temperatures hover around 70°F in the summer and between 40°F and 60°F during the off-season.

San Juans residents are a blend of highly educated sophisticates and '60s-era (or thusly inspired) folk who have sought alternative lifestyles in a rustic setting. Fishing, farming, and tourism are the only industries. Creative chefs operate small restaurants here, but though the food is as contemporary as anything in Seattle, other aspects of island life haven't changed substantially in 30 years. Each of the islands has a distinct character, yet all share basic features: serene farmland, mysteriously charmed light, the velvet-green waters of the Strait of Juan de Fuca, and vistas framed by either Mount Baker and the Cascade Range to the east or the Olympics to the south.

## Lopez Island

**4** *45 mins by ferry from Anacortes.*

The first ferry stop is at quiet and relatively flat Lopez Island, a favorite of bicyclists. Of the three islands that accommodate visitors, Lopez has the smallest population (approximately 1,800) and with old orchards, weathered barns, and pastures of sheep and cows is the most rustic. There is only one main town, Lopez Village, which has a few shops, some galleries that exhibit local artists' works, and the post office.

The **Lopez Island Historical Museum** (⊠ Weeks Rd. at Washburn Rd., ☎ 360/468–2049), across the street from the island's only bank, has some impressive ship and small-boat models. The museum—open from noon to 4 Wednesday to Sunday in July and August and Friday to Sunday in May, June, and September—has maps of local landmarks.

Beaches, trails, and wildlife are the draws at 130-acre **Spencer Spit State Park** (⊠ Rte. 2, ☎ 360/468–2251), on the northeast shore just over 2 mi from Lopez Village. Popular **Odlin County Park** (⊠ Rte. 2, ☎ 360/ 468–2496) is 1 mi from the ferry landing. You'll likely spot marine life—perhaps seals, sea otters, and heron, or smaller creatures among the tide pools—at craggy, isolated **Shark Reef.** Park in the lot south of the village on Shark Reef Road and follow the unmarked trail (it begins next to the outhouse) for about 15 minutes through a thick forest to the water's edge.

The **Lopez Island Vineyard** (⊠ Fisherman Bay Rd. north of Cross Rd., ☎ 360/468–3644), the only vineyard on the San Juans, has a tasting room that is open from Memorial Day to Labor Day Wednesday to Sunday from 12 to 5 (call for hours rest of year).

### Dining and Lodging

**$$**  ✕ **Bay Café.** At this colorful restaurant you'll find everyone from locals and vacationers to movie stars filming on the island; many customers sail over and dock their boats at the restaurant's edge. Menu highlights include the seafood tapas: basil-and-goat-cheese stuffed prawns with saffron rice, a ricotta corn cake with smoked salmon and blackberry ketchup, and sea scallops with sun-dried tomatoes. All entrées include soup and salad. Homemade sorbet and a fine crème

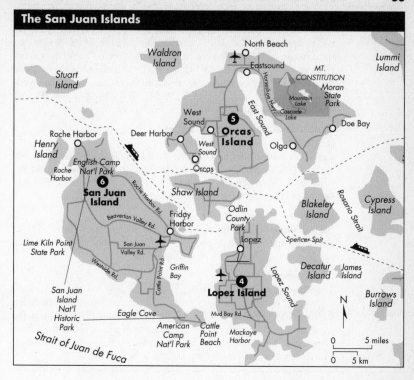

caramel are among the desserts. ✉ *Lopez Village,* ☎ *360/468–3700. MC, V. No lunch.*

**$$$** 🏠 **Edenwild.** A large gray Victorian-style farmhouse surrounded by gardens and framed by Fisherman's Bay looks as if it's been restored, but it dates from 1990, not 1890. The rooms at handsome, orderly Edenwild are airy, each painted in a bold color. Some rooms have fireplaces, and all are furnished with simple antiques. Tiny roses fill the trellis on the wraparound ground-floor veranda. Well-selected contemporary art adorns the ocher-color hallways, bright lobby, and dining room. Rates here include a full breakfast. The inn welcomes children. ✉ *Eades La. at Lopez Village Rd., 98261,* ☎ *360/468–3238,* 🇫🇦🇽 *360/468–4080. 8 rooms. AE, D, MC, V.*

**$$–$$$** 🏠 **Inn at Swifts Bay.** New owners Rob Aney and Mark Adcock are continuing this inn's tradition of mellow hospitality. Their Tudor-style house has eclectic furnishings, a fascinating collection of books, and an exhaustive video library. Bay windows in the living and dining areas overlook well-kept gardens, and a crackling fire warms the living room on winter evenings. Robes, thongs, and flashlights are available for your walk through the garden to a hot tub under the stars. The downstairs rooms have heavy floral drapes and elaborate bed dressings, but are small and share baths. The downstairs suite has more space and a private entrance, but even better are the two upstairs suites, which are long and narrow, with high, sloping ceilings. Gourmet breakfasts include exotic creations such as pumpkin eggnog muffins. ✉ *Rte. 2, Box 3402, 98261,* ☎ *360/468–3636,* 🇫🇦🇽 *360/468–3637. 2 rooms with shared bath, 3 suites. Hot tub, beach. AE, D, MC, V.*

**$$** 🏠 **Mackaye Harbor Inn.** This two-story inn, a frame 1920s sea-captain's house with ½ mi of beach, is at the south end of Lopez Island. Rooms have golden-oak and brass details and wicker furniture; three have views of Mackaye Harbor. Breakfast often includes Finnish pancakes and other Scandinavian specialties. Three rooms share 2½ baths; two suites have private baths, small decks, and fireplaces. A new carriage house has a two-bedroom suite with a steam room and a full kitchen; a small studio here also has a kitchen. Breakfast is not included for guests in the carriage house. Boats and mountain bikes are available for rent. ⊠ *Rte. 1, Box 1940, 98261,* ☎ *360/468–2253,* FAX *360/468–3293. 5 rooms, 2 with bath, 2 suites. Beach. MC, V.*

## Outdoor Activities and Sports

BICYCLING

**Cycle San Juans Tours and Rentals** (⊠ Rte. 1, ☎ 360/468–3251) advertises this tour: "Cycle with bald Lopezian to discover island curiosities." **Lopez Bicycle Works** (⊠ Fisherman Bay Rd., ☎ 360/468–2847) provides free bicycle delivery all year.

MARINAS

**Islands Marine Center** (⊠ Fisherman Bay Rd. north of Hummel Lake Rd. near Lopez Village, ☎ 360/468–3377) has standard marina amenities, repair facilities, and transient moorage.

## Shopping

The **Chimera Gallery** (⊠ Lopez Village, ☎ 360/468–3265), a local artists' cooperative, exhibits crafts, jewelry, and fine art. **Grayling Gallery** (⊠ 3630 Hummel Lake Rd., ☎ 360/468–2779) displays the paintings, prints, sculptures, and pottery of about 10 artists from Lopez Island, some of whom live and work on the gallery's premises. The gallery is open Friday and weekends from 10 to 5.

# Shaw Island

*20 mins by ferry from Lopez; 65 mins from Anacortes.*

At tiny Shaw Island local nuns wear their traditional habits while running the ferry dock. Few tourists get off here; the island is mostly residential. **King Salmon Charters** (☎ 360/468–2314) operates saltwater fishing excursions.

# Orcas Island

**❺** *10 mins from Shaw Island by ferry; 75 mins from Anacortes.*

The roads on horseshoe-shape Orcas Island sweep down through wide valleys and rise to marvelous hilltop views. The wealthy landowners on this mostly privately owned island mix with a visible arts-oriented countercultural community. Public access to the waterfront is limited.

Shops in **Eastsound Village,** in the middle of the horseshoe and the island's business and social center, showcase the jewelry, pottery, and other crafts of local artisans. Along Prune Alley you'll find a handful of small shops and restaurants. Pick up free maps and brochures at the unstaffed **Travel Infocenter** (⊠ Main St., ☎ 360/376–2273), next to the Orcas Island Museum (worth a stop if you're a history buff). Nearby is the simple yet stately **Emmanuel Church,** built in 1886 to resemble an English countryside chapel. The church's **Brown Bag Concerts** (☎ 360/376–2352)—you'll hear anything from a piano sonata to the vocalizing of a barbershop quartet—take place on summer Thursdays at noon.

**Moran State Park** contains 151 campsites, 14 hiking trails, some sparkling lakes, 5,000 acres of old-growth forests, and **Mount Constitution.** Exhilarating views of the San Juan Islands, the Cascades, the Olympics, and Vancouver Island can be had from the mountain's

2,400-ft summit, the tallest on all the islands. ⊠ *Star Rte. 22; from Eastsound, head northeast on Horseshoe Hwy. and follow signs (mailing address: ⊠ Box 22, Eastsound 98245), ☎ 360/376–2326 for park, 800/452–5678 for camping reservations.* 🏕 *Camping: $11 fee, plus $6 per night.*

## Dining and Lodging

**$$$** ✗ **Christina's.** The modern decor at the premier Orcas restaurant includes original artworks and copper-top tables. The seasonal menu changes daily but generally emphasizes fresh local fish and seafood. You're almost certain to encounter a salmon entrée, delicately prepared and served with grilled vegetables. Other possibilities include a seafood stew with a saffron broth and rouille (a peppery garlic sauce), and lamb shank with white beans, rosemary, and root vegetables. The extensive wine list highlights Pacific Northwest vintages. Expect a wait in-season at Christina's, which has fine views from its rooftop terrace and enclosed porch. ⊠ *N. Beach Rd. and Horseshoe Hwy., Eastsound, ☎ 360/376–4904. AE, DC, MC, V. Closed Tues. Oct.–mid-June. No lunch.*

**$–$$** ✗ **Bilbo's Festivo.** Stucco walls, Mexican tiles, wood benches, and weavings from New Mexico betray this restaurant's culinary inclinations. Munch on burritos, enchiladas, and other Mexican favorites like orange-marinated chicken grilled over mesquite and served with fresh asparagus, potatoes, and salad. In warm weather, it's pleasant to sip fresh lime margaritas in the courtyard. ⊠ *N. Beach Rd. and A St., Eastsound, ☎ 360/376–4728. Reservations not accepted. AE, MC, V. No lunch Oct.–May.*

**$$$–$$$$** 🏨 **Rosario Spa & Resort.** Shipbuilding magnate Robert Moran built this Mediterranean-style mansion on Cascade Bay in 1906. Told he had six months to live, Moran pulled out all the stops on his last extravagance—then lived another 30 years. Now his mansion is on the National Register of Historic Places. The original Mission-style furniture, displayed for the public, is worth a look even if you're not staying here. The house's centerpiece, an Aeolian pipe organ with 1,972 pipes, is used for summer music concerts. The resort is renovating the villas and hotel units that were added in 1960 when Rosario was converted from a private residence. The rooms completed so far are comfortable, with gas fireplaces and other modern amenities. The spa offers everything from aerobic instruction to herbal wraps and massage. A shuttle meets every ferry and provides transportation into Eastsound. When an expansion project is finished, the resort's marina will have 200 slips. ⊠ *1 Rosario Way, off Horseshoe Hwy., Eastsound 98245, ☎ 360/376–2222 or 800/562–8820. 131 rooms. Dining room, indoor pool, 2 outdoor pools, 2 tennis courts, hot tub, sauna, spa, hiking, dock, boating, fishing. AE, DC, MC, V.*

**$$$–$$$$** 🏨 **Spring Bay Inn.** Sandy Playa and Carl Burger, former park rangers, ★ run this B&B on acres of woodland surrounding private Spring Bay. All rooms have bay views (this is the only Orcas B&B actually on the water), wood-burning fireplaces, feather beds, and private sitting areas; one room has an outdoor hot tub. Walking trails meander through the property. Mornings begin with coffee, fresh muffins, and croissants outside your door—fortification for a two-hour kayaking experience, should you care to partake. While one of your hosts is out on the water— expect to see bald eagles, herons, or other wildlife—the other is preparing a full breakfast that includes fresh-squeezed orange juice and smoothies. ⊠ *Obstruction Pass Trailhead Rd. off Obstruction Pass Rd., Olga 98279, ☎ 360/376–5531, FAX 360/376–2193. 5 rooms. Refrigerators, hot tub, kayaking. D, MC, V.*

$$$     🏨 **Deer Harbor Inn.** The original 1915 log lodge here, on a knoll over-looking Deer Harbor, was the island's first resort. The lodge is now the inn's dining room. A log cabin built later holds eight rooms with peeled-log furniture and meadow views from balconies. Three newer cottages have whirlpool tubs and propane fireplaces. A complimentary Continental breakfast is delivered to the door in a picnic basket. The large but cozy dining room, which serves seafood, has an adjoining deck for outdoor eating. ⊠ *Box 142, Deer Harbor 98243,* ☎ *360/ 376–4110,* 𝖥𝖠𝖷 *360/376–2237. 11 rooms. Restaurant. AE, MC, V.*

$$–$$$     🏨 **Orcas Hotel.** Construction began in 1900 on this three-story red-roof Victorian hotel on a hill across from the Orcas ferry landing. The building, complete with a wraparound porch and a white picket fence, is on the National Register of Historic Places. Guest rooms have feather beds, down comforters, and wicker, brass, and antique furnishings; many rooms have water views. All second-floor rooms share baths. Two suites have whirlpool tubs. The dining room—open in season (from June to October) to guests and nonguests—overlooks gardens and the ferry landing. In-season room rates include a full breakfast; lower off-season rates do not, but you can grab an espresso or baked goods at the on-site café. ⊠ *Horseshoe Hwy., Box 155, Orcas 98280,* ☎ *360/376–4300,* 𝖥𝖠𝖷 *360/ 376–4399. 12 rooms, 2 with bath, 3 with half bath. Restaurant, bar, café. AE, D, MC, V.*

$$–$$$     🏨 **Turtleback Farm Inn.** Eighty acres of meadow, forest, and farmland in the shadow of Turtleback Mountain surround this forest-green inn that dates from the late 1800s. Guest rooms have easy chairs, good beds with woolen comforters made from the fleece of resident sheep, some antiques, and views of meadows and forest. Breakfast, cooked by Susan Fletcher and served by her husband Bill, can be taken in the dining room or on the deck overlooking the valley. ⊠ *R.R. 1, Box 650, Eastsound 98245,* ☎ *360/376–3914 or 800/376–4914. 7 rooms. D, MC, V.*

$–$$     🏨 **Doe Bay Village Resort.** A haven for neohippies and outdoorsy families, this property at the eastern tip of Orcas morphed from a nudist colony into a commune, a youth hostel, and finally a resort. Prices for the patchwork of accommodations—campsites, yurts, a hostel, and cabins tucked between two forested hills—start as low as $12, and there's a mostly vegetarian café on site. The resort's small beach is perfect for kayak launches. Guests staying in the cabins may also use the resort's mineral baths and sauna for free ($3 fee for hostel guests and campers). ⊠ *Star Rte. 86 off Pt. Lawrence Rd. near Olga 98279,* ☎ *360/376–2291,* 𝖥𝖠𝖷 *360/376–4755. 30 cabins and structures, 24 campsites. Café, hot tubs, massage, mineral baths, sauna, volleyball, beach. AE, MC, V.*

## Outdoor Activities and Sports

### BICYCLING

**Dolphin Bay Bicycles** (⊠ Eastsound, ☎ 360/376–4157) is at the ferry landing. **Key Moped Rental** (⊠ Eastsound, ☎ 360/376–2474) rents mopeds during the summer. **Wildlife Cycles** (⊠ Eastsound, ☎ 360/376–4708) also has bikes for rent.

### FISHING

Three lakes at **Moran State Park** (☞ *above*) are open for fishing from late April to October.

### MARINAS

**Deer Harbor Resort & Marina** (☎ 360/376–3037) and **West Sound Marina** (☎ 360/376–2240) have standard marina facilities. **Island Petroleum** (⊠ Orcas, ☎ 360/376–3883) has gas and diesel at the ferry landing. **Rosario Resort** (⊠ Eastsound, ☎ 360/376–2222) has boat slips.

**Shopping**

**Darvill's Rare Print Shop** (⊠ Eastsound, ☎ 360/376–2351) specializes in maps and bird and floral prints.

# San Juan Island

**❻** *45 mins by ferry from Orcas; 75 mins from Anacortes by express ferry.*

The story goes that Friday Harbor got its name when an explorer rounding San Juan Island called from the boat "What bay is this?" A man on shore heard "What day is this?" and called back "Friday." The islands' county seat and the only incorporated town on San Juan Island is the most convenient destination for visitors traveling on foot.

Standing at the ferry dock facing the bluff and downtown, you'll recognize the modest **Whale Museum** by the whale mural painted on its exterior. To reach the entrance, walk up Spring Street and turn right on 1st Street. Models of whales and whale skeletons, recordings of whale sounds, and videos of whales are the attractions. Workshops survey marine-mammal life and San Juan ecology. ⊠ *62 1st St. N,* ☎ *360/378–4710.* ☜ *$3.* ☉ *June–Sept., daily 10–5; Oct.–May, daily 11–4.*

For an opportunity to see whales cavorting in the Strait of Juan de Fuca, head to **Lime Kiln Point State Park,** on San Juan's west side, just 6 mi from Friday Harbor. The best months for sighting whales are from the end of April through August. ⊠ *6158 Lighthouse Rd.,* ☎ *360/378–2044.* ☜ *Free.* ☉ *Daily 8 AM–10 PM.*

The **San Juan Island National Historic Park** (☎ 360/378–2240) is a remnant of the "Pig War," a prolonged scuffle between American and British troops that were brought in after a Yank killed a Brit's pig in 1859. The mere presence of the soldiers was pretty much the extent of the hostilities (no gunfire was ever exchanged), although troops from both countries remained on the island until 1872. The park, which is open daily from dawn to 11 PM, encompasses two separate areas: a British camp on the west side of the island (follow Roche Harbor Road north from Friday Harbor), containing a blockhouse, a commissary, and barracks; and an American camp (follow Cattle Point Road south from Friday Harbor) with a laundry, fortifications, and a visitor's center. From June through August the park conducts hikes and reenacts 1860s-era military life.

Snazzy **Roche Harbor** at the northern end of San Juan began as a limestone quarrying village. The Roche Harbor Lime and Cement Company, the oldest incorporated company in Washington, still maintains its original location on the docks. Painted like a Mississippi River boat, it's hard to miss. With its rose gardens, cobblestone waterfront, and well-manicured lawns, Roche Harbor retains the flavor of its days as a hangout for the world's elite—Teddy Roosevelt and many other notables stopped here.

The historic **Hotel de Haro** (☞ Roche Harbor Resort, *below*) displays period photographs and artifacts in its lobby. If you're interested, ask the staff for a map that points out remnants of the quarrying industry and **The Mausoleum,** an eerie Greek-inspired memorial to businessman and Roosevelt confidant John S. McMillin.

## Dining and Lodging

**$$$** ✕ **Duck Soup Inn.** Everything the Duck Soup Inn serves is made from scratch daily—fresh bread, Mediterranean-inspired entrées, vegetarian dishes, and delicious ice cream. Start with apple-wood-smoked West-

cott Bay oysters, followed by pan-seared sea scallops in a red-curry coconut sauce on a bed of cashews and greens. Northwest, California,
and European wines are on the list here. ⊠ *3090 Roche Harbor Rd.,
near town of Roche Harbor,* ☎ *360/378–4878. MC, V. Closed Mon.–
Tues. Apr.–Oct.; closed entirely Nov.–Mar. No lunch.*

$$–$$$     ✕ **Springtree Café.** Chef James Boyle devises his daily menu around
fresh seafood and Waldron Island organic produce and herbs, creating savory dishes that you won't soon forget. Begin with the Caesar
salad—made with tofu instead of eggs—and continue with the king
salmon in pesto sauce, the ginger shrimp with mango and dark rum,
or other fish and meat entrées. Vegetarian options abound, and there's
a full bar and an extensive wine selection. ⊠ *310 Spring St., Friday
Harbor,* ☎ *360/378–4848. MC, V. Closed Sun.–Mon. mid-Oct.–
Apr.*

$     ✕ **Front Street Ale House.** The English-style ale house serves sandwiches,
salads, and traditional pub fare—lamb stew, meat pasties, steak-and-
kidney pie, and the like. For vegetarians there's a vegetable patty
lightly sautéed, then stacked with cheese, mushrooms, lettuce, tomato,
and onions. On-tap brews from the San Juan Brewing Company carry
such locally inspired names as Pig War Stout. ⊠ *1 Front St., Friday
Harbor,* ☎ *360/378–2337. Reservations not accepted. MC, V.*

$$$–$$$$     ✕⌂ **Mariella Inn & Cottages.** This impeccably maintained property sits
on 8 acres on a cove just outside Friday Harbor. Rooms inside a 100-
year-old country house have English antique furniture. Each room has
a private bath and a view of either the water or the exquisite gardens,
but some are small. Some of the private cottages and waterfront suites
scattered throughout the grounds have modern amenities such as VCRs
and kitchenettes. Especially romantic are the contemporary solarium
suites with private whirlpool tubs inside glass-enclosed atriums. Break-
fast and the newspaper are delivered to the cottages each morning. Din-
ner might include lamb chops, pancetta-wrapped filet mignon, or
oven-roasted Pacific salmon. ⊠ *630 Turn Point Rd., Friday Harbor
98250,* ☎ *360/378–6868 or 800/700–7668,* ℻ *360/378–6822. 8
rooms, 3 suites, 12 cottages. Restaurant, bicycles. AE, MC, V.*

$$$     ✕⌂ **Friday Harbor House.** The ceiling-to-floor windows of this con-
temporary bluff-top villa hotel were designed to take advantage of its
views of the marina, ferry landing, and San Juan Channel—as was the
placement of whirlpool tubs in the center of each room. Slate tiles, fireplaces, cable TV, and sleek modern wood wall units all contribute to
the casually upscale atmosphere. Dinners, primarily local seafood, include greens from San Juan's Zion Farm. Guests take their elaborate
complimentary Continental breakfasts at the intimate harbor-view
dining room. ⊠ *130 West St., Friday Harbor 98250,* ☎ *360/378–8455,*
℻ *360/378–8453. 20 rooms. Restaurant, refrigerators. AE, DC, MC,
V.*

$$–$$$     ⌂ **Hillside House.** This split-level house less than a mile from Friday
Harbor has views of the waterfront and Mount Baker from a large deck.
Rooms have either sophisticated or more whimsical decor. Some over-
look the 10,000-square-ft full-flight aviary. Breakfast—made with resident hens' eggs, island jams, and fresh berries—is often served on the
large deck that rings the house. ⊠ *365 Carter Ave., Friday Harbor 98250,*
☎ *360/378–4730 or 800/232–4730,* ℻ *360/378–4715. 6 rooms, 1
suite. AE, D, MC, V.*

$$–$$$     ⌂ **Roche Harbor Resort.** The choice here is between nondescript cot-
tages and condominiums or rooms in the 1886 restored Hotel de
Haro. The old hotel building is better to look at than to stay in; its
guest rooms are somewhat shabby (or rustic, depending on your point

of view). On the other hand, the resort has extensive facilities, including slips for a few hundred boats, a full-service marina, and a 4,000-ft airstrip. Whale-watching and day cruises, plus kayaking tours are available. ⊠ *4950 Tarte Memorial Dr., 10 mi northwest of Friday Harbor off Roche Harbor Rd., Roche Harbor 98250,* ☎ *360/378–2155 or 800/451–8910,* FAX *360/378–6809. 59 rooms, 5 with bath. Restaurant, grocery, pool, tennis court, boating, motorbikes. AE, MC, V.*

$$ ☷ **San Juan Inn.** Rooms in this restored 1873 property ½ block from the ferry landing may be smallish, but there's an air of authenticity here that most island accommodations can't match: This site has been operated as an inn for more than 100 years. All rooms have brass, iron, or wicker beds, Queen Anne eyelet bedspreads, and some antiques. A breakfast of muffins, coffee, and juice is served each morning in a parlor overlooking the harbor. The garden suite behind the inn has a TV and VCR, a full kitchen, and a fireplace. ⊠ *50 Spring St., Box 776, Friday Harbor 98250,* ☎ *360/378–2070 or 800/742–8210,* FAX *360/378–6437. 9 rooms, 4 with bath; 1 suite. Outdoor hot tub, car rental. AE, D, MC, V.*

## Outdoor Activities and Sports

### BEACHES

**American Camp** has 6 mi of public beach. You'll find 10 acres of beachfront at **San Juan County Park** (⊠ 380 Westside Rd. N, Friday Harbor, ☎ 360/378–2992).

### BICYCLING

**San Juan Island Bicycles** (⊠ 380 Argyle St., Friday Harbor, ☎ 360/378–4941) has a reputation for good service and equipment. **Susie's Mopeds** (⊠ Friday Harbor, ☎ 360/378–5244 or 800/532–0087), at the top of the hill behind the line to board the ferry, rents mopeds.

### BOATING

**Port of Friday Harbor** (☎ 360/378–2688), **Roche Harbor Resort** (☎ 360/378–2155), and **Snug Harbor Resort Marina** (☎ 360/378–4762) have standard marina facilities.

### FISHING

You can fish year-round for bass and trout at Egg and Sportsman lakes, both north of Friday Harbor off Roche Harbor Road. **Buffalo Works** (☎ 360/378–4612) arranges saltwater fishing trips. Licenses are required.

### WHALE-WATCHING

**San Juan Excursions** (☎ 360/378–6636 or 800/809–4253) cruises the waters around the islands. **Western Prince Cruises** (☎ 360/378–5315 or 800/757–6722) operates a four-hour narrated tour.

## Shopping

**Boardwalk Bookstore** (⊠ 5 Spring St., Friday Harbor, ☎ 360/378–2787) is strong in the classics and has a good collection of popular literature. **Dan Levin** (⊠ 50 1st St., ☎ 360/378–2051) stocks original jewelry. **Island Wools & Weaving** (⊠ 30 1st St. S, Friday Harbor, ☎ 360/378–2148) carries yarns, imaginative buttons, quilting supplies, and some hand-knit items. **Napier Sculpture Gallery** (⊠ 232 A St., ☎ 360/378–2221) exhibits bronze and steel sculptures. **Waterworks Gallery** (⊠ 315 Argyle St., Friday Harbor, ☎ 360/378–3060) represents eclectic contemporary artists.

# San Juan Islands Essentials

## Arriving and Departing

### BY CAR

To reach the San Juan Islands from Seattle, drive north on I–5 to Exit 230 (Mount Vernon), go west on Highway 20, and follow signs to Anacortes, where you can pick up a Washington State Ferries (☞ *below*) boat. It is convenient to have a car in the San Juan Islands, but taking your car with you may mean waiting in long lines at the ferry terminals. With prior arrangement, most B&B owners will pick up guests without cars at the ferry terminals.

### BY FERRY

**Washington State Ferries** (☎ 206/464–6400; 800/843–3779 in Washington only) vessels depart from Anacortes, about 76 mi north of Seattle, for the San Juan Islands. Departures vary during the year, starting from 5 AM to 7 AM and continuing regularly until 8 PM or 10 PM. Sunny weekends can be particularly crowded westbound on Friday evening and Saturday morning, and eastbound on Sunday evening. Some weekday ferries are crowded during commuter hours.

You pay for only westbound trips headed for the San Juans—prices vary depending on your point of departure and destination. Since no reservations are accepted on Washington State Ferries (except for the Sidney to Anacortes run during summer), arriving at least a half hour before a scheduled departure is always advised. Prior to boarding, lower your antenna. Only parking lights should be used at night, and it is considered bad form to start your engine before the ferry docks. Walk-on passengers and bicycles always load first unless otherwise instructed.

**San Juan Islands Shuttle Express** (✉ Alaska Ferry Terminal, 355 Harris Ave., No. 105, Bellingham 98225, ☎ 360/671–1137) takes passengers from Bellingham to Orcas Island and Friday Harbor.

### BY PLANE

**West Isle Air** (☎ 800/874–4434) flies to Friday Harbor on San Juan Island from Sea-Tac and Bellingham airports. **Kenmore Air** (☎ 206/486–1257 or 800/543–9595) flies floatplanes from Lake Union in Seattle to the San Juan Islands.

## Contacts and Resources

### CAMPING

**Marine State Parks** (☎ 360/753–2027) are accessible by private boat only. No moorage or camping reservations are available, and fees are charged at some parks from May through Labor Day. Fresh water, where available, is limited. Island parks are Blind, Clark, Doe, James, Jones, Matia, Patos, Posey, Stuart, Sucia, and Turn. All have a few campsites; there are no docks at Blind, Clark, Patos, Posey, or Turn islands.

### CHARTERS

**Amante Sail Tours** (☎ 360/376–4231). **Charters Northwest** (☎ 360/378–7196). **Harmony Sailing Charters** (☎ 360/468–3310). **Kismet Sailing Charters** (☎ 360/468–2435). **Nor'wester Sailing Charters** (☎ 360/378–5478).

### KAYAKING

If you are kayaking on your own, beware of the ever-changing conditions, ferry and shipping landings, and strong tides and currents. Go ashore only on known public property. **Shearwater Sea Kayak Tours** (☎ 360/376–4699), **Doe Bay Resort** (☎ 360/376–2291), **San Juan Kayak Expeditions** (☎ 360/378–4436), and **Seaquest** (☎ 360/378–5767) conduct day trips and longer expeditions.

VISITOR INFORMATION
**San Juan Island Chamber of Commerce** (⊠ Friday Harbor 98250, ☎ 360/378–5240). **San Juan Islands Tourism Cooperative and Visitors Information Service** (⊠ Lopez 98261, ☎ 360/468–3663).

# SNOQUALMIE AND LEAVENWORTH

Interstate 90 heading east from Seattle winds through bucolic farmland with snowcapped mountains in the background. Nestled in the foothills is Snoqualmie Falls, one of the area's most popular attractions. Small mining towns dot the mountains, and to the north of the main I–90 route, you'll find Leavenworth, an alpine-style village with excellent sporting opportunities.

## Snoqualmie

*28 mi east of Seattle on I–90.*

★ Spring and summer snowmelt turns the Snoqualmie River into the thundering torrent known as **Snoqualmie Falls** as it cascades through a 268-ft rock gorge (100 ft higher than Niagara Falls) to a 65-ft-deep pool below. The falls, which were considered sacred by the native people who lived along the river bank, are Snoqualmie's biggest attraction (though some visitors come to see locations David Lynch used in his TV series *Twin Peaks*). A 2-acre park, including an observation platform 300 ft above the Snoqualmie River, offers a view of Snoqualmie Falls and the surrounding area. You can hike the **River Trail**, a 3-mi round-trip route through trees and open slopes that ends at the base of the falls. Be prepared for an uphill workout on the return to the trailhead.

The vintage cars of the **Snoqualmie Valley Railroad,** built in the mid-1910s for the Spokane, Portland, and Seattle Railroad, travel between the landmark **Snoqualmie Depot** and a depot in North Bend. The 50-minute (round-trip) excursion passes through woods and farmland. The **Northwest Railway Museum** within Snoqualmie's depot displays memorabilia and has a bookstore. ⊠ *Snoqualmie Depot: 38625 S.E. King St., at Hwy. 202,* ☎ *206/746–4025 (Seattle) or 425/888–0373 (Snoqualmie).* ☎ *$6.* ☉ *Trains: May–Sept., weekends and holidays; Oct., Sun. only; on the hr 11–4 from Snoqualmie and on the ½ hr 11:30–3:30 from North Bend. Museum, depot, and bookstore: Thurs.–Mon. 10–5.*

Winding north through heavy forest from Snoqualmie, Highway 203 becomes plain old Main Street when it reaches the unassuming town of **Duvall,** a good place to stop for a little antiquing or bookshop browsing, a glimpse of the Snoqualmie River, or a mid-afternoon latte. To return to Seattle you can backtrack to Snoqualmie or head west on the Woodinville–Duvall Road.

### Dining and Lodging

$$$$ ✕ **The Herbfarm.** If there is such a thing as Northwest cuisine, then
★ this intimate restaurant must rank as its temple. A nine-course meal served at two to three seatings a night includes five glasses of Northwest wine and takes between four and five hours. Try such delicacies as goat's-milk-cheese and parsley biscuits, green pickled walnuts in the husk, fresh salmon with a sauce of fresh garden herbs, and sorbet of rose geranium and lemon verbena. The Herbfarm is often booked up months ahead of time. A devastating fire swept through the restaurant in early 1997, but renovations should be completed by the time you read this. ⊠ *32804 Issaquah-Fall City Rd. (from I–90 Exit 22 head*

## Northwestern Washington

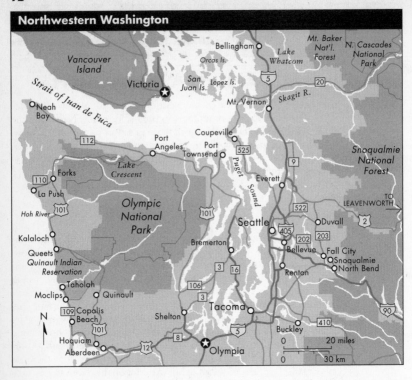

*left, then take right onto Preston–Fall City Rd.; follow this 3 mi to Y in road, then go left over bridge and another ½ mi), Fall City,* ☎ *206/ 784–2222. Reservations essential. MC, V. Closed most weekdays and for a few wks between mid-Feb. and Mar. No lunch.*

**$$$$** ✕🖼 **★ Salish Lodge.** One of Seattleites' favorite weekend getaways consistently rates high in polls of the best resorts in *Condé Nast Traveler* and other publications. Eight of the 91 rooms at the Salish look out over Snoqualmie Falls; others have a view upriver. All have an airy feeling, wood furniture, whirlpool baths, and wood-burning fireplaces. Pampering at the on-site spa includes massage, sea-algae wraps, and sea-salt cleansing scrubs. The restaurant's elaborate Saturday and Sunday brunches include eggs, bacon, fish, fresh fruit, pancakes, and the Salish's renowned oatmeal. Jacket and tie are required for dinner; reservations are essential. Breakfast is served weekdays. ⌧ *6501 Railroad Ave. SE, 98065,* ☎ *425/888–2556 or 800/826–6124,* ℻ *425/888– 2420. 91 rooms. 2 restaurants, bar, room service, health club, spa, laundry service, concierge, business services, meeting rooms. AE, D, DC, MC, V.*

### Nightlife and the Arts

**Snoqualmie Falls Forest Theater** (☎ 425/222–7044) presents two or three plays, usually melodramas performed by acting students and community performers, in a 250-seat outdoor amphitheater near Fall City—from I–90 take Exit 22 and go 4 mi; take a right on David Powell Road, follow signs, and continue through the gate to the parking area. Tickets are $13; for another $12, you can enjoy a salmon or steak barbecue after the matinee or before the evening performance. Reservations are required for dinner.

## Outdoor Activities and Sports

Snoqualmie Pass has three downhill and cross-country ski areas—
**Alpental, Ski Acres, and Snoqualmie Summit** (✉ Mailing address for
all three: 3010 77th St. SE, Mercer Island 98040, ☎ 206/232–8182).
Each area rents equipment and has a full restaurant and lodge facilities.

# Leavenworth

★ *128 mi from Seattle, I–5 north to U.S. 2 east.*

Participants in a 1997 poll conducted by *Seattle* magazine voted Leavenworth one of their favorite weekend getaways. And it's easy to see
why: The charming (if occasionally *too* cute) Bavarian-style village, home
to creative restaurants and attractive lodgings, is a hub for some of Northwest's best skiing, hiking, rock climbing, rafting, canoeing, and snow-
shoeing.

Leavenworth was a railroad and mining center for many years, but by
the 1960s had fallen on hard times. Civic leaders, looking for ways to
capitalize on the town's setting in the heart of the Central Cascade Range,
convinced shop owners and other businesspeople to maintain a gin-
gerbread Tyrolean style—even the Safeway supermarket and the
Chevron gas station carry out the theme. Restaurants prepare Bavar-
ian-influenced dishes, candy shops sell gourmet Swiss-style chocolates,
and stores and boutiques stock music boxes, dollhouses, and other Bavarian items. Events held throughout the year, modeled after those in a
typical Bavarian village, foster a European spirit of simple elegance in
a setting that is never short of spectacular.

The **Marlin Handbell Ringers** keep alive an 18th-century English tradition that evolved into a musical form. Twelve ringers play 107 bells
covering 5½ chromatic octaves. The bells are rung as part of the town's
Christmas festivities and also in early May. Also noteworthy is the
**Nutcracker Museum** (✉ 735 Front St., ☎ 509/548–4708), which contains more than 2,500 different kinds of antique and present-day
nutcrackers. The museum is open from May through October, daily
from 2 to 5.

## Dining and Lodging

$$$ ✕ **Lorraine's Edel House.** The candlelit rooms at this modest restau-
rant, a rare Leavenworth eatery that doesn't focus on German food,
are quiet and cozy. From the appetizer of mussels sautéed in an orange
cream sauce to exotic dessert wines and a homespun white- and dark-
chocolate creation, you'll savor imaginatively mouthwatering combi-
nations. The entrées include Asian-accented pastas, game and fish, and
more obscure offerings like grilled wild boar or braised oxtail with
caramelized purple onions, celery, and baby carrots. ✉ *320 9th St.,*
☎ *509/548–4412. D, DC, MC, V.*

$$–$$$ ✕ **Restaurant Osterreich.** Chef Leopold Haas, who hails from Austria,
prepares haute German cuisine—authentic Austrian and European
dishes such as the appetizer of marinated duck breast in a dumpling
coating or an elk stew entrée. The menu changes daily. The atmosphere
is infinitely more casual than the food. ✉ *Tyrolean Ritz Hotel, 633A
Front St.,* ☎ *509/548–4031. MC, V. Closed Mon.*

$$ ✕ **Cougar Inn.** This family restaurant, established in 1890, is on the
shores of Lake Wenatchee, about 25 mi from Leavenworth. Locals often
come by boat and tie up at the restaurant's dock. Great views of the
lake can be had, especially in summer from the big outdoor deck. Breakfast, lunch, and dinner are served daily; the hearty American-style
Sunday brunch is especially popular. The dinner menu includes a sir-

loin steak for two, fried and baked fish, burgers, and standard pastas. ⊠ *23379 Hwy. 207, Lake Wenatchee,* ☎ *509/763–3354. AE, MC, V.*

**$$**   ✕ **Pewter Pot.** This intimate restaurant with lace curtains and fresh flowers is worth the 10-mi drive from Leavenworth to Cashmere. Start with one of the great soups and follow it up with an entrée of stuffed breast of chicken with an apple-cider sauce, turkey and dressing, or sour-cream beef potpie. The deep-dish marionberry pie is memorable. ⊠ *124½ Cottage Ave., Cashmere,* ☎ *509/782–2036. Reservations essential. MC, V. Closed Sun. and Mon.*

**$**   ✕ **Baren Haus.** The cuisine served at this spacious, noisy, and often crowded beer-hall-style room may not be haute, or even particularly interesting, but the generous servings and low prices will appeal to those traveling on a budget. House specialties include German-style sandwiches and pizzas. ⊠ *208 9th St.,* ☎ *509/548–4535. MC, V.*

**$**   ✕ **Danish Bakery.** Come to this small shop for tasty homemade pastries, strong espresso drinks, and friendly service. ⊠ *731 Front St.,* ☎ *509/548–7514. Reservations not accepted. No credit cards.*

**$**   ✕ **Leavenworth Brewery.** The only brewery in Leavenworth pours 8 to 10 fresh brews—the selection changes every two to three weeks. The highly trained brew masters provide detailed descriptions of their beers (daily brewery tours are given at 2 PM). Sandwiches and bar food are available. ⊠ *636 Front St.,* ☎ *509/548–4545. Reservations not accepted. MC, V.*

**$$–$$$**   🏨 **Pine River Ranch.** Mountains completely surround this B&B on 32 acres 16 mi outside Leavenworth. Two extremely private suites have kitchens, gas fireplaces, whirlpool tubs, stereos, televisions with VCRs, and decks. Four rooms in the farmhouse in front are significantly less spacious and private but still quite nice. A full breakfast is served in the dining room, but guests staying in the suites can have it delivered to them. ⊠ *19668 Hwy. 207, 98826,* ☎ *509/763–3959,* FAX *509/763–2073. 6 rooms. AE, D, MC, V.*

**$$–$$$**   🏨 **Pension Anna.** Rooms and suites at this family-run Austrian-style pension in the heart of the village are decorated with sturdy antique pine furniture; added touches include fresh flowers and comforters on the beds. Two of the suites have whirlpool baths, and all except the ground-level rooms have small balconies. The two largest suites have fireplaces and handsome four-poster beds. A hearty European-style breakfast (cold cuts, meats, cheeses, soft-boiled eggs), included in the lodging rate, is served in a room decorated in traditional European style with crisp linens, pine decor, dark-green curtains, and a cuckoo clock. ⊠ *926 Commercial St., 98826,* ☎ *509/548–6273 or 800/509–2662,* FAX *509/548–4656. 12 rooms, 3 suites. AE, D, MC, V.*

**$$–$$$**   🏨 **Run of the River.** Pierre Cardin bathrobes, toothpaste and toothbrushes, and private whirlpool tubs are among the amenities at this luxury accommodation. Each room is decorated with handmade willow furnishings and plush carpeting and is equipped with a TV. Innkeepers Monty and Karen Turner live in the house next door and are readily at hand to meet your needs. Breakfast is served in an enormous dining room on the main floor. ⊠ *9308 E. Leavenworth Rd., 98826,* ☎ *509/548–7171 or 800/288–6491,* FAX *509/548–7547. 6 rooms. Dining room, refrigerators. AE, D, MC, V.*

**$$**   🏨 **Evergreen Motel.** Popular with hikers and skiers, the Evergreen was built in the 1930s. The property still has much of the charm of the downtown roadside inn it once was. Some of its two-bedroom suites have fireplaces or kitchens (though no utensils); others have multiple beds and can sleep up to six comfortably. The room rates include a Continental breakfast served by the very friendly staff. ⊠ *1117 Front St.,*

98826, ☎ 509/548–5515 or 800/327–7212, FAX 509/548–6556. 39 rooms. AE, D, DC, MC, V.

$$ 🏨 **Haus Rohrbach.** This alpine-style B&B sits on the side of a hill with an unobstructed view of the village and the entire surrounding valley. The center of activity is a large lodgelike room with a wood stove, a kitchen area, and tables for dining, playing games, socializing, or taking in the scenery. Guest rooms have double or queen-size beds (some have a sofa bed or daybed as well), down comforters, and pine furniture. The suites have king-size beds, whirlpool tubs, a gas fireplace, easy chairs, and small but fully equipped kitchens. The full breakfast served here typically includes Dutch babies or sourdough pancakes and sausage. ✉ 12882 Ranger Rd., 98826, ☎ 509/548–7024 or 800/ 548–4477, FAX 509/548–5038. 7 rooms, 5 with bath; 3 suites. Pool, hot tub. AE, D, MC, V.

$$ 🏨 **Linderhoff Motor Inn.** This non-Bavarian–style motel at the west end of Leavenworth is one of the nicest in town for the money. Rooms have contemporary decor, locally crafted pine furnishings, and TVs and phones. Options include standard rooms, honeymoon suites with whirlpool tubs and fireplaces, and town-house units that sleep up to eight and have fully equipped kitchens and two bathrooms. You can have your complimentary Continental breakfast—fresh fruit juice, muffins, and Danish pastries—in your room or outside on the inn's balcony. ✉ 690 Hwy. 2, 98826, ☎ 509/548–5283 or 800/828–5680, FAX 509/548–6705. 34 rooms. Pool, hot tub. AE, D, DC, MC, V.

$ 🏨 **Edelweiss Hotel.** The hotel above the restaurant of the same name has small, plainly furnished rooms. It's not the place to go for a romantic weekend, but if you're on a budget and simply need a place to lay your head, the price ($19.45 for a single room; no windows or TV) is hard to beat. The service is genial if occasionally harried. ✉ 843 Front St., 98826, ☎ 509/548–7015, FAX 509/548–2104. 14 rooms, 5 with bath. MC, V.

## Outdoor Activities and Sports

### FISHING

Trout and salmon are plentiful in many streams and lakes around Lake Wenatchee. **Leavenworth Ranger Station** (☎ 509/782–1413) issues permits for the Enchantment Lakes and Alpine Lake Wilderness area.

### GOLF

**Leavenworth Golf Club** (✉ 9101 Icicle Rd., ☎ 509/548–7267) has an 18-hole, par-71 course. The greens fee is $20, plus $20 for an optional cart.

### HIKING

The Leavenworth Ranger District contains more than 320 mi of scenic trails, among them Hatchery Creek, Icicle Ridge, the Enchantments, Tumwater Canyon, Fourth of July Creek, Snow Lake, Stuart Lake, and Chatter Creek. Contact the Leavenworth Ranger District (✉ 600 Sherburne St., 98826, ☎ 509/782–1413) or the Lake Wenatchee Ranger Station (✉ 22976 Hwy. 207, ☎ 509/763–3101) for more information.

### HORSEBACK RIDING

Hourly and daily horseback rides and pack trips are available at **Eagle Creek Ranch** (✉ 7951 Eagle Creek Rd., ☎ 509/548–7798).

### SKIING

More than 20 mi of cross-country ski trails lace the Leavenworth area. **Mission Ridge** (☎ 800/374–1693) has 35 major downhill runs and night skiing from late December to early March. **Stevens Pass** (☎ 360/973–2441 or 360/634–1645) has 36 major downhill runs, and slopes and lifts for skiers of every level. Several shops in Leavenworth rent and sell ski equipment. For more information, contact the **Leavenworth Winter Sports Club** (☎ 509/548–5115).

WHITE-WATER RAFTING

Rafting is a popular sport from March to July; the prime high-country runoff occurs in May and June. The Wenatchee River, which runs through Leavenworth, is generally considered the best white-water river in the state—a Class 3 on the International Canoeing Association scale. Depending on the season and location, anything from a relatively calm scenic float to an invigorating white-water shoot is possible on the Wenatchee or on one of several other nearby rivers.

Rafting outfitters and guides in the area include **All Rivers Adventures/Wenatchee Whitewater** (☎ 509/782–2254 or 800/743–5628), **Alpine Adventures** (☎ 800/926–7238 or 509/548–4159), **Leavenworth Outfitters** (☎ 509/763–3733 or 800/347–7934), and **Northern Wilderness River Riders** (☎ 509/548–4583).

## Snoqualmie and Leavenworth Essentials

### Arriving and Departing

BY BUS

**Metro Bus 210** originates in downtown Seattle (☞ Seattle A to Z *in* Chapter 2) and travels to Snoqualmie and North Bend. The ride takes just over an hour. Call **Greyhound Lines** (☎ 800/231–2222) about buses from downtown Seattle to Snoqualmie and Leavenworth. The ride to Leavenworth takes three hours.

BY CAR

Snoqualmie is a 35-minute drive on I–90 east from Seattle. The quickest route from Seattle to Leavenworth is I–5 north to U.S. 2 east; the drive usually takes a little more than two hours. Leavenworth is 54 mi north of I–90 on U.S. 97.

### Visitor Information

**Leavenworth Chamber of Commerce** (✉ 894 U.S. 2, 98826, ☎ 509/548–5807). **Upper Snoqualmie Valley Chamber of Commerce** (✉ Box 356, North Bend 98045, ☎ 425/888–4440).

# 4 Vancouver

*The spectacular setting of cosmopolitan Vancouver has drawn people from around the world to settle here. The ocean and mountains form a dramatic backdrop to downtown's gleaming towers of commerce and make it easy to pursue all kinds of outdoor pleasures. You can trace the city's history in Gastown and Chinatown, savor the wilderness only blocks from the city center in Stanley Park, or dine on superb ethnic or Pacific Northwest cuisine before you sample the city's vibrant nightlife.*

Updated by
Melissa Rivers

**V**ANCOUVER IS A YOUNG CITY, even by North American standards. It was not yet a town when British Columbia became part of the Canadian confederation in 1870. The city's history, such as it is, remains visible to the naked eye: Eras are stacked east to west along the waterfront, from cobblestone late-Victorian Gastown to shiny postmodern glass cathedrals of commerce.

The Chinese were among the first to recognize the possibilities of Vancouver's setting. They came to British Columbia during the 1850s seeking the gold that inspired them to name the province Gum-shan, or Gold Mountain. As laborers they built the Canadian Pacific Railway, giving Vancouver a purpose—one beyond the natural splendor that Royal Navy captain George Vancouver admired during his lunchtime cruise around its harbor on June 13, 1792. The transcontinental railway, along with the city's Great White Fleet of clipper ships, gave Vancouver a full week's edge over the California ports in shipping tea and silk to New York at the dawn of the 20th century.

Vancouver's natural charms are less scattered than those in many other cities. On clear days, the mountains appear close enough to touch. Two 1,000-acre wilderness parks lie within the city limits. The salt water of the Pacific and fresh water direct from the Rocky Mountain Trench form the city's northern and southern boundaries.

Bring a healthy sense of reverence when you visit: Vancouver is a spiritual place. For its original inhabitants, the Coast Salish peoples, it was the sacred spot where the mythical Thunderbird and Killer Whale flung wind and rain all about the heavens during their epic battles—how else to explain the coast's fits of meteorological temper? Devotees of a later religious tradition might worship in the sepulchre of Stanley Park or in the rough-hewn interior of Christ Church Cathedral, the city's oldest church.

Vancouver, with a metropolitan area population of 1.7 million people, is booming. A tremendous number of Asians have migrated here, including many from Hong Kong who are drawn to the city because of its supportive business environment and protective banking regulations. The mild climate, exquisite natural scenery, and thriving cultural scene also bring new residents to British Columbia's business center. The number of visitors is increasing because of the city's scenic attractions and its proximity to outdoor activities. Many people get their first glimpse of Vancouver when catching an Alaskan cruise, and many return at some point to spend more time here.

## Pleasures and Pastimes

### Dining
The gastronomical experience here is satisfyingly diverse; restaurants—from the bustling downtown area to trendy beachside neighborhoods—have enticing locales in addition to succulent cuisine. The wave of Asian immigration and tourism has brought a proliferation of upscale Chinese, Japanese, Korean, Thai, and Vietnamese restaurants. Cutting-edge establishments perfecting and defining Pacific Northwest fare—including homegrown regional favorites such as salmon and oysters, accompanied by British Columbia and Washington State wines—have become some of the city's leading attractions.

## The Great Outdoors

Nature has truly blessed this city, surrounding it by verdant forests, towering mountains, coves, inlets, rivers, and the wide sea. Biking, hiking, skiing and snowboarding, rafting, and sailing are among the many outdoor activities available throughout the city. Whether you prefer to relax on a beach by yourself or join a kayaking tour with an outfitter, Vancouver has plenty to offer.

## Nightlife and the Arts

Vancouverites support the arts enthusiastically. Touring musicals, serious dramas, and experimental theatrical pieces are presented year-round, as are film, performing-arts, and other cultural festivals. The city's opera, ballet, and symphonic companies are thriving. And there's a complete range of live music, from jazz and blues to heavy metal.

# EXPLORING VANCOUVER

Vancouver may be small when compared to New York or even San Francisco, but it still takes time to explore. You can see a lot of the city in two days, but a day or two more will give you time to explore sights in the larger Vancouver area and the surrounding countryside.

Many sights of interest are concentrated in the hemmed-in peninsula of downtown Vancouver. The heart of Vancouver—which includes the downtown area, Stanley Park, and the West End high-rise residential neighborhood—sits on this peninsula bordered by English Bay and the Pacific Ocean to the west; by False Creek, the inlet home to Granville Island, to the south; and by Burrard Inlet, the working port of the city, to the north, past which loom the North Shore mountains. The oldest part of the city—Gastown and Chinatown—lies at the edge of Burrard Inlet, around Main Street, which runs north–south and is roughly the dividing line between the east side and the west side. All the avenues, which are numbered, have east and west designations. One note about printed Vancouver street addresses: Suite numbers often appear *before* the street number, followed by a hyphen.

## Great Itineraries

### IF YOU HAVE 1–2 DAYS

If you have only one day in Vancouver, start with an early morning drive through Stanley Park to see the Vancouver Aquarium and other sights such as Second Beach on English Bay. Head northeast from the park on Denman Street to Robson Street to lunch and meander on foot through the trendy shops lining the street between Denman and Burrard, then walk northeast on Burrard Street to view the many buildings of architectural interest. Stop along the way at the Vancouver Art Gallery, the Canadian Craft Museum, and the tiny Sri Lankan Gem Museum.

On day two take a more leisurely paced walking tour of the shops, eateries, and cobblestone streets of Gastown and Chinatown. There are plenty of places to eat and shop in both districts.

### IF YOU HAVE 3–4 DAYS

If you have another day to tour Vancouver following your exploration of Stanley Park, Robson Street, Gastown, and Chinatown, head to the south side of False Creek and English Bay on day three to delve into the many boutiques, dining outlets, theaters, and lively public markets of Granville Island. Buses and ferries provide easy transit. Parking is plentiful should you prefer to drive, but touring Granville Island is best accomplished on foot.

**Greater Vancouver** *(Boxes Refer to Detail Maps)*

**Stanley Park**

49 Cap
50 Cap
51 Gra

1A
99A

*STANLEY PARK*

Lions Gate Br.

Denman St.

*Burrard Inlet*

*English Bay*

Vancouver Aquatic Centre

Thurl

Vancouver Maritime Museum

Vancouver Museum

Pacific Spa Centre

41

39 40

Burrard Br.

Ogden Ave.

Chestnut St.

Vanier Park

Cypress St.

Burrard St.

Granville

Gra Isl

*Kitsilano Beach Park*

*Jericho Beach Park*

Point Grey Rd.

Gran Isl

Museum of Anthropology

42

4th Ave.

4th Ave.

Nitobe Memorial Garden

43

Alma St.

**KITSILANO**

Balsam St.

Broadway

Granville St.

Hemlock St.

8th Ave.

10th Ave.

*Connaught Park*

12th Ave.

16th Ave.

Macdonald St.

*Shaughne Park*

Ave.

99

Wallace St.

Dunbar St.

Blenheim St.

*Carnarvon Park*

Trafalgar St.

Valley Dr.

Arbutus St.

Cypress St.

Matthews

Discovery St.

King Edward Ave.

27th Ave.

*Chaldercott Park*

McKenzie St.

Eddington Dr.

*Quilchena Park*

*Balaclava Park*

*Memorial Park West*

NORTH VANCOUVER

...lano Suspension Bridge and Park
...ano Salmon Hatchery
...se Mountain

Burrard Inlet

N

0                    1 mile
0              1 km

**Downtown Vancouver**
**Ford Centre for**
**the Performing Arts**

Pender St.
Georgia St.
Robson St.
Haro St.
Burrard St.
Howe St.
Hornby St.
Dunsmuir St.
Hastings St.
Seymour St.
Homer St.
Cambie St.
Cordova St.
Centennial
Powell St.
Hastings St.
7A
Clark
Victoria

■
**46** Library Square

Davie St.
Granville St.
Richards St.
Pacific Blvd.

**B.C. Sports**
**Hall of Fame**
**47 and Museum**

Dunlevy Ave.
Powell St.
*Strathcona*
*Park*

**Science World**
**48**

Terminal Ave.

...nville
...nd

**...ille**
**...nd**

*False Creek*

Cambie Br.

2nd Ave.

Quebec St.

Commercial Dr.

Broadway

Oak St.

Heather St.

12th Ave.

7

*Cedar*
*Cottage*
*Park*

16th Ave.

Cambie St.

Manitoba St.

Main St.

Fraser St.

Windsor St.

*Clarke*
*Park*

Knight St.

28th Ave.

King Edward

1A
99A

Victoria Dr.

**VanDusen**
**Botanical Garden**
**44**
↓  33rd Ave.

**45**
**Queen Elizabeth**
**Park**

On day four, you'll need a car to tour the far-flung sights south of downtown Vancouver. Museum and history buffs will want to tour the Museum of Anthropology on the campus of the University of British Columbia, and the Vancouver Museum, the high-tech Pacific Space Centre, and the Vancouver Maritime Museum, all just south of downtown in the Kitsilano area.

IF YOU HAVE 5–7 DAYS

If you have another two days to explore and you've already seen Stanley Park, Robson Street, Gastown, Chinatown, Granville Island, and the museums and gardens of Vancouver and parks on the North Shore, don't miss a side trip to beautiful Whistler (☞ Chapter 5) in the mountains north of the city. Although it's ranked as one of the top ski destinations in the world, this growing resort has an ever-expanding array of outdoor activities and festivals that make it worth a visit any time of year.

## Robson to the Waterfront

*Numbers in the text correspond to numbers in the margin and on the Downtown Vancouver map.*

### A Good Walk

Begin your tour of Vancouver on **Robson Street** ①, also referred to as Vancouver's Rodeo Drive because of the sheer number of see-and-be-seen sidewalk cafés and high-end boutiques, and as Robson Strasse because of its European flavor. Start at the northwest end near the cross streets of Bute or Thurlow and follow Robson southeast to Hornby to reach landscaped **Robson Square** ② and the outstanding **Vancouver Art Gallery** ③. On the north side of the gallery across Hornby Street sits the **Hotel Vancouver** ④, one of the city's best-known landmarks. Cathedral Place, a spectacular office tower, stands across the street on the corner of Hornby and Georgia. Three large sculptures of nurses at the corners of the building are replicas of the statues that ornamented the art deco Georgia Medical-Dental Building, the site's previous structure. To the left of Cathedral Place is the Gothic-style **Christ Church Cathedral** ⑤, the oldest church in Vancouver. Head east up Burrard and you'll see on your right a restored terra-cotta arch—formerly the front entrance to the medical building—and frieze panels showing scenes of individuals administering care; these decorate the **Canadian Craft Museum** ⑥, one of the first national cultural facilities dedicated to crafts. Farther still up Burrard, on the opposite side of the street, is the **Marine Building** ⑦, its terra-cotta bas-reliefs making it one of Canada's best examples of art deco architecture.

Across the street (due east, on the corner of Burrard and Hastings) is the elaborate **Vancouver Club** ⑧, the private haunt of the city's top business movers and shakers. This marks the start of the old financial district, which runs southeast along Hastings, where temple-style banks, investment houses, and businesspeople's clubs survive as evidence of the city's sophisticated architectural advances prior to World War I. Until the period between 1966 and 1972, when the first of the bank towers and underground malls on West Georgia Street were developed, this was Canada's westernmost business terminus. **Sinclair Centre** ⑨, at Hastings and Howe streets, is a magnificently restored complex of government buildings that now houses offices and retail shops. Near Granville Street you'll find the former headquarters of the **Canadian Imperial Bank of Commerce (CIBC)** ⑩. The more Gothic **Royal Bank** ⑪ stands directly across the street.

Head northeast up Seymour toward Burrard Inlet to the **Waterfront Station** ⑫. From here, you can either meander through the station and the courtyards to its left or turn north up Cordova, take a right on Howe, and you'll face the soaring canopies of **Canada Place** ⑬, site of Vancouver's primary cruise-ship pier, the Trade and Convention Center, and the luxurious Pan Pacific Hotel (☞ Lodging, *below*). Here you can stop for a snack in one of the dining outlets on the water or catch a film at the Imax theater. Stop off at the **Vancouver Tourist Info Centre** ⑭ across the street (next door to the Waterfront Centre Hotel) to pick up brochures on other Vancouver attractions and events before leaving the area.

TIMING
This walking tour, with time to take in the intriguing architecture along the route, will take approximately two to three hours if you're not drawn into all the shops along the way. Allow about an hour at the Canadian Craft Museum, and another two to three to see the collections at the Vancouver Art Gallery.

## Sights to See

⑬ **Canada Place.** Originally built on an old cargo pier to be the off-site Canadian pavilion in Expo '86, Canada Place was later converted into Vancouver's trade and convention center. The shore end is dominated by the luxurious **Pan Pacific Hotel** (☞ Lodging, *below*), which has a three-story lobby and waterfall. The fabric roof shaped like 10 sails that covers the convention space has become a landmark of Vancouver's skyline. Below is a cruise-ship facility, and at the north end are an Imax theater, a restaurant, and an outdoor performance space. A promenade runs along the pier's west side, affording views of the Burrard Inlet harbor and Stanley Park. ⊠ *999 Canada Pl.,* ☎ *604/775–8687.*

⑥ **Canadian Craft Museum.** Opened in 1992, the museum is one of the first national cultural facilities dedicated to crafts—historical and contemporary, functional and decorative. Craft embodies the human need for artistic expression in everyday life, and examples here range from elegantly carved utensils with decorative handles to colorful hand-spun and handwoven garments. The two-level museum has exhibits, lectures, and the Museum Shop. The structure was once a medical building, still evident outside in the restored terra-cotta arch and frieze panels showing scenes of individuals administering care. The restful courtyard is a quiet place to take a break. ⊠ *639 Hornby St.,* ☎ *604/687–8266.* ☞ *$5.* ☺ *Apr.–Oct., Mon.–Sat. 10–5, Sun. noon–5; Nov.–Mar., Mon. and Wed.–Sat. 10–5, Sun. noon–5.*

⑩ **Canadian Imperial Bank of Commerce (CIBC).** Built between 1906 and 1908, the former headquarters of one of Vancouver's oldest and most powerful chartered banks has columns, arches, and details that reflect a typically Roman influence. It now houses a jewelry store. ⊠ *698 W. Hastings St.*

⑤ **Christ Church Cathedral.** This tiny church, built in 1895, is the oldest in Vancouver. Constructed in Gothic style with buttresses and pointed-arch windows, it looks like the parish church of an English village from the outside. By contrast, the cathedral's rough-hewn interior is that of a frontier town, with Douglas-fir beams and ornate woodwork that provide excellent acoustics for the vespers, carols, and Gregorian chants frequently sung here. ⊠ *690 Burrard St.,* ☎ *604/682–3848.* ☺ *Weekdays 10–4.*

④ **Hotel Vancouver.** Completed in 1939, the Hotel Vancouver (☞ Lodging, *below*) is one of the last railway-built hotels (the final one was the

## Downtown Vancouver

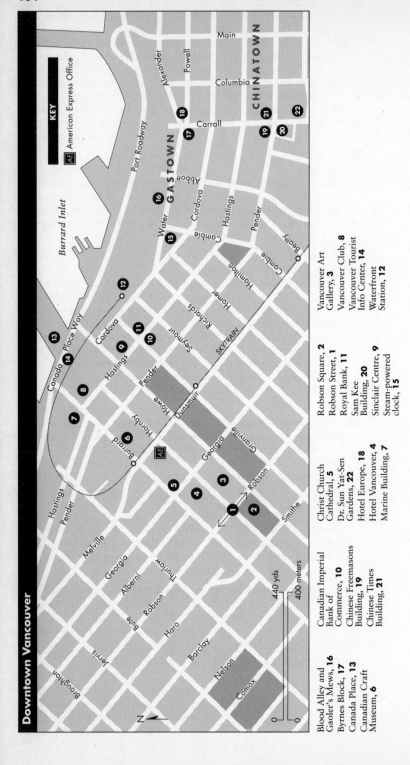

**KEY**

AE American Express Office

Blood Alley and
Gaoler's Mews, **16**
Byrnes Block, **17**
Canada Place, **13**
Canadian Craft
Museum, **6**

Canadian Imperial
Bank of
Commerce, **10**
Chinese Freemasons
Building, **19**
Chinese Times
Building, **21**

Christ Church
Cathedral, **5**
Dr. Sun Yat-Sen
Gardens, **22**
Hotel Europe, **18**
Hotel Vancouver, **4**
Marine Building, **7**

Robson Square, **2**
Robson Street, **1**
Royal Bank, **11**
Sam Kee
Building, **20**
Sinclair Centre, **9**
Steam-powered
clock, **15**

Vancouver Art
Gallery, **3**
Vancouver Club, **8**
Vancouver Tourist
Info Center, **14**
Waterfront
Station, **12**

Chateau Whistler, in 1989). Its château style, with details reminiscent of a medieval French castle, has been incorporated into hotels in almost every major Canadian city. The Depression slowed construction, which began in 1937, and the hotel was finished only in time for the visit of King George VI in 1939. It has been renovated three times, most recently in 1996. The exterior of the building, one of the most recognizable on Vancouver's skyline, has carvings of malevolent-looking gargoyles at the corners, an ornate chimney, native chiefs on the Hornby Street side, and an assortment of grotesque mythological figures. ⊠ *900 W. Georgia St.,* ☎ *604/684–3131.*

**➐ Marine Building.** This art deco building erected in 1931 is ornamented with terra-cotta bas-reliefs depicting the history of transportation: airships, steamships, locomotives, and submarines. Because most buildings were still using classical or Gothic ornamentation, these motifs were once considered radical and modernistic. From the east, the Marine Building is reflected in bronze by 999 West Hastings, and from the southeast it is mirrored in silver by the Canadian Imperial Bank of Commerce. Stand on the corner of Hastings and Hornby streets for the best view of the building. ⊠ *355 Burrard St.*

**➋ Robson Square.** Built in 1975 and designed by architect Arthur Erickson to be *the* gathering place of downtown Vancouver, Robson Square functions from the outside as a park. Here you'll find the **Vancouver Art Gallery** (☞ *below*), government offices, and law courts woven together by landscaped walkways, as well as a block-long glass canopy over one of the walkways and a waterfall. An ice-skating rink and restaurants occupy the below-street level. ⊠ *800 Robson St.*

**➊ Robson Street.** If you're up for a day of shopping, amble down this street (☞ Shopping, *below*) whose stores carry everything from souvenirs to high fashions. There are plenty of places to stop for tea, espresso, or lunch. Europeans of diverse backgrounds settled west of Burrard Street in the 1950s and 1960s, and their influence can still be felt.

**⓫ Royal Bank.** Gothic in style, this building was intended to be half of a symmetrical building that because of the Depression was never completed. Striking, though, is the magnificent hall, reminiscent of a European cathedral. The building is still a bank. ⊠ *685 W. Hastings St.*

**➒ Sinclair Centre.** Outstanding Vancouver architect Richard Henriquez knitted four government office buildings into Sinclair Centre, an office-retail complex. The two Hastings Street buildings—a 1905 **Post Office** with an elegant clock tower and the 1913 **Winch Building**—are linked with the **Post Office Extension** and **Customs Examining Warehouse** to the north. Painstaking and costly restoration involved finding master masons—the original terrazzo suppliers in Europe—and uncovering and refurbishing the pressed-metal ceilings. ⊠ *757 W. Hastings St.,* ☎ *604/666–4438.*

**➌ Vancouver Art Gallery.** The city's best art museum has sculpture and modern art, as well as some native works, but paintings by artist Emily Carr of British Columbia make up the most popular permanent collection. This museum was a classical-style 1912 courthouse until architect Arthur Erickson converted it to a spacious gallery in 1980. The lions that guard the majestic front steps and the use of columns and domes are some of the features borrowed from ancient Roman architecture. ⊠ *750 Hornby St.,* ☎ *604/662–4719.* 🎟 *$9.50.* ☉ *Mon.–Wed. and Fri. 10–6, Thurs. 10–9, Sat. 10–5, Sun. noon–5.*

**➑ Vancouver Club.** The architecture of this gathering place for the city's elite evokes that of private clubs in England inspired by Italian Renaissance palaces. The Vancouver Club, built between 1912 and 1914, is still the private haunt of city businesspeople. ⊠ *915 W. Hastings St.,* ☎ *604/685–9321.*

**⑭ Vancouver Tourist Info Centre.** Here you'll find brochures and personnel to answer questions, as well as an attractive Northwest Coast native art collection. ⊠ *200 Burrard St.,* ☎ *604/683–2000.* ☼ *Sept.–June, weekdays 8:30–5, Sat. 9–5; July–Aug., daily 8–6.*

**⑫ Waterfront Station.** The third and most imposing of three Canadian Pacific Railway passenger terminals in Vancouver was constructed from 1912 to 1914. It replaced the other two as the western terminus for Canada's transcontinental railway. After Canada's railways merged, the station became obsolete until a 1978 renovation turned it into an office-retail complex and SeaBus terminal. Murals in the waiting rooms (now used by Skytrain, SeaBus, West Coast Express, and BC Transit passengers) show the scenery travelers once saw on journeys across Canada. ⊠ *601 W. Cordova St.,* ☎ *604/521–0400 for BC Transit.*

## Chinatown and Gastown

Gastown is where Vancouver originated after smooth talker "Gassy" Jack Deighton arrived at Burrard Inlet in 1867 with his wife, some whiskey, and few amenities, and managed to con local loggers and trappers into building him a saloon for a barrel of whiskey. When the transcontinental train arrived in 1887, Gastown became the transfer point for trade with the Far East and was soon crowded with hotels and warehouses. The Klondike gold rush encouraged further development until 1912, when the "Golden Years" ended. From the 1930s to the 1950s hotels were converted into rooming houses, and the warehouse district shifted elsewhere. The neglected area gradually became run down. However, both Gastown and Chinatown were declared historic districts in the late 1970s and have been revitalized. Gastown is now chockablock with boutiques, cafés, loft apartments, and souvenir shops.

The Chinese were among the first inhabitants of Vancouver. There was already a sizable Chinese community in British Columbia because of the 1858 Cariboo gold rush in central British Columbia, but the greatest influx from China came in the 1880s, during construction of the Canadian Pacific Railway, when 15,000 laborers were imported. Even while doing the hazardous work of blasting the rail bed through the Rocky Mountains, however, the Chinese were discriminated against. The Anti-Asiatic Riots of 1907 stopped growth in Chinatown for 50 years, and immigration from China was discouraged by more and more restrictive policies, climaxing in a $500 head tax during the 1920s. In the 1960s the city council planned bulldozer urban renewal for Strathcona, the residential part of Chinatown, as well as freeway connections through the most historic blocks of the district. Fortunately, the project was halted, and today Chinatown is an expanding, vital neighborhood fueled by investment from Vancouver's most notable newcomers—immigrants from Hong Kong. The best way to view the buildings in Chinatown is from the south side of Pender Street, where the Chinese Cultural Center stands. From here you'll see the important details that adorn the upper stories. The style of architecture in Vancouver's Chinatown is patterned on that of Canton.

*Numbers in the text correspond to numbers in the margin and on the Downtown Vancouver map.*

## A Good Walk

Pick up Water Street at Richards Street and head east into Gastown.
At the corner of Water and Cambie streets, you can see and hear the
world's first **steam-powered clock** ⑮ (it chimes on the quarter hour).
Along the way you'll pass **Blood Alley and Gaoler's Mews** ⑯, which
are tucked behind 12 Water Street. Two buildings of historical and architectural note are the **Byrnes Block** ⑰ on the corner of Water and Carrall streets and the **Hotel Europe** ⑱ (1908–09) at Powell and Alexander
streets. A statue of Gassy Jack stands on the west side of Maple Tree
Square, at the intersection of Water, Powell, Alexander, and Carrall
streets, where he built his first saloon.

From Maple Tree Square it's only three blocks south on Carrall Street
to Pender Street, where Chinatown begins. This route passes through
a rough part of town, so it's far safer to backtrack two blocks on Water
Street through Gastown to Cambie Street, then head south to Pender
and east to Carrall. The corner of Carrall and Pender streets, now the
western boundary of Chinatown, is one of the neighborhood's most
historic and photogenic spots. It's here that you'll find the **Chinese
Freemasons Building** ⑲ (circa 1901) and the **Sam Kee Building** ⑳ (circa
1913), and, directly across Carrall Street, the **Chinese Times Building** ㉑
(circa 1902). Across Pender are the first living classical Chinese gardens built outside China, the **Dr. Sun Yat-Sen Gardens** ㉒, tucked behind the Chinese Cultural Center, which houses exhibition space,
classrooms, and the occasional mah-jongg tournament. Finish up by
poking around in the open-front markets and import shops that line
several blocks of Pender running east.

TIMING

The walk itself will take from two to three hours depending on your
pace; allow extra time for the guided tour of the garden in Chinatown.
Daylight hours are best, although shops and restaurants are open into
the night in both areas. There are few traffic signals for safe crossings
in Gastown, so avoid commuter rush hours.

## Sights to See

★ ⑯ **Blood Alley and Gaoler's Mews.** Once the site of the city's first civic
buildings—the constable's cabin and customs house, and a two-cell log
jail—today the cobblestone street with antique lighting is home to architectural offices. ⊠ *Behind 12 Water St.*

⑰ **Byrnes Block.** This building was constructed on the site of Gassy Jack's
second saloon after the 1886 Great Fire. The date is just visible at the
top of the building above the door where it says "Herman Block," which
was its name for a short time. ⊠ *Water and Carrall Sts.*

⑲ **Chinese Freemasons Building.** Two completely different facades dis-
tinguish a fascinating structure on the northwest corner of Pender and
Carrall streets: The side facing Pender presents a fine example of Can-
tonese-imported recessed balconies; the Carrall Street side displays
the standard Victorian style common throughout the British Empire.
Dr. Sun Yat-Sen hid for months in this building from agents of the
Manchu dynasty while he raised funds for its overthrow, which he accomplished in 1911. ⊠ *W. Pender St.*

㉑ **Chinese Times Building.** This building, on the north side of Pender Street
just east of Carrall, dates from 1902. Police officers could hear the click-
ing sounds of clandestine mah-jongg games played after sunset on the
building's hidden mezzanine floor. But attempts by vice squads to en-
force restrictive policies against the Chinese gamblers proved fruitless,
because police were unable to find the players. Meandering down Pen-

der Street, you can still hear mah-jongg games going on behind the colorful facades of other buildings in Chinatown. ⊠ *1 E. Pender St.*

★ ㉒ **Dr. Sun Yat-Sen Gardens.** Fifty-two artisans from Suzhou, China, using no power tools, screws, or nails, constructed these gardens in the 1980s. Their design incorporates elements and traditional materials from several of Suzhou's centuries-old private gardens. Free guided tours are conducted throughout the day; telephone for times. ⊠ *578 Carrall St.,* ☎ *604/689–7133.* 🖃 *$5.50.* ◷ *Daily 10–7:30.*

⑱ **Hotel Europe.** Once billed as the best hotel in the city, this circa 1908–1909 flatiron building was Vancouver's first reinforced concrete structure. Designed as a functional commercial building, the hotel lacks ornamentation and fine detail, its style unusually utilitarian for the time. ⊠ *Alexander and Powell Sts.*

⑳ **Sam Kee Building.** *Ripley's Believe It or Not!* recognizes this 6-ft-wide structure as the narrowest building in the world. Its bay windows overhang the street and the basement burrows under the sidewalk. ⊠ *8 W. Pender St.*

★ ⑮ **Steam-powered clock.** An underground steam system powers the world's first steam clock. Every quarter hour the whistle blows, and on the hour a huge cloud of steam spews from the clock. It was built by Ray Saunders of Landmark Clocks (⊠ 123 Cambie St., ☎ 604/669–3525). ⊠ *Water and Cambie Sts.*

---

# Stanley Park

A 1,000-acre wilderness park just blocks from the downtown section of a major city is both a rarity and a treasure. In the 1860s, because of a threat of American invasion, the area that is now Stanley Park was designated a military reserve (though it was never needed). When the city of Vancouver was incorporated in 1886, the council's first act was to request that the land be set aside for a park. In 1888 permission was granted and the grounds were named Stanley Park after Lord Stanley, then governor general of Canada.

Spend a morning or afternoon in Stanley Park and you'll get a capsule tour of Vancouver that includes beaches, the ocean, the harbor, Douglas fir and cedar forests, and a good look at the North Shore mountains. The park sits on a peninsula, and along the shore is a pathway 9 km (5½ mi) long called the seawall. You can drive or bicycle the mostly flat route all the way around. Bicycles are for rent at the foot of Georgia Street near the park entrance. Cyclists must ride in a counterclockwise direction and stay on their side of the path.

*Numbers in the text correspond to numbers in the margin and on the Stanley Park map.*

## A Good Biking or Driving Tour

A good place to start is at the foot of Alberni Street beside Lost Lagoon. Go through the underpass and veer right to the seawall past **Malkin Bowl** ㉓, an open amphitheater. Just past the amphitheater is a cutoff to the left that leads to the renowned **Vancouver Aquarium** ㉔; the main road continues on to the rest of the park's sights. The old wood structure that you pass next is the Vancouver Rowing Club, a private athletic club established in 1903; a bit farther along is the Royal Vancouver Yacht Club. About ½ km (⅓ mi) away is the causeway to **Deadman's Island** ㉕.

If you continue straight past the causeway, ahead at the water's edge is the **Nine O'Clock Gun** ㉖. To the north is Brockton Point and its small but functional lighthouse and foghorn. The **totem poles** ㉗, which are a bit farther down the road and slightly inland on your left, are a popular photo stop. Continue on and you'll pass the miniature steam train, five minutes northwest of the aquarium; it's a big hit with children. The children's water park across the road is also popular throughout the summer.

At km 3 (mi 2) is **Lumberman's Arch** ㉘, a huge log archway. About 2 km (1 mi) farther is the Lions Gate Bridge—the halfway point of the seawall. Just past the bridge is **Prospect Point** ㉙, where cormorants build nests. Continuing around the seawall, you'll come to the English Bay side and the beginning of sandy beaches. The imposing rock just offshore is **Siwash Rock** ㉚, the focus of a native legend.

The next attraction along the seawall is the large saltwater pool at **Second Beach** ㉛. You can take a shortcut from here back to Lost Lagoon by walking along the perpendicular road behind the pool, which cuts into the park. The wood footbridge that's ahead will lead you to a path along the south side of the lagoon to your starting point at the foot of Alberni or Georgia street. If you continue along the seawall, you will emerge from the park into a high-rise residential neighborhood, the West End. You can walk back to Alberni Street along Denman Street, where there are places to stop for coffee, ice cream, or a drink.

TIMING

You'll find parking near most of the sights in the park; expect a driving tour to take about an hour. Your biking time will depend on your speed, but with stops to see the sights, expect it to take several hours. Add at least two hours to see the aquarium thoroughly, and you've filled a half- to full-day tour. Stanley Park becomes crowded on weekends; on weekday afternoons the local jogging and biking traffic is at its lowest.

## Sights to See

㉕ **Deadman's Island.** A former burial ground for the local Salish people and the early settlers is now a small naval training base called H.M.C.S. *Discovery* and is not open to the public.

㉘ **Lumberman's Arch.** Made of logs, this large archway is dedicated to the workers in Vancouver's first industry. Beside the arch is an asphalt path that leads back to Lost Lagoon and the Vancouver Aquarium.

㉓ **Malkin Bowl.** An open amphitheater becomes a theater under the stars during the summer. ⊠ *1st right off Pipeline Rd. past park entrance,* ☎ *604/687–0174.*

㉖ **Nine O'Clock Gun.** This cannonlike apparatus by the water was originally used to alert fishermen to a curfew ending weekend fishing; now it signals 9 o'clock every night.

㉙ **Prospect Point.** Here cormorants build their seaweed nests along the cliff's ledges. The large black diving birds are distinguished by their long necks and beaks; when not nesting, they often perch atop floating logs or boulders. Another remarkable bird found along the park's shore is the beautiful great blue heron, which reaches up to 4 ft tall and has a wing span of 6 ft. Herons prey on passing fish in the waters here; the oldest heron rookery in British Columbia is in the trees near the aquarium.

㉛ **Second Beach.** In summer a draw is the big saltwater children's pool with lifeguards, but in winter, when the pool is drained, skateboarders perform stunts here.

## Stanley Park

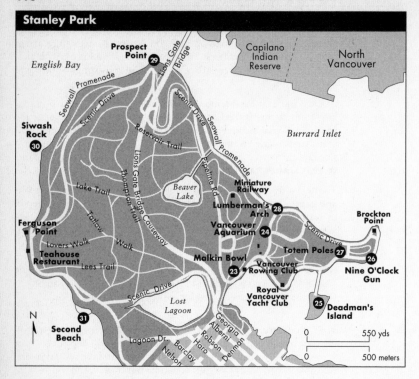

**30 Siwash Rock.** Legend tells of a young Native American who, about to become a father, bathed persistently to wash his sins away so that his son could be born pure. For his devotion he was blessed by the gods and immortalized in the shape of Siwash Rock, just offshore. Two small rocks, said to be his wife and child, are on the cliff above the site.

**27 Totem poles.** Totem poles were not made in the Vancouver area; these, carved of cedar by the Kwakiutl and Haida peoples late in the last century, were brought to the park from the north coast of British Columbia. The carved animals, fish, birds, and mythological creatures are like family coats-of-arms or crests.

★ ☺ **24 Vancouver Aquarium.** The humid Amazon rain-forest gallery has piranhas, giant cockroaches, alligators, tropical birds, and jungle vegetation. Other displays show the underwater life of coastal British Columbia, the Canadian arctic, and other areas of the world. Huge tanks (populated with orca and beluga whales and playful sea otters) have large windows for underwater viewing. ☎ 604/682–1118. ☜ $12. ☼ July–Labor Day, daily 9:30–8; Labor Day–June, daily 10–5:30.

## Granville Island

Granville Island was just a sandbar until World War I, when the federal government dredged False Creek for access to the sawmills that lined the shore. The sludge from the creek was heaped up onto the sandbar to create the island and to house much-needed industrial- and logging-equipment plants. By the late 1960s, however, many of the businesses that had once flourished on Granville Island had deteriorated. Buildings were rotted, rat-infested, and dangerous. In 1971 the federal government bought up leases from businesses that wanted to leave and proposed an imaginative plan to refurbish the island with a public market, marine activities, and artisans' studios. The opposite shore of False Creek was the site of the Expo '86 and is now part of the largest urban redevelopment plan in North America.

The small island has no residents except for a houseboat community. Most of the former industrial buildings and tin sheds have been retained but are painted in upbeat reds, yellows, and blues. Through a committee of community representatives, the government regulates the types of businesses on Granville Island; most of the businesses permitted involve food, crafts, marine activities, and the arts.

*Numbers in the text correspond to numbers in the margin and on the Granville Island map.*

## A Good Walk

To reach Granville Island on foot, make the 15-minute walk from downtown Vancouver to the south end of Hornby Street. Aquabuses (☎ 604/689–5858) depart here and deliver passengers across False Creek to Granville Island Public Market. The Granville Island Ferries (☎ 604/684–7781), which leave every five minutes from a dock behind the Vancouver Aquatic Centre, are another option. Still another way to reach the island is to take a 20-minute ride on a B.C. Transit (☎ 604/521–0400) bus; to do this take a University of British Columbia (U.B.C.), Granville, Arbutus, Cambie, or Oak bus from downtown to Granville and Broadway, and transfer to Granville Island Bus 51 or False Creek Bus 50 from Gastown or stops on Granville Street. Parking is free for up to three hours; paid parking is available in garages on the island.

The ferry will drop you off at the **Granville Island Public Market** ㉜, which contains fast-food outlets and produce, meat, coffee, liquor, and flower stalls. The **Granville Island Information Centre** ㉝ is catercorner to the market.

Walk south on Johnston Street to begin a clockwise loop tour of the island. Ocean Cement is one of the last of the island's former industries; its lease does not expire until the year 2004. Next door is the **Emily Carr Institute of Art and Design** ㉞. Past the art school, on the left, is Sea Village, one of the only houseboat communities in Vancouver. Take the boardwalk that starts at the houseboats and continues partway around the island.

As you circle around to Cartwright Street, stop in Kakali at Number 1249, where you can watch the fabrication of fine handmade paper from such materials as blue jeans, herbs, and sequins. Another unusual artisan on the island is the glassblower at the New-Small Sterling Glass Studio (✉ 1404 Old Bridge St.), around the corner. The next two attractions will make any child's visit to Granville Island a thrill. First, on Cartwright Street, is the **Granville Island Water Park** ㉟. A bit farther down the street, beside Isadora's restaurant, is the **Kids Only Market** ㊱, selling anything and everything a child could desire. Cross Anderson Street and walk down Duranleau Street. On your left are the seafaring stores of the **Maritime Market** ㊲. The last place to explore on Granville Island is the **Net Loft** ㊳, a collection of small, high-quality stores. Once you have come full circle, you can either take the ferry back to downtown Vancouver or stay for dinner and catch a play at the Arts Club (☎ 604/687–1644) or the Waterfront Theater (☎ 604/685–6217).

### TIMING

If your schedule is tight, you can tour Granville Island in three to four hours; if you're a shopping fanatic, plan for a full day here.

## Sights to See

**❸❹ Emily Carr Institute of Art and Design.** The institute's three main build-ings—wooden structures formerly used for industrial purposes—were renovated in the 1970s. The **Charles H. Scott Gallery,** just inside the front door to your right, hosts contemporary exhibitions in various media. ⊠ *1399 Johnston St.,* ☎ *604/687–3800.* ⚏ *Free.* ☉ *Daily noon–5.*

**❸❸ Granville Island Information Centre.** Maps are available here, and a slide show depicts the evolution of Granville Island. Ask about special-events days; boat shows, outdoor concerts, and dance performances often occur on the island. ⊠ *1592 Johnston St.,* ☎ *604/666–5784.* ☉ *Daily 8–6.*

**★ ❸❷ Granville Island Public Market.** Because no chain stores are allowed in this 50,000-square-ft building, each outlet is unique; most sell high-quality merchandise. You can pick up a snack, espresso, or fixings for lunch on the wharf here, and year-round you'll see mounds of rasp-berries, strawberries, blueberries, and more exotic fruits like persim-mons. There's plenty of outdoor seating on the water side of the market. ⊠ *1669 Johnston St., under Granville St. bridge, 2nd floor,* ☎ *604/666–6477.* ☉ *Memorial Day–Labor Day, daily 9–6; Labor Day–Memorial Day, Tues.–Sun. 9–6.*

**❸❺ Granville Island Water Park.** This kids' paradise has a wading pool, sprinklers, and a fire hydrant made for children to shower one another. ⊠ *1318 Cartwright St.,* ☎ *604/257–8195.* ⚏ *Free.* ☉ *Late May–early Sept., daily 10–6.*

**❸❻ Kids Only Market.** Yet another slice of kids' heaven on Granville Is-land, the Kids Only Market has two floors of small shops selling toys, arts-and-crafts materials, dolls, records and tapes, chemistry sets, and other good kid stuff. ⊠ *1496 Cartwright St.,* ☎ *604/689–8447.* ☉ *Daily 10–6.*

**❸❼ Maritime Market.** These businesses are all geared to the sea. The first walkway to the left, Maritime Mews, leads to marinas and dry docks. ⊠ *1650 Duranleau St.,* ☎ *604/687–1556.*

**❸❽ Net Loft.** In this blue building is a collection of small, high-quality stores, including a bookstore, a crafts store-gallery, a kitchenware shop, a post-card shop, a custom-made hat shop, a handmade paper store, a British Columbian native art gallery, and a do-it-yourself jewelry store. ⊠ *1666 Johnston St., across from Public Market,* ☎ *604/876–6637.*

# Greater Vancouver

The metropolis of Vancouver includes North Vancouver across Bur-rard Inlet and the larger, more residential peninsula south of down-town bordered by English Bay to the north, the Strait of Georgia to the west, and the Fraser River to the south. There are wonderful mu-seums, gardens, and natural sights sprinkled throughout Greater Van-couver, but you'll need a car to maximize your time.

*Numbers in the text correspond to numbers in the margin and on the Greater Vancouver map.*

## A Good Drive

South of the Burrard Bridge in Vanier Park is the **Vancouver Museum** ㊴, which showcases the city's history in cheerful, life-size displays. Also here are the high-tech **Pacific Space Centre** ㊵ and the **Vancouver Mar-itime Museum** ㊶. After visiting one or more of the museums, follow Cypress Street south out of the park to 4th Avenue, then head west to the University of British Columbia to visit the amazing **Museum of An-**

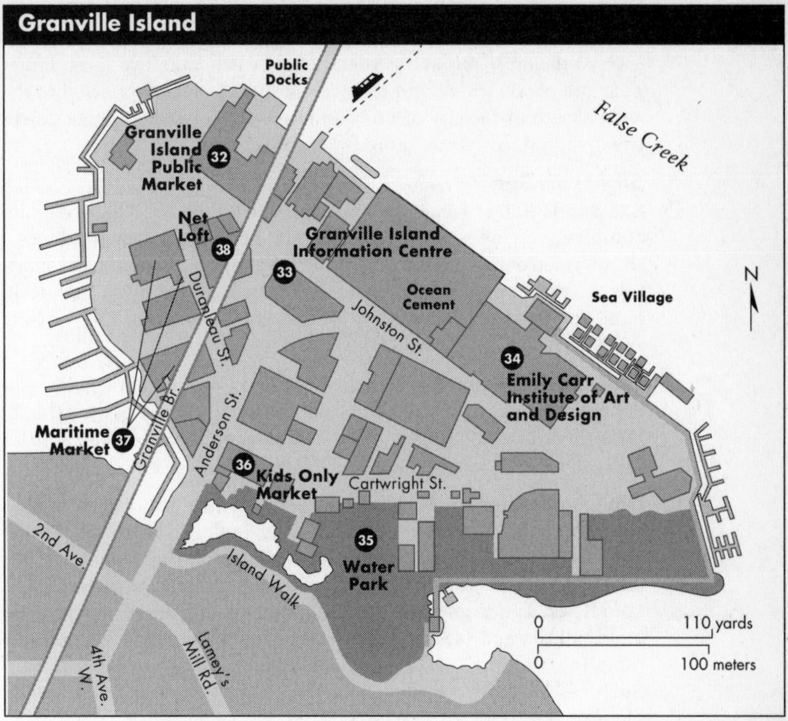
Granville Island
Public Docks
False Creek
Granville Island Public Market 32
Net Loft 38
Granville Island Information Centre
33
Ocean Cement
Sea Village
N
Duranleau St.
Johnston St.
34 Emily Carr Institute of Art and Design
Anderson St.
Granville Br.
Maritime Market 37
36 Kids Only Market
Cartwright St.
2nd Ave.
Island Walk
35 Water Park
0 110 yards
0 100 meters
4th Ave. W.
Lamey's Mill Rd.

**thropology** ㊷. You can pause for a moment of reflection at the **Nitobe Memorial Garden** ㊸, also on campus.

Follow Southwest Marine Drive through the university campus and turn left on 41st Avenue. Turn left again on Oak Street to reach the entrance of the **VanDusen Botanical Garden** ㊹ (it'll be on your left). Return to 41st Avenue, continue farther east, and then turn left on Cambie Street to reach **Queen Elizabeth Park** ㊺, which overlooks the city.

Head back downtown across the Cambie Bridge (stay in the right lane), which flows onto Smithe Street. Turn right onto Homer Street and look for parking in the next few blocks so that you can stop to see **Library Square** ㊻, the city's multimillion-dollar central library project that resembles Rome's Colosseum. From there it's only three more blocks to B.C. Place, where you'll find the **B.C. Sports Hall of Fame and Museum** ㊼. Turn south on Cambie and follow it to Pacific Boulevard (don't cross the Cambie Bridge), which winds east around False Creek and turns into Quebec Street at the head of the creek. Turn right here, and right again into the parking lot of **Science World** ㊽.

From Science World head straight across Quebec to Main Street, turn left, and make a second left at the Georgia Viaduct, which leads onto Dunsmuir. Follow it for eight or so blocks. Turn left onto Howe Street and then right onto Georgia, which winds through town and Stanley Park and across the Lions Gate Bridge to North Vancouver. Follow the signs into the mountains of the North Shore to see the **Capilano Suspension Bridge and Park** ㊾, where a cedar-plank footbridge swings high above the Capilano River. Nearby in the Capilano Regional Park, the **Capilano Salmon Hatchery** ㊿ is another good spot to visit. Up the hill a bit farther, at the end of Nancy Greene Way, is **Grouse Mountain** (51), where a funicular gives you great city views.

TIMING

To cover all the sights of Greater Vancouver, taking sufficient time at each of the museums and gardens, could easily take two days. Either pick and choose those you really want to see, or limit yourself to the sights south of the city one day and save the remaining sights downtown and on the North Shore for another day.

## Sights to See

**47** **B.C. Sports Hall of Fame and Museum.** Part of the B.C. Place Stadium complex, this museum celebrating the province's sports achievers shows video documentaries and has photographs, costumes, and sporting equipment on display. Bring tennis shoes to wear in the high-tech, hands-on participation gallery. ⊠ *B.C. Pl., 777 Pacific Blvd. S, Gate A,* ☎ *604/687–5525.* ☒ *$6.* ☉ *Daily 10–5.*

**50** **Capilano Salmon Hatchery.** In the Capilano Regional Park, the hatchery has viewing areas and exhibits about the life cycle of the salmon. ⊠ *4500 Capilano Park Rd., North Vancouver,* ☎ *604/666–1790.* ☒ *Free.* ☉ *Call for seasonal hrs.*

**49** **Capilano Suspension Bridge and Park.** At this, Vancouver's oldest tourist attraction (the original bridge was built in 1889), you can get a taste of the mountains and test your mettle on the swaying, 450-ft cedar plank suspension bridge that hangs 230 ft above the rushing Capilano River. The amusement park also has viewing decks, nature trails amid tall firs and cedars, a gift shop, a totem-carving shed, and displays for the kids. ⊠ *3735 Capilano Rd., North Vancouver,* ☎ *604/ 987–7474.* ☒ *Call for admission fees.* ☉ *Summer, daily 8–dusk; winter, daily 9–5; call for exact hrs.*

**51** **Grouse Mountain.** The Skyride to the top is a great way to take in stunning city, sea, and mountain vistas. In the theater at the peak you can catch a film on Vancouver's transformation from a string of scattered native, trapper, and logger settlements to a bustling modern metropolis. ⊠ *6400 Nancy Greene Way, North Vancouver,* ☎ *604/984–0661.* ☒ *Ride and theater $15.* ☉ *Call for seasonal hrs.*

**46** **Library Square.** Built to evoke images of the Colosseum in Rome, the spiraling library building, open plazas, frescoed waterfall, and shaded atriums of the new Library Square were completed in 1995. This architectural stunner is a favorite backdrop for movie productions. The book collection is moved about on motorized shelving systems in the ultra-high-tech library that fills the core of the structure; the outer edge of the spiral houses trendy boutiques, coffee shops, and a fine book and gift shop. ⊠ *350 W. Georgia St.,* ☎ *604/331–3600.* ☉ *Mon.– Tues. 10–9, Thurs.–Sat. 10–6; also Oct.–Apr., Sun. 1–5.*

★ **42** **Museum of Anthropology.** The MOA is Vancouver's most spectacular museum, focusing on the arts of the Pacific Northwest natives and aboriginals from around the world, including the works of Bill Reid, Canada's most respected Haida carver. Reid's *The Raven and the First Men,* which took five carvers more than three years to complete, is its centerpiece. Arthur Erickson designed the award-winning structure that houses the museum. In the Great Hall are large and dramatic totem poles, ceremonial archways, and dugout canoes—all adorned with carvings of frogs, eagles, ravens, bears, and salmon. You'll also find exquisite carvings of gold, silver, and argillite (a black stone found in the Queen Charlotte Islands), as well as masks, tools, and costumes from many other cultures. The museum's ceramics wing contains several hundred pieces from 15th- to 19th-century Europe. ⊠ *University of British Columbia, 6393 N.W. Marine Dr.,* ☎ *604/822–5087.* ☒ *$5, free Tues.* ☉ *Tues. 11–9, Wed.–Sun. 11–5.*

# 30%*
# more
# charming.

*(*depending on the exchange rate)*

Air Canada can't take credit for the very generous exchange rate on American currency. But, in all modesty, we do pride ourselves on getting a lot of other things right. *Like more nonstops* between the USA and Canada than any other airline. Not to mention convenient connections to our vast global network. We even offer you your choice of Mileage Plus[®1], OnePass[®2] or our own Aeroplan[®3] miles.

So to say that we are eager to please would be a remarkable understatement. However, this may help to explain why Americans polled by Business Traveler International Magazine declared Air Canada *The Best Airline to Canada*. For the fifth year in a row (wow, thanks guys). And why more people fly Air Canada from the USA to Canada than any other airline. Air Canada. We're like a regular airline, only nicer.

For more details, please call your travel agent or Air Canada at **1-800-776-3000**. For great holiday packages, call **Air Canada's Canada at 1-800-774-8993 (ext. 8045)**. And feel free to visit us on our Internet site at this address: http://www.aircanada.ca

[1]Mileage Plus is a registered trademark of United Airlines. [2]OnePass is a registered trademark of Continental Airlines. [3]Aeroplan is a registered trademark of Air Canada.

*The* **nicer** *way to fly.*

# Pick up the phone.
# Pick up the miles.

**1-800-FLY-FREE**

Now when you sign up with MCI you can receive up to 8,000 bonus frequent flyer miles on one of seven major airlines.

Then earn another 5 miles for every dollar you spend on a variety of MCI services, including MCI Card® calls from virtually anywhere in the world.*

You're going to use these services anyway. Why not rack up the miles while you're doing it?

**Is this a great time, or what? :-)**

**43** **Nitobe Memorial Garden.** This 2½-acre garden is considered the most authentic Japanese garden outside Japan. The circular path around the park symbolizes the cycle of life and provides a tranquil view from every direction. In April and May cherry blossoms are the highlight, and in June the irises are magnificent. ✉ *University of British Columbia, 1903 West Mall,* ☎ *604/822–6038.* 🎫 *$3.* ☉ *Summer, daily 10–6; winter, weekdays 10–3.*

**40** **Pacific Space Centre.** A virtual reality Cyberwalk and a kinetic space-ride simulator are among the interactive exhibits and high-tech learning systems at this fascinating facility that's so advanced it was granted status as a NASA Teacher Resource Center. Films screening at the on-site theater highlight Canada's achievements in space, and astronomy shows take place at the **H. R. MacMillan Planetarium.** If the sky is clear, the half-meter telescope at the **Gordon MacMillan Southam Observatory** is focused on whatever stars or planets are worth watching that night. ✉ *Vanier Park, 1100 Chestnut St.,* ☎ *604/738–7827; 604/738–2855 special-events schedule.* 🎫 *Observatory free, planetarium fee varies.* ☉ *Observatory daily 7 PM–11 PM; planetarium shows daily June–Aug. (times vary), Sept.–May, Tues.–Sun.*

**45** **Queen Elizabeth Park.** Besides views of downtown, the park has lavish gardens brimming with roses and other flowers, an abundance of grassy picnicking spots, and illuminated fountains. In the **Bloedel Conservatory,** you can see tropical and desert plants and 35 species of free-flying tropical birds. Other park facilities include 20 tennis courts, a pitch-and-putt golf course, and a restaurant. ✉ *Cambie St. and 33rd Ave.,* ☎ *604/872–5513.* 🎫 *Conservatory $3.* ☉ *Apr.–Sept., weekdays 9–8, weekends 10–9; Oct.–Mar., daily 10–5.*

**48** **Science World.** In a gigantic shiny dome built over an Omnimax Theater for Expo '86, this hands-on museum encourages visitors to touch and participate in the theme exhibits. The special Search Gallery is aimed at younger children, as are the fun-filled demonstrations given in Center Stage. ✉ *1455 Quebec St.,* ☎ *604/268–6363.* 🎫 *Science World $9, Omnimax $9, combination ticket $12.* ☉ *Weekdays 10–5, weekends 10–6.*

**41** **Vancouver Maritime Museum.** This museum on English Bay traces the history of marine activities on the West Coast. Permanent exhibits depict the port of Vancouver, the fishing industry, and early explorers; the model ships on display are a delight. Traveling exhibits vary but always have a maritime theme. Guided tours are led through the double-masted schooner *St. Roch,* the first ship to sail in both directions through the treacherous Northwest Passage. Restored heritage boats from different cultures are moored behind the museum, and a huge Kwakiutl totem pole stands out front. ✉ *1905 Ogden Ave., north end of Cypress St., also accessible via Granville Island Ferry,* ☎ *604/257–8300.* 🎫 *$5.* ☉ *May–Aug., daily 10–5; Sept.–Apr., Tues.–Sun. 10–5.*

**39** **Vancouver Museum.** Life-size replicas of a trading post, a Victorian parlor, and an 1897 Canadian Pacific Railway passenger car, as well as a real dugout canoe, are the highlights at this museum whose exhibits focus on the city's early history and native art and culture. ✉ *1100 Chestnut St., Vanier Park,* ☎ *604/736–4431.* 🎫 *$5, extra charge for special exhibitions.* ☉ *Summer, daily 10–5; winter, Tues.–Sun. 10–5.*

**44** **VanDusen Botanical Garden.** On what was once a 55-acre golf course grows one of the largest collections of ornamental plants in Canada. Native and exotic plant displays include a shrubbery maze and herb gardens; rhododendrons bloom in May and June. For a bite to eat, stop in Sprinklers Restaurant (☎ 604/261–0011), on the grounds. ⊠ *5251 Oak St., at 37th Ave., ☎ 604/878–9274. ⊠ $5, ½ price Oct.–May. ☉ July–Aug., daily 10–9; Oct.–Apr., daily 10–4; May–June, Sept., daily 10–6.*

# DINING

Vancouver dining is usually fairly informal; casual but neat dress is appropriate everywhere except a few expensive restaurants that require jacket and tie (indicated in the text). *See* the Downtown Vancouver Dining map to locate downtown restaurants and the Greater Vancouver Dining map to locate restaurants in Kitsilano, Granville Island, and other neighborhoods away from downtown.

| CATEGORY | COST* |
|----------|-------|
| $$$$ | over C$40 |
| $$$ | C$30–C$40 |
| $$ | C$20–C$30 |
| $ | under C$20 |

*per person for a three-course meal, excluding drinks, service, and sales tax*

## Downtown

### American

$$  ✕ **Griffin's.** Sunday brunch here is cheerful, energetic, and kid-oriented: A special buffet is chockablock with favorite foods for the younger set. The rest of the week the emphasis is on the adult crowd. This brasserie uniquely blends the charm of old Italy with sophisticated design. Squash-yellow walls, bold black-and-white tiles, and splashy food art keep it lively. The open kitchen prepares inspired cuisine from fresh, regional ingredients, including buffet selections such as convict bread (a round loaf stuffed with goat cheese, olives, tomatoes, and peppers in olive oil), smoked salmon, chicken pasta al pesto, and baked Pacific cod. ⊠ *900 W. Georgia St., ☎ 604/662–1900. Reservations essential. AE, D, DC, MC, V.*

### California

$$  ✕ **Delilah's.** Cherubs dance on the ceiling, candles flicker on the ta-
★   bles, and martini glasses clink in toasts at this incredibly popular restaurant. Under the direction of chef Peg Montgomery, the nouvelle California cuisine is delicious, innovative, and beautifully presented. The menu, which changes seasonally, lets you choose two- or five-course prix-fixe dinners. Try the pancetta, pine nut, Asiago, and mozzarella fritters with sun-dried tomato aioli and the grilled swordfish with blueberry-lemon compote if they're available. Patrons have been known to line up before Delilah's opens for dinner. ⊠ *1739 Comox St., ☎ 604/687–3424. Reservations not accepted. DC, MC, V. No lunch.*

### Chinese

$$–$$$  ✕ **Imperial Chinese Seafood.** This elegant Cantonese restaurant in the
★   art deco Marine Building has two-story floor-to-ceiling windows with stupendous views of Stanley Park and the North Shore mountains across Coal Harbour. Any dish featuring lobster, crab, or shrimp from the live tanks is recommended, as is the dim sum served every day from 11 to 2:30. Portions tend to be small and pricey (especially the abalone, shark's fin, and bird's nest delicacies) but never fail to please. ⊠ *355 Burrard St., ☎ 604/688–8191. Reservations essential. AE, MC, V.*

# Downtown Vancouver Dining

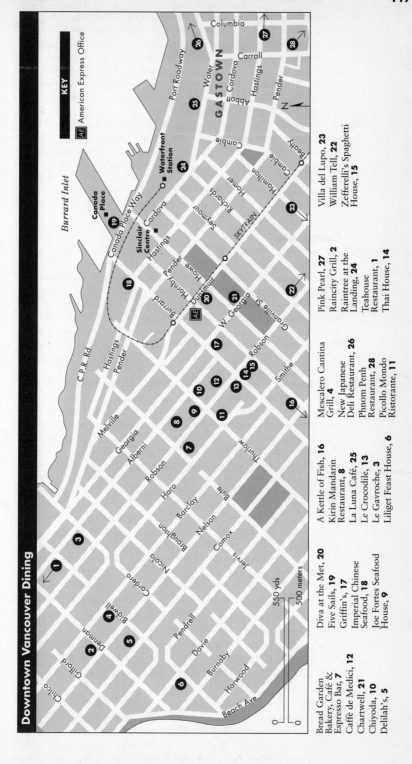

Bread Garden
Bakery, Café &
Espresso Bar, **7**
Caffè de Medici, **12**
Chartwell, **21**
Chiyoda, **10**
Delilah's, **5**

Diva at the Met, **20**
Five Sails, **19**
Griffin's, **17**
Imperial Chinese
Seafood, **18**
Joe Fortes Seafood
House, **9**

A Kettle of Fish, **16**
Kirin Mandarin
Restaurant, **8**
La Luna Café, **25**
Le Crocodile, **13**
Le Gavroche, **3**
Liliget Feast House, **6**

Mescalero Cantina
Grill, **4**
New Japanese
Deli Restaurant, **26**
Phnom Penh
Restaurant, **28**
Picollo Mondo
Ristorante, **11**

Pink Pearl, **27**
Raincity Grill, **2**
Raintree at the
Landing, **24**
Teahouse
Restaurant, **1**
Thai House, **14**

Villa del Lupo, **23**
William Tell, **22**
Zefferelli's Spaghetti
House, **15**

$$ ✕ **Kirin Mandarin Restaurant.** Fish swim in tanks set into the slate-green walls, part of the lavish decorations of this restaurant serving a smattering of northern Chinese cuisines. Dishes include Shanghai-style smoked eel, Peking duck, and Szechuan hot-and-spicy scallops. Kirin is just two blocks from most of the major downtown hotels. A second location at Cambie focuses on milder Cantonese seafood creations. ⊠ *102–1166 Alberni St.,* ☎ *604/682–8833; 555 W. 12th Ave., 2nd floor,* ☎ *604/879–8038. Reservations essential. AE, DC, MC, V.*

$$ ✕ **Pink Pearl.** This noisy, 680-seat Cantonese restaurant has tanks of live seafood—crab, shrimp, geoduck, oysters, abalone, rock cod, lobsters, and scallops. Menu highlights include clams in black-bean sauce, crab sautéed with five spices (a spicy dish sometimes translated as crab with peppery salt), and Pink Pearl's version of crisp-skinned chicken. Arrive early for dim sum on the weekend if you don't want to wait in a long line. ⊠ *1132 E. Hastings St.,* ☎ *604/253–4316. Reservations essential. AE, DC, MC, V.*

## Continental

$$$–$$$$ ✕ **Chartwell.** Named after Sir Winston Churchill's country home (a
   ★   painting of which hangs over the green marble fireplace), the flagship dining room at the Four Seasons hotel (☞ Lodging, *below*) looks like an upper-class British club. Floor-to-ceiling dark wood paneling, deep leather chairs, and a quiet setting make this the city's top spot for a power lunch. The chefs cook robust, inventive Continental food as well as lighter offerings and low-calorie, low-fat entrées. Favorites include tomato basil soup with gin, rack of lamb, and a number of salmon offerings. ⊠ *791 W. Georgia St.,* ☎ *604/844–6715. Reservations essential. Jacket and tie. AE, DC, MC, V.*

$$$–$$$$ ✕ **William Tell.** Silver service plates, embossed linen napkins, and a silver vase on each table set the tone of Swiss luxury in this establishment in the Georgian Court Hotel. Chef Christian Lindner offers excellent sautéed veal sweetbreads with red-onion marmalade and marsala sauce and Swiss specialties such as cheese fondue, pickled herring with apples, and thinly sliced veal with mushrooms in a light white wine sauce. A bar and bistro area caters to a more casual crowd. Reserve in advance for the all-you-can-eat Swiss Farmer's Buffet on Sunday night. ⊠ *765 Beatty St.,* ☎ *604/688–3504. Reservations essential. Jacket and tie. AE, DC, MC, V.*

$$$ ✕ **Teahouse Restaurant.** The best of the Stanley Park restaurants is perfectly poised for watching sunsets over the water, especially from a glassed-in wing that resembles a conservatory. The country French and seafood menu includes cream of carrot soup, lamb with herb crust, and the perfectly grilled fish. ⊠ *7501 Stanley Park Dr., Ferguson Point, Stanley Park,* ☎ *604/669–3281. Reservations essential. AE, MC, V.*

## Deli

$ ✕ **La Luna Café.** This unpretentious bi-level deli in the heart of Gastown serves fragrant coffees and teas and soup-and-salad lunches, but the luscious sourdough cinnamon rolls steal the show. Have one heated and slathered with butter if you plan to eat in at one of the small tables, or get one to go: These rolls are not to be missed! ⊠ *117 Water St.,* ☎ *604/687–5862. AE, MC, V.*

## Eclectic

$$ ✕ **Diva at the Met.** The multitiered restaurant at the Metropolitan Hotel is quickly becoming a local favorite. The innovative nouvelle cuisine served here is as appealing as the Impressionist art adorning the walls. Top creations from the glass-walled kitchen include charred ahi tuna on a warm bean salad with grilled asparagus and red pepper aioli, and veal London broil with foie gras, mushroom risotto, and balsamic re-

duction. The after-theater crowd heads here for dessert: Fresh sorbets, chocolate anise crème brûlée, and Stilton cream cheesecake draw rave reviews. ⊠ *645 Howe St.,* ☎ *604/687–7788. AE, DC, MC, V.*

## French

$$$ ✕ **Le Gavroche.** At this century-old house, a woman dining with a man will be offered a menu without prices. The classic French cooking, lightened—but by no means reduced—to nouvelle cuisine, includes simple dishes such as smoked salmon with blini and sour cream and more complex offerings like grilled veal tenderloin with chanterelles and lobster sauce. The excellent wine list stresses Bordeaux. Tables by the front window have mountain and water views. ⊠ *1616 Alberni St.,* ☎ *604/ 685–3924. Reservations essential. AE, DC, MC, V. No lunch weekends.*

$$ ✕ **Le Crocodile.** In a roomy location off Burrard Street, chef Michael Jacob serves simple food at reasonable prices—innards, a caramel-sweet onion tart, and old standards like duck à l'orange. ⊠ *100–909 Burrard St.,* ☎ *604/669–4298. Reservations essential. AE, DC, MC, V. Closed Sun. No lunch Sat.*

## Italian

$$$ ✕ **Caffè de Medici.** This somewhat formal restaurant has ornate molded ceilings, green-velvet curtains and chair coverings, portraits of the Medici family, and a courtly, peaceful atmosphere. Although an enticing antipasto table sits in the center of the room, consider the *bresaola* (air-dried beef marinated in olive oil, lemon, and pepper) as an appetizer, followed by the rack of lamb entrée in a mint, mustard, and vermouth sauce. ⊠ *1025 Robson St.,* ☎ *604/669–9322. Reservations essential. AE, D, DC, MC, V. No lunch weekends.*

$$$ ✕ **Villa del Lupo.** Ask the top chefs in town where they head for Ital-
★ ian, and Villa del Lupo is the answer more often than not. Country-house decor sets a romantic tone, but come prepared to roll up your sleeves and mop up the sauce with a chunk of crusty bread. Pasta stuffed with roasted duck, veggies, and ricotta cheese; rabbit loin with mushrooms, black olives, and thyme; and braised lamb osso buco in a sauce of tomatoes, red wine, cinnamon, and lemon are favorites here. ⊠ *869 Hamilton St.,* ☎ *604/688–7436. Reservations essential. AE, MC, V. No lunch weekends.*

$$ ✕ **Picollo Mondo Ristorante.** Soft candlelight, bountiful flower arrangements, and fine European antiques create a romantic mood at this intimate northern Italian restaurant on a quiet street one block off Robson. Start with the seafood puff pastry with chive-vermouth cream sauce and follow up with the classic osso buco or the linguine tossed with smoked Alaskan cod, capers, and red onions. The award-winning wine cellar stocks more than 3,000 bottles. ⊠ *850 Thurlow St.,* ☎ *604/ 688–1633. Reservations essential. AE, DC, MC, V. Closed Sun. No lunch Sat.*

$$ ✕ **Zefferelli's Spaghetti House.** As you might guess from the name, spaghetti, penne, fusilli, tortellini, and fettuccine dressed in creative but subtle sauces—from roasted garlic, broccoli, feta cheese, and tomato sauce to traditional meat sauce—play first string at Zefferelli's, but grilled prawns and chicken saltimbocca (with prosciutto and sage in marsala wine) are strong competition. Done up in forest green, mustard, and persimmon, the trendy dining room has an open kitchen at one end and a wall of windows overlooking busy Robson Street at the other. ⊠ *1136 Robson St.,* ☎ *604/687–0655. Reservations essential. AE, DC, MC, V. No lunch weekends.*

## Japanese

**$$**  ✕ **Chiyoda.** The *robata* (grill) bar curves through Chiyoda's main room: On one side are the customers and an array of flat baskets full of the day's offerings; on the other side are the chefs and grills. There are 35 choices of things to grill, from squid, snapper, and oysters to eggplant, mushrooms, onions, and potatoes. The finished dishes, dressed with sake, soy sauce, or *ponzu* (vinegar and soy sauce), are dramatically passed over on the end of a long wooden paddle. ⊠ *200–1050 Alberni St.,* ☎ *604/688–5050. Reservations essential. AE, DC, MC, V. Closed Sun. No lunch Sat.*

**$**  ✕ **New Japanese Deli Restaurant.** The least expensive sushi in town is served in the high-ceilinged main-floor room of a turn-of-the-century building on Powell Street, once the heart of Vancouver's Japantown. The food is especially fresh and good if you can make it an early lunch: sushi rectangles and rolls are made at 11 AM for the 11:30 opening, and there are all-you-can-eat sushi and tempura lunch specials on weekdays. ⊠ *381 Powell St.,* ☎ *604/662–8755. No credit cards. Closed Sun.*

## Mexican/Spanish

**$$–$$$**  ✕ **Mescalero Cantina Grill.** The look and feel here is of Santa Fe, from
**★**  stucco walls and leather chairs inside to a charming greenery-draped patio for open-air dining. Tapas are the main draw—Cajun beef and black bean tostada; panfried blue cornmeal-crusted oysters; roast chicken and chorizo chimichangas; and grilled salmon, asparagus, and goat-cheese burritos—but dinner selections such as blackened red snapper with avocado, corn, black-bean, and vodka salsa with crème fraîche are equally good. The Bandito Brunch on weekends draws a crowd. ⊠ *1215 Bidwell St.,* ☎ *604/669–2399. Reservations essential. AE, MC, V.*

## Pacific Northwest

**$$**  ✕ **Liliget Feast House.** Only a few blocks from English Bay, this downstairs "longhouse" serves the original Northwest Coast cuisine: Bannock bread, baked sweet potato with hazelnuts, alder-grilled salmon, toasted seaweed with rice, steamed fern shoots, barbecued venison, and soapberries for dessert. Try the authentic but odd dish—"oolichan grease"—that's prepared from candlefish. Native music is piped in, and Northwest Coast native masks (for sale) peer from the walls. ⊠ *1724 Davie St.,* ☎ *604/681–7044. Reservations essential. AE, MC, V. No lunch.*

**$$**  ✕ **Raincity Grill.** This West End hot spot across the street from English Bay is a neighborhood favorite. The setting, with candlelit tables, balloon-back chairs, cushioned banquettes, and enormous flower arrangements, is very sophisticated. All the same, it plays second fiddle to a creative weekly menu that highlights the best regional seafood, meats, and produce. Grilled romaine spears are used in the Caesar salad, giving it a delightful smoky flavor. Varying preparations of salmon and duck are usually available, as is at least one vegetarian selection. ⊠ *1193 Denman St.,* ☎ *604/685–7337. Reservations essential. AE, DC, MC, V.*

**$$**  ✕ **Raintree at the Landing.** In a beautifully renovated heritage building in busy Gastown, this spacious restaurant has waterfront views, a local menu, and a wine list with Pacific Northwest vintages. The kitchen, focusing on healthy cuisine, teeters between willfully eccentric and exceedingly simple; it bakes its own bread and makes luxurious soups. Main courses, which change daily, may include salmon and crab gnocchi, smoked Fraser Valley duck breast, and grilled marlin with basil risotto cakes. ✉ *375 Water St.,* ☎ *604/688–5570. Reservations essential. AE, DC, MC, V. No lunch weekends.*

## Pacific Rim

**$$$$** ✕ **Five Sails.** On the fourth floor of the Pan Pacific Hotel, this special-occasion restaurant has a stunning panoramic view of Canada Place, Lions Gate Bridge, and the lights of the north shore across the bay. Austrian chef Ernst Dorfler has a special flair for presentation, from the swan-shape butter served with breads early in the meal to the chocolate ice-cream bonbon served at the end. The broad-reaching, seasonally changing Pacific Rim menu often includes caramelized swordfish, ahi in red Thai curry vinaigrette, terrine of duck, and old favorites like medallions of British Columbia salmon or lamb from Salt Spring Island. ✉ *Pan Pacific Hotel, 300–999 Canada Pl.,* ☎ *604/662–8211. Reservations essential. AE, DC, MC, V. No lunch.*

## Seafood

**$$** ✕ **Joe Fortes Seafood House.** Reserve a table on the second-floor balcony at this Vancouver seafood hot spot to take in the view of the broad
★ wall murals, the mounted blue marlins, and, most especially, the boy-meets-girl scene at the noisy bar downstairs. The signature panfried Cajun oysters, clam and corn fritters, salmon with smoked apple and cider chutney, and seared sea scallops in a sesame and oyster glaze are tasty and filling, but are often overlooked in favor of the reasonably priced blue-plate special. ✉ *777 Thurlow St.,* ☎ *604/669–1940. Reservations essential. AE, D, DC, MC, V.*

**$$** ✕ **A Kettle of Fish.** Since opening in 1979, this family-run restaurant at the northeast end of Burrard Bridge has attracted a strong local following; count on getting top-quality seafood here. The menu varies daily according to market availability, but there are generally 15 kinds of fresh seafood that are either grilled, sautéed, poached, barbecued, or blackened Cajun-style. The British Columbia salmon and the seafood combo plate are always good choices. ✉ *900 Pacific Blvd.,* ☎ *604/ 682–6661. AE, DC, MC, V. No lunch weekends.*

## Southeast Asian

**$** ✕ **Phnom Penh Restaurant.** Part of a small cluster of Southeast Asian
★ shops on the fringes of Chinatown, this eatery has potted plants and framed views of Angkor Wat. The hospitable staff serves unusually robust Vietnamese and Cambodian fare, including crisp, peppery garlic prawns fried in the shell and a salad with sliced warm beef crusted with ground salt and pepper. ✉ *244 E. Georgia St.,* ☎ *604/253–8899; 955 W. Broadway,* ☎ *604/734–8988. AE, MC, V. Closed Tues.*

**$** ✕ **Thai House.** This sun-filled second-floor diner overlooking Robson Street offers a great lunch deal from 11 to 3: For less than $8, patrons feast on a spring roll, soup, salad, rice, and a choice of 18 typical Thai dishes for the main course. The mild, smoky flavor of *kai pad khing* (boneless chicken with ginger, mushroom, and onions) is satisfying, but the tangy Thai garlic chicken is even better. ✉ *1116 Robson St.,* ☎ *604/683–3383. AE, MC, V.*

# Greater Vancouver

## American

**$** ✕ **Isadora's.** Not only does Isadora's offer good coffee and a "West Coast–fresh" menu that ranges from lox and bagels to vegetarian pastas and seafood platters, but it also has children's specials (the pizzas come with faces here) and an inside play area packed with toys. In summer the restaurant opens onto Granville Island's water park. Service can be slow, but the staff is friendly. The restaurant is no-smok-

# Greater Vancouver Dining

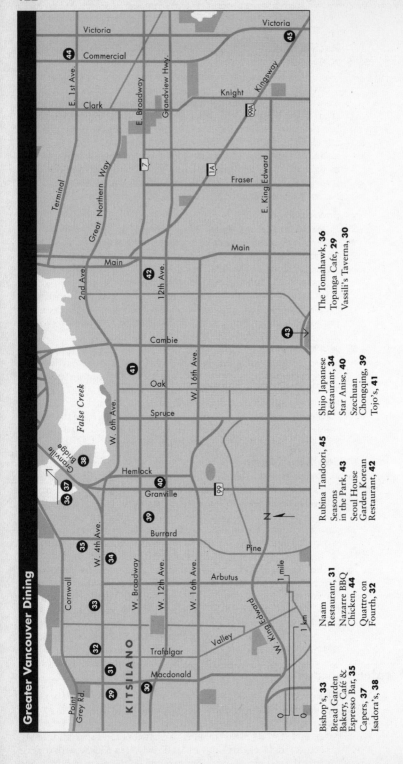

Bishop's, **33**
Bread Garden Bakery, Café & Espresso Bar, **35**
Capers, **37**
Isadora's, **38**

Naam Restaurant, **31**
Nazarre BBQ Chicken, **44**
Quattro on Fourth, **32**

Rubina Tandoori, **45**
Seasons in the Park, **43**
Seoul House Garden Korean Restaurant, **42**

Shijo Japanese Restaurant, **34**
Star Anise, **40**
Szechuan Chongqing, **39**
Tojo's, **41**

The Tomahawk, **36**
Topanga Cafe, **29**
Vassili's Taverna, **30**

ing. Vegan dishes (prepared without animal products) are available on request. ⊠ *1540 Old Bridge St., Granville Island,* ☎ *604/681–8816. DC, MC, V. No dinner Mon. Sept.–May.*

$ ✕ **Nazarre BBQ Chicken.** The best barbecued chicken in town comes from this funky storefront on Commercial Avenue in the Little Italy neighborhood. Owner Gerry Moutal massages his chickens for tenderness before he puts them on the rotisserie and bastes them with a mixture of rum and spices. Chicken comes with roasted potatoes and a choice of mild, hot, or extra spicy garlic sauce. You can eat in, at one of four rickety tables, but the service can be surly at times; we recommend takeout. ⊠ *1859 Commercial Dr.,* ☎ *604/251–1844. Reservations not accepted. No credit cards.*

## Bakery

$ ✕ **Bread Garden Bakery, Café & Espresso Bar.** Once a croissant bakery, this is now the ultimate Kitsilano 24-hour hangout. Salads, quiches, elaborate cakes and pies, giant muffins, and cappuccino draw a steady stream of the young and fashionable. The wait in line may be long here or at any of its other locations. Reports indicate that quality has suffered with the rapid expansion, but the Garden's following is still strong. ⊠ *1880 W. 1st Ave., Kitsilano,* ☎ *604/738–6684;* ⊠ *2996 Granville St.,* ☎ *604/736–6465;* ⊠ *812 Bute St.,* ☎ *604/688–3213. AE, MC, V.*

## Chinese

$ ✕ **Szechuan Chongqing.** At this unpretentious, white-tablecloth restaurant, try the Szechuan-style crunchy green beans tossed with garlic or the Chongqing chicken—a boneless chicken served on a bed of spinach cooked in dry heat until crisp, giving it the texture of dried seaweed and a salty, rich, and nutty taste. ⊠ *1668 W. Broadway,* ☎ *604/734– 1668. Reservations essential. AE, MC, V.*

## Continental

$$$ ✕ **Seasons in the Park.** Seasons, in Queen Elizabeth Park, has a commanding view over gardens to the city lights and the mountains beyond. A comfortable room with light wood and white tablecloths sets the mood for conservative Continental standards like grilled salmon with fresh mint and roast duck with sun-dried cranberry sauce. Weekend brunch is popular. ⊠ *Queen Elizabeth Park, 33rd and Cambie St.,* ☎ *604/874–8008. Reservations essential. AE, MC, V.*

## East Indian

$$ ✕ **Rubina Tandoori.** For the best East Indian food in the city, try Ru-
★ bina Tandoori, 20 minutes from downtown. The large menu spans most of the subcontinent's cuisines, and the especially popular *chevda* (an East Indian salty snack) is shipped to fans all over North America. Nonsmokers sit in the smaller, funkier back room with paintings of coupling gods and goddesses; smokers dine in the slightly more subdued front room. ⊠ *1962 Kingsway,* ☎ *604/874–3621. Reservations essential. DC, MC, V. Closed Sun.*

## Greek

$$ ✕ **Vassili's Taverna.** The menu in this family-run restaurant in the heart of the city's small Greek community is almost as conventional as the decor: checked tablecloths and mandatory paintings of fishing villages and the blue Aegean Sea. At Vassili's, though, even standards become memorable because of the flawless preparation. The house specialty is a deceptively simple *kotopoulo* (a half chicken, pounded flat, herbed, and charbroiled). ⊠ *2884 W. Broadway,* ☎ *604/733–3231. Reservations essential. AE, DC, MC, V. Closed Mon. No lunch weekends.*

## Health Food

**$** ✕ **Capers.** Hidden in the back of the most lavish health food store in
**★** the Lower Mainland, Capers drips with earth-mother chic: wood tables, potted plants, and heady aromas from the store's bakery. Breakfast starts at 8: bacon (with no additives) and eggs (from free-range
chickens), or featherlight blueberry pancakes. Top choices from the lunch
and dinner menu include roasted squash soup and local mushrooms
with *capellini* (thin pasta). The newer 4th Avenue location, with its dining room above the store, is by far the nicer of the two; the West Vancouver store is somewhat old and dingy. ⊠ *2496 Marine Dr., West
Vancouver, ☎ 604/925–3374; 2285 W. 4th Ave., ☎ 604/739–6685.
MC, V. No dinner Sun. at Marine Dr.*

**$** ✕ **Naam Restaurant.** Vancouver's oldest organic eatery is open 24 hours,
so if you need to satisfy a late-night tofu-burger craving, rest easy. The
Naam also serves wine, beer, cappuccino, fresh juices, and wicked
chocolate desserts, along with vegetarian stir-fries. Wood tables and
kitchen chairs help create a homey atmosphere. On warm summer
evenings, try the outdoor courtyard at the back of the restaurant. ⊠
*2724 W. 4th Ave., ☎ 604/738–7151. MC, V.*

## Italian

**$$** ✕ **Quattro on Fourth.** This northern Italian restaurant in Kitsilano
shot to stardom quickly. A mosaic floor, mustard-color walls with stark-
green-and-mauve-stenciled borders, cherry-stained tables, and a
wraparound covered porch for alfresco dining enhance the Mediter-
ranean atmosphere. Mushroom lovers usually jump at the truffle fet-
tuccine, but if you can't make up your mind, there's the antipasto platter
and *combinazione* (a plate for two with the five most popular pastas
and sauces). The gelato trio is a perfect topper. ⊠ *2611 W. 4th Ave.,
☎ 604/734–4444. Reservations essential. AE, DC, MC, V. No lunch.*

## Japanese

**$$$** ✕ **Tojo's.** Hidekazu Tojo is a sushi-making legend here, with more than
**★** 2,000 preparations tucked away in his creative mind. His handsome
blond-wood tatami rooms, on the second floor of a modern green-glass
tower on West Broadway, provide the proper ambience for intimate
dining, but Tojo's 10-seat sushi bar stands as the centerpiece. With Tojo
presiding, it offers a convivial ringside seat for watching the creation
of edible art. Although tempura and teriyaki dinners will satisfy, the
seasonal menu is more exciting. In fall, ask for *dobin mushi,* a soup
made from pine mushrooms. In spring, try salad made from scallops
and pink cherry blossoms. ⊠ *202–777 W. Broadway, ☎ 604/872–
8050. Reservations essential. AE, DC, MC, V. Closed Sun. No lunch.*

**$$** ✕ **Shijo Japanese Restaurant.** Shijo has an excellent and very large sushi
bar, a smaller robata bar, tatami rooms, and a row of tables overlooking
4th Avenue. The epitome of modern urban Japanese chic is conveyed
through the jazz music, handsome lamps with a bronze finish, and lots
of black wood. Count on creatively prepared sushi in generous pro-
portions, eggplant *dengaku* (topped with light and dark miso paste and
broiled), and shiitake foil *yaki* (fresh shiitake mushrooms cooked in
foil with lemony ponzu sauce). ⊠ *1926 W. 4th Ave., ☎ 604/732–4676.
Reservations essential. AE, DC, MC, V. No lunch weekends.*

## Korean

**$** ✕ **Seoul House Garden Korean Restaurant.** This bright restaurant, dec-
orated in Japanese style, serves a full menu of Japanese and Korean
food, including sushi. The best bet is the Korean barbecue, which you
cook at your table; the dinner of marinated beef, pork, chicken, or fish
comes complete with a half dozen side dishes—kimchi, salads, stir-fried
rice, and pickled vegetables—as well as soup and rice. Service can be

chaotic. ⊠ *36 E. Broadway,* ☎ *604/874–4131. Reservations essential. MC, V. No lunch Sun.*

### Mexican

$ ✕ **Topanga Cafe.** Arrive before 6:30 or after 8 PM to avoid waiting in line for this 40-seat Kitsilano classic. The Tex-Mex food hasn't changed much since 1978, when the Topanga started dishing up fresh salsa and homemade tortilla chips. Quantities are still huge and prices low. Kids can color blank menu covers while waiting for food; one hundred of their best efforts are framed on the walls. ⊠ *2904 W. 4th Ave.,* ☎ *604/ 733–3713. Reservations not accepted. MC, V. Closed Sun.*

### Pacific Northwest

$$$–$$$$ ✕ **Bishop's.** John Bishop established this restaurant as a favorite in 1985 by serving West Coast Continental cuisine with an emphasis on British Columbia seafood. The seasonal menu might include medallions of venison, smoked Alaskan black cod, seared lamb loin, roast rabbit leg, or linguine tossed with fresh acorn squash. The small white rooms—their only ornament some splashy expressionistic paintings—are favored by Pierre Trudeau, Robert De Niro, and other celebrity patrons. ⊠ *2183 W. 4th Ave.,* ☎ *604/738–2025. Reservations essential. AE, DC, MC, V. Closed 1st wk in Jan. No lunch.*

$ ✕ **The Tomahawk.** North Vancouver was mostly trees in 1926, when the Tomahawk first opened. Over the years, the original hamburger stand grew and mutated into part Northwest Coast native kitsch museum, part gift shop, and part restaurant. Renowned for its Yukon breakfast—five slices of back bacon, two eggs, hash browns, and toast—the Tomahawk also serves gigantic muffins, excellent French toast, and pancakes. At lunch and dinner, the menu switches to oysters, trout, and burgers named for native chiefs. ⊠ *1550 Philip Ave.,* ☎ *604/988–2612. AE, MC, V.*

### Pacific Rim

$$$ ✕ **Star Anise.** When Sammy Lalji left the highly regarded Bishop's (☞
★ *above*) to open his own restaurant, he built a faithful following in record time. His superior skills in attentive service, imaginative presentation, and excellent preparation of Pacific Rim cuisine with French flair shine in this intimate, no-smoking location just off Granville. Don't miss the crab and shrimp sausage on wilted spinach salad or the grilled enoki mushrooms with tomato risotto; the juniper-marinated venison with raspberry vinegar and crème fraîche is another fine choice. ⊠ *1485 W. 12th Ave.,* ☎ *604/737–1485. Reservations essential. AE, D, DC, MC, V. No lunch weekends.*

# LODGING

Vancouver hotels, especially the more expensive properties downtown, are fairly comparable in facilities. Unless otherwise noted, expect to find the following amenities: minibars, in-room movies, no-smoking rooms/floors, room service, massage, exercise room, baby-sitting, laundry service and dry cleaning, concierge, business services, meeting rooms, and parking (for which there is usually an additional fee). Lodgings in the moderate to inexpensive category do not generally offer much in the way of amenities (no in-room minibar, restaurant, room service, pool, exercise room, and so on).

| CATEGORY | COST* |
|----------|-------|
| $$$$ | over C$300 |
| $$$ | C$200–C$300 |
| $$ | C$125–C$200 |
| $ | under C$125 |

*All prices are for a standard double room for two, excluding 10% provincial accommodation tax, 15% service charge, and 7% GST.*

**$$$$**    🖾 **Four Seasons.** This 28-story hotel adjacent to the Vancouver Stock Exchange is attached to the Pacific Centre shopping mall. Standard rooms are average in size and comforts; roomier corner rooms are recommended. Service at this luxury property is top notch, and the attention to detail is outstanding. The formal dining room, Chartwell (☞ Dining, *above*), is one of the best in the city. Even pets receive red-carpet treatment here—they're served Evian and pet treats in silver bowls. ⊠ *791 W. Georgia St., V6C 2T4,* ☎ *604/689–9333, 800/268–6282 in Canada, 800/332–3442 in the U.S.,* ㏌ *604/844–6744. 274 rooms, 111 suites. 2 dining rooms, bar, lobby lounge, indoor-outdoor pool, hot tub, sauna, aerobics, shops, piano. AE, DC, MC, V.*

**$$$$**    🖾 **Hyatt Regency.** The standard rooms of this 34-story hotel are spacious and decorated in deep, dramatic colors and dark wood; all are equipped with irons and boards, coffeemakers, bathrobes, and voice mail. Ask for a corner room with a balcony on the north or west side for the best view. Automated check-in service (via a kiosk) is available in the bustling lobby. For a small fee, the Regency Club gives you the exclusivity of a floor accessed by keyed elevators; your own concierge; a private lounge; and complimentary breakfast. ⊠ *655 Burrard St., V6C 2R7,* ☎ *604/683–1234 or 800/233–1234,* ㏌ *604/689–3707. 612 rooms, 34 suites. Restaurant, 2 bars, café, in-room modem lines, in-room safes, pool, sauna, shops, children's programs (ages 6–12), travel services, car rental. AE, D, DC, MC, V.*

**$$$$**    🖾 **Pan Pacific Hotel.** Sprawling Canada Place, on a pier right by the financial district, houses the luxurious Pan Pacific, the Vancouver Trade and Convention Centre, and a cruise-ship terminal. The hotel's three-story atrium lobby has a dramatic totem pole and waterfall, and the lounge, restaurant, and café all have huge expanses of glass with views of the harbor and mountains. Earth tones and varied textures give the rooms an understated elegance. Corner rooms overlooking the harbor are favorites. ⊠ *300–999 Canada Pl., V6C 3B5,* ☎ *604/662–8111, 800/663–1515 in Canada, 800/937–1515 in the U.S.,* ㏌ *604/685–8690. 467 rooms, 39 suites. 3 restaurants, coffee shop, lobby lounge, in-room modem lines, in-room safes, in-room VCRs, pool, barbershop, beauty salon, hot tubs, saunas, steam rooms, aerobics, health club, indoor track, paddle tennis, racquetball, squash, shops, convention center, travel services. AE, DC, MC, V.*

**$$$$**    🖾 **Sutton Place.** The feel here is more exclusive guest house than large
**★**    hotel: The lobby has sumptuously thick carpets, enormous displays of flowers, and European furniture. The rooms are furnished with rich, dark woods reminiscent of 19th-century France. Despite its size, this hotel maintains a significant level of intimacy and exclusivity. The Fleuri Restaurant serves a great Sunday brunch; Le Club, a fine Continental restaurant, is for special occasions. Le Grande Residence, a luxury apartment hotel suitable for extended stays, adjoins the hotel. ⊠ *845 Burrard St., V6Z 2K6,* ☎ *604/682–5511 or 800/961–7555,* ㏌ *604/682–5513. 350 rooms, 47 suites. Restaurant, bar, café, lobby lounge, kitchenettes, indoor pool, beauty salon, sauna, spa, steam room, health club, bicycles, piano. AE, D, DC, MC, V.*

# Vancouver Lodging

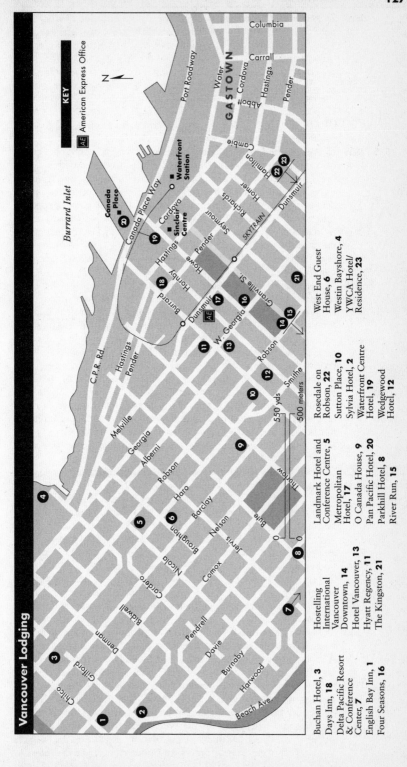

**KEY**

AE American Express Office

N

Burrard Inlet

GASTOWN

Columbia
Carrall
Water
Cordova
Hastings
Pender
Abbott
Cambie
Hamilton
Homer
Richards
Seymour
Howe
Hornby
Burrard
Melville
Georgia
Alberni
Robson
Haro
Barclay
Nelson
Comox
Pendrell
Davie
Burnaby
Harwood
Beach Ave.
Chilco
Gilford
Denman
Bidwell
Cardero
Nicola
Broughton
Jervis
Bute
Thurlow
Smithe
Granville St.
Dunsmuir
W. Georgia
Robson
SKYTRAIN
Pender
Hastings
Cordova
Canada Place Way
Canada Place
Waterfront Station
Sinclair Centre
Port Roadway
C.P.R. Rd.

550 yds
500 meters

---

Buchan Hotel, **3**
Days Inn, **18**
Delta Pacific Resort & Conference Center, **7**
English Bay Inn, **1**
Four Seasons, **16**

Hostelling International Vancouver Downtown, **14**
Hotel Vancouver, **13**
Hyatt Regency, **21**
The Kingston, **21**

Landmark Hotel and Conference Centre, **5**
Metropolitan Hotel, **17**
O Canada House, **9**
Pan Pacific Hotel, **20**
Parkhill Hotel, **8**
River Run, **15**

Rosedale on Robson, **22**
Sutton Place, **10**
Sylvia Hotel, **2**
Waterfront Centre Hotel, **19**
Wedgewood Hotel, **12**

West End Guest House, **6**
Westin Bayshore, **4**
YWCA Hotel/Residence, **23**

**$$$$** ⊡ **Waterfront Centre Hotel.** Dramatically elegant, the 23-story glass
★ hotel opened in 1991 across from Canada Place, which can be reached
from the hotel by an underground walkway. Views from the caramel-
color lobby and 70% of the guest rooms are of Burrard Inlet. The rooms
are attractively furnished with contemporary artworks; armoires con-
ceal the TV. Large corner rooms have the best views. A string quartet
entertains in the lobby restaurant, Herons, during Sunday brunch. ⊠
*900 Canada Pl. Way, V6C 3L5,* ☎ *604/691–1991 or 800/441–1414,*
℻ *604/691–1999. 460 rooms, 29 suites. Restaurant, pool, steam
room, shops, travel services, car rental. AE, D, DC, MC, V.*

**$$$–$$$$** ⊡ **Wedgewood Hotel.** An owner who cares fervently about her guests
★ runs this small hotel whose intimate lobby is decorated with polished
brass, beveled glass, a fireplace, tasteful artworks, and fine antiques.
Expect all the extra touches: nightly turndown service, afternoon ice
delivery, flowers on the balcony, robes, and a morning newspaper. No
tour groups or conventions stop here; the Wedgewood's clients are al-
most exclusively corporate, except on weekends, when the place turns
into a couples' retreat. ⊠ *845 Hornby St., V6Z 1V1,* ☎ *604/689–7777
or 800/663–0666,* ℻ *604/608–5348. 59 rooms, 34 suites. Restaurant,
bar, in-room safes, sauna, piano, travel services. AE, D, DC, MC, V.*

**$$$** ⊡ **Delta Pacific Resort & Conference Center.** Its facilities are what make
this property on 14 acres a resort: swimming pools (one indoor, with
a three-story tubular water slide), tennis courts with a pro, an outdoor
fitness circuit, aqua-exercise classes, outdoor volleyball nets, a play center and summer camps for children, and a playground. In spite of the
hotel's size, the atmosphere is casual and friendly. Guest rooms are modern, with contemporary decor and a pleasant blue and green color
scheme. ⊠ *10251 St. Edwards Dr., Richmond V6X 2M9,* ☎ *604/278–
9611, 800/268–1133 in Canada, 800/877–1133 in the U.S.,* ℻ *604/
276–1121. 453 rooms, 5 suites. 2 restaurants, lobby lounge, in-room
modem lines, indoor pool, 2 outdoor pools, barbershop, beauty salon,
hot tub, saunas, putting green, squash, bicycles, children's programs
(ages 5–12), convention center, travel services, car rental, free parking. AE, DC, MC, V.*

**$$$** ⊡ **Hotel Vancouver.** The copper roof of this grand château-style hotel
★ dominates Vancouver's skyline. Opened in 1939 by the Canadian Na-
tional Railway, the hotel commands a regal position in the center of
town. Even the standard guest rooms have an air of prestige, with ma-
hogany furniture, attractive linens, and the original, deep bathtubs. Suites,
with French doors and graceful wing-back chairs, take up two floors
and come with extra services and amenities. Afternoon tea in the lobby
lounge is a real treat. ⊠ *900 W. Georgia St., V6C 2W6,* ☎ *604/684–
3131 or 800/441–1414,* ℻ *604/662–1937. 504 rooms, 46 suites. 3
restaurants, lobby lounge, in-room modem lines, indoor lap pool, hot
tub, spa, steam rooms, shops, piano, travel services, car rental. AE, D,
DC, MC, V.*

**$$$** ⊡ **Metropolitan Hotel.** This 18-story hotel built in 1984 by the Hong
Kong Mandarin chain is now a member of the Preferred Hotels group.
Although the rates went down, the surroundings were improved during 1996 renovations: The lobby, still restrained and tasteful, now has
a view of the hotel's new restaurant, Diva at the Met (☞ Dining, *above*),
through an etched-glass wall. A slight Asian theme touches the rich dark-
mahogany furnishings. Standard rooms are surprisingly spacious and
have narrow balconies, but the even bigger studio suites are only
slightly more expensive than a standard room. Rooms on the business
floor have in-room faxes, printers, and modem lines. ⊠ *645 Howe St.,
V6C 2Y9,* ☎ *604/687–1122 or 800/667–2300,* ℻ *604/689–7044.*

*179 rooms, 18 suites. Restaurant, bar, indoor lap pool, men's steam room, racquetball, squash. AE, DC, MC, V.*

$$$ &#9974; **Westin Bayshore.** The Bayshore, perched right on the best part of the harbor adjacent to Stanley Park, has truly fabulous views. It's the perfect place to stay in summer, especially for a family, because of its huge outdoor pool, sundeck, grassy areas, and extensive recreational facilities. The tower rooms have the best views of the water. &#9993; *1601 W. Georgia St., V6G 2V4,* &#9742; *604/682–3377 or 800/228–3000,* &#70;&#65;&#88; *604/687–3102. 484 rooms, 33 suites. Restaurant, café, 2 bars, indoor pool, outdoor pool, barbershop, beauty salon, steam rooms, boating, fishing, bicycles, billiards, piano, travel services, airport shuttle, car rental. AE, D, DC, MC, V.*

$$–$$$ &#9974; **Parkhill Hotel.** Cool pastel shades echo the colors of the Impressionist prints decorating the surprisingly spacious rooms in this West End hotel just a block from the seawall and sandy Sunset Beach. Large, comfortable sitting areas, half-moon balconies with city or bay views, minirefrigerators, hair dryers, and complimentary downtown shuttle services are part of the package. &#9993; *1160 Davie St., V6E 1N1,* &#9742; *604/685–1311 or 800/663–1525,* &#70;&#65;&#88; *604/681–0208. 191 rooms. 2 restaurants, lounge, in-room safes, pool, sauna, travel services, car rental. AE, D, DC, MC, V.*

$$–$$$ &#9974; **Rosedale on Robson.** If you plan to be in town a while and want
★ to keep expenses down by doing some of your own cooking, look into a room at the all-suite Rosedale on Robson. Rooms in shades of peach and light green are generous in size and have European kitchens, bleached hemlock furniture, and garden patios or balconies overlooking the city. Rooms on upper floors on the north side have views of Coal Harbour. You'll find charming gardens with strolling paths on the second and third floors of the complex. &#9993; *838 Hamilton St., V6B 5W4,* &#9742; *604/689–8033 or 800/661–8870,* &#70;&#65;&#88; *604/689–4426. 275 suites. Restaurant, bar, kitchenettes, refrigerators, room service, indoor lap pool, hot tub, sauna, steam room, coin laundry. AE, DC, MC, V.*

$$ &#9974; **English Bay Inn.** This renovated 1930s Tudor house is one block from
★ the ocean and Stanley Park. The guest rooms have wonderful sleigh beds (in all but one room) with matching armoires and Ralph Lauren linens. The common areas of this no-smoking inn are furnished with museum-quality antiques: The sophisticated but cozy parlor has wing-back chairs, a fireplace, a gilt Louis XIV clock and candelabra, and French doors overlooking the front garden. Breakfast is served in a rather formal room with a Gothic dining room suite, a fireplace, and a 17th-century grandfather clock. &#9993; *1968 Comox St., V6G 1R4,* &#9742; *604/683–8002. 4 rooms, 1 suite. Free parking. AE, MC, V.*

$$ &#9974; **Landmark Hotel and Conference Center.** The towering Landmark is still the tallest hotel (42 stories) in downtown Vancouver and contains some of the prettiest guest rooms in town. The bold jewel tones (emerald, sapphire, and ruby) of paintings by British Columbia's beloved Emily Carr (whose works hang in every room) are repeated on walls and furnishings. All rooms enjoy a fine view, but the Cloud Nine revolving restaurant on the top floor is a great place for an unobstructed view of Vancouver over an early breakfast buffet (in summer only); go elsewhere for dinner. &#9993; *1400 Robson St., V6G 1B9,* &#9742; *604/687–0511 or 800/325–3535,* &#70;&#65;&#88; *604/687–2801. 351 rooms, 7 suites. Restaurant, café, sports bar, saunas, travel services. AE, DC, MC, V.*

$$ &#9974; **O Canada House.** New to the growing list of bed-and-breakfasts in Vancouver, O Canada House is a beautifully restored 1897 Victorian oozing with period charm inside and out. Each bedroom is fairly spacious and appointed in late-Victorian antiques; modern touches, including a TV with VCR, a refrigerator, and a phone, are discreetly tucked out

of sight. Guests often gather in the evening near the fireplace in the front parlor and assemble again in the morning in the formal dining room for a gourmet breakfast—though breakfast served on the wraparound porch is also an option. ✉ *1114 Barclay St., V6E 1H1,* ☎ *604/688–0555,* FAX *604/488–0556. 5 rooms. Free parking. AE, MC, V.*

**\$\$**  ☷ **West End Guest House.** This Victorian house, built in 1906, is a true
**★**  "painted lady," from its front parlor, cozy fireplace, and early 1900s furniture to its green-trimmed pink exterior. Most of the small but handsome rooms have high brass beds, antiques, and gorgeous linens. The basement suite has a gas fireplace in the sitting area and a side garden view. The inn's genial host, Evan Penner, adds small touches such as a pre-dinner glass of sherry, duvets and feather mattress pads, terry bathrobes, and turndown service. The inn is in a residential neighborhood two minutes from Robson Street. Room rates at this no-smoking establishment include a full breakfast. ✉ *1362 Haro St., V6E 1G2,* ☎ *604/681–2889,* FAX *604/688–8812. 7 rooms. Bicycles, free parking. AE, D, MC, V.*

**\$–\$\$**  ☷ **Days Inn.** Business travelers looking for a bargain will find this location convenient. The six-story hotel, which opened as the Abbotsford in 1920, is the only moderately priced hotel in the business core. Recent renovations of the guest rooms and the lobby have made it even more agreeable. Rooms are bright, clean, and utilitarian; standard units are large, but there is no room service and few amenities. Suites 310, 410, 510, and 610 have a harbor view. ✉ *921 W. Pender St., V6C 1M2,* ☎ *604/681–4335,* FAX *604/681–7808. 74 rooms, 11 suites. Restaurant, 2 bars, in-room safes, billiards, coin laundry, free off-site parking. AE, D, DC, MC, V.*

**\$–\$\$**  ☷ **River Run.** This unique bed-and-breakfast inn rests in the serene Fraser River delta in the village of Ladner, 30 minutes drive south of downtown Vancouver and 10 minutes north of the ferries to Vancouver Island. You can choose among a little gem of a floating house; a room in the owner's larger floating home; a net loft (complete with Japanese soaking tub on the deck and a cozy captain's bed tucked away in the rafters); and a river's-edge cottage with a two-person whirlpool tub, full kitchen, fireplace, and deck. A canoe and a kayak are available to guests. Afternoon refreshments and breakfast are included in the tariff at this no-smoking inn. ✉ *4551 River Rd. W, Ladner V4K 1R9,* ☎ *604/946–7778,* FAX *604/940–1970. 1 room, 3 suites. Kitchenettes, bicycles, free parking. MC, V.*

**\$**  ☷ **Buchan Hotel.** This three-story 1930s building is conveniently set in a tree-lined residential street a block from Stanley Park. For the budget price, you rent tiny, institutional rooms with very basic furnishings, ceiling fans, and color TV, but no telephone or air-conditioning. There's also a TV lounge, a public telephone, and storage for bikes and skis. The pension-style rooms with shared bath down the hall are perhaps the most affordable accommodations in downtown. This is a no-smoking hotel. ✉ *1906 Haro St., V6G 1H7,* ☎ *604/685–5354 or 800/668–6654,* FAX *604/685–5367. 60 rooms, 30 with bath. Coin laundry. AE, DC, MC, V.*

**\$**  ☷ **Hostelling International Vancouver Downtown.** Vancouver's newest
**★**  hostel, conveniently located in the West End, is just blocks from Sunset Beach on English Bay, within walking distance of Stanley Park and a quick ferry ride to Granville Island. The hostel itself is tidy and secure; access to the wings of private rooms and the men's and women's dorms requires a card key. Amenities include a shared kitchen and dining room, a TV room, a garden patio and rooftop garden, a games room, and storage for luggage and bikes. The staff here is extremely friendly and informative, and the low price can't be beat. ✉ *1114 Burnaby St.,*

*V6E 1P1,* ☎ *604/684–4565,* FAX *604/684–4540. 23 rooms, 7 with private bath, 224 dormitory beds. Dining room, no-smoking floors, bicycles, library, coin laundry.*

$ ☎ **The Kingston.** The Kingston is a small budget hotel convenient to shopping. It's an old-style, four-story building, with no elevator—the type of establishment you'd find in Europe. The spartan rooms are small and immaculate and share a bathroom down the hall. All rooms have phones and a few have TVs and private baths. Rooms on the south side are sunnier. The room rate includes a Continental breakfast. ⊠ *757 Richards St., V6B 3A6,* ☎ *604/684–9024,* FAX *604/684–9917. 56 rooms, 8 with bath. Sauna, coin laundry, free overnight parking (fee during day). AE, MC, V.*

$ ☎ **Sylvia Hotel.** To stay at the Sylvia Hotel from June through August you'll need to book six months to a year ahead. This older, ivy-covered hotel is popular because of its low rates and near-perfect location: about 25 ft from the beach on scenic English Bay, 200 ft from Stanley Park, and a 20-minute walk from Robson Street. The unadorned rooms have worn, plain furnishings. Suites are huge, and all have kitchens. ⊠ *1154 Gilford St., V6G 2P6,* ☎ *604/681–9321. 97 rooms, 18 suites. 2 restaurants, lounge, laundry service, dry cleaning. AE, DC, MC, V.*

$ ☎ **YWCA Hotel/Residence.** A secured 12-story building in the heart of
★ the entertainment district, the YWCA has bright, airy, and very comfortable rooms. All have cheery floral bedspreads, white laminated nightstands and desks, minirefrigerators, and phones. Some have sinks and share a bath down the hall, others share adjacent baths, and still others have private baths. The hotel is open to men and women and offers discounts for seniors, students, and YWCA members. ⊠ *733 Beatty St., V6B 2M4,* ☎ *604/895–5830, 800/663–1424 in British Columbia and Alberta,* FAX *604/681–2550. 155 rooms, 30 with private bath. No-smoking floors, refrigerators, coin laundries, meeting rooms. MC, V.*

# NIGHTLIFE AND THE ARTS

For **information on events,** pick up a free copy of the *Georgia Straight* (available at cafés and bookstores around town), or look in the entertainment section of the *Vancouver Sun* (Thursday's paper has listings in the "What's On" column). Call the **Arts Hotline** (☎ 604/ 684–2787) for the latest lineups in entertainment. For tickets, book through **Ticketmaster** (☎ 604/280–3311).

## Nightlife

### Bars and Lounges

DOWNTOWN

The **Bacchus Lounge** (⊠ Wedgewood Hotel, 845 Hornby St., ☎ 604/ 689–7777) is stylish and chic, with a pianist providing soothing background music. The **Garden Lounge** (⊠ Four Seasons, 791 W. Georgia St., ☎ 604/689–9333) is bright and airy with African flora and a waterfall, plus big soft chairs you won't want to get out of; a pianist plays here on the weekends. The **Gérard Lounge** (⊠ Sutton Place Hotel, 845 Burrard St., ☎ 604/682–5511), a major film-industry hangout, is probably the nicest in the city because of its fireplaces, wing-back chairs, dark wood, and leather. The sophisticated lobby bar at the **Hotel Vancouver** (⊠ 900 W. Georgia St., ☎ 604/684–3131) is the place to see and be seen; musicians perform live in the evenings from 4 PM, and 55 wines are available by the glass.

One of the city's "hot" pool halls is the **Automotive Billiards Club** (⊠ 1095 Homer St., ☎ 604/682–0040). For a lively atmosphere, try **Joe**

**Fortes** (⊠ 777 Thurlow St., ☎ 604/669–1940), known in town as the local "meet market." The **Soho Café and Billiards** (⊠ 1144 Homer St., ☎ 604/688–1180) is the place to go to sip and shoot.

GRANVILLE ISLAND

The **Backstage Lounge** (⊠ 1585 Johnston St., ☎ 604/687–1354), behind the main stage at the Arts Club Theatre and the hangout for local and touring musicians and actors, stocks many Scotches. The after-work crowd heads to **Bridges** (☎ 604/687–4400), near the Public Market overlooking False Creek. **Pelican Bay** (⊠ Granville Island Hotel, ☎ 604/683–7373) is a somewhat upscale lounge.

## Brew Pubs

The brewmasters at **Steam Works** (⊠ 375 Water St., ☎ 604/689–2739) on the edge of bustling Gastown use an age-old steam process and large copper kettles (visible through glass walls in the dining room downstairs) to whip up six to nine brews; the espresso ale is interesting. The **Yaletown Brewing Company** (⊠ 1111 Mainland St., ☎ 604/681–2739) is based in a huge renovated warehouse with a glassed-in brewery turning out eight tasty microbrews; it also has a darts and billiards pub and a restaurant with an open-grill kitchen.

## Casinos

Vancouver has a few casinos; proceeds go to local charities and arts groups. No alcohol is served. The **Great Canadian Casino** (⊠ Holiday Inn, 2477 Heather St., ☎ 604/872–5543) is in downtown Vancouver. The **Royal Diamond Casino** (⊠ 106B-750 Pacific Blvd. S, ☎ 604/685–2340) is in the Plaza of Nations Expo site downtown.

## Comedy Clubs

The cheerful **Punchlines Comedy Theatre** (⊠ 15 Water St., ☎ 604/684–3015) is in Gastown. **Yuk Yuks** (⊠ 750 Pacific Blvd., ☎ 604/687–5233) is good for a few laughs.

## Gay and Lesbian Nightlife

**Celebrities** (⊠ 1022 Davie St., ☎ 604/689–3180) is a multilevel space with dancing, billiards, and Wednesday-night drag shows.

**Denman Station** (⊠ 860 Denman St., ☎ 604/669–3448), a friendly and low-key pub, is patronized by gay men and lesbians.

**Odyssey** (⊠ 1251 Howe St., ☎ 604/689–5256) is one of Vancouver's most popular gay discos.

## Music

DANCE CLUBS

**Graceland** (⊠ 1250 Richards St., ☎ 604/688–2648), featuring progressive European, North American, and tribal dance music, attracts a youngish dance crowd. The nitrogen fog screen, automated lighting, and go-go dancers at **Mars** (⊠ 1320 Richards St., ☎ 604/662–7707) get dancers into the swing of things. Dance clubs come and go, but lines still form every weekend at **Richard's on Richards** (⊠ 1036 Richards St., ☎ 604/687–6794) for live and taped dance tunes.

JAZZ

A jazz and blues hot line (☎ 604/682–0706) has information on concerts and clubs. Beatnik poetry readings would seem to fit right in at the **Chameleon Urban Lounge** (⊠ 801 W. Georgia St., ☎ 604/669–0806) in the basement of the Hotel Georgia, but it's the sophisticated mix of jazz, R&B, and Latin tunes that draws the crowds. The **Alma Street Café** (⊠ 2505 Alma St., ☎ 604/222–2244), a restaurant, is a traditional venue with good mainstream jazz; live performances have the spotlight Wednesday through Saturday. The **Glass Slipper** (⊠ 185 E.

11th Ave., ☎ 604/877–0066) presents jazz, from the mainstream to the contemporary, to a hushed crowd there to listen to the music. A Big Band dance sound carries into the night at **Hot Jazz** (✉ 2120 Main St., ☎ 604/873–4131).

ROCK

The **Commodore Ballroom** (✉ 870 Granville St., ☎ 604/681–7838), a Vancouver institution restored to its original art deco style, presents live musicians ranging from B.B. King to zydeco bands. Taped classic rock, plenty of music memorabilia, and specialty salads and sandwiches are dished up at Vancouver's edition of the **Hard Rock Cafe** (✉ 686 W. Hastings St., ☎ 604/687–7625). **The Rage** (✉ 750 Pacific Blvd. S, ☎ 604/685–5585) nightclub has alternative music and draws a young crowd. The **Town Pump** (✉ 66 Water St., ☎ 604/683–6695) is the main venue for local and touring rock bands.

# The Arts

## Dance

**Ballet British Columbia** (☎ 604/732–5003) mounts productions and hosts out-of-town companies from September to April. Local modern dance companies worth seeing are Karen Jamison, Judith Marcuse, and JumpStart. Most performances by these companies can be seen at the Queen Elizabeth Theatre (☞ Theater, *below*). Two other top dance venues are the Fireside Arts Centre (✉ 280 E. Cordova, ☎ 604/689–0926) and the Vancouver East Cultural Centre (☞ Theater, *below*).

## Film

For **foreign films and original works,** try the Park Theater (✉ 3440 Cambie St., ☎ 604/876–2747), the Ridge Theatre (✉ 3131 Arbutus St., ☎ 604/738–6311), and the Varsity Theater (✉ 4375 W. 10th Ave., ☎ 604/222–2235). Tickets are half price on Tuesdays at all **Cineplex Odeon** theaters. **Pacific Cinémateque** (✉ 1131 Howe St., ☎ 604/688–8202) shows esoteric foreign and art films. The **Vancouver International Film Festival** (☎ 604/685–0260) is held during September or October in several theaters around town.

## Music

CHAMBER MUSIC AND SMALL ENSEMBLES

The **Early Music Society** (☎ 604/732–1610) performs medieval, Renaissance, and Baroque music throughout the year and hosts the Vancouver Early Music Summer Festival, one of the most important early music festivals in North America. Concerts by the **Friends of Chamber Music** (no phone) are worth watching for. Programs of the **Vancouver Recital Society** (☎ 604/736–6034) are always of excellent quality.

CHORAL GROUPS

**Choral groups** like the Bach Choir (☎ 604/921–8012), the Vancouver Cantata Singers (☎ 604/921–8588), and the Vancouver Chamber Choir (☎ 604/738–6822) play a major role in Vancouver's classical music scene.

ORCHESTRAS

The **CBC (Canadian Broadcasting Company) Orchestra** (☎ 604/662–6000) performs at the restored Orpheum Theatre. The **Vancouver Symphony Orchestra** (☎ 604/684–9100) is the resident company at the Orpheum..

## Opera

**Vancouver Opera** (☎ 604/682–2871) stages five high-caliber productions a year, usually in October, November, February, March, and June, at the Queen Elizabeth Theatre (✉ 600 Hamilton St.).

## Theater

**Arts Club Theatre** (⊠ 1585 Johnston St., ☎ 604/687–1644) has two stages on Granville Island and theatrical performances all year.

**Back Alley Theatre** (⊠ 751 Thurlow St., ☎ 604/738–7013) hosts *Theatresports,* a hilarious improv event.

**Bard on the Beach** (☎ 604/739–0559) is a summer series of Shakespeare's plays performed under a huge tent on the beach at Vanier Park.

**Carousel Theatre** (☎ 604/669–3410) performs off-off Broadway shows at the Waterfront Theatre (⊠ 1405 Anderson St.) on Granville Island.

**Ford Centre for the Performing Arts** (⊠ 777 Homer St., ☎ 604/844–2808) attracts major productions and top touring companies.

**The Fringe** (☎ 604/873–3646), Vancouver's annual live theatrical arts festival, is staged in September at churches, dance studios, and theater halls around town.

**Queen Elizabeth Theatre** (⊠ 600 Hamilton St., ☎ 604/665–3050) is a major venue in Vancouver for traveling Broadway musicals as well as opera and other events.

**Vancouver East Cultural Centre** (⊠ 1895 Venables St., ☎ 604/254–9578) is a multipurpose performance space.

**Vancouver Playhouse** (⊠ 160 W. 1st St., ☎ 604/872–6622) is the leading venue in Vancouver for mainstream theatrical shows.

# OUTDOOR ACTIVITIES AND SPORTS

## Beaches

An almost continuous string of beaches runs from Stanley Park to the University of British Columbia. The water is cool, but the beaches are sandy, edged by grass. Liquor is prohibited in parks and on beaches. For information, call the **Vancouver Board of Parks and Recreation** (☎ 604/257–8400).

**Kitsilano Beach,** over the Burrard Bridge from downtown, has a lifeguard and is the city's busiest—portable radios, volleyball games, and sleek young people are ever present. The part of the beach nearest the Maritime Museum is the quietest. Facilities include a playground, tennis courts, a heated saltwater pool, concession stands, and nearby restaurants and cafés.

The **Point Grey beaches** give you a number of different options. Jericho, Locarno, and Spanish Banks, which begin at the end of Point Grey Road, offer a huge expanse of sand, especially in summer and at low tide. The shallow water here, warmed slightly by sun and sand, is best for swimming. Farther out, toward Spanish Banks, you'll find the beach less crowded, but the last concession stand and rest rooms are at Locarno. If you keep walking along the beach just past Point Grey, you'll hit Wreck Beach, Vancouver's nude beach.

Among the **West End beaches,** Second Beach and Third Beach, along Beach Drive in Stanley Park, draw families. Second Beach has a guarded saltwater pool. Both have concession stands and rest rooms. The liveliest of the West End beaches is English Bay Beach, at the foot of Denman Street. A water slide, live music, a windsurfing outlet, and other concessions here stay jumping all summer long. Farther along Beach Drive, Sunset Beach, surprisingly quiet considering the location, has a lifeguard but no facilities.

# Participant Sports

## Biking

**Stanley Park** (☞ Stanley Park *in* Exploring Vancouver, *above*) is the most popular spot for family cycling. Rentals are available here from **Bayshore Bicycles** (✉ 745 Denman St., ☎ 604/688–2453) or **Spokes Bicycle Rentals & Espresso Bar** (✉ 1798 W. Georgia St., ☎ 604/688–5141).

A good summer biking route is along the north or south shores of **False Creek.** For bikes, try **Granville Island Bike Rentals** (✉ 1496 Cartwright, ☎ 604/669–2453) or **Granville Island Water Sports** (✉ Charter Boat Dock, ☎ 604/662–7245).

**Cycling British Columbia** (✉ 1367 W. Broadway, Suite 332, ☎ 604/737–3034) is the best source for bike route maps and biking guidebooks.

## Boating

Several charter companies offer a cruise-and-learn vacation, usually to the Gulf Islands. **Sea Wing Sailing Group, Ltd.** (✉ Granville Island, ☎ 604/669–0840) offers a five-day trip teaching the ins and outs of sailing. If you'd rather rent a speedboat to zip around the bay for a day, contact **Granville Island Boat Rentals** (☎ 604/682–6287).

## Fishing

You can fish for salmon all year in coastal British Columbia. **Sewell's Marina Horseshoe Bay** (✉ 6695 Nelson St., Horseshoe Bay, ☎ 604/921–3474) organizes a daily four-hour trip on Howe Sound and has hourly rates on U-drives. **Bayshore Yacht Charters** (✉ 1601 W. Georgia St., ☎ 604/691–6936) has fishing charters.

## Golf

Lower Mainland golf courses are open all year. Spacious **Fraserview Golf Course** (✉ 7800 Vivian St., ☎ 604/280–1818), an 18-hole municipal course, is under renovation until July 1998. Call for updated course information and fees. The 18-hole, par-72 course at **Furry Creek Golf and Country Club** (✉ Hwy. 99, Furry Creek, ☎ 604/896–2224), north of Vancouver overlooking scenic Howe Sound, is challenging but forgiving. The greens fee ranges from $45 to $85 and includes a mandatory cart.

**Northview Golf and Country Club** (✉ 6857 168th St., Surrey, ☎ 604/574–0324), easily accessible from Vancouver, has two Arnold Palmer–designed 18-hole courses (both par 72) and is the home of the Greater Vancouver Open. The greens fee for the Ridge course, where the PGA tour plays, ranges from $40 to $75, the fee for the Canal course from $30 to $55; an optional cart at either costs $28.50. **Peace Portal Golf Course** (✉ 6900 4th Ave., South Surrey, ☎ 604/538–4818), near White Rock, a 45-minute drive from downtown, is a fine 18-hole, par-72 course. The greens fee ranges from $25 to $45; an optional cart costs $27. The 18-hole, par-72 course at **Westwood Golf and Country Club** in nearby Coquitlam (✉ 3251 Plateau Blvd., ☎ 604/552–0777) was a runner-up in the "Best New Course in Canada" category in *Golf Digest*. The greens fee ranges from $60 to $100 and includes a cart. The course is closed in November.

## Health and Fitness Clubs

The **YMCA** (✉ 955 Burrard St., ☎ 604/681–0221) downtown has daily rates; facilities include pools and weight rooms, as well as racquetball, squash, and handball courts. The **YWCA** (✉ 580 Burrard St., ☎ 604/662–8188) has drop-in rates that let you participate in all activities for the day; the facility has pools, weight rooms, and fitness classes. The **Bentall Centre Athletic Club** (✉ 1055 Dunsmuir St., lower level, ☎ 604/689–4424), has racquetball and squash courts, weight rooms, and aerobics.

### Hiking

**Pacific Spirit Park** (✉ 4915 W. 16th Ave., ☎ 604/224–5739), more rugged than Stanley Park, has 61 km (38 mi) of trails, a few rest rooms, and a couple of signboard maps. Go for a wonderful walk in the West Coast arbutus and evergreen woods only 15 minutes from downtown Vancouver. The **Capilano Suspension Bridge and Park** (☞ Greater Vancouver *in* Exploring Vancouver, *above*), on the North Shore, provides a scenic hike.

### Jogging

The seawall around **Stanley Park** (☞ Stanley Park *in* Exploring Vancouver, *above*) is 9 km (5½ mi) long and gives an excellent minitour of the city. You can take a shorter run of 4 km (2½ mi) in the park around Lost Lagoon. The **Running Room** (✉ 1519 Robson St., ☎ 604/684–9771) is a good source for information on fun runs in the area.

### Tennis

There are 180 free public courts around town; contact the **Vancouver Board of Parks and Recreation** (☎ 604/257–8400) for locations. **Stanley Park** has 15 well-surfaced outdoor courts near English Bay Beach; many of the other city parks have public courts as well.

### Water Sports

KAYAKING

Rent a kayak from **Ecomarine Ocean Kayak Center** (✉ 1668 Duranleau St., ☎ 604/689–7575) on Granville Island to explore the waters of False Creek and the shoreline of English Bay.

WINDSURFING

Sailboards and lessons are available at **Windsure Windsurfing School** (✉ Jericho Beach, ☎ 604/224–0615) and **Windmaster** (✉ English Bay Beach, ☎ 604/685–7245). The winds aren't very heavy on English Bay, making it a perfect locale for learning the sport. You'll have to travel north to Squamish for more challenging high-wind conditions.

## Spectator Sports

Vancouver's in-line roller-hockey team and professional basketball and hockey teams play at **General Motors Place** (✉ 800 Griffith Way, ☎ 604/899–7400). **Ticketmaster** (☎ 604/280–4400) sells tickets to many local sports events.

### Baseball

The **Canadians** (☎ 604/872–5232) of the AAA Pacific Coast League play in old-time Nat Bailey Stadium (✉ 4601 Ontario St.), which has one of the few remaining manual scoreboards in Canada.

### Basketball

The **Vancouver Grizzlies** (☎ 604/899–4666) of the National Basketball Association play at General Motors Place.

### Football

The **B.C. Lions** (☎ 604/583–7747) of the Canadian Football League play at B.C. Place Stadium (✉ 777 Pacific Blvd., ☎ 604/669–2300).

### Hockey

The **Vancouver Canucks** (☎ 604/899–4600) of the National Hockey League play at General Motors Place.

### In-Line Roller Hockey

New to Vancouver is an in-line roller hockey team, the **Vancouver Voodoo** (☎ 604/899–7400); they scrimmage June to August at General Motors Place.

### Soccer

The **Vancouver Eighty-Sixers** (☎ 604/273–0086) play soccer in Swangard Stadium (✉ Central Park, Kingsway and Boundary St., Burnaby, ☎ 604/435–7121).

# SHOPPING

Unlike many cities where suburban malls have taken over, Vancouver is full of individual boutiques and specialty shops. Antiques stores, ethnic markets, art galleries, high-fashion outlets, and fine department stores dot the city. Store hours are generally from 9:30 to 6 on Monday, Tuesday, Wednesday, and Saturday, from 9:30 to 9 on Thursday and Friday, and from noon to 5 on Sunday.

## Shopping Districts and Malls

**Fourth Avenue,** from Burrard to Balsam streets, has an eclectic mix of stores selling everything from sophisticated women's clothing to surfboards. **Oakridge Shopping Centre** (✉ 650 W. 41st Ave., at Cambie St., ☎ 604/261–2511) has chic, expensive stores that are fun to browse. The immense **Pacific Centre Mall** (✉ 550–750 W. Georgia St., ☎ 604/688–7236), on two levels and mostly underground, in the heart of downtown, connects the Eaton's and Bay department stores, which stand at opposite corners of Georgia and Granville streets. Stores around **Sinclair Centre** (✉ 757 W. Hastings St., ☎ 604/666–4483) cater to sophisticated and upscale tastes. **Robson Street,** stretching from Burrard to Bute streets, is chockablock with small boutiques and cafés. Vancouver's liveliest street is not only for the fashion-conscious; it also provides many excellent corners for people-watching and attracts an array of street performers.

The huge **Vancouver Flea Market** (✉ 703 Terminal Ave., ☎ 604/685–0666), with more than 360 stalls, is held weekends and holidays from 9 to 5. It is easily accessible from downtown on the SkyTrain, if you exit at the Main Street station.

### Ethnic Districts

**Chinatown**—centered on Pender and Main streets—is an exciting, bustling place for restaurants, exotic foods, and distinctive architecture (☞ Chinatown and Gastown *in* Exploring Vancouver, *above*). Commercial Drive (around East 1st Avenue) is the heart of the Italian community, here called **Little Italy.** You can sip cappuccino in coffee bars where you may be the only one speaking English, or buy sun-dried tomatoes, real Parmesan, or an espresso machine. **Little India** is on Main Street around 50th Avenue. Curry houses, sweetshops, grocery stores, discount jewelry, and silk shops abound. A small **Japantown** on Powell Street at Dunlevy Street contains grocery stores, fish stores, and a few restaurants.

## Department Stores

Among Vancouver's top department stores is Canadian-owned **Eaton's** (✉ 701 Granville St., ☎ 604/685–7112), which carries everything: clothing, appliances, furniture, jewelry, accessories, and souvenirs. Many malls have branches. **Holt Renfrew** (✉ 633 Granville St., ☎ 604/681–

3121) is smaller, focusing on high fashion for men and women. You'll find this Canadian store in most malls as well.

## Auction Houses

On Wednesday at noon and 7 PM, art and antiques auctions are held at **Love's** (⊠ 1635 W. Broadway, ☎ 604/733–1157). **Maynard's** (⊠ 415 W. 2nd Ave., ☎ 604/876–6787) auctions home furnishings on Wednesday at 7 PM.

## Specialty Stores

### Antiques
A stretch of antiques stores runs along Main Street from 19th to 35th avenues. **Folkart Interiors** (⊠ 3715 W. 10th Ave., ☎ 604/228–1011) specializes in whimsical British Columbia folk art and Western Canadian antiques. **The Vancouver Antique Center** (⊠ 422 Richards St., ☎ 604/681–3248) has two floors of antiques and collectibles dealers under one roof. For Oriental rugs, go to **Granville Street** between 7th and 14th avenues.

### Art Galleries
There are many private galleries throughout Vancouver. **Buschlen/Mowatt** (⊠ 1445 W. Georgia St., No. 111, ☎ 604/682–1234), among the best in the city, is a showcase for Canadian and international artists. **Diane Farris** (⊠ 1565 W. 7th Ave., ☎ 604/737–2629; call first) often spotlights hot new artists. **The Inuit Gallery of Vancouver** (345 Water St., ☎ 604/688-7323) features an array of coastal native art.

### Books
**Bollum's Books** (⊠ 710 Granville St., ☎ 604/689–1802) carries 250,000 books and CD-ROM titles, all nicely displayed and well lit, with several comfortable sitting areas, including a little café, for browsers. **Duthie's** (⊠ 919 Robson St., ☎ 604/684–4496; Library Square, 205–345 Robson St., ☎ 604/602–0610), downtown and near the university, is a book-lovers' favorite in Vancouver. **World Wide Books and Maps** (⊠ 736A Granville St., downstairs, ☎ 604/687–3320), one of several specialty bookstores in town, sells travel books and maps that cover the world.

### Clothes
For unique women's clothing, try **Dorothy Grant** (⊠ 757 W. Hastings St., ☎ 604/681–0201), where traditional Haida native designs meld with modern fashion in a boutique that looks more like an art gallery than a store. Handmade Italian suits, cashmere, and leather for men are sold at stylish **E. A. Lee** (⊠ 466 Howe St., ☎ 604/683–2457); there are also a few women's items to browse through. **George Straith** (⊠ Hotel Vancouver, 900 W. Georgia St., ☎ 604/685–3301) carries traditional tailored designer fashions for men and women.

Ultrachic **Leone** (⊠ 757 W. Hastings St., ☎ 604/683–1133) carries designer collections. Trendy men's and women's casual wear by Ralph Lauren is available at **The Polo Store** (⊠ 375 Water St., ☎ 604/682–7656). At the architecturally stunning **Versus** (⊠ 1008 W. Georgia St., ☎ 604/688–8938) boutique, ladies and gents sip cappuccino as they browse through the designs of the late Gianni Versace. Buttoned-down businesswomen shop at **Wear Else?** (⊠ 789 W. Pender St., ☎ 604/662–7890).

### Gifts
One of the best places in Vancouver for good-quality souvenirs (West Coast native art, books, music, jewelry, and so on) is the **Clamshell Gift**

**Shop** (⊠ Vancouver Aquarium, ☎ 604/685–5911) in Stanley Park. **Hill's Indian Crafts** (⊠ 165 Water St., ☎ 604/685–4249), in Gastown, sells Haida, Inuit, and Salish native art. **Leona Lattimer's** (⊠ 1590 W. 2nd Ave., ☎ 604/732–4556) shop, near Granville Island and built like a longhouse, is full of native arts and crafts ranging from cheap to priceless. At the **Salmon Shop** (☎ 604/666–6477) in the Granville Island Public Market you can pick up smoked salmon wrapped for travel.

# VANCOUVER A TO Z

## Arriving and Departing

### By Bus

**Greyhound Lines** (☎ 604/662–3222; 800/661–8747 in Canada; 800/231–2222 in the U.S.) is the largest bus line serving Vancouver. The Pacific Central Station (⊠ 1150 Station St.) is the depot. **Quick Shuttle** (☎ 604/244–3744; 800/665–2122 in the U.S.) bus service runs between Vancouver and Seattle five times a day in winter and up to eight times a day in summer. The depot is at 180 West Georgia Street.

### By Car

Interstate 5 becomes **Highway 99** at the U.S.–Canada border. Vancouver is a three-hour drive (226 km/140 mi) from Seattle. It's best to avoid border crossings during peak times such as holidays and weekends. Highway 1, the **Trans-Canada Highway,** enters Vancouver from the east. To avoid traffic, arrive after rush hour (8:30 AM).

### By Ferry

**B.C. Ferries** (☎ 250/386–3431; 888/223–3779 in British Columbia only) serves Vancouver, Victoria, and other cities in British Columbia. For more information about the system and other ferries that serve the area, *see* Ferry Travel *in* the Gold Guide.

### By Plane

**Vancouver International Airport** (⊠ Grant McConachie Way, ☎ 604/276–6101) is on Sea Island, about 14 km (9 mi) south of downtown of Highway 99. An airport improvement fee is assessed on all flight departures: $5 for flights within British Columbia, $10 for flights within Canada, and $15 for international flights. American, Continental, Delta, Horizon Air, Northwest, Reno, and United serve the airport. The two major domestic carriers are Air Canada and Canadian. *See* Air Travel *in* the Gold Guide for airline numbers.

**Air B.C.** (☎ 604/688–5515 or 800/776–3000) operates 30-minute harbor-to-harbor service (downtown Vancouver to downtown Victoria) several times a day. Planes leave from near the Westin Bayshore Hotel (⊠ 1601 W. Georgia St.). **Helijet Airways** (☎ 604/682–1468) has helicopter service from downtown Vancouver to downtown Victoria. The heliport is near Vancouver's Pan Pacific Hotel (⊠ 300–999 Canada Pl.).

BETWEEN THE AIRPORT AND DOWNTOWN

The drive from the airport to downtown takes 20 to 45 minutes, depending on the time of day. Airport hotels offer free shuttle service to and from the airport.

The **Vancouver Airporter Service** (☎ 604/244–9888) bus leaves the international and domestic arrivals levels of the terminal building approximately every half hour, stopping at major downtown hotels. It operates from 6 AM until midnight. The fare is $9 one way and $15 round-trip.

Taxi stands are in front of the terminal building on domestic and international arrivals levels. The taxi fare to downtown is about $22. Area cab companies are **Yellow** (☎ 604/681–1111) and **Black Top** (☎ 604/681–2181).

Limousine service from **Airlimo** (☎ 604/273–1331) costs a bit more than the taxi fare to downtown: The current rate is about $30.

### By Train

The **Pacific Central Station** (✉ 1150 Station St.) is the hub for rail, bus, and SkyTrain service. The **VIA Rail** (☎ 800/561–8630) station is at Main Street and Terminal Avenue. VIA provides transcontinental service through Jasper to Toronto three times a week. Passenger trains leave the **B.C. Rail** (☎ 604/631–3500) station in North Vancouver for Whistler and the interior of British Columbia. **Amtrak** (☎ 800/835–8725 in the U.S. or 800/872–7245 in B.C.) has one round-trip per day between Seattle and Vancouver.

## Getting Around

### By Bus

Exact change is needed to ride **B.C. Transit** (☎ 604/521–0400) buses: $1.50. Books of 25 tickets are sold at convenience stores and newsstands; look for a red, white, and blue "Fare Dealer" sign. Day passes, good for unlimited travel after 9:30 AM, cost $4.50 for adults. They are available from fare dealers and any SeaBus or SkyTrain station. Transfers are valid for 90 minutes and allow travel in both directions. Because of traffic and overcrowding, this mode can be time-consuming and uncomfortable; however, you can get just about anywhere you need to go in the city by bus.

### By Car

Because no freeways cross Vancouver, rush-hour traffic still tends to be horrendous. The worst bottlenecks outside the city center are the North Shore bridges, the George Massey Tunnel on Highway 99 south of Vancouver, and Highway 1 through Coquitlam and Surrey. Parking downtown is expensive and tricky to find. Right turns are allowed on most red lights after you've come to a full stop.

### By Ferry

The **SeaBus** is a 400-passenger commuter ferry that crosses Burrard Inlet from the foot of Lonsdale (North Vancouver) to downtown. The ride takes 13 minutes and costs the same as the transit bus (and it's much faster). With a transfer, connection can be made to any B.C. Transit bus or SkyTrain. **Aquabus Ferries** (☎ 604/689–5858) connect several stations on False Creek including Science Center, Granville Island, Stamp's Landing, and the Hornby Street dock.

### By Rapid Transit

Vancouver has a one-line, 25-km (16-mi) rapid transit system called **SkyTrain,** which travels underground downtown and is elevated for the rest of its route to New Westminster and Surrey. Trains leave about every five minutes. Tickets, sold at each station from machines (correct change is not necessary), must be carried with you as proof of payment. You may use transfers from SkyTrain to SeaBus (☞ *above*) and B.C. Transit buses and vice versa. The SkyTrain is convenient for transit between Gastown and Science World, but that's about it for points of interest.

## By Taxi

It is difficult to hail a cab in Vancouver; unless you're near a hotel, you'd have better luck calling a taxi service. Try **Yellow** (☎ 604/681–1111) or **Black Top** (☎ 604/683–4567).

# Contacts and Resources

## B&B Reservation Agencies

**A Home Away From Home** (✉ 1441 Howard Ave., V5B 3S2, ☎ 604/294–1760, FAX 604/294–0799). **Best Canadian Bed and Breakfast Network** (✉ 1090 W. King Edward Ave., V6H 1Z4, ☎ 604/738–7207). **Town & Country Bed and Breakfast** (✉ 2803 W. 4th Ave., V6K 1K2, ☎ 604/731–5942).

## Car Rental

**Avis** (☎ 604/606–2847 or 800/331–1212). **Budget** (☎ 604/668–7000; 800/527–0700 in the U.S.). **Thrifty Car Rental** (☎ 604/606–1666 or 800/367–2277).

## Consulates

**United States** (✉ 1075 W. Pender St., ☎ 604/685–4311). **United Kingdom** (✉ 800–1111 Melville St., ☎ 604/683–4421).

## Emergencies

**Ambulance** (☎ 911). **Fire** (☎ 911). **Police** (☎ 911).

Doctors are on call through the emergency ward at **St. Paul's Hospital** (✉ 1081 Burrard St., ☎ 604/682–2344), a downtown facility open around the clock. **Medicentre** (✉ 1055 Dunsmuir St., lower level, ☎ 604/683–8138), a drop-in clinic in the Bentall Centre, is open weekdays. Dentists are on call at **Dentacentre** (✉ 1055 Dunsmuir St., lower level, ☎ 604/669–6700), which is next door and is also open weekdays.

## Guided Tours

Tour prices fluctuate, so inquire about current rates when booking tours. Kids are generally charged half the adult fare.

AIR

Tour the mountains and fjords of the North Shore by helicopter for around $200 per person (minimum of three people) for 50 minutes: **Vancouver Helicopters** (☎ 604/270–1484) flies from the Harbour Heliport downtown. You can see Vancouver from the air for $70 for 30 minutes: **Harbour Air**'s (☎ 604/688–1277) seaplanes leave from beside the Westin Bayshore Hotel.

BOAT

**Aquabus Ferries** (✉ 1656 Duranleau St., ☎ 604/689–5858) runs a 25-minute City Skyline cruise departing from Hornby dock or Granville Island for $6. Their English Bay Cruise runs 50 minutes from Granville Island out into the bay, passing Siwash Rock and Stanley Park, and returning along the Kitsilano shoreline; the fare is $15.

**Fraser River Connection** (✉ 810 Quayside Dr., in the Information Centre at Westminster Quay, ☎ 604/525–4465) will take you on a seven-hour tour of a fascinating working river—past log booms, tugs, and houseboats. Between May and October ride from New Westminster to Fort Langley aboard a convincing replica of an 1800s-era paddle wheeler for less than $50.

**Harbour Ferries** (✉ 1 N. Denman St., ☎ 604/688–7246) has several worthwhile excursions, including one on the Royal Hudson, Canada's only functioning steam train, which heads along the mountainous coast up Howe Sound to the logging town of Squamish. After a break here, you sail back to Vancouver on the M.V. *Britannia*. The trip costs about $75 and takes 6½ hours; reservations are advised.

Harbour Ferries also operates a 1½-hour narrated tour of Burrard Inlet aboard the paddle wheeler M.V. *Constitution*; the tour operates from Wednesday to Sunday and costs less than $20. Sunset cruises are also available.

### ECOLOGY

**English Bay Sea Kayaking Company** (☎ 604/898–4979) has guided half-day ($75) and sunset ($45) sea kayaking tours for a closer look at the inlets and bays of Vancouver's waterfront. **Lotus Land Tours** (☎ 604/684–4922) runs a six-hour sea canoe (similar to, but wider than a kayak) trip that visits Twin Island (an uninhabited provincial marine park) to explore the marine life that populates the area's intertidal zone; cost is $120 and includes a salmon barbecue lunch. A good operator with a number of interpretative day hikes around Vancouver is **Path of Logic Wilderness Adventures** (☎ 604/802–2082). Guided hikes (for $35 and up) through the rain forests and canyons surrounding Vancouver are available through **Rockwood Adventures** (☎ 604/926–7705). A unique way to see the heights of the city with an environmental focus is the Grouse Mountain downhill mountain biking trip offered by **Velo-City Cycle Tours** (☎ 604/924–0288).

**Bluewater Adventures** (☎ 604/980–3800) has a multiday natural history cruise to the Gulf Islands and Queen Charlotte Islands, including an Orca and Totems trip that visits long-abandoned Haida native villages to see the fallen totem poles slowly being reclaimed by the landscape. Call for pricing. **Nunatak Expeditions** (☎ 604/987–6727) offers three- to six-day guided sea kayaking trips to the islands and sounds in Canada's Inside Passage, including a fantastic six-day trip in Johnstone Strait in search of orca (killer whale) encounters. The fees range from $350 to $850. **Wild West Adventures** (☎ 604/688–2008) has a weekend camping tour to Mayne Island that incorporates interpretative hikes, sea kayaking around the island, and wildlife watching (seals, otters, eagles, and more); the cost is $200. The company also schedules whale-watching trips to Tofino, using Zodiac boats to explore Clayquote Sound and seek out migrating gray whales each spring; the cost is $210.

### ORIENTATION

**Gray Line** (☎ 604/879–3363) conducts a 3½-hour Grand City bus tour year-round. Departing from the Sandman Inn in winter and the Plaza of Nations in summer, the tour includes Stanley Park, Chinatown, Gastown, English Bay, and Queen Elizabeth Park and costs about $31. Between June and September, Gray Line has a narrated city tour aboard double-decker buses; passengers can get on and off as they choose and are allowed to ride free the following day if they haven't had their fill. The adult fare is about $20. Using minibuses departing from downtown hotels and transit stations, **Vance Tours** (☎ 604/941–5660) has a highlights tour (3½ hours, $33) that includes a visit to the University of British Columbia and a shorter city tour (2½ hours, $30, hotel pickup included).

The **Vancouver Trolley Company** (☎ 604/451–5581) runs turn-of-the-century-style trolleys through Vancouver from April through October on a two-hour narrated tour of Stanley Park, Gastown, English Bay, Granville Island, and Chinatown, among other sights. A day pass allows you to complete one full circuit, getting off and on as often as you like. Start the trip at any of the sights and buy a ticket on board.

The adult fare is less than $20. During the rest of the year, the trolley runs the same circuit on a 2½-hour trip, but no on-off option is available. During spring, summer, and fall, **Westcoast City and Nature Sightseeing** (☎ 604/451–1600) accommodates up to 31 people in vans that run a 3½-hour city-highlights tour for about $30 (pickup available from all major hotels downtown).

**North Shore tours** usually include any or several of the following: a gondola ride up Grouse Mountain, a walk across the Capilano Suspension Bridge, a stop at a salmon hatchery, a visit to the Lonsdale Quay Market, and a ride back to town on the SeaBus. Half-day tours cost between $45 and $55 and are offered by Landsea Tours (☎ 604/255–7272), Harbour Ferries (☎ 604/688–7246), Gray Line (☎ 604/879–3363), and Pacific Coach Lines (☎ 604/662–7575).

PERSONAL GUIDES

**Early Motion Tours** (☎ 604/687–5088) will pick you up at your hotel for a tour of Vancouver in a Model-A Ford convertible. For about $70 or $80, up to four people can take an hour-long trip around downtown, Chinatown, and Stanley Park; longer tours can also be arranged. **AAA Horse & Carriage** (☎ 604/681–5115) has a one-hour tour of Stanley Park, along the waterfront and through a cedar forest and a rose garden. The cost is $10 per person ($30 for a family of four); the tour departs from the information booth near the zoo. Individualized tours are available from **VIP Tourguide Services,** run by Marcel Jonker (☎ 604/214–4677).

WALKING

The **Gastown Business Improvement Society** (⊠ 12 Water St., ☎ 604/683–5650) sponsors free 90-minute historical and architectural walking tours daily from June to August. Meet the guide at 2 PM at the statue of Gassy Jack in Maple Tree Square.

## Late-Night Pharmacy

**Shopper's Drug Mart** (⊠ 1125 Davie St., ☎ 604/669–2424) is open around the clock.

## Road Emergencies

**BCAA** (☎ 604/293–2222) has 24-hour emergency road service for members of AAA or CAA.

## Travel Agencies

**American Express Travel Service** (⊠ 666 Burrard St., ☎ 604/669–2813). **Mirage Holidays** (⊠ 14–200 Burrard St., ☎ 604/685–4008). **P. Lawson Travel** (⊠ 409 Granville St., Suite 150, ☎ 604/682–4272).

## Visitor Information

**Super, Natural B.C.** (☎ 800/663–6000). **Vancouver Tourist Info Centre** (⊠ 200 Burrard St., V6C 3L6, ☎ 604/683–2000, FAX 604/682–6839).

# 5 Side Trips from Vancouver

*Victoria, the capital of British Columbia, is one of several destinations within easy reach of Vancouver. Often called the most British city in Canada, it is indeed an Anglophile's dream, both for its architecture and its cuisine. For more rustic excursions, consider a trip to one of the Gulf Islands or the inland town of Whistler.*

**C**OSMOPOLITAN VANCOUVER IS BRITISH COLUMBIA'S urban star, but to appreciate the province's most dramatic natural attractions, you'll need to travel beyond the city limits. No matter how modern British Columbia may appear, evidence remains of the earliest settlers: Pacific coast natives (Haida, Kwakiutl, Nootka, Salish, and others) who occupied the land for more than 12,000 years before the first Europeans arrived en masse in the late 19th century. British Columbia's roots show throughout the province, in native arts such as the wood-carved objects and etched-silver jewelry sold in small-town boutiques, and in the authentic culinary delights from traditional recipes of big-city dining establishments.

Updated by
Melissa Rivers

## Pleasures and Pastimes

### Dining

Restaurants are generally casual in the region. For price ranges on Vancouver Island and the Gulf Islands, refer to the chart below; a separate chart in the Whistler section outlines meal costs in that city.

| CATEGORY | COST* |
|---|---|
| $$$$ | over C$35 |
| $$$ | C$25–C$35 |
| $$ | C$15–C$25 |
| $ | under C$15 |

*per person, excluding drinks, service, and 7% GST*

### Lodging

Accommodations across the province range from bed-and-breakfasts and rustic cabins to deluxe chain hotels. For price ranges on Vancouver Island and the Gulf Islands, refer to the chart below; a separate chart in the Whistler section outlines room costs in that city.

| CATEGORY | COST* |
|---|---|
| $$$$ | over C$180 |
| $$$ | C$110–C$180 |
| $$ | C$70–C$110 |
| $ | under C$70 |

*All prices are for a standard double room, excluding 10% provincial accommodation tax, service charge, and 7% GST.*

### Whale-Watching

Three resident and several transient pods of orca whales travel in the waters around Vancouver Island and are the primary focus of charter boat tours that depart from Victoria between May and October. June and July are the best months to see the whales—harbor seal, sea lion, porpoise, and marine bird sightings are likely anytime.

# VICTORIA

Victoria was the first European settlement on Vancouver Island. Originally known as Fort Victoria, it's the oldest city on Canada's west coast. James Douglas chose it in 1843 to be the Hudson's Bay Company's westernmost outpost; it became the capital of British Columbia in 1868. The city is 71 km (44 mi) south of Vancouver and a 2½-hour ferry ride from Seattle.

**Southern Vancouver Island**

## Exploring Victoria

*Numbers in the text correspond to numbers in the margin and on the Downtown Victoria map.*

### A Good Walk

Begin on the waterfront at the **Visitors Information Centre** ①. Across the way on Government Street is the majestic **Empress Hotel** ②. A short walk south on Government Street will bring you to the **Parliament Buildings** ③ complex on Belleville Street. Follow Belleville one block east to reach the **Royal British Columbia Museum** ④, where you can explore thousands of years of history. Behind the museum and bordering Douglas Street is Thunderbird Park, where totem poles and a ceremonial longhouse stand in one corner of the garden of the **Helmcken House** ⑤. A walk east on Superior Street to Douglas Street leads to **Beacon Hill Park** ⑥. From the park, go north on Douglas Street and stop at the glass-roof **Crystal Gardens Conservatory** ⑦.

From Crystal Gardens, continue north on Douglas Street to View Street, then west to **Bastion Square** ⑧, with its gas lamps, restaurants, cobblestone streets, and small shops. While you're here, you can stop in at the **Maritime Museum of British Columbia** ⑨ and learn about an important part of the province's history. West of Government Street, between Pandora Avenue and Johnson Street, is the **Market Square** ⑩ shopping district. Around the corner from Market Square is Fisgard Street, the heart of **Chinatown** ⑪. A 15-minute walk or a short drive east on Fort Street will take you to Joan Crescent and lavish **Craigdarroch Castle** ⑫.

### TIMING

Many of the sights are within easy walking distance of one another and could be covered in half a day, but there's so much to see at the

Royal British Columbia Museum and the other museums that you should plan on a full day downtown. This will allow time for some shopping and a visit to Craigdarroch Castle.

## Sights to See

**Anne Hathaway's Cottage.** A full-size replica of Shakespeare's wife's original thatched home in Stratford-upon-Avon, England, is part of the English Village, a complex with re-created period buildings. The 16th-century antiques inside are typical of Shakespeare's era. The Olde England Inn here is a pleasant spot for tea or an English-style meal, and you can also stay in one of the 50 antiques-furnished rooms. Guided tours leave from the inn in winter and the cottage in summer. The village is touristy but appeals to many people. From downtown Victoria, you can take the Munro bus to the cottage. ✉ *429 Lampson St.,* ☎ *250/388–4353.* ☜ *$6.50.* ☉ *June–Sept., daily 9–8; Oct.–May, daily 10–4.*

**Art Gallery of Greater Victoria.** This fine museum houses large collections of Chinese and Japanese ceramics and contains the only authentic Shinto shrine in North America. A permanent exhibit of British Columbia native Emily Carr's work is on display. The gallery is a few blocks west of Craigdarroch Castle, off Fort Street. ✉ *1040 Moss St.,* ☎ *250/384–4101.* ☜ *$5, Mon. by donation.* ☉ *Mon.–Wed., Fri., and Sat. 10–5, Thurs. 10–9, Sun. 1–5.*

**⑧ Bastion Square.** James Douglas chose this spot for the original Fort Victoria and Hudson's Bay Company trading post. Fashion boutiques and restaurants occupy the old buildings, and the cobblestone streets are lighted by gas lamps. ✉ *Bordered by Yates, Wharf, Government, and Fort Sts.*

**⑥ Beacon Hill Park.** The southern lawns of this spacious park have great views of the Olympic Mountains and the Strait of Juan de Fuca. Also here are lakes, jogging and walking paths, abundant flowers and gardens, a wading pool, a petting zoo, and an outdoor amphitheater for Sunday afternoon concerts. ✉ *East of Douglas St.*

OFF THE BEATEN PATH

**BUTCHART GARDENS –** More than 700 varieties of flowers grow in this impressive site that contains Italian, Japanese, and English rose gardens. In summer, many of the exhibits are illuminated at night, and fireworks light the sky over the gardens on Saturday night. Also on the premises are a teahouse and restaurants. ✉ *800 Benvenuto Ave., 21 km (13 mi) north of downtown Victoria (take Hwy. 17A from downtown), Brentwood Bay,* ☎ *250/652–5256 or 250/652–4422.* ☜ *$14.50, discounts in winter.* ☉ *Call for seasonal hrs.*

**⑪ Chinatown.** The Chinese were responsible for building much of the Canadian Pacific Railway in the 19th century, and their influence still marks the region. If you enter Chinatown (one of the oldest in Canada) from Government Street, you'll walk under the elaborate **Gate of Harmonious Interest,** made from Taiwanese ceramic tiles and decorative panels. Along the street, merchants display paper lanterns, embroidered silks, imported fruits, and vegetables. Narrow **Fan Tan Alley,** off Fisgard Street, was the gambling and opium center of Chinatown.

★ **⑫ Craigdarroch Castle.** This lavish mansion was built as the home of British Columbia's first millionaire, Robert Dunsmuir, who oversaw coal mining for the Hudson's Bay Company. He died in 1889, just a few months before the castle's completion. Converted into a museum depicting turn-of-the-century life, the castle has elaborately framed landscape paintings, stained-glass windows, carved woodwork—precut in Chicago for

# Downtown Victoria

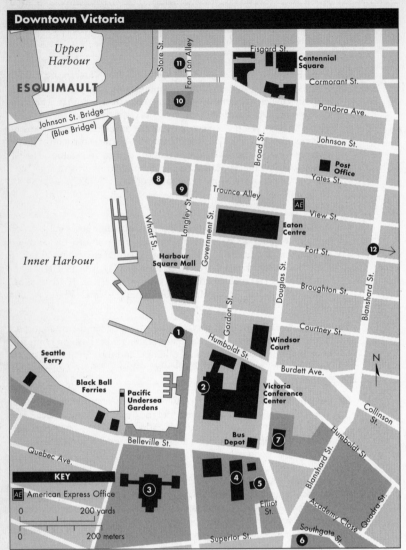

Upper Harbour

ESQUIMAULT

Johnson St. Bridge (Blue Bridge)

Inner Harbour

Store St.

Fan Tan Alley

Fisgard St.

Centennial Square

Cormorant St.

Pandora Ave.

Johnson St.

Broad St.

Post Office

Yates St.

Trounce Alley

View St.

AE

Wharf St.

Langley St.

Government St.

Eaton Centre

Harbour Square Mall

Fort St.

Broughton St.

Blanshard St.

Gordon St.

Douglas St.

Courtney St.

Humboldt St.

Windsor Court

Burdett Ave.

Seattle Ferry

Black Ball Ferries

Pacific Undersea Gardens

Victoria Conference Center

Collinson St.

Belleville St.

Bus Depot

Humboldt St.

Quebec Ave.

KEY

AE  American Express Office

0        200 yards

0        200 meters

Elliot St.

Blanshard St.

Academy Close

Quadra St.

Superior St.

Southgate St.

N

Dunsmuir and sent by rail—and rooms for billiards and smoking. There's a wonderful view of downtown Victoria from the fourth-floor tower. ⊠ *1050 Joan Crescent,* ☎ *250/592–5323.* ⌑ *$6.50.* ⊘ *Mid-June–early Sept., daily 9–7:30; mid-Sept.–mid-June, daily 10–4:30.*

**❼ Crystal Gardens Conservatory.** Opened in 1925 as the largest saltwater swimming pool in the British Empire, this glass-roof building—owned by the provincial government—houses flamingos, macaws, 75 varieties of other tropical birds, monkeys, and hundreds of blooming flowers. At street level there are several boutiques and popular Rattenbury's Restaurant. ⊠ *713 Douglas St.,* ☎ *250/381–1213.* ⌑ *$7.* ⊘ *Dec.–Apr., daily 10–4:30; May–Aug., daily 8–8; Sept.–Nov., daily 9–6.*

**❷ Empress Hotel.** Originally opened in 1908, the Empress (☞ Lodging, *below*) is a symbol of both the city and the Canadian Pacific Railway. Designed by Francis Rattenbury, whose works dot Victoria, the property is another of the great châteaus built by Canadian Pacific, still the owners. Stop in for high tea, served at hour-and-a-half intervals during the afternoon (no jeans, shorts, or T-shirts are permitted in the tea lobby). ⊠ *721 Government St.,* ☎ *250/384–8111.*

**★ ❺ Helmcken House.** The oldest house in British Columbia was built in 1852 by pioneer doctor and statesman John Sebastian Helmcken. The holdings here include early Victorian furnishings and an intriguing collection of 19th-century medical tools. Audio tours last 20 minutes. **Thunderbird Park,** with totem poles and a ceremonial longhouse constructed by Kwakiutl Chief Mungo Martin, occupies one corner of the house's garden. ⊠ *10 Elliot St.,* ☎ *250/361–0021.* ⌑ *$4.* ⊘ *May–Sept., daily 10–5; call for winter hrs.*

**❾ Maritime Museum of British Columbia.** The dugout canoes, model ships, Royal Navy charts, photographs, uniforms, and ship's bells at this museum inside Victoria's original courthouse chronicle the city's seafaring history. A seldom-used 100-year-old cage lift, believed to be the oldest in North America, ascends to the third floor. ⊠ *28 Bastion Sq.,* ☎ *250/385–4222.* ⌑ *$5.* ⊘ *Daily 9:30–4:30.*

**❿ Market Square.** The many specialty shops and boutiques here are enhanced by the historic setting. At the end of the 19th century this area, once part of Chinatown, provided everything a visitor desired: food, lodging, entertainment. ⊠ *West of Government St., between Pandora Ave. and Johnson St.*

**★ ❸ Parliament Buildings.** These massive stone structures, completed in 1897, dominate the Inner Harbour. Two statues flank them, one of Sir James Douglas, who chose the site where Victoria was built, the other of Sir Matthew Baille Begbie, the man in charge of law and order during the gold-rush era. Atop the central dome is a gilded statue of Captain George Vancouver, the first European to sail around Vancouver Island. A statue of Queen Victoria reigns over the front of the complex; more than 3,000 lights outline the buildings at night. Another of Francis Rattenbury's creations, the Parliament Buildings typify the rigid symmetry and European elegance of much of the city's architecture. ⊠ *501 Belleville St.,* ☎ *250/387–3046.* ⌑ *Free.* ⊘ *Sept.–May, weekdays 8:30–5; June–Aug., daily 9–5.*

**★ ⊘ ❹ Royal British Columbia Museum.** At what is easily the best attraction in Victoria, you can spend hours wandering through the centuries, back 12,000 years. In the prehistoric exhibit, you can actually smell the pines and hear the calls of mammoths and other ancient wildlife. Or you can explore a turn of-the-century town, with trains rumbling past. The smell of cedar envelops the Kwakiutl longhouse, while piped-in potlatch songs relate the origins of the genuine ceremonial house before you. The museum also has fine interpretative displays of native artifacts, including an impressive collection of masks. ⊠ *675 Belleville St.,* ☎ *250/387–3014.* 🖾 *$7.* 🕙 *Sept.–June, daily 10–5:30; July and Aug., daily 9:30–7.*

❶ **Visitors Information Centre.** A convenient waterfront location adds to the center's appeal. The bridge immediately to the south has a grand view of the Inner Harbour and, across the water on Songhees Point, the 182½-ft **Welcome Totem** (now the tallest totem pole in the world) erected in 1994 for the Commonwealth Games. ⊠ *812 Wharf St.,* ☎ *250/953–2033.* 🕙 *July and Aug., Mon.–Sat. 9–9, Sun. 9–7; May, June, and Sept., daily 9–7; Oct.–Apr., daily 9–5.*

---

## Dining

### CHINESE

$$ ✗ **Don Mee's.** A large neon sign invites you inside this traditional Chinese restaurant with an expansive dining room. Szechuan and Cantonese entrées include sweet-and-sour chicken, almond duck, and bean curd with broccoli. Dim sum is served daily during lunch hours. ⊠ *538 Fisgard St.,* ☎ *250/383–1032. AE, DC, MC, V.*

### FRENCH

$$$ ✗ **Chez Daniel.** One of Victoria's old standbys, Chez Daniel serves rich French dishes, though the nouvelle influence has found its way into some creations. The award-winning wine list is varied, and the menu has a wide selection of basic dishes including rabbit, salmon, duck, and steak. The romantic atmosphere here encourages you to linger. ⊠ *2524 Estevan Ave.,* ☎ *250/592–7424. Reservations essential. AE, MC, V. Closed Sun. and Mon. No lunch.*

### GREEK

$ ✗ **Periklis.** You can order standard Greek cuisine in this warm, taverna-style restaurant, but steaks and ribs are also on the menu. The dolmas and baklava are especially good. At night there's Greek dancing and belly dancing. ⊠ *531 Yates St.,* ☎ *250/386–3313. Reservations essential. AE, MC, V. No lunch weekends.*

### ITALIAN

$$ ✗ **Il Terrazzo.** The locals' choice for romantic alfresco dining prepares
★ baked garlic served with warm *cambozola* cheese and focaccia; scallops dipped in roasted pistachios and garnished with arugula, Belgian endive, and mango salsa; grilled lamb chops on angel-hair pasta with tomatoes, garlic, mint, and black pepper; and other hearty northern Italian dishes, all piping hot from the restaurant's authentic wood oven. ⊠ *555 Johnson St., off Waddington Alley (call for directions),* ☎ *250/361–0028. Reservations essential. AE, MC, V.*

$$ ✗ **Pagliacci's.** Quiches, veal, and chicken in marsala sauce with fettuccine are among the standout dishes served at this fine trattoria where the pastas are all made in-house. You'll dine surrounded by orange walls covered with photos of Hollywood movie stars. Save room for the cheesecake. ⊠ *1011 Broad St.,* ☎ *250/386–1662. Reservations not accepted. AE, MC, V.*

### JAPANESE

$$ ✗ **Tomoe.** A long sushi bar, a few tatami rooms, and tables set comfortably apart are the elements of this low-key restaurant. Choose from satisfying seafood dishes (watch for the occasional exotic offering flown in from Japan) as well as standards such as tempura and teriyaki. ⊠ *726 Johnson St.,* ☎ *250/381–0223. AE, MC, V. Closed Sun.*

### MEXICAN

$ ✗ **Cafe Mexico.** Hearty portions of Mexican food, such as *pollo chipotle* (grilled chicken with melted cheddar and spicy sauce on a bed of rice) are served at a spacious, redbrick dining establishment just off the waterfront. ✉ *1425 Store St.,* ☎ *250/386–5454. AE, DC, MC, V.*

### PACIFIC NORTHWEST

$$$–$$$$ ✗ **Empress Room.** For a special-occasion dinner, reserve a fireside table in the elegant Empress Room. Beautifully presented Pacific Northwest cuisine vies for attention with the setting when candlelight dances on the tapestried walls beneath an intricately carved mahogany ceiling. Fresh local ingredients go into imaginative seasonal dishes such as house-cured Pacific salmon with wild blackberry–ginger butter, pan-roasted Arctic char with wild-rice polenta and gooseberry chutney, or peppered Vancouver Island venison with a black-currant sauce. ✉ *Empress Hotel, 721 Government St.,* ☎ *250/381–8111. Reservations essential. AE, D, DC, MC, V. No lunch.*

$$ ✗ **Camille's.** Smoked Gruyère cheese and carrot cake (an appetizer), roast loin of venison with wild mushroom polenta, and grainy Dijon-and-mint-crusted lamb with a blackberry port reduction are among the specialties of this intimate restaurant. Camille's has an extensive wine cellar; wine tasting dinners are offered once each week. ✉ *45 Bastion Sq.,* ☎ *250/381–3433. Reservations essential. AE, MC, V. No lunch.*

### SEAFOOD

$$–$$$ ✗ **Marina Restaurant.** This round restaurant overlooking the Oak Bay
★ Marina is so popular with locals that it's always crowded and a bit noisy. The best bets on the imaginative menu are warm salmon salad, grilled marlin in a citrus-sesame vinaigrette, rack of lamb in a port glaze, and crab served with drawn butter and Indonesian hot-and-sour sauce. The Café Deli downstairs sells Mediterranean picnic foods prepared by the chefs upstairs. ✉ *1327 Beach Dr.,* ☎ *250/598–8555. Reservations essential. AE, DC, MC, V.*

$$–$$$ ✗ **Pescatore's Fish House and Oyster Bar.** Upbeat Pescatore's specializes in fresh seafood (grilled wild Coho salmon, fresh spinach, and smoked Gruyère on Italian flat bread) and Pacific Northwest preparations like rosemary-and-garlic-marinated lamb and oyster mushrooms on angel-hair pasta. Daily blue-plate specials tend to be reasonably priced and creative—for example, pan-seared chicken breast in chanterelle sauce with crushed potatoes and vegetables. ✉ *614 Humboldt St.,* ☎ *250/385–4512. Reservations essential. AE, MC, V.*

$ ✗ **Barb's Place.** This funky take-out shack, a Victoria institution, is on Fisherman's Wharf, on the south side of Victoria Harbour, west of the Inner Harbour, just off Marine Drive. Locals consider the authentic fish (halibut) and chips to be the city's best: Pick up an order before taking a quick ride on the little harbor ferry across the bay to Songhees Point for a picnic. ✉ *310 Lawrence St.,* ☎ *250/384–6515. No credit cards. Closed Nov.–Mar.*

### THAI

$ ✗ **Siam.** The Thai chefs at Siam work wonders with hot and mild dishes. The *phad Thai goong* (fried rice noodles with prawns, tofu, peanuts, eggs, bean sprouts, and green onions), *panang* (choice of meat in curry and coconut milk), and *satay* (grilled, marinated cubes of meat served with a spicy peanut sauce) are particularly good options. ✉ *512 Fort St.,* ☎ *250/383–9911. Reservations essential. MC, V. No lunch Sun.*

VIETNAMESE

**$–$$** ✕ **Le Petit Saigon.** The fare is Vietnamese with French influences at this intimate restaurant. The crab, asparagus, and egg swirl soup is a house specialty, and combination meals are cheap and tasty. ✉ *1010 Langley St.,* ☎ *250/386–1412. AE, MC, V.*

# Lodging

**$$$$** ▣ **The Aerie.** The million-dollar view of Finlayson Arm and the Gulf
★ Islands persuaded Leo and Maria Schuster to build their small, luxury resort here, 30 km (19 mi) north of Victoria. Some of the plush rooms in the Mediterranean-style villa have a patio; others have fireplaces and whirlpool tubs tucked into window nooks. The dining room (no lunch served) is open to the public for stunning views and outstanding cuisine. The maple-smoked salmon, pheasant consommé, and medallions of venison in morel sauce are more than worth the drive from Victoria. A full gourmet breakfast is included in the tariff. ✉ *600 Ebedora La., Malahat V0R 2L0,* ☎ *250/743–7115,* ℻ *250/743–4766. 11 rooms, 11 suites. Dining room, no-smoking rooms, indoor pool, indoor and outdoor hot tubs, sauna, spa, tennis court, exercise room, library, meeting room, helipad. AE, MC, V.*

**$$$$** ▣ **Beaconsfield Inn.** Built in 1905 and restored in 1984, the Beaconsfield has retained its Old World charm. Dark mahogany wood appears throughout the house; down comforters and some canopy beds adorn the rooms, reinforcing the Edwardian style. Some rooms in this no-smoking inn have fireplaces and whirlpool bathtubs. The room rates include a full breakfast with homemade croissants or scones, afternoon tea, and evening sherry. ✉ *998 Humboldt St., V8V 2Z8,* ☎ *250/384–4044,* ℻ *250/721–2442. 5 rooms, 4 suites. Breakfast room, no-smoking rooms, library. MC, V.*

**$$$$** ▣ **Clarion Hotel Grand Pacific.** One of Victoria's newest and finest hotels has mahogany woodwork and an elegant ambience. Overlooking the harbor and adjacent to the legislative buildings, the hotel accommodates business travelers and vacationers looking for comfort, convenience, and great scenery; all rooms have terraces, with views of either the harbor or the Olympic Mountains. ✉ *450 Québec St., V8V 1W5,* ☎ *250/386–0450 or 800/663–7550,* ℻ *250/386–8779. 130 rooms, 15 suites. Dining room, lounge, no-smoking rooms, room service, indoor pool, massage, sauna, aerobics, racquetball, squash, bicycles, laundry service and dry cleaning, business services, convention center, meeting rooms, free parking. AE, D, DC, MC, V.*

**$$$$** ▣ **Empress Hotel.** Stained glass, carved archways, and hardwood floors are among the noteworthy design elements of Victoria's dowager queen, which opened in 1908. Newer rooms added in 1989 are more spacious than the original ones. The Empress is the city's primary meeting place for politicians, locals, and tourists. ✉ *721 Government St., V8W 1W5,* ☎ *250/384–8111 or 800/441–1414,* ℻ *250/381–4334. 466 rooms, 17 suites. Restaurant, café, 2 lounges, no-smoking rooms, room service, indoor pool, sauna, health club, laundry service and dry cleaning, concierge, business services, convention center, parking (fee). AE, D, DC, MC, V.*

**$$$–$$$$** ▣ **Ocean Pointe Resort.** Across the "blue bridge" (Johnson Street
★ Bridge) from downtown Victoria, the Ocean Pointe opened in 1992 on the site of an old shingle mill in an area once claimed by the Songhees natives. From here you have the best possible view of the lights of the Parliament buildings across the Inner Harbour. Public rooms and half the guest rooms have romantic evening views of downtown Victoria. Amenities include the only full European aesthetics spa in western Canada, with all kinds of beauty treatments. ✉ *45 Songhees Rd.,*

V9A 6T3, ☎ 250/360–2999 or 800/667–4677, ⅋ 250/360–5856. *213 rooms, 37 suites. 2 restaurants, lounge, kitchenettes, no-smoking rooms, indoor pool, sauna, spa, 2 tennis courts, exercise room, racquetball, squash, laundry service and dry cleaning, business services, meeting rooms, parking (fee). AE, DC, MC, V.*

**$$$–$$$$** 🏨 **Victoria Regent Hotel.** Originally built as an apartment house, this is now a posh hotel with views of the harbor or city. The outside is plain, with a glass facade, but the interior is sumptuously decorated with warm earth tones and modern furnishings; each suite has a living room, a dining room, a deck, a kitchen, and one or two bedrooms with bath (some with hot tubs). It's a good choice for families. ✉ *1234 Wharf St., V8W 3H9, ☎ 250/386–2211 or 800/663–7472, ⅋ 250/386–2622. 10 rooms, 34 suites. Restaurant, kitchenettes, no-smoking rooms, refrigerators, coin laundry, meeting room, free parking. AE, D, DC, MC, V.*

**$$$** 🏨 **Abigail's Hotel.** The elegant informality in this no-smoking hotel is
★ especially noticeable in the guest library and sitting room, where hors d'oeuvres are served each evening. Breakfast, included in the room rate, is served in the downstairs dining room. ✉ *906 McClure St., V8V 3E7, ☎ 250/388–5363 or 800/561–6565, ⅋ 250/361–1905. 16 rooms. Breakfast room, library, concierge, free parking. MC, V.*

**$$$** 🏨 **Bedford Regency.** This European-style hotel in the heart of downtown is reminiscent of San Francisco's small hotels, with personalized service and careful attention to details. Rooms are in earth colors, and many have goose-down comforters, fireplaces, and whirlpool bathtubs. Four rooms on the west side have views of the harbor and are much quieter than those facing the traffic on Government Street. ✉ *1140 Government St., V8W 1Y2, ☎ 250/384–6835 or 800/665–6500, ⅋ 250/386–8930. 40 rooms. Restaurant, pub, no-smoking rooms, laundry service and dry cleaning, business services, free parking. AE, MC, V.*

**$$$** 🏨 **Haterleigh Heritage Inn.** Leaded- and stained-glass windows, intricate moldings, and ornate plasterwork on 11-ft ceilings transport guests here to a more gracious time. Mounds of pillows and plump down comforters dress the beds. Extras like sherry and chocolates delivered to your room on check-in are nice touches indeed, as are the hearty family-style breakfasts. ✉ *243 Kingston St., V8V 1V5, ☎ 250/384–9995, ⅋ 250/384–1935. 5 double rooms, 1 2-bedroom room, 1 suite. Whirlpool tubs in several rooms. MC, V.*

**$$$** 🏨 **Oak Bay Beach Hotel.** Beside the ocean in Oak Bay on the southwest side of the Saanich Peninsula, this Tudor-style hotel is just 10 minutes from the bustle of downtown. The hotel overlooks Haro Strait; the antiques and flower prints decorating the rooms echo the dreamy landscaped grounds above the pebble beach. Most of the highly individual rooms have antiques (lots of slipper chairs and high brass or canopy beds), though a 1992 renovation brought contemporary styling, furniture, and fixtures to some. ✉ *1175 Beach Dr., V8S 2N2, ☎ 250/598–4556 or 800/668–7758, ⅋ 250/598–6180. 51 rooms. Restaurant, pub, no-smoking rooms, limited room service, boating, meeting room, free parking. AE, DC, MC, V.*

**$$–$$$** 🏨 **Coast Victoria Harbourside.** West of the Inner Harbour in a residential
★ section of the waterfront, the Coast Victoria has marine views but is away from the traffic on Government Street. Serene relaxation in modern comfort is a theme here, from the warm mahogany-paneled lobby and soothing shades in average-size guest rooms to an extensive health club. ✉ *146 Kingston St., V8V 1V4, ☎ 250/360–1211 or 800/663–1144, ⅋ 250/360–1418. 118 rooms, 14 suites. Restaurant, lounge, no-smoking rooms, room service, indoor-outdoor pool, hot tub, sauna,*

*health club, business services, meeting rooms, free parking. AE, DC, MC, V.*

**$$–$$$**  🖭 **Holland House Inn.** Two blocks from the Inner Harbour, legislative buildings, and ferry terminals, this no-smoking hotel surrounded by a picket fence exudes a casual elegance. Some of the individually designed rooms have original fine art created by local artists; some have four-poster beds and fireplaces. All but two rooms have balconies. The room rates include a lavish breakfast. ⊠ *595 Michigan St., V8V 1S7,* ☎ *250/384–6644,* FAX *250/384–6117. 10 rooms. No-smoking rooms. AE, MC, V.*

**$$**  🖭 **Mulberry Manor.** The last building designed by Victoria architect Samuel McClure has been restored and decorated to magazine-cover perfection with antiques, sumptuous linens, and tile baths. The Tudor-style mansion sits behind a high stone wall on an acre of carefully manicured grounds. Charming hosts Susan and Tony Temple serve sumptuous breakfasts with homemade jams and great coffee. ⊠ *611 Foul Bay Rd., V8S 1H2,* ☎ *250/370–1918,* FAX *250/370–1968. 3 rooms, 1 suite. Breakfast room, no-smoking rooms. MC, V.*

**$$**  🖭 **Swans.** Extensive renovations have given a 1913 brick warehouse a new look: There's a brewery, bistro, and pub on the first floor; large apartmentlike guest rooms decorated with Pacific Northwest art fill the upper floors. Swans is a good choice for families. ⊠ *506 Pandora Ave., V8W 1N6,* ☎ *250/361–3310 or 800/668–7926,* FAX *250/361–3491. 29 rooms. Restaurant, pub, no-smoking rooms, coin laundry. AE, DC, MC, V.*

**$–$$**  🖭 **Admiral Motel.** On Victoria harbor along the tourist strip, this modern motel is in the center of things but relatively quiet in the evening. The amiable owners take good care of the rooms, and small pets are permitted. Children under 12 stay free in their parents' room. ⊠ *257 Belleville St., V8V 1X1,* ☎ FAX *250/388–6267. 29 rooms. Kitchenettes, no-smoking rooms, coin laundry, free parking. AE, D, MC, V.*

**$**  🖭 **Cats Meow.** Dorm space at this youth hostel costs less than $20 a night; a private room costs about $45 for two people. ⊠ *1316 Grant St., V8R 1M3,* ☎ FAX *250/595–8878. 1 dorm with 6 beds shares bath, 2 private rooms share bath. No credit cards.*

# Nightlife and the Arts

## Bars and Clubs

**Harpo's** (⊠ 15 Bastion Sq., ☎ 250/385–5333) hosts rock, blues, and jazz performers. Call the **Jazz Hotline** (☎ 250/658–5255) for jazz updates. In addition to live music, darts, and brewery tours, **Spinnakers Brew Pub** (⊠ 308 Catherine St., ☎ 250/386–2739) pours plenty of British Columbian microbrewery beer. For dancing, head to **Sweetwater's** (⊠ 27-560 Johnson St., ☎ 250/383–7844), where a younger crowd moves on two dance floors to taped techno and Top 40.

## Music

The **Victoria International Music Festival** (☎ 250/736–2119) presents internationally acclaimed musicians each summer from the first week in July to late August. The **Victoria Symphony** plays in the Royal Theatre (⊠ 805 Broughton St., ☎ 250/386–6121) and at the University Centre Auditorium (⊠ Finnerty Rd., ☎ 250/721–8480).

## Opera

The **Pacific Opera Victoria** performs three productions a year in the 900-seat McPherson Playhouse (⊠ 3 Centennial Sq., ☎ 250/386–6121), adjoining the Victoria City Hall.

# Outdoor Activities and Sports

## Golf

The **Cordova Bay Golf Course** (✉ 5333 Cordova Bay Rd., ☎ 250/658–4444) is an 18-hole, par-72 course set on the shoreline. The greens fee ranges from $30 to $45, plus $27 for an optional cart.

## Whale-Watching

To see the pods of orcas that travel in the waters around Vancouver Island, you can take charter boat tours from Victoria from May to October. These three-hour Zodiac (motor-powered inflatable boat) excursions cost about $75 per person: **Great Pacific Adventures** (☎ 250/386–2277), **Ocean Explorations** (☎ 250/383–6722), and **Seacoast Expeditions** (☎ 250/383–2254) are the top operators.

# Shopping

## Shopping Centers

**Eaton Centre** (✉ 1 Victoria Eaton Centre, at Government and Fort Sts., ☎ 250/382–7141), a department store and mall, has about 100 boutiques and restaurants. **Market Square** (✉ 560 Johnson St., ☎ 250/386–2441) has three stories of specialty shops and offbeat stores. You'll find many specialty stores on Government Street downtown, particularly in the blocks between 800 and 1400.

# Victoria Essentials

## Arriving and Departing

### BY BOAT

**B.C. Ferries** (☎ 250/386–3431; 888/223–3779 in British Columbia only) operates daily service between Vancouver and Victoria. The Vancouver terminal is in Tawwassen, 38 km (24 mi) southwest of downtown at the end of Highway 17. In Victoria, ferries arrive at and depart from Swartz Bay Terminal at the end of Pat Bay Highway, 32 km (20 mi) north of downtown Victoria. The tickets cost about $8 per passenger, and $30 per vehicle. Rates fluctuate depending on the season.

There is year-round passenger service between Victoria and Seattle on the *Victoria Clipper* (☎ 250/382–8100 in Victoria; 206/448–5000 in Seattle; 800/888–2535 in the U.S. only).

**Washington State Ferries** (☎ 250/381–1551; 206/464–6400 in the U.S.; 800/843–3779 in WA only) cross daily, year-round, between Sidney, just north of Victoria, and Anacortes, Washington. **Black Ball Transport** (☎ 250/386–2202; 206/457–4491 in the U.S.) operates between Victoria and Port Angeles, Washington.

Direct passenger and vehicle service between Victoria and Seattle is available from mid-May to mid-September on the *Princess Marguerite III*, operated by **Clipper Navigation** (☎ 250/480–5555 in Victoria; 206/448–5000 in Seattle; 800/888–2535 in the U.S. only). The boat departs from Ogden Point in Victoria each morning at 7:30 AM and arrives at Seattle's Pier 48 at 12 noon. It departs from Seattle at 1 PM, arriving back at Odgen Point at 5:30. Reservations are advised if you're traveling with a vehicle.

### BY BUS

**Pacific Coach Lines** (☎ 800/661–1725) operates daily connecting service between Victoria and Vancouver on B.C. Ferries.

### BY CAR

**Highway 17** connects the Swartz Bay ferry terminal on the Saanich Peninsula with downtown Victoria. **Island Highway** (Highway 1, also known as the Trans-Canada Highway) runs south from Nanaimo to Victoria. **Highway 14** connects Sooke to Port Renfrew, on the west coast of Vancouver Island, with Victoria.

BY HELICOPTER

**Helijet Airways** (☎ 604/628–1468 or 250/382–6222) helicopter service is available from downtown Vancouver to downtown Victoria.

BY PLANE

**Victoria International Airport** (✉ Willingdon Rd. off Hwy. 17, Sidney, ☎ 250/953–7500) is served by Air B.C., Air Canada, Canadian, Horizon, and Westjet. *See* Air Travel *in* the Gold Guide for airline numbers. Air B.C. provides airport-to-airport service from Vancouver to Victoria at least hourly. Flights take about 35 minutes.

BY TRAIN

**VIA Rail** (☎ 800/835–3037) serves Victoria's VIA Rail Station (✉ 450 Pandora Ave., at the east end of the Johnson Street Bridge).

## Getting Around

BY BUS

The **B.C. Transit System** (☎ 250/382–6161) serves Victoria and the surrounding areas. An all-day pass costs $5.

BY TAXI

**Empress Taxi** (☎ 250/381–2222). **Victoria Taxi** (☎ 250/383–7111).

## Contacts and Resources

CAR RENTAL

**ABC Rent a Car** (☎ 250/388–3153, ℻ 250/388–0111).

EMERGENCIES

**Ambulance** (☎ 911). **Police** (☎ 911).

**Victoria General Hospital** (✉ 35 Helmcken Rd., ☎ 250/727–4212).

GUIDED TOURS

**Gray Line** (☎ 250/388–5248) conducts city tours on double-decker buses that visit the city center, Chinatown, Antique Row, Oak Bay, and Beacon Hill Park; a combination tour stops at Butchart Gardens as well. See the sights of the Inner Harbour by **Harbour Gondola** (☎ 250/480–8841), complete with an authentically garbed gondolier to narrate the tour. **Tally-Ho Horsedrawn Tours** (☎ 250/479–1113) operates a get-acquainted tour with downtown Victoria that includes Beacon Hill Park. **Victoria Carriage Tours** (☎ 250/383–2207) has horse-drawn tours of the city.

LATE-NIGHT PHARMACY

**McGill and Orme Pharmacies** (✉ 649 Fort St., ☎ 250/384–1195).

VISITOR INFORMATION

**Discover B.C.** (☎ 800/663–6000). **Tourism Victoria** (✉ 812 Wharf St., V8W 1T3, ☎ 250/953–2033).

# SOUTHERN VANCOUVER ISLAND

The largest island on Canada's west coast, Vancouver Island stretches 450 km (279 mi) from Victoria in the south to Cape Scott in the north. Thick conifer forests blanket it down to soft, sandy beaches on the eastern shoreline and rocky, wave-pounded grottoes and inlets along the western shore. The cultural heritage of the island is from the Kwakiutl, Nootka, and Coastal Salish native groups. Arts and other centers flourish throughout the region, enabling you to catch a glimpse of contemporary native culture.

Mining, logging, and tourism are the important island industries. Environmental issues, such as the logging practices of British Columbia's lumber companies, are becoming important to islanders—both native and nonnative. Residents are working to establish a balance between the island's wilderness and its economy.

# Sooke

*42 km (26 mi) west of Victoria on Hwy. 14.*

Sooke is a logging, fishing, and farming community. **East Sooke Park,** on the east side of the harbor, has 350 acres of beaches, hiking trails, and wildflower-dotted meadows.

You can also visit the **Sooke Regional Museum and Travel Infocentre,** which holds displays of Salish and Nootka crafts and artifacts from 19th-century Sooke. In summer, food fests of barbecued salmon and strawberry shortcake are sometimes held on the front lawn. ✉ *2070 Phillips Rd., Box 774, V0S 1N0,* ☎ *250/642–6351,* FAX *250/642–7089.* 🖾 *Donations accepted.* ☉ *June–Aug., daily 9–6; Sept.–May, Tues.–Sun. 9–5.*

## Dining and Lodging

$ ✕ **Seventeen Mile House.** Stop here on the road between Sooke and Victoria for British pub fare, a beer, or fresh local seafood. Built as a hotel, the house is a study in turn-of-the-century island architecture. ✉ *5121 Sooke Rd.,* ☎ *250/642–5942. MC, V.*

$$$$ ✕🖾 **Sooke Harbour House.** This oceanfront 1931 clapboard farmhouse–
★ turned–country inn has three suites, a 10-room addition, and a dining room—all of which exude elegance. The restaurant is one of the finest in British Columbia: The seafood is just-caught fresh, and the herbs are grown on the property. In the romantic guest rooms, natural wood and white finishes add to each unit's unique theme. French doors in the Herb Garden Room, which is decorated in shades of mint, open onto a private patio. Native American furnishings grace the Longhouse Room. The room rates include breakfast and lunch. At press time an additional 10 rooms were slated to be added by winter 1998. ✉ *1528 Whiffen Spit Rd., R.R. 4, V0S 1N0,* ☎ *250/642–3421 or 250/642–4944,* FAX *250/642–6988. 13 rooms. Restaurant, no-smoking rooms, beach, meeting room. AE, MC, V.*

$$–$$$ ✕🖾 **Ocean Wilderness.** A large 1940s log cabin sits on 5 forested, beach-front acres, 13 km (8 mi) west of Sooke. Owner Marion Rolston built a rough cedar addition in 1990; she furnishes her home with Victorian antiques she picks up at auction. Romantic canopies and ruffled linens on high beds dominate the spacious guest rooms, which have sitting areas with views of either the Strait of Juan de Fuca or the pretty gardens in the back, as well as private decks or patios. The dining room fare is innovative West Coast treatments of fresh local fish and meats. ✉ *109 W. Coast Rd., R.R. 2, V0S 1N0,* ☎ FAX *250/646–2116. 9 rooms. Dining room, no-smoking rooms, hot tub, hiking. MC, V.*

## Shopping

Watercolor artist and author **Sue Coleman** (☎ 250/478–0380) in Metchosin, 35 minutes west of Victoria on the road to Sooke, invites visitors to the island to tour her studio by appointment.

# Duncan

*60 km (37 mi) north of Victoria on the Trans-Canada Hwy. (Hwy. 1).*

Duncan is nicknamed City of Totems for the many totem poles that dot the small community. The two carvings behind the City Hall are worth a short trip off the main road.

The **Native Heritage Centre** covers 13 acres on the banks of the Cowichan River. The center includes a native longhouse, a theater, occasional interpretative dance presentations, an arts-and-crafts gallery that focuses on carvings and weaving traditions, and native fare served in the Bighouse Restaurant. ⊠ *200 Cowichan Way,* ☎ *250/746–8119,* FAX *250/746–4143.* ✑ *$8.* ◔ *Mid-May–mid-Oct., daily 9:30–5:30; mid-Oct.–mid-May, daily 10–4:30.*

The **British Columbia Forest Museum,** more a park than a museum, spans 100 acres, combining indoor and outdoor exhibits that focus on the history of forestry in the province. You ride an original steam locomotive around the property and over an old wood trestle bridge. The exhibits show logging and milling equipment. ⊠ *Trans-Canada Hwy.,* ☎ *250/746–1251,* FAX *250/715–1113.* ✑ *$7.50.* ◔ *May–Sept., daily 9:30–6; Oct.–Apr. by appointment.*

### Shopping

Duncan is the home of Cowichan wool sweaters, hand knitted by the Cowichan people. A large selection of sweaters is available from **Hills Indian Crafts** (☎ 250/746–6731) on the main highway, about 1½ km (1 mi) south of Duncan. **Modeste Wool Carding** (⊠ 2615 Modeste Rd., ☎ 250/748–8983), about a half mile off the highway, also carries a selection of handmade knitwear.

## Chemainus

*85 km (53 mi) north of Victoria, 27 km (17 mi) south of Nanaimo.*

Chemainus is known for the bold epic murals that decorate its townscape. Once dependent on the lumber industry, the small community began to revitalize itself in the early 1980s when its mill closed down. Since then, the town has brought in international artists to paint more than 30 murals depicting local historical events around town. Footprints on the sidewalk lead you on a self-guided tour of the murals. Restaurants, shops, tearooms, coffee bars, art galleries, antiques dealers, and the new **Chemainus Theater** (☎ 250/246–9820 or 800/565–7738), which presents live theater (matinees and shows with dinner included), have added to the town's growth.

### Lodging

$$$ ▨ **Little Inn on Willow.** This fairy-tale-looking little cottage, complete with gingerbread and turret, is a romantic delight. Built for two, it has a lavishly draped bed, a whirlpool tub for two, and a fireplace. The cottage is managed by the Pacific Shores Inn next door, which caters more to families, with simpler accommodations with fully equipped kitchens. ⊠ *Chemainus Rd., Box 958, V0R 1K0,* ☎ *250/246–4987,* FAX *250/246–4785. 1 cottage, 3 rooms (Pacific Shores). MC.*

## Nanaimo

*110 km (68 mi) northwest of Victoria, 115 km (71 mi) southeast of Courtenay, 155 km (96 mi) southeast of Campbell River, 23 km (14 mi) on land plus 38 nautical mi west of Vancouver.*

Petroglyphs (rock carvings) throughout the Nanaimo area represent humans, birds, wolves, lizards, sea monsters, and supernatural creatures. The **Nanaimo District Museum** (⊠ 100 Cameron St., ☎ 250/753–1821) will give you information about local carvings. Eight kilometers (5 miles) south of town at **Petroglyph Provincial Park** (⊠ Hwy. 1, ☎ 250/387–5002), you can follow marked trails that begin at the parking lot to see designs carved thousands of years ago.

## Dining and Lodging

**$$** ✕ **Mahle House.** This casually elegant place serves innovative North-
★ west cuisine, such as braised rabbit with Dijon mustard and red wine
sauce. Among the items on the regular menu are a succulent carrot and
ginger soup and a catch of the day. Attention to detail, an intimate set-
ting, and three country-style rooms make this one of the finest dining
experiences in the region. ⊠ *Cedar and Heemer Rds.,* ☎ *250/722–
3621. MC, V. Closed Mon.–Tues. No lunch.*

**$–$$** ✕ **The Grotto.** A Nanaimo institution that specializes in a variety of
★ seafood has a casual waterfront setting. Try oysters on the half shell,
spareribs, garlic prawn pasta, or the seafood platter that's big enough
for two. The Kitchen Sink, a heaping bowl of clams, shrimp, and
salmon steamed in white wine, herbs, and butter, is a favorite. ⊠ *1511
Stewart Ave.,* ☎ *250/753–3303. AE, MC, V. No lunch.*

**$$–$$$** ✕🏨 **Coast Bastion Inn Nanaimo.** This convenient hotel is downtown
near the ferry terminal and train and bus stations. Rooms with balconies and modern furnishings have views of the old Hudson's Bay fort
and the ocean. There's an Irish deli-pub. ⊠ *11 Bastion St., V9R 2Z9,*
☎ *250/753–6601; 800/663–1144 in the U.S.;* ℻ *250/753–4155.
179 rooms. Restaurant, lounge, no-smoking rooms, room service, hot
tub, sauna, exercise room, laundry service and dry cleaning, meeting
rooms. AE, DC, MC, V.*

**$$$** 🏨 **Yellow Point Lodge.** Yellow Point is a very popular resort area on
★ a spit of land 24 km (15 mi) south of Nanaimo, 13 km (8 mi) north-
east of Ladysmith. Rebuilt in 1986 after a fire destroyed the original,
the lodge lost almost nothing of its homey, summer-camp ambience.
Nine large lodge rooms and a range of cottages all have private baths;
most are available year-round. Perched on a rocky knoll overlooking
the Stuart Channel are beach cabins, field cabins, and beach barracks
for the hardy; these are closed from mid-October to mid-April, have
no running water, and share a central bathhouse. You can stroll the
lodge's 178 acres, and there are canoes and kayaks for exploring the
shoreline. The room rate includes three full meals and snacks. ⊠ *3700
Yellow Point Rd., R.R. 3, Ladysmith V0R 2E0,* ☎ *250/245–7422,* ℻
*250/245–7411. 50 rooms. Restaurant (for guests only), no-smoking
rooms, saltwater pool, hot tub, sauna, 2 tennis courts, badminton, jog-
ging, volleyball, boating, mountain bikes. MC, V.*

**$$–$$$** 🏨 **Best Western Dorchester Hotel.** Upbeat Mediterranean tones of
champagne, ocher, and teal brighten the exterior of the Dorchester. Once
the Nanaimo Opera House, this elegant hotel in the city center over-
looking the harbor has a distinctive character, with gold knockers on
each of the doors, winding hallways, and a rooftop patio. The rooms
are small but exceptionally comfortable, and most have views of the
harbor. ⊠ *70 Church St., V9R 5H4,* ☎ *250/754–6835 or 800/528–
1234,* ℻ *250/754–2638. 65 rooms. Restaurant, lounge, no-smoking
rooms, room service, library, laundry service and dry cleaning, meet-
ing rooms. AE, D, DC, MC, V.*

## Outdoor Activities and Sports

CANOEING AND KAYAKING

**Wild Heart Adventures** (⊠ Site P, C-5, R.R. 4, V9R 5X9, ☎ 250/722–
3683) conducts multiple-day guided sea-kayak expeditions.

# Southern Vancouver Island Essentials

## Arriving and Departing

### BY BUS

**Island Coach Lines** (☎ 250/385–4411) serves the Vancouver Island area. **Laidlaw Coach Lines** (☎ 250/385–4411) operates buses from Victoria to Sooke, Duncan, Chemainus, and Nanaimo. **Maverick Coach Lines** (☎ 604/662–8051) provides service between Vancouver and Nanaimo.

### BY CAR

The Island Highway (Highway 1), which becomes Highway 19 in Nanaimo, is the main road up the east side of Vancouver Island.

### BY FERRY

**B.C. Ferries** (☎ 250/386–3431; 888/223–3779 in British Columbia only) provides service from outside Vancouver and Victoria to Nanaimo.

### BY TRAIN

**VIA Rail** (☎ 800/835–3037) provides service between Victoria and Nanaimo.

## Getting Around

### BY CAR

To reach Nanaimo from the Departure Bay ferry terminal, take Stewart Avenue south to Terminal Avenue, which intersects with the downtown core.

## Contacts and Resources

### CAR RENTAL

Most major agencies, including **Avis, Budget,** and **Hertz,** serve cities throughout the province. *See* Car Rental *in* the Gold Guide for company numbers.

### EMERGENCIES

Dial 0 for an ambulance or the police.

### GOLF BOOKINGS

**Tee-Time Central Booking Service** (✉ 412–4004 Bluebird Rd., Kelowna V1W 1X3, ☎ 250/764–4118 or 800/930–4622), a service for out-of-town golfers, lists courses throughout Vancouver Island and mainland British Columbia. It's open between mid-May and mid-October, weekdays from 9 to 5.

### VISITOR INFORMATION

**Tourism Association of Vancouver Island** (✉ 302–45 Bastion Sq., Victoria, V8W 1J1, ☎ 250/382–3551).

# THE GULF ISLANDS

A temperate climate, scenic beaches, towering promontories, rolling pasturelands, and virgin forests are common to many of the Gulf Islands—Galiano, Mayne, and Saltspring are among the most popular. Marine birds are numerous, and unusual vegetation such as arbutus trees (also known as madrones, a leafy evergreen with red peeling bark) and Garry oaks differentiate the islands from other areas around Vancouver.

## Galiano Island

*20 nautical mi (almost 2 hrs by ferry due to interisland stops) from Swartz Bay (32 km/20 mi north of Victoria), 13 nautical mi (a 50-min ferry ride) from Tsawwassen (39 km/24 mi south of Vancouver).*

The activities on Galiano Island are almost exclusively of the outdoor type. The long, unbroken eastern shoreline is perfect for leisurely beach walks, while the numerous coves and inlets along the western coast make it a prime area for kayaking. Miles of trails through forests of Douglas fir beg for exploration by foot or bike. Hikers can climb to the top of **Mount Galiano** for a view of the Olympic Mountains in Washington or trek the length of **Bodega Ridge.** The best spots to view **Active Pass** and the surrounding islands are Bluffs Park, Bellhouse Park, and Centennial Park; these are also good areas for picnicking and bird-watching.

Biological studies show that the straits between Vancouver Island and the mainland of British Columbia are home to the largest variety of marine life in North America. The frigid waters offer superb visibility, especially in winter. Acala Point, Porlier Pass, and Active Pass are top locations for scuba diving. Fisherman head to the point at Bellhouse Park to cast for salmon from shore, or head by boat to Porlier Pass and Trincomali Channel.

## Lodging

$$$ ⊞ **Woodstone Country Inn.** This serene inn sits on the edge of a forest overlooking a meadow that's fantastic for bird-watching. Stenciled walls and tall windows bring the pastoral setting into spacious bedrooms furnished in a mixture of wicker, antiques, and English country prints. Most rooms have fireplaces and patios, and a few have oversize soaker tubs. The room rates include a hearty gourmet breakfast. Guests and nonguests can have four-course dinners here by advance reservation. Smoking is not permitted at the inn. ⊠ *Georgeson Bay Rd., R.R. 1, V0N 1P0,* ☎ *250/539–2022 or 250/539–5198. 12 rooms. AE, MC, V.*

$ ⊞ **Sutil Lodge.** The simple guest rooms at this 1927 British colonial bungalow have throw rugs on dark hardwood floors and beds tucked into window nooks; the shared bathrooms have antique ball-foot tubs and small corner sinks. The kayak center on the property attracts folks from around the world who want to paddle the still coves of the Gulf Islands (rentals and guided trips are available). The room rates include breakfast. ⊠ *637 Southwind Rd., Montague Harbour, V0N 1P0,* ☎ *250/539–2930,* ⨳ *250/539–5390. 7 rooms share 3 baths. Dining room, hiking. MC, V.*

## Outdoor Activities and Sports

### BICYCLES

Bike rentals are available from **Galiano Bicycle** (☎ 250/539–9906).

### BOATING, DIVING, AND FISHING

For dive charters on Galiano, contact **Martin Karakas** (☎ 250/539–5186) or **George Parson** (☎ 250/539–3109). Call **Mel-n-i Fishing Charters** (☎ 250/539–3171) or **Bert's Charters** (☎ 250/539–3109) to charter a fishing boat.

### GOLF

The nine-hole, par-32 course at **Galiano Golf and Country Club** (☎ 250/539–5533) is moderate in difficulty. The greens fee is $17; power carts are not available.

### KAYAKING

For equipment rentals and guided kayak tours, contact **Gulf Islands Kayaking** (☎ 250/539–2442). **Canadian Gulf Islands Seakayaking** (☎ 250/539–2930) has rentals and tours.

# Mayne Island

*28 nautical mi from Swartz Bay (32 km/20 mi north of Victoria), 22 nautical mi from Tsawwassen (39 km/24 mi south of Vancouver).*

Middens of clam and oyster shells give evidence that tiny Mayne Island—only 21 square km (13 square mi)—was inhabited as early as 5,000 years ago. It later became the stopover point for miners headed from Victoria to the gold fields of Fraser River and Barkersville, and by the mid-1800s it had developed into the communal center of the inhabited Gulf Islands, with the first school, post office, police lockup, church, and hotel. Farm tracts and orchards established in the 1930s and 1940s and worked by Japanese farmers until their internment during World War II continue to thrive today, and a farmer's market is open each Saturday during harvest season. There are few stores, restaurants, or historic sites here, but Mayne's manageable size (even if you're on a bicycle) and slow pace make it very popular.

Starting at the ferry dock at Village Bay, head toward Miners Bay on Village Bay Road. About ½ mi from the ferry landing on the left is the unmarked path to **Helen Point** (pull off on the shoulder near the grouping of power lines that cross the road), previously a native reservation but currently without inhabitants. You'll pass middens by the bay and the remains of log cabins in the woods on the hour-long hike out to Helen Point, where you can look out across Active Pass (named for the turbulent waters).

A quarter mile farther on the right side of Village Bay Road is the entrance to **Mount Parke,** declared a wilderness park in 1989. Drive as far as the gate and the sign that reads NO VEHICLES PAST THIS POINT. From here it's a 15- to 20-minute hike to the highest point on the island and a stunning, almost 360-degree view of Vancouver, Active Pass, and Vancouver Island.

Continue on Village Bay Road toward **Miners Bay,** a little town 2 km (1 mi) away. Here, you'll find Plumbers Pass Lockup (closed from September to June), built in 1896 as a jail and now a minuscule museum chronicling the island's history.

From Miners Bay head east on Georgia Point Road to **St. Mary Magdalene Church,** a pretty stone chapel built in 1898 that now doubles as an Anglican and United church. The graveyard beyond is also interesting; generations of islanders—the Bennets, Georgesons, Maudes, and Deacons (whose names are all over the Mayne Island map)—are buried. A stairway across the road stairway leads down to the beach.

At the end of Georgia Point Road is the **Active Pass Lighthouse,** built in 1855, which still signals ships into the busy waterway. The grassy grounds, open to the public daily from 1 to 3, are great for picnicking.

Head back down Georgia Point Road and turn left on Waugh Road, which turns into Campbell Bay Road. There's a great pebble beach for beachcombing at shallow (and therefore warmer) **Campbell Bay.** Look for a pull-out on the left just past the bottom of the hairpin turn. A fencepost marks the entrance to the path leading to the beach. Campbell Bay Road ends at Fernhill Road; turn right here and you'll end up back in Miners Bay.

## Dining and Lodging

$$$–$$$$ ✕▥ **Oceanwood Country Inn.** This Tudor-style house on 10 forested
★ acres overlooking Navy Channel has English country decor throughout. Fireplaces, ocean-view balconies, and whirlpool or soaking tubs

make several rooms deluxe; all are inviting, with cozy down comforters on comfortable beds, cheerful wall stenciling, and cushioned chairs in brightly lighted reading areas. The waterfront dining room, which is open to the public for dinner, serves outstanding regional cuisine. Afternoon tea and breakfast are included in the room rates. ⊠ *630 Dinner Bay Rd., V0N 2J0,* ☎ *250/539–5074,* ℻ *250/539–3002. 12 rooms. Restaurant, no-smoking rooms, hot tub, sauna, hiking, jogging, beach, bicycles, library, meeting room. MC, V.*

**$$–$$$** ✕🔟 **Fernhill Lodge.** Constructed of wood from the property, this 1983 West Coast cedar structure has fantastic theme rooms—Moroccan, East Indian, Edwardian, Japanese, Colonial, Jacobean, and French. Two of them have outdoor hot tubs. Hosts Mary and Brian Crumblehulme prepare historical dinners (Rome, Chaucer, and Cleopatra, to name a few themes) several nights a week; nonguests must reserve in advance. Breakfasts, included in the room rate, are less exotic. This is a no-smoking inn, and pets are not allowed. ⊠ *Fernhill Rd., R.R. 1 C-4, V0N 2J0,* ☎ *250/539–2544. 7 rooms. Dining room, no-smoking rooms, sauna, bicycles, library. MC, V.*

### Outdoor Activities and Sports

You can rent bicycles at the **Miner's Bay gas station.**

## Saltspring Island

*28 nautical mi from Swartz Bay (32 km/20 mi north of Victoria), 22 nautical mi from Tsawwassen (39 km/24 mi south of Vancouver).*

Named for the saltwater springs at its north end, Saltspring is the largest and most developed of the Gulf Islands. Among its first nonnative settlers were black Americans who came here to escape slavery in the 1850s. The agrarian tradition they and other immigrants established remains strong, but tourism and art now support the local economy. A government wharf, two marinas, and a waterfront shopping complex at Ganges serve a community of more than 8,500 residents.

In **Ganges,** a pedestrian-oriented seaside village and the island's cultural and commercial center, you'll find dozens of smart boutiques, galleries, and restaurants. Mouat's Trading Company (Fulford–Ganges Road), built in 1912 and still functioning as a community store, is worth a peek. Ganges is the site of **ArtCraft,** a summer-long festival of arts, crafts, theater, music, and dance. Dozens of artists' studios are open to the public; pick up a studio tour map at the Chamber of Commerce on Lower Ganges Road.

From Ganges, you can circle the northern tip of the island by bike or car (on Vesuvius Bay Road, Sunset Road, North End and North Beach roads, Walker Hook Road, and Robson Road) past fields and peekaboo marine views. You can take a shortcut on North End Road past **St. Mary Lake,** your best bet for warm-water swimming.

Near the center of Saltspring, the summit of **Mount Maxwell Provincial Park** (⊠ Mt. Maxwell Rd., off Fulford–Ganges Rd.) affords spectacular views of south Saltspring, Vancouver Island, and other of the Gulf Islands. It's also a great picnic spot. The last portion of the drive is steep, winding, and unpaved.

From Mount Maxwell, follow Fulford–Ganges Road south, then turn east on Beaver Point Road to reach **Ruckle Provincial Park,** site of an 1872 heritage homestead and extensive fields still being farmed by the Ruckle family. The park also has camping and picnic spots and trails leading to rocky headlands.

## Saltspring Island

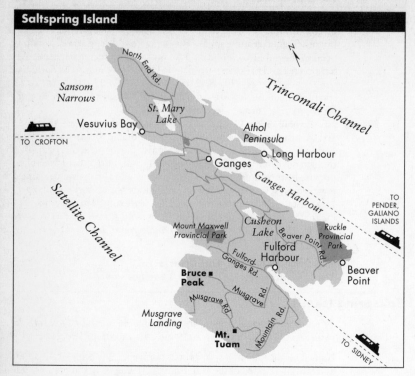

## Dining and Lodging

**$$** ✕ **House Piccolo.** Broiled sea scallop brochette, roasted British Columbia venison with juniper berries, and the salmon du jour are good choices for dinner at this casual restaurant. But save room for homemade ice cream or the signature chocolate terrine. ⊠ *108 Hereford Ave., Ganges,* ☎ *250/537–1844. Reservations essential. AE, DC, MC, V. Closed Jan. No lunch.*

**$–$$** ✕ **Pomodori.** Earthenware pots with dried flowers, antique farm implements, battered wooden tables, bent-willow chairs, and international folk music set an eclectic tone for an eatery with a menu that changes daily. Roasted tomato, red pepper, and Italian feta in balsamic-vinegar and olive-oil dressing with home-baked focaccia for dipping; chicken, prawn, and mussel jambalaya; and fresh vegetable and herb stew appear often. ⊠ *Booth Bay Resort, 375 Baker Rd., Ganges,* ☎ *250/537–2247. Reservations essential. MC, V. No lunch Mon.–Sat.*

**$$$$** ✕▤ **Hastings House.** The centerpiece of this luxurious 30-acre seaside farm estate is a Tudor-style manor built in 1940. Guest quarters are in the manor or the farmhouse, in cliffside or garden cottages and in suites in the reconstructed barn. All are furnished with fine antiques in an English country theme, with extras such as eiderdowns, fireplaces, and covered porches or decks. Elegant prix-fixe dinners in the manor house are formal and open to the public. ⊠ *160 Upper Ganges Rd., Box 1110, Ganges, V0S 1E0,* ☎ *250/537–2362 or 800/661–9255,* FAX *250/537–5333. 3 rooms, 7 suites, 2 2-bedroom suites. Restaurant, minibars, no-smoking rooms, croquet, beach, mountain bikes. AE, MC, V. Closed Jan.–mid-Mar.*

$$$  ⊞ **Beach House on Sunset.** Two upstairs rooms in this B&B have private entrances and balconies; a romantic cedar-lined cottage with a wraparound porch sits over the boathouse at water's edge. There's also a suite with a cathedral ceiling, broad windows framing lovely sea views, and a private deck with an outdoor shower. Extras include eiderdown comforters, thick terry robes, slippers, fruit platters, decanters of sherry, fresh flowers, and a bountiful breakfast. ⊠ *930 Sunset Dr., V8K 1E6,* ☎ *250/537–2879,* FAX *250/537–4747. 4 rooms. Library. MC, V. Closed Dec.–Feb.*

$$$  ⊞ **Old Farmhouse Bed and Breakfast.** The style of the main house, a registered historic property built in 1895, is echoed in a four-room wing added in 1989 that has rooms furnished with pine bedsteads, down comforters, lace curtains, and wicker chairs. Breakfast in the dining room begins with fresh-baked goods followed by a hot entrée such as a smoked salmon soufflé. ⊠ *1077 Northend Rd., V8K 1L9,* ☎ *250/ 537–4113,* FAX *250/537–4969. 4 rooms. Breakfast room, no-smoking rooms, boating. MC, V.*

$$$  ⊞ **Salty Springs Resort.** Perched on a 50-ft bluff on the northern shore of Saltspring, this is the only property to take advantage of the island's natural mineral springs. The one-, two-, and three-bedroom Ponderosa pine cabins have arched Gothic ceilings, fireplaces, kitchenettes, and whirlpool massage bathtubs that tap into the mineral springs. ⊠ *1460 N. Beach Rd., V8K 1J4,* ☎ *250/537–4111,* FAX *250/537–2939. 12 units. Picnic areas, kitchenettes, refrigerators, boating, bicycles, recreation room, coin laundry. MC, V.*

### Outdoor Activities and Sports

For bicycle rentals on Saltspring, try **Island Spoke Folk** (☎ 250/537–4664) at the Trading Company Building in Ganges.

### Shopping

There are bargains galore at Saltspring Island's **Saturday markets,** held from April to October. Fresh produce, seafood, crafts, clothing, herbs and aromatherapy mixtures, candles, toys, home-canned items, and more are available at two markets; one is at the top of the hill (next to the Harbour House) overlooking Ganges Harbour, the other in the center of town between Fulford–Ganges Road and Centennial Park.

## Gulf Islands Essentials

### Arriving and Departing

#### BY BOAT

**B.C. Ferries** (☎ 250/386–3431; 888/223–3779 in British Columbia only) provides service from outside Vancouver and Victoria to Galiano Island, Mayne Island, and Saltspring Island (reserve ahead). When you travel with a vehicle in summer, arrive at the terminal well in advance of the scheduled sailing time.

#### BY PLANE

**Harbour Air Ltd.** (☎ 250/537–5525 or 800/665–0212) and **Hanna Air Saltspring** (☎ 250/537–9359; 800/665–2359 in British Columbia only) operate 20- to 30-minute daily floatplane flights from Ganges on Saltspring Island to Coal Harbour in downtown Vancouver and to the Vancouver airport.

### Getting Around

#### BY BUS

**Salt Spring Transit** (☎ 250/537–4737) routes include one between the ferry terminal and Ganges.

## Contacts and Resources

### CAR RENTAL
Car rentals are available on Saltspring Island through **Heritage Rentals** (☎ 250/537–4225).

### EMERGENCIES
**Ambulance** (☎ 911). **Police** (☎ 911).
**Lady Minto Hospital** (✉ Ganges, Saltspring Island, ☎ 250/537–5545).

### GUIDED TOURS
**Ecological: Ecosummer Expeditions** (✉ 1516 Duranleau St., Vancouver V6H 3S4, ☎ 604/669–7741 or 800/465–8884, FAX 604/669–3244) and the **Canadian Outback Adventure Company** (✉ 1110 Hamilton St., Vancouver V6C 3L6, ☎ 604/688–7206) run ecological tours of the Gulf Islands.

**Orientation: Classic Holidays Tour & Travel** (✉ 102–75 W. Broadway, Vancouver V5Y 1P1, ☎ 604/875–6377) and **Sea to Sky** (✉ 1928 Nelson Ave., West Vancouver V7V 2P4, ☎ 604/922–7339) offer tours throughout British Columbia.

**Whale-Watching: Jamie's Whaling Station** (✉ Box 590, Tofino V0R 2Z0, ☎ 250/725–3919; 800/667–9913 in Canada), **Tofino Sea-Kayaking Company** (✉ Box 620, Tofino V0R 2Z0, ☎ 250/725–4222) on the west coast.

### VISITOR INFORMATION
**Galiano Island Visitor Information Centre** (✉ Sturdies Bay, Box 73, Galiano V0N 1P0, ☎ 250/539–2233). **Mayne Island Chamber of Commerce** (✉ General Delivery, Mayne Island V0N 2J0, no phone). **Saltspring Island Visitor Information Centre** (✉ 121 Lower Ganges Rd., Ganges V8K 2T1, ☎ 250/537–5252).

# WHISTLER

Whistler and Blackcomb mountains, part of the Whistler Resort (☎ 800/944–7853), are the two largest ski mountains in North America and are consistently ranked the first- or second-best ski destinations on the continent. There's winter and summer glacier skiing, the longest vertical drop in North America, and one of the most advanced lift systems in the world. Whistler has also grown in popularity as a summer destination, with a range of outdoor activities and events.

## Whistler Village

*120 km (74 mi) north of Vancouver, Hwy. 1 to Hwy. 99.*

At the base of the mountains are Whistler Village Town Plaza, Market Place, and Upper Village—a rapidly expanding, interconnected community of lodgings, restaurants, pubs, gift shops, and boutiques. Locals generally refer to the entire area as Whistler Village. With dozens of hotels and condos within a five-minute walk of the mountains, the site is frenzied with activity, though all on foot: Whistler Village is a pedestrian-only community.

### Dining
Dining at Whistler is informal; casual dress is appropriate everywhere. Japanese and Mediterranean offerings are strong in the village.

| CATEGORY | COST* |
|---|---|
| $$$$ | over C$40 |
| $$$ | C$30–C$40 |
| $$ | C$20–C$30 |
| $ | under C$20 |

*per person for a three-course meal, excluding drinks, service, and sales tax*

$$$ ✕ **Il Caminetto di Umberto, Trattoria di Umberto.** Umberto offers home-style Italian cooking in a relaxed atmosphere; he specializes in pasta dishes such as crab-stuffed cannelloni. Il Caminetto is known for its veal, osso buco, and zabaglione. The Trattoria has a Tuscan-style rotisserie. A pasta dish is served with a tray of chopped tomatoes, hot pepper, basil, olive oil, anchovies, and Parmesan so that you can mix it as spicy and flavorful as you like. ⊠ *Il Caminetto, 4242 Village Stroll,* ☎ *604/932–4442; Trattoria, Mountainside Lodge, 4417 Sundial Pl.,* ☎ *604/932–5858. Reservations essential. AE, DC, MC, V.*

$$$ ✕ **Les Deux Gros.** The name means "the two fat guys," which may ex-
★ plain the restaurant's motto, "Never trust a skinny chef." Portions of the country French cuisine are generous indeed. Alsatian onion pie, steak tartare, juicy rack of lamb, and salmon Wellington are all superbly crafted and presented, and service is friendly but unobtrusive. Just southwest of the village, this is the spot for a special romantic dinner; request one of the prime tables by the massive stone fireplace. ⊠ *1200 Alta Lake Rd.,* ☎ *604/932–4611. Reservations essential. AE, MC, V. No lunch.*

$$ ✕ **La Rúa.** One of the brightest lights on the Whistler dining scene is
★ on the ground floor of Le Chamois (☞ Lodging, *below*). Reddish flag-stone floors and sponge-painted walls, a wine cellar behind a wrought-iron door, modern oil paintings, and sconce lighting give the restaurant an intimate, Mediterranean ambience. Favorites from the Continental menu include charred rare tuna, loin of deer, rack of lamb, and baked sea bass fillet in a red-wine and herb sauce. ⊠ *4557 Blackcomb Way,* ☎ *604/932–5011. Reservations essential. AE, DC, MC, V. No lunch.*

$ ✕ **Zeuski's.** This friendly taverna, now in new digs at the Whistler Town
★ Plaza, introduced tasty, inexpensive Greek fare to Whistler. Wall murals of the Greek islands surround candlelit tables, helping create a Mediterranean atmosphere. There's a patio for alfresco dining. It's hard to pass on the spanikopita, souvlaki, and other standards, but the house special, *katapoulo* (chicken breast rolled in pistachios and roasted), is not to be missed, nor are the tender, herb-battered calamari. ⊠ *4314 Main St.,* ☎ *604/932–6009. Reservations essential. AE, MC, V.*

## Lodging

Accommodations in Whistler, including hundreds of time-share condos, can be booked through the **Whistler Resort Association** (☎ 604/932–3928 or 800/944–7853); summer rates are discounted. The **Pan Pacific Lodge,** managed by Pan Pacific Hotels (☎ 800/937–1515) was scheduled for completion in December 1997. The lodge will be in Whistler Village, at the base of Blackcomb and Whistler mountains.

| CATEGORY | COST* |
|---|---|
| $$$$ | over C$300 |
| $$$ | C$200–C$300 |
| $$ | C$125–C$200 |
| $ | under C$125 |

*All prices are for a standard double room for two, excluding 10% provincial accommodation tax, 15% service charge, and 7% GST.*

$$$$ 🏨 **Chateau Whistler.** Canadian Pacific built and runs this large and friendly-looking fortress in the Upper Village at the foot of Blackcomb Mountain. The standard rooms are average, but the suites are fit for royalty, with specially commissioned quilts and artworks, comple-

mented by antique furnishings. Expansion to be completed sometime in 1998 will add 220 more rooms and new meeting space. ✉ *4599 Chateau Blvd., Box 100, V0N 1B0,* ☎ *604/938–8000, 800/441–1414 in the U.S. and Canada,* ℻ *604/938–2055. 307 rooms, 36 suites. Restaurant, lobby lounge, tapas bar, indoor-outdoor pool, saunas, steam rooms, 18-hole golf course, 3 tennis courts, mountain bikes, ski shop, shops, piano, travel services. AE, D, DC, MC, V.*

**$$$$** 🏨 **Delta Whistler Resort.** The resort at the base of Whistler Mountain is a large complex, complete with shopping, dining, and fitness facilities. Rooms are very generous in size (almost all will easily sleep four). There are a few standard rooms, but most have fireplaces, whirlpool bathtubs, balconies, and/or kitchens. ✉ *4050 Whistler Way, Box 550, V0N 1B0,* ☎ *604/932–1982, 800/877–1133 in the U.S., 800/268–1133 in Canada,* ℻ *604/932–7318. 276 rooms, 24 suites. Restaurant, sports bar, kitchenettes, pool, indoor and outdoor hot tubs, steam room, 2 indoor/outdoor tennis courts, shops, video games, coin laundries. AE, DC, MC, V.*

**$$$$** 🏨 **Edgewater.** Next to Green Lake nestles this intimate cedar lodge. In traditional Canadian shades of olive, crimson, pale yellow, and cloudy blue, the interior is simple and relaxing, a true country retreat. An extended Continental breakfast (juice, granola, fruit, and breads) is included in the tariff at this no-smoking establishment. ✉ *Off Hwy. 99, 2½ km (1½ mi) north of village, Box 369, V0N 1B0,* ☎ *604/932–0688,* ℻ *604/932–0686. 6 rooms, 6 suites. Dining room, bar, outdoor hot tub, hiking, boating, cross-country skiing, ski storage. MC, V.*

**$$$–$$$$** 🏨 **Le Chamois.** This luxury hotel enjoys a prime ski-in, ski-out loca-
**★** tion at the base of the Blackcomb runs. Of the spacious guest rooms with convenience kitchens, the most popular are the studios with Jacuzzi tubs set in front of the living room's bay windows overlooking the slopes. Guests can also keep an eye on the action from the glass elevators and the heated outdoor pool. ✉ *4557 Blackcomb Way, V0N 1B0,* ☎ *604/932–8700, 800/777–0185 in the U.S. and Canada,* ℻ *604/905–2576. 47 suites, 6 studios. 2 restaurants, kitchenettes, refrigerators, limited room service, pool, coin laundry. AE, DC, MC, V.*

**$$$** 🏨 **Durlacher Hof.** Custom fir woodwork and doors, exposed ceiling beams, a *kachelofen* (tiled oven), and antler chandeliers hung over fir benches and tables carry out the rustic European theme of this fancy Tyrolean inn. The green and maroon bedrooms, all named for European mountains, contain more fine examples of custom-crafted wooden furniture. Two upgraded rooms on the third floor have added amenities such as double whirlpool tubs. A hearty European breakfast is included in the tariff. ✉ *7055 Nesters Rd., V0N 1B0,* ☎ *604/932–1924,* ℻ *604/938–1980. 7 double rooms, 1 suite. No-smoking rooms, hot tub, sauna, ski storage, airport shuttle. MC, V. Closed Nov.*

**$$$** 🏨 **Pension Edelweiss.** Rooms here have a crisp, spic-and-span feel in keeping with the Bavarian chalet style of the house; some have balconies and telephones. Breakfast is included in the room rate. A bus stop just outside provides easy access to Whistler Village. ✉ *7162 Nancy Greene Way, Box 850, V0N 1B0,* ☎ *604/932–3641 or 800/665–2003,* ℻ *604/938–1746. 8 rooms, 1 suite. No-smoking rooms, hot tub, sauna, bicycles, ski storage. AE, MC, V.*

**$** 🏨 **Hostelling International Whistler Youth Hostel.** Although it's nothing to write home about, the hostel is the cheapest sleep in town, and there's a kitchen. ✉ *Alta Lake Rd., V0N 1B0,* ☎ *604/932–5492,* ℻ *604/932–4687. 30 beds in 5 dorms, 1 private room (no bath). Ski storage. No credit cards.*

## Outdoor Activities and Sports

CANOEING, KAYAKING, RAFTING, AND WINDSURFING

Canoe, kayak, and sailboard rentals are available at **Alta Lake** at both Lakeside Park and Wayside Park. A spot that's perfect for canoeing is the **River of Golden Dreams,** either from Meadow Park to Green Lake or upstream to Twin Bridges. Kayakers looking for a thrill may want to try **Green River** from Green Lake to Pemberton. **Whistler River Adventures** (☎ 604/932–3532) operates a variety of half- and full-day rafting trips priced from $50 to $150.

The breezes are reliable for windsurfing on Alpha, Alta, and Green lakes. Call **Whistler Outdoor Experience** (☎ 604/932–3389), **Whistler Sailing and Water Sports** (☎ 604/932–7245), **Whistler Windsurfing** (☎ 604/932–3589), or **Sea to Sky Kayaking** (☎ 604/898–5498) for equipment or guided trips.

FISHING

**Whistler Backcountry Adventures** (✉ No. 36, 4314 Main St., ☎ 604/938–1410) or **Whistler Fishing Guides** (✉ Carlton Lodge, 4218 Mountain Sq. [base of both gondolas], ☎ 604/932–4267) will take care of anything you need—equipment, guides, and transportation. All five lakes around Whistler are stocked with trout.

GOLF

Robert Trent Jones II designed the championship 18-hole, par-72 course at the **Chateau Whistler Golf Club** (✉ 4612 Blackcomb Way, ☎ 604/938–2092). The greens fee runs from $70 to $105, which includes a mandatory cart. The scenery at the 18-hole, par-72 course at the **Whistler Golf Club** (✉ 4010 Whistler Way, ☎ 604/932–4544) is as beautiful as the back nine is difficult. The greens fee at this Arnold Palmer–designed course runs from $50 to $85, plus $25 for an optional cart.

RAFTING

**Canadian River Expeditions** (✉ 301–9571 Emerald Dr., Whistler, V0N 1B9, ☎ 604/938–6651; 800/898–7238 in Canada only).

## Skiing

CROSS-COUNTRY

The meandering trail around the Whistler Golf Course in the village is an ideal beginners' route. For more advanced skiing, try the 28 km (17 mi) of track-set trails that wind around Lost Lake, Chateau Whistler Golf Course, and the Nicklaus North Golf Course and Green Lake. Trail maps and equipment rental information are available at the **Whistler Activity and Information Center** (☎ 604/932–2394) in the village.

DOWNHILL

The vertical drops and elevations at **Blackcomb** (☎ 604/938–7743, FAX 604/938–7527) and **Whistler** (☎ 604/932–3434, FAX 604/938–9174) mountains are perhaps the most impressive features here. The resort covers 6,998 acres of skiable terrain in 12 alpine bowls on three glaciers and on more than 200 marked trails, served by the most advanced high-speed lift system on the continent. Blackcomb has a 5,280-ft vertical drop, North America's longest, while Whistler comes in second, with a 5,020-ft drop. The top elevation is 7,494 ft on Blackcomb and 7,160 on Whistler. Blackcomb and Whistler have more than 100 marked trails each and receive an average of 360 inches of snow per year; Blackcomb is open from June to August for summer glacier skiing. Whistler Ski School and Blackcomb Ski School provide lessons.

**Mountain Heli-Sports** (☎ 604/932–2070), **Tyax Heli-Skiing** (☎ 604/932–7007 or 800/663–8126), and **Whistler Heli-Skiing** (☎ 604/932–4105) have guided day trips with up to four glacier runs, or 12,000 vertical feet of skiing, for experienced skiers; the cost is about $350.

## Whistler Essentials

### Arriving and Departing

BY BUS

**Maverick Coach Lines** (☎ 604/255–1171, FAX 604/255–5770) has buses leaving every couple of hours for Whistler Village from the depot in downtown Vancouver. The fare is about $34 round-trip. During ski season, the last bus leaves Whistler at 9:45 PM. **Perimeter Bus Transportation** (☎ 604/266–5386, FAX 604/266–1628) has daily service, from November to April and June to September, from Vancouver International Airport to Whistler. Prepaid reservations are necessary 24 hours in advance; the ticket booth is on Level One of the airport. The fare is around $40 one way. **Westcoast City and Nature Sightseeing** (☎ 604/451–1600 in Vancouver) operates a sightseeing tour to Whistler that allows passengers to stay over and return on their date of choice to Vancouver; call for seasonal rates.

BY CAR

Whistler is 120 km (74 mi), or 2½ hours, north of Vancouver on winding Highway 99, the Sea-to-Sky Highway.

BY TRAIN

**B.C. Rail** (☎ 604/984–5246) travels north from Vancouver to Whistler along a beautiful route. The Vancouver Bus Terminal and the North Vancouver Station are connected by bus shuttle. Rates are under $60 round-trip for the train only.

### Getting Around

The streets surrounding **Whistler Village** are clearly marked and easy to negotiate by car, and pay parking is readily available. However, there's really no reason to use a car because the resort association operates a free public transit system that loops throughout the resort; call 604/932–4020 for information and schedules.

### Contacts and Resources

B&B RESERVATION AGENCIES

**Whistler Bed and Breakfast Inns** (☎ 604/932–3282 or 800/665–1892) represents the leading inns of Whistler.

CAR RENTAL

**Budget Rent-A-Car** (☎ 604/932–1236, FAX 604/932–3026). **Thrifty Car Rental** (☎ 604/938–0302 or 800/367–2277, FAX 604/938–1228).

EMERGENCIES

Dial 911 for **police, ambulance,** or **poison control.**

GUIDED TOURS

**Alpine Adventure Tours** (☎ 604/683–0209) conducts a Whistler history tour of the valley and a Squamish day trip. **Whistler Nature Guides** (☎ 604/932–4595) operates guided alpine hiking tours. Budget-priced, guided camping trips out of Vancouver are available through **Bigfoots Backpacker Adventure Express** (☎ 604/739–1025).

VISITOR INFORMATION

**Whistler Resort Association** (✉ 4010 Whistler Way, Whistler V0N 1B4, ☎ 604/932–4222, 604/664–5625 in Vancouver, or 800/944–7853 in the U.S. and Canada).

# INDEX

X = restaurant, 🏨 = hotel

# WHEREVER YOU TRAVEL, *H*ELP IS NEVER FAR AWAY.

From planning your trip to providing travel assistance along the way, American Express® Travel Service Offices are always there to help you do more.

## *Seattle and Vancouver*

American Express Vacation Travel Service
900-1166 Alberni Street
Vancouver, BC
604/691-7740

American Express Travel Service
666 Burrard Street
Vancouver, BC
604/669-2813

American Express Travel Service
Plaza 600 Building
600 Stewart Street
Seattle, WA
206/441-8622

do more AMERICAN EXPRESS

**Travel**

http://www.americanexpress.com/travel